AF782148

De Gruyter Handbook of Rural Entrepreneurship

De Gruyter Handbook of Rural Entrepreneurship

Edited by
Chyi-Lyi (Kathleen) Liang and Thomas S. Lyons

DE GRUYTER

ISBN 978-3-11-079128-0
e-ISBN (PDF) 978-3-11-079139-6
e-ISBN (EPUB) 978-3-11-079149-5
ISSN 2748-016X

Library of Congress Control Number: 2025934016

Bibliographic information published by the Deutsche Nationalbibliothek
The Deutsche Nationalbibliothek lists this publication in the Deutsche Nationalbibliografie; detailed bibliographic data are available on the internet at http://dnb.dnb.de.

© 2025 Walter de Gruyter GmbH, Berlin/Boston, Genthiner Straße 13, 10785 Berlin
Typesetting: Integra Software Services Pvt. Ltd.

www.degruyter.com
Questions about General Product Safety Regulation:
productsafety@degruyterbrill.com

De Gruyter Handbooks in Business, Economics and Finance

De Gruyter Handbook of Disability and Management
Edited by: Joy E. Beatty, Sophie Hennekam and Mukta Kulkarni

De Gruyter Handbook of Sustainable Entrepreneurship Research
Edited by: Gjalt de Jong, Niels Faber, Emma Folmer, Tom Long and Berfu Ünal

De Gruyter Handbook of SME Entrepreneurship
Edited by: Marina Dabić and Sascha Kraus

De Gruyter Handbook of Degrowth
Edited by: Lauren Eastwood and Kai Heron

De Gruyter Handbook of Media Economics
Edited by: Ulrike Rohn, M. Bjørn von Rimscha and Tim Raats

De Gruyter Handbook of Migrant Entrepreneurship
Edited by: Beata Glinka and Jörg Freiling

De Gruyter Handbook of Digital Entrepreneurship
Edited by: Wadid Lamine, Sarah Jack, Alain Fayolle and David Audretsch

De Gruyter Handbook of Social Entrepreneurship
Edited by: Bryan C. Boots, Lane G. Perry, III, and Benjamin J. Williams

De Gruyter Handbook of Poverty, Disadvantage and Entrepreneurship
Edited by: Michael H. Morris and Susana C. Santos

De Gruyter Handbook of Media Technology and Innovation
Edited by: Richard A. Gershon

De Gruyter Handbook of Women Entrepreneurs in Emerging Economies
Edited by: Helle Neergaard, Maribel Guerrero and Breda Kenny

For more information, scan QR code below or visit
https://www.degruyterbrill.com/serial/dghbef-b/html

Contents

About the Authors

Arjan van Dorsselaer is a doctoral candidate in social and community entrepreneurship at the Utrecht School of Economics (USE), Utrecht University (UU). His PhD is part of the Scentiss project, a Dutch research consortium exploring social impact scaling strategies and entrepreneurial ecosystems for social and community-driven entrepreneurs (SCEs). Yet, being generally interested in contextualizing entrepreneurship, Arjan further examines spatial dimensions, like rural social entrepreneurship, and multi-stakeholder approaches, such as civic wealth creation.

Bryan Collins is an Assistant Professor in the Department of Geography and Environmental Sustainability at SUNY Oneonta. He is broadly interested in how spatial models can be used to address societal challenges. Current research interests include movements toward sustainable agricultural systems in the United States and Canada, as well as the issue of equitable land access for farmers. Recent journal articles have been published in the journal of *Applied Economics Teaching Resources*, the *Small Business Institute Journal*, and *The Professional Geographer*.

Christina Theodoraki is Full professor in Entrepreneurship at IAE Aix-Marseille University. She is elected Program Chair at the Academy of Management, Entrepreneurship Division. She is Advisory Board Member at the Institute for Development Strategies at Indiana University, Research associate at the Chair of Entrepreneurship Territory Innovation (ETI) – IAE Paris-Sorbonne, Business Development Manager at the Entrepreneurial Ecosystem Research Network (EERN), Editor of Small Business Economics, Associate editor of the Journal of Small Business Management, Management & Prospective – Gestion 2000, and Revue internationale PME, and member of several editorial boards.

Chyi-Lyi (Kathleen) Liang who is the W.K. Kellogg Distinguished Professor of Sustainable Agriculture, and currently serving as the Director of the Center for Environmental Farming Systems at North Carolina Agricultural and Technical State University in Greensboro, North Carolina, USA. Dr. Liang is an award-winning scholar who has more than 40 years of experiences designing and implementing innovative strategies to support entrepreneurs. Her research fields include entrepreneurship, sustainable agriculture, food systems, and rural development. She is the Founder of Dollar Enterprise, one of the best entrepreneurship programs in the US to create and energize new opportunities for start-ups using limited resources.

Dax Jacobson is Dean of the Bill & Vieve Gore School of Business at Westminster University in Salt Lake City, Utah. As Dean, Dax is focused on strengthening entrepreneurial ecosystems. Dax's teaching and research interests include leadership, entrepreneurship, and strategy. He advises business big and small, urban and rural, private and non-profit. He has a passion for rural entrepreneurs in the American West and is involved in programming, research, and podcasts related to rural and other overlooked entrepreneurial ecosystems. Dax has a dual degree in Finance & History from Utah State University and an MBA and PhD from Bentley University.

Don Macke is the founder of **e2 Entrepreneurial Ecosystems,** formerly the national Center for Rural Entrepreneurship where he was a co-founder with Dr. Deborah Markley. e2 over the past three decades has worked with state, regional and community partners to advance rural community-centered entrepreneur-focused community economic development. Core to e2's success, is it's ***e2 Development Framework and Process***. Over the past 50 years Don has worked throughout North America. He lives in Lincoln, Nebraska with his wife Jenny Carver, a retired public-school teacher. Don is now evolving into retirement continuing to conduct research, analysis, provide advising, and writing in this new stage of his life.

Elias G. Carayannis is Full Professor of Science, Technology, Innovation and Entrepreneurship, as well as co-Founder and co-Director of the Global and Entrepreneurial Finance Research Institute (GEFRI) and Director of Research on Science, Technology, Innovation and Entrepreneurship, European Union Research

https://doi.org/10.1515/9783110791396-203

Center, (EURC) at the School of Business of the George Washington University in Washington, DC. Dr. Carayannis' teaching and research activities focus on the areas of strategic Government-University-Industry R&D partnerships, technology road-mapping, technology transfer and commercialization, international science and technology policy, technological entrepreneurship and regional economic development.

Emi Makino is an Associate Professor at Ritsumeikan Asia Pacific University in Beppu, Japan. She has been teaching and developing entrepreneurship programs at Japanese universities since 2013. Her book Innovation Makers examined how campus makerspaces combined with co-curricular programs are sparking innovative student ventures in Japan. She has a PhD in management and MBA from Claremont Graduate University's Drucker School of Management, and an MS in journalism from Columbia Graduate School of Journalism.

Hassan Shahraki is an assistant professor in University of Zabol, Iran. He has earned his bachelor degree in Agriculture Machinery from Ferdowsi University of Mashhad, Iran, the Master of Science in Rural Development form Razi University, Iran, and PhD in Rural Development from Bu-Ali-Sina University, Hamedan, Iran. Also, he has been a visiting researcher at the Department of Development Studies, University of Vienna, Austria, from 2015 to 2016. Right now, he is a visiting scholar in the Department of Sociology and Anthropology in Carleton University. Shahraki's main academic interests include the wide range from critical development studies, Critical Discourse Analysis (CDA), Situational Analysis (SA), to the sociology of development, post-modernism, rural development (entrepreneurship), and the sociology of body and embodiment. His main intention as a visiting scholar in Carleton is to search about the Buen Vivir (Collective well-being in English) as a Latin American development approach, and redefine it according to the sociological, historical, and cultural circumstances, conditions, and situations in Iran as an Islamic country. He named this revised version of Buen Vivir the IBV (Islamic Buen Vivir).

Karim Messeghem is a Full Professor of Entrepreneurship and Strategy at the University of Montpellier. He contributed to the founding of the Montpellier Management Institute and the Labex Entreprendre. He is the Co-Director of the Master's program in Entrepreneurship and Project Management and serves as the Director of the Entrepreneurial Ecosystem Lab. He conducts his research within the MRM Laboratory. His work focuses on entrepreneurial ecosystems, entrepreneurial support, and SME strategies. He has published approximately 60 articles in journals such as *Small Business Economics*, the *Journal of Small Business Management*, and *European Management Review*.

Kelly Cowan holds a Ph.D. in Engineering Management from Portland State University, as well as a Masters in Management of Technology, and a Bachelors in Management Information Systems from the University of New Mexico. His work combines scholarship and practice. He has published many highly cited articles in leading journals in the field of Technology Management. He also has significant experience helping companies bring technology to market, working for Sandia National Laboratories' department of Licensing and Intellectual Property, and a number of business incubators and accelerators. Kelly has worked primarily in industries related to clean energy, smart grid, and sustainability.

Mara van Twuijver is a lecturer in the Department of Food, Business, and Development at Cork University Business School (CUBS), University College Cork (UCC). As a former Marie Skłodowska-Curie Fellow with the RurAction network, her PhD focused on rural social entrepreneurship and the role these organisations play in local development. Her continued research focuses on social entrepreneurship, rural and community development, and entrepreneurial ecosystems, with a particular interest in how change can be created in our food system.

Marcus Taylor is a Professor and Head of the Department of Global Development Studies at Queen's University where he teaches on rural development and sustainable livelihoods. Based on his research in southern India, he is a contributing author to the forthcoming Intergovernmental Panel on Climate Change (IPCC) AR6 report on climate-resilient development. Recent books include *The Political Ecology of*

Climate Change Adaptation (2015), *Global Labour Studies* (2018) and a forthcoming volume on *Climate Smart Agriculture*.

Maria I. Marshall is a Professor and the James and Lois Ackerman Endowed Chair in Agricultural Economics in the Department of Agricultural Economics at Purdue University. She is the director of the Purdue Institute for Family Business and the North Central Regional Center for Rural Development. Dr. Marshall has a nationally and internationally recognized program focused on small and family business development and small business disaster recovery. Her program's goal is to increase the viability and sustainability of small and family businesses as they develop and mature through their life cycles.

Michael W-P Fortunato currently serves as founding partner of the engagement firm Creative Insight Community Development and is an instructor in the Penn State Masters of Professional Studies program for Community and Economic Development (CEDEV). He is a scholar, lecturer, writer, and strategic analyst as well as being a community-based entrepreneur, arts enthusiast, and incremental developer. A part-time professional musician since age 15, he applies insights from art and music to his community development practice to build relationships that inspire action and creativity.

Niels Bosma is full professor Social Entrepreneurship and Director of Studies with Utrecht University School of Economics. His research interests revolve around the nexus of institutions, entrepreneurial ecosystems and entrepreneurial activity, with a particular focus on social entrepreneurship. He is currently Senior Research Advisor with the Global Entrepreneurship Monitor (GEM). He has also acted GEM's research director, member of the Board of Directors and has co-authored various GEM Global Reports between 2006 and 2025.

Simona Zollet is an Assistant Professor at Hiroshima University, Japan, and was a USASBE (US Association for Small Business and Entrepreneurship) Rural Research Fellow for two consecutive terms in 2021-2023. Her interdisciplinary research background includes sustainability science, rural sociology, sociology of agriculture and food systems, and rural entrepreneurship. Her current research includes urban-to-rural migration, lifestyle entrepreneurship and sustainable rural community revitalization in Japan and Italy.

Steven Deller is Vilas Distinguished Achievement Professor and Extension Specialist in the Department of Agricultural and Applied Economics at the University of Wisconsin-Madison. Steve's work focuses on rural economic growth and development with an eye toward policies that can be implemented at the local level. His work has explored the implications of retirement migration, tax and spending patterns of local governments, natural amenities and quality of life, and small business development on rural communities. His work has appeared in *Review of Economics and Statistics, American Journal of Agricultural Economics, International Regional Science Review, Economic Development Quarterly, Journal of Planning Literature,* and *Public Administration Review,* among others. His latest co-authored book is entitled *Understanding Municipal Fiscal Health: A Model for Local Governments in the USA.*

Tessa Conroy is an Associate Professor and Extension Specialist in the Department of Agricultural and Applied Economics at the University of Wisconsin-Madison. Tessa's work explores patterns of rural economic growth and development with a focus on entrepreneurship. Specific topic areas included assessing the influence of broadband access and entrepreneurship, community level social capital and business survival rates, access to finance and rural entrepreneurship, and availability of childcare services and rates of women entrepreneurship, among others. Her work has been published in *Small Business Economics, Regional Science and Urban Economics, American Journal of Agricultural Economics,* and *Journal of Banking and Finance*, among others. She has been quoted in *U.S. News and World Report, Fortune, The Wall Street Journal, MarketWatch, Milwaukee Journal Sentinel* and is a frequent guest on *Wisconsin Public Radio.*

Theodore R. Alter is a recently retired professor of agricultural, environmental, and regional economics and former co-director of the Center for Economic and Community Development in the Department of

Agricultural Economics, Sociology, and Education at Penn State University. He is a former co-editor of the *Entrepreneurship Research Journal (2018–21)* and currently founding partner of Creative Insight Community Development. Alter's research, teaching, and community engagement work focuses on community and rural development, regional economics, entrepreneurship, resource and environmental economics, community engagement for natural resource management, behavioral and public sector economics, and the political economy of democracy.

Thomas S. Lyons, Ph.D. is the Clarence E. Harris Chair of Excellence in Entrepreneurship, Professor of Marketing & Entrepreneurship, and Executive Director of the Center for Innovation and Entrepreneurship in the Gary W. Rollins College of Business at the University of Tennessee at Chattanooga. His research interests are entrepreneurship skills measurement and development, the relationship between entrepreneurship and community economic development, and social entrepreneurship. He is the co-author of fifteen books; has published numerous articles, book chapters and papers on these subjects; and has edited a three-volume set on social entrepreneurship (*Social Entrepreneurship: How Businesses Can Transform Society*).

Chyi-Lyi (Kathleen) Liang and Thomas S. Lyons

Introduction

It is our purpose in this *Handbook of Rural Entrepreneurship* to specifically frame the unique contribution of entrepreneurs to rural economic development based on the characteristics, challenges, and opportunities within entrepreneurial ecosystems in rural communities from an interdisciplinary and global perspective. The COVID-19 pandemic, for example, shifted the individual's mindset and career trajectory significantly. With unpredictable numbers of furloughed and displaced workers, many people chose to start their own businesses. Rural areas became affordable and less-stressful alternatives for people who were seeking new opportunities to survive and thrive. The in-migration of talented and skilled workers retreating from previous urban or suburban employment brought new ideas and activities to rural communities.

With this in mind, we believe this is an ideal time to document and explore the dynamics of rural entrepreneurship to capture the momentum of these changes. Our objectives herein are to (1) provide a comprehensive overview of the issues, challenges, barriers, and opportunities related to rural entrepreneurship; (2) establish sufficient theoretical frameworks to guide research in rural entrepreneurship; and (3) identify empirical research topics using various methods to examine rural entrepreneurship from an interdisciplinary and global perspective.

Currently, there is a limited theoretical framework, or body of literature, that defines the domain of rural entrepreneurship (Pato & Teixeira, 2014). Some theoretical frameworks exist in discussing general entrepreneurship, and many scholars have examined the relationships between entrepreneurial decision making, innovation, desire to take control, and seeking higher values through change (e.g., Volery & Mazzarol, 2015; Kickul & Lyons, 2025). However, the concepts of general entrepreneurship might not accurately and fully represent or explain the behaviors, decisions, choices, and social networks of rural entrepreneurs. The most recent review of the rural entrepreneurship literature indicates that the prominent scholars of rural entrepreneurship research are from Europe. Most of the existing literature focuses on developed countries, and there are only limited empirical studies examining rural entrepreneurship associated with undeveloped or underdeveloped countries (Kulawiak, Suliborski & Rachwat, 2022). This handbook largely builds on the extant literature seeking to understand rural entrepreneurship in developed countries, with the exception of a chapter that provides insights from the Middle East.

Rural economic development and rural entrepreneurship have largely been explored through interdisciplinary research. Economists, sociologists, geographers, and historians have recognized issues in rural communities – a declining labor force and wages, decreasing social and economic capital, reduced investment in education and professional development, and a lack of catalytic industries or public policies to stim-

https://doi.org/10.1515/9783110791396-001

ulate growth and wealth creation (e.g., Gladwin et al., 1989; Lyons, Lyons & Jolley, 2020). In the face of these challenges, many scholars applaud the efforts of small businesses to revitalize rural prosperity and economic mobility (Faggian, Partridge & Malecki, 2017; Wojan, 2022). Rural small businesses also seem to be more resilient during economic shocks (Liang & Goetz, 2016).

Some of the most popular topics in rural entrepreneurship research relate to identifying key factors associated with entrepreneurial actions in rural areas, examining barriers and challenges imposed by institutions, analyzing gaps and opportunities related to infrastructure, and socio-demographic variables correlated to the likelihood of new venture creation in rural communities. For example, Kolawole and Torimiro (2005) applied factor analysis to identify key variables influencing rural entrepreneurship development and employment promotion. This study examined selected socio-economic variables such as work experiences and education. They also studied institutional and infrastructural situations as enhancers or barriers, other constraints and challenges, and ways to encourage rural entrepreneurship among local residents. The conclusions suggested that a lack of accredited facilities and the high cost of labor are major constraints, and other influential factors included social status, personal experience, infrastructure functionality, and educational advantage. Yu and Artz (2019) investigated entrepreneurship and location choices among college-educated individuals in the US. These researchers modeled the location and entrepreneurship decisions jointly, demonstrating that individuals who chose a rural residence were more likely to become entrepreneurs. Sharma et al. (2013) presented similar findings that entrepreneurship was more likely to exist in economically distressed regions, although rural entrepreneurs encountered more challenges surrounding access to knowledge, financing, technology, human resources, and management and marketing expertise.

Harpa (2017) analyzed four factors influencing rural entrepreneurship from a macroeconomic perspective – educational institutions, clusters and associates, innovation support institutions, and state institutions. Determinants included policies, competence, skills, motivation, culture, natural resources, human resources, location, infrastructure, technology, suppliers, competitors, local networks, markets, etc. Soleymani et al. (2021) examined sustainable rural entrepreneurship for development, growth, and prosperity. Several sets of indicators were identified related to social, economic, and ethical domains in supporting rural entrepreneurship. Social trust, social altruism, and empathy significantly influenced rural entrepreneurs' network capacity. Rural enterprise development positively related to effectiveness of utilization of facilities, cost management, and services to business stability and market management. Finally, sustainable rural entrepreneurship development was positively linked to ethical practices such as financial business transparency, ethics in using biological resources, and ethics in managing human resources.

Many scholars have offered insight to create rural entrepreneurship theory that would link to knowledge creation and wealth creation in rural communities. Newbery et al. (2017) discussed gaps and facilitated beneficial flows of knowledge linking to the importance of networks, communities, and the supply chain. Authors in sociology, regional economic development, and political science have discussed the role of policies, regional development strategies, social capital building, and learning experiences that could hinder or strengthen rural entrepreneurship (Goetz et al., 2010; Fortunato, 2014; Koyana & Mason, 2017; Lyons, Miller & Mann, 2018; Lang & Fink, 2019; Lyons, Lyons & Jolley, 2020; Lyons, 2022). Many studies have explored how gender, age, and experiences trigger rural entrepreneurship, more specifically, empowering women and youth to create new opportunities (de Guzman et al., 2020; Elkafrawi, Roos & Refai, 2022; Ahl et al., 2024). Younger and older migrants tended to have the largest impacts on rural business start-ups. Older, retired people, who preferred a rural lifestyle, were more likely to emerge as entrepreneurs (Deller et al., 2019).

Most recently, there is a burgeoning interest among entrepreneurship researchers in the concept of entrepreneurial ecosystems (EEs). The idea of place-based local or regional systems that engage and support entrepreneurs has taken root. There is now a growing literature focused on the unique characteristics of rural EEs. and insights into how to build and sustain these rural entrepreneurship systems (Lyons, Lyons & Jolley, 2020; Aguilar, 2021; Reynolds, 2022; Hammer & Frimanslund, 2022; Asmit et al., 2024).

Researchers seem to agree that there are significant differences between rural entrepreneurship and general entrepreneurship – how entrepreneurs think, act, and interact with others while facing various influential social, economic, political, and environmental forces. This handbook's objectives are important and timely because of the growing interest in studying rural entrepreneurship at local, regional, national, and global levels. Given recent multiple shocks in our society and economy, rural entrepreneurship deserves a broader and deeper investigation through an interdisciplinary view to generate new ideas, theories, and best practices.

Toward achieving this handbook's objectives, we have curated eleven chapters from leading scholars in the rural entrepreneurship field from around the world. Relative to providing a comprehensive overview of the issues, challenges, barriers, and opportunities related to rural entrepreneurship, we have chapters that address defining and measuring entrepreneurship in rural areas, developing entrepreneurship skills, fostering sustainable development, effectively utilizing technology, and the impact of economic globalization. Regarding our second objective of establishing sufficient theoretical frameworks to guide research in rural entrepreneurship, we provide coverage of frameworks for reconceptualizing rural entrepreneurial ecosystems, fostering rural resilience and development, and defining the role of universities in rural ecosystems. Our third objective of identifying empirical research topics using various methods to examine rural entrepreneurship from an interdisciplinary and global perspective is fulfilled by our authors' use of case studies, other qualitative approaches, and large data set-quantitative research. The work embodied here was conducted mostly in the European and North American contexts, giving it an international perspective. This is further enhanced by a chapter that provides global insights from the view of an author from Iran.

Whether the reader is an academic researcher, a teacher, a student, an entrepreneurship support provider or a policymaker, we hope the material in this handbook is challenging, thought-provoking, and inspiring.

References

Aguilar, E.C. (2021). Rural entrepreneurial ecosystems: A systematic literature review advancing conceptualisation. Entrepreneurial Business and Economic Review, 9(4), 101–114.

Ahl, H., Berglund, K., Pettersson, K., & Tillmar, M. (2024). Women's contributions to rural development: Implications for entrepreneurship policy. International Journal of Entrepreneurial Behavior & Research, 30(7), 1652–1677.

Asmit, B., Simatupang, T.M., Rudito, B., & Novani, S. (2024). Uncovering the building blocks of rural entrepreneurship: A comprehensive framework for mapping the components of a rural entrepreneurial ecosystem. Heliyon, 10(1). https://doi.org/10.1016/j.heliyon.2024.e24139.

de Guzman, M.R.T., Kim, S., Taylor, S., & Padasas, I. (2020). Rural communities as context for entrepreneurship: Exploring perceptions of youth and business owners. Journal of Rural Studies, 80, 45–52.

Deller, S., Kures, M., & Conroy, T. (2019). Rural entrepreneurship and migration. Journal of Rural Studies, 66, 30–42.

Elkafrawi, N., Roos, A., & Refai, D. (2022). Contextualizing rural entrepreneurship: A strong structuration perspective on gendered local agency. International Small Business Journal, 40(8), 1019–1040.

Faggian, A., Partridge, M., & Malecki, E.J. (2017). Creating an environment for economic growth: Creativity, entrepreneurship or human capital? International Journal of Urban and Regional Research, 41(6), 997–1009.

Fortunato, M. (2014). Supporting rural entrepreneurship: A review of conceptual developments from research to practice. Community Development, 45(4), 387–408. doi: 10.1080/15575330.2014.935795.

Gladwin, C.H., Long, B.F., Mabb, E.M., Beaulieu, L.J., Moseley, A., Mulkey, D., & Zimet, D.J. (1989). Rural entrepreneurship: One key to rural revitalization. American Journal of Agricultural Economics, Proceedings Issue, December, 71(5), 1305–1314.

Goetz, S., Partrige, M., Deller, S., & Fleming, D. (2010). Evaluating US rural entrepreneurship policy. The Journal of Regional Analysis & Policy, 40(1), 20–33.

Hammer, S., & Frimanslund, T. (2022). Lessons from a rural ecosystem. Local Economy, 37(5), 348–363.

Harpa, E. (2017). Macroeconomic analysis of the competitive factors which influence innovation in rural entrepreneurship. Procedia Engineering, 181, 965–968.

Kickul, J., & Lyons, T.S. (2025). Understanding social entrepreneurship: The relentless pursuit of mission in an ever changing world, Fourth Edition. Routledge.

Koyana, S., & Mason, R. (2017). Rural entrepreneurship and transformation: The role of learnerships. International Journal of Entrepreneurial Behavior & Research.

Kolawole, O.D., & Torimiro, D.O. (2005). Participatory rural entrepreneurship development for grassroots transformation: A factor analysis. Journal of Human Ecology, 28(3), 193–198.

Kulawiak, A., Suliborski, A., & Rachwat, T. (2022). Research on rural entrepreneurship in terms of the literature: Definition problems and selected research issues. Questiones Geographicae, 41(2), 7–19.

Lang, R., & Fink, M. (2019). Rural social entrepreneurship: The role of social capital within and across institutional levels. Journal of Rural Studies, 70, 155–168.

Liang, J.C., & Goetz, S.J. (2016). Self-employment and trade shock mitigation. Small Business Economics, 46(1), 45–56.

Lyons, T.S. (2022). Social capital building for rural innovation. In C. French, Building rural community resilience through innovation and entrepreneurship (pp. 62–81). Routledge.

Lyons, T.S., Lyons, J.S., & Jolley, G.J. (2020). Entrepreneurial skill-building in rural ecosystems: A framework for applying the Readiness Inventory for Successful Entrepreneurship (RISE). Journal of Entrepreneurship and Public Policy, 9(1), 112–136.

Lyons, T.S., Miller, S., & Mann, J. (2018). A new role for land grant universities in the rural innovation ecosystem? Journal of Regional Analysis and Policy, 48(2), 32–47.

Newbery, R., Siwale, J., & Henley, A. (2017). Rural entrepreneurship theory in the developing and developed world. The International Journal of Entrepreneurship and Innovation, Special edition.

Pato, M., & Teixeira, A. (2014). Twenty years of rural entrepreneurship: A bibliometric survey, European Society for Rural Sociology. Sociologia Ruralis, 56(1), 12058.

Reynolds, J. (2022). Building an entrepreneurial ecosystem to catalyze innovation in rural places. In C. French, Building rural community resilience through innovation and entrepreneurship (pp. 31–48). Routledge.

Sharma, M., Chaudhary, V., Bala, R., & Chauhan, R. (2013). Rural entrepreneurship in developing countries: Challenges, problems, and performance appraisal. Global Journal of Management and Business Studies, 3(9), 1035–1040.

Soleymani, A., Farani, A.Y., Karimi, S., Azadi, H., Nadiri, H., & Scheffran, J. (2021). Identifying sustainable rural entrepreneurship indicators in the Iranian context. Journal of Cleaner Production, 290, 125186.

Volery, T., & Mazzarol, T. (2015). The evolution of the small business and entrepreneurship field: A bibliometric investigation of articles in the International Small Business Journal. International Small Business Journal, 33(4), 374–396.

Wojan, T.R. (2022). Rural flourishing through artistic imagination: Unleashing the advantages of nonmetropolitan America. In C. French, Building rural community resilience through innovation and entrepreneurship (pp. 131–152). Routledge.

Yu, L., & Artz, G.M. (2019). Does rural entrepreneurship pay? Small Business Economics, 53, 647–668.

Tessa Conroy and Steven Deller

Rural Entrepreneurship is Declining . . . or Is It?

Abstract: Start-up activity in the U.S., and specifically in rural communities, has been declining for decades. The decline is concerning giving the growing evidence that entrepreneurship is an important driver of economic growth and development, especially in rural communities that have experienced tepid employment, income, and population growth. We explore whether the rural classification system distorts our understanding of rural entrepreneurial patterns. We find that the classification system does skew low performing counties, in terms of business growth, toward the rural classification. We also find that, while the declining start-up rate is remarkably stable across counties, the definition of a start-up or "new" firm is important. As most start-up activity focuses only on businesses with employees, the vast majority of start-up activity from small businesses with no paid employees (nonemployer establishments) is unaccounted for. This is particularly important for rural areas where nonemployer establishments are the only source of business growth.

Keywords: entrepreneurship, start-up, rural, nonemployers, growth

> . . . rural areas have been facing significant demographic challenges. Chronic migration loss, selective to the younger cohorts, have been the reality for most of these communities since 1950, if not longer. (Kulcsár, 2019: p.14)

> . . . results support pessimistic conclusions about the economic status of rural America's workforce, and the ability of rural Americans to meet the basic requisites of the good life through work. (Thiede, Lichter & Slack, 2018: p.183)

1 Introduction

Rural economies have, by several measures, lagged their urban counterparts, particularly in the years following the Great Recession (Deller & Conroy, 2023). Rural areas have struggled with traditional metrics of economic growth such as population, employment, and income as well as more nuanced economic measures such as poverty. From 2010 to 2020, rural counties lost population on net, with the highest rates of population loss in the most remote rural counties (Pender et al., 2019), while urban counties grew

Tessa Conroy, Department of Agricultural and Applied Economics, Community Development Institute, University of Wisconsin-Madison, email: tessa.conroy@wisc.edu
Steven Deller, Department of Agricultural and Applied Economics, Community Development Institute, University of Wisconsin-Madison, email: scdeller@wisc.edu

https://doi.org/10.1515/9783110791396-002

(Dobis et al., 2021). Though rural counties did add jobs on average in every year of the last decade, it was often at less than half the rate of urban counties (Cromartie, 2020; Deller & Conroy, 2023). The most remote rural counties, again, faced the most significant challenges, with employment losses in these rural counties (Pender et al., 2019). Labor force participation is also lower in nonmetro counties, largely explained by an older, less educated population with higher rates of disability (Pender et al., 2019). Income was lower and grew slower in nonmetropolitan counties (Pender et al., 2019). Undoubtedly, relatively low agricultural prices and the decline in farm income during the period partly explain the nonmetro income trend. It is perhaps unsurprising then that rural areas were also more likely to be in persistent poverty than urban areas (Dobis et al., 2021), with the highest rates of poverty in the most remote rural locations – the same places that struggled the most with high rates of population loss.

These economic trends highlight both the challenges for rural communities and the variation across counties across the rural spectrum with the most rural places having the greatest need for economic development assistance. Economic development has historically emphasized large industry as a key strategy for growth with current thinking being traced back to the Great Depression–era Mississippi Balance Agriculture with Industry (BAWI) policies of 1933. To address the severe economic hardships of the Great Depression and shift away from extensive dependency on production agriculture, the State of Mississippi implemented a series of policies to encourage manufacturers in the northern states to relocate to Mississippi. The BAWI policies focused on the availability of cheap labor, cheap land, limited regulation, and low taxes in Mississippi relative to the northern states. Together, these policies constituted what was viewed at the time as a "positive business climate" and served as a precursor to a coming competition between states to recruit businesses during the first wave of economic development (Deller, 2014, 2021; Deller & Goetz, 2009).

What is widely considered the "first wave" of economic development (e.g., Eisinger, 1998; Olberding, 2002) focused on industry recruitment where places tried to recruit large businesses, mostly manufacturers, to their location with a positive business climate – cheap land and labor, low taxes, and few regulations. This strategy proliferated across states and has persisted for nearly a century. The narrative of advancing a strong business climate has motivated countless incentive packages and tax exemptions, as well as public investment in infrastructure. Recent examples of this approach include Wisconsin's $3.5 billion incentive package to lure Foxconn to southeast Wisconsin in 2017, South Carolina's 2021 announcement that it will actively target the recruitment of pharmaceutical and medical supply manufacturers, or the recent announcement by Amazon that it is seeking "bids" to locate what it referred to as its World Headquarters II.

Indeed, in the name of economic growth many states still argue that their "positive business climate" makes their state attractive to businesses looking to relocate. As noted by Deller (2021), the North Carolina economic development organization, for example, promotes the state as having "the lowest corporate income tax rate in the country" and "business costs rank among the lowest in the nation" and "less red tape and litigation." The Tennessee economic development organization notes that Tennessee is "a right-to-work state with no personal income tax on wages," and "local tax burdens are among the lowest in the country." The Idaho Department of Commerce concisely states that they "keep our costs and taxes low, and we remove the burdensome regulations . . ." This notion of what drives a positive business climate retains the logic of the first wave of economic growth and development thinking.

In the latter half of the twentieth century many economic development policymakers and practitioners, particularly at the local level, began to move away from the first wave of business recruitment by offering low costs to a focus on small businesses. As the examples above note, industrial recruitment never receded entirely from practice, particularly at the state level, but more and more places started to embrace small businesses as important engines of economic growth. This emphasis on small businesses was fueled by the work of David Birch (1981, 1987), who found evidence that job growth in the United States comes predominately from smaller, rather than larger, businesses. Birch's work, along with the work of others (e.g., Wojan & Pulver, 1995), documented that much economic growth (i.e., employment growth) is not driven by large companies but rather by smaller firms. Thus, the focus on large businesses at the core of the first-wave approach may be misplaced and the focus should shift toward small businesses. This shift resulted in the second wave of economic growth and development strategies which emphasized the role of small firms. One example of this shift in thinking is reflective in the growth of business retention and expansion or "BRE"-type strategies and policies. Broadly speaking these strategies are focused on existing businesses – retaining those that are already in a community and helping them expand or grow (Loveridge & Smith, 1992; Loveridge, Smith & Morse, 1991). Many communities also began to embrace the importance of new business formation, or entrepreneurship, as an integral part of their economic growth and development efforts.

The work of the Harvard business economist Michael Porter (1998, 2000) expanded on the notions of regional comparative advantages and reintroduced the notion of economic clusters to the policy thinking around economic growth and development. The implication at the local or regional level is that communities should be strategic in the types of businesses which are the focus of their efforts. Rather than cast a wide net, efforts should be focused on industries that are unique to the community or region as defined by the comparative advantages of the area. An integral part of a dynamic economic cluster is the networking among businesses that compose the cluster and the public sector. The ensuing third wave of economic development strategy has focused on public-private partnerships and cluster development.

With this more focused approach to economic growth and development thinking, policies and strategies, it became more common for government entities and private organizations to collaborate in support of interconnected businesses along supply chains. Importantly, this strategy emphasizes more than a positive climate in the conventional sense. The role of social capital also became a consideration. That is, beyond taxes, labor costs, land prices, and regulations, practitioners began to incorporate a much more complex set of factors that affect business location. Relationships, interconnectedness, trust, and collaboration are central to the success of many firms both in terms of how they interact with other businesses and the community at large. This was likely the early signs of a pivot toward a "systems" or "ecosystem" approach to economic development that emphasized business in the context of many community-level factors that contribute to the overall quality of life.

2 Entrepreneurship as an Economic Development Strategy

Flowing out of the second wave of economic growth and development thinking, new business formation, or entrepreneurship, gained popularity as an economic development strategy. We know now that new businesses, which happen to be small, are responsible for a disproportionately large share of job creation, including in rural areas (Haltiwanger et al., 2016; Deller & Conroy, 2023). In other words, it is the newness of businesses more so than the smallness that explains job creation. There is also evidence that entrepreneurship is linked to income growth across the rural-urban continuum and poverty alleviation in rural counties (Rupasingha & Goetz, 2011; Si et al., 2020).

Innovation has long been a hallmark of entrepreneurial activity, and there is greater emphasis on the benefits of the value-added created by entrepreneurs as they bring new products and services to market. We know now too that the entrepreneurial community can lend itself to a more stable economy. Whereas relying on one industry or one large employer can make a region vulnerable to the downturns of a particular sector of the economy, developing entrepreneurs means supporting a diversity of businesses that can offset the negative effects of a decline in any one industry (Wagner & Deller, 1998; Dissart, 2003; Watson & Deller, 2017). Entrepreneurs can also contribute to the local quality of life by offering important services, especially in rural markets with fewer offerings. These may include simple amenities like a coffee shop or a café to essential services like child care and home health aides. Given the benefits of job creation, income growth, poverty alleviation, innovation, stability, and quality of life, it is not surprising to see the appeal of entrepreneurship as an economic development strategy especially for rural areas that appear to lag on many of these aspects of economic performance (Deller, 2010).

The growing emphasis on new firms has been influenced by the rise of systems-thinking and ecosystem development. More and more rural communities are focused on their entrepreneurial ecosystem. This approach is a departure from earlier emphasis on business costs alone. The entrepreneurial ecosystem includes elements of human capital development, financial services, community culture, local leadership, access to markets, and infrastructure, in addition to the regulatory and tax considerations. Within each element there are potentially many features of the community that can be leveraged to support entrepreneurship. For example, in considering the human capital resources within the ecosystem, there may be a range of technical assistance providers, colleges, apprenticeships, and mentors that are meant to educate and assist entrepreneurs directly. Some of these same entities may also be educating the workforce, building the talent pool so that entrepreneurs can find the labor they need to support their businesses. In that sense the ecosystem would include high schools and youth programs that not only educate the future workforce but also influence the career paths of young people and have the chance to encourage business ownership as a viable option. In considering financial capital resources, there are similarly many entities that could strategically rally around entrepreneurs. While banks are critically important in offering loan financing, credit unions, community development financial institutions, rotating loans funds, independent investors, and sponsored competitions can all offer access to capital for entrepreneurs. In working together, these organizations can more efficiently match with the entrepreneurs they are best able to serve in a cohesive, strategic approach that benefits the broader entrepreneurial community.

Entrepreneurship as an economic development strategy especially makes sense in rural communities because it builds on an existing asset. Rural communities by some measures are quite entrepreneurial and, given the traditions of farming and self employment, could be considered more entrepreneurial than urban areas (Deller & Conroy, 2016). In the United States, there are more proprietorships, a legal status for businesses that correlates with entrepreneurial activity, per capita in rural counties compared to urban. There is also evidence that businesses in rural counties are more likely to survive to the critical five-year threshold than are businesses in urban counties (Deller & Conroy, 2016, 2017). While this may be the result of weak competition and few employment alternatives in rural markets, it also speaks to a certain resourcefulness and persistence that can be viewed as entrepreneurial strengths. Many rural areas are also home to the farming community which is inherently entrepreneurial and represents another asset that could be further leveraged to grow rural entrepreneurship.

Despite these relatively positive entrepreneurial indicators for rural regions, the start-up rate has been declining in the rural U.S. The downward trend began at least 40 years ago when the U.S. Census Bureau began tracking businesses by age with the Business Dynamic Statistics. The most recent trend in declining entrepreneurship is somewhat surprising given the research suggesting a U-shaped pattern of entrepreneurial activity along the continuum of economic development. Acs et al., 1994; Blau, 1987; Verheul et al., 2006; Wennekers et al., 2005 all find a U-shaped relationship between national income and entrepreneurship with income on the x-axis and entrepreneurial activity on the y-axis. This pattern suggests that entrepreneurship is prevalent in the early stages of development when income per capita is relatively low, declines as income increases, but increases again with higher income per capita. These studies identify a common trend in developed countries in that in the early twentieth century, especially from the 1950s to the 1970s, entrepreneurship declined. The trend reversed as countries' income level grew, and they reached higher levels of development. The logic behind this pattern is the movement from agriculture, which tends to be dominated by smaller scale entrepreneurial businesses, to manufacturing which tends to be dominated by fewer and larger firms and hence less entrepreneurial, to the modern service economy which should be conducive to more new business formation activity. The decline in the start-up rate, however, suggests there may be another structural shift causing a new trend.

Explanations for the decline in new firm formation have highlighted the role of slowing population growth and business consolidation (Hathaway & Litan, 2014). Yet these explanations result from a study focused on country level regions as well as metropolitan areas and may not apply to rural areas. Some have further speculated that the share of prime-age individuals (35–44 years old) who tend to start new businesses is declining and therefore leading to fewer new firms. Still others have explored the roll of the business environment, namely taxes and regulation. Salfado (2020) finds that the declining share of entrepreneurs in U.S. households is mostly accounted for by a decline in entrepreneurship among college graduates and argues that it may be a positive sign. The trend could signal that, due to technical change, skilled workers have relatively lucrative options in the wage-and-salary sector and that is promising for productivity and growth from a macroeconomic perspective. Even with this new evidence, the exact causes of the decline, and how they may be unique in rural settings, remain far from settled. In a study of female entrepreneurs in the rural U.S., Conroy and Low (2022) found a similar U-shaped pattern and hypothesize that at low income levels women are drawn self-employment as a means of economic survival, but as wage and salary employment opportunities expand the need for self-employment declines. As community or regional incomes grow, there is a larger market for specialized businesses which can be a draw for rural women entrepreneurships. The shift from entrepreneurship out of necessity to entrepreneurship of opportunity drives the U-shaped pattern that is commonly observed. The challenge for most rural areas is if the market for entrepreneurship of opportunity is sufficient to drive new business formation.

Regardless of the causes, the decline in entrepreneurship is concerning given the widespread benefits already discussed. In rural regions this decline is especially worrisome as it has come alongside trailing employment, population, and income metrics relative to urban areas. In the next section, we explore the long-run trend for rural counties in the context of the rural classification system. We show how the method of classifying rural counties will systematically define lower-performing places, in terms of population, employment and income, and, most important for our analysis, businesses growth, as rural. Conversely, over time high-performing counties are more likely to be classified as urban. The result is that rural places will almost necessarily trail behind urban places across a range of metrics when looking at a recent cross-section.

3 The Changing Definition of Rural

There are many definitions of "rural" (Deller & Conroy, 2023). The mix of definitions can lead to ambiguity, making it difficult to have a well-understood concept of rural. Further, the definitions we use often do not reflect the perception of people who live and in and near so called "rural" communities. For example, the way in which the Office of Management and Budget (OMB) defines a metropolitan area has two fundamental components: a county has at least one place (municipality) with a population of at least 50,000 or more and adjacent counties that have a high degree of economic and social integration with that core county. The degree of integration is directly tied to commuting: if 25% of the labor force in a county adjacent to a metropolitan county commute to the core county, then the adjacent county is defined as metropolitan and part of the larger metropolitan area.

These latter criteria can lead to counties where residents view themselves as living in a rural community, and most observers would think of the county as rural, yet they are classified as metropolitan. This notion of what constituted rural as opposed to urban could be considered "in the eyes of the beholder" (e.g., Cloke, 2006; Cloke & Little, 2005; Little, 1999). Consider the Madison, Wisconsin metropolitan area which is set within Dane County which has a population of 542,500 (the City of Madison's population is 258,400). But the Madison Metropolitan area is composed of Dane County itself, Columbia County (north), Green County (south), and Iowa County (west). Each of these three counties is widely described and considered as rural. Columbia County has a total population of 58,500, and the largest place is the city of Portage which has a population of 10,600, Green County has a population of 37,100, and the largest place is the city of Monroe with a population of 10,700 and Iowa County with a population of only 23,700 and its two largest places are Dodgeville with a population of 4,900 and Mineral Point with a population of 2,600. Thus, there are at least three counties in Wisconsin that are, for all practical purposes, rural but are classified as metropolitan by the OMB.

In the U.S., there are more than 10 definitions of rural used by federal agencies and national organizations (Center on Rural Innovation, 2019). Among the most common are the Core Based Statistical Areas (CBSAs) from the Office of Management and Budget (OMB) and the Rural Urban Continuum Codes from the United States Department of Agriculture (USDA). To address some of the concerns about the basic definition of metropolitan, the CBSAs system defines Metropolitan (metro) areas as those regions with a population core of 50,000 or more plus adjacent territories with a high degree of social and economic integration as measured by commuting. Micropolitan (micro) areas are those regions with a population core of 5,000 to 50,000 plus highly integrated adjacent territory. All areas outside the defined metro- and micropolitan regions are defined as "nonmetropolitan" (nonmetro) – a term often used interchangeably with "rural."

The Rural Urban Continuum Codes (often referred to as the Beale Codes) subdivide the metro and nonmetro categories from the OMB into a finer gradient from urban to rural. The metro category is divided into three categories based on the population size of their core metro area (United States Department of Agriculture, 2020). All other areas are divided into six nonmetro categories classified by their degree of urbanization and adjacency to a metro area. The result is a nine-part system for classifying all U.S. counties along the rural-urban continuum. The most urban counties in the system are part of a metropolitan area with one million people or more, followed by those with 250,000 to one million people and, last, those with a population under 250,000. The nonmetro counties are classified first by their urban population into three categories: 20,000 or more, 2,500 to 19,999, and less than 2,500. Second, they are classified by adjacency to one or more metro areas. Nonmetro, nonadjacent counties are the most rural in the system.

The definitions of "rural" have also changed over time. Consider the CBSAs produced by OMB which are generally updated after each decennial census. There are some definitional shifts over time. For example, between the 1990 and 2000 standards, there was an effort to include adjacent territories with a high degree of social and economic integration into metropolitan areas. As a result of these changes in standards, counties could be reclassified to reflect this more inclusive definition of metropolitan.

In general, however, the periodic updates to the CBSA standards mean that counties will be reclassified based on their current size and extent of urbanization. Nonmetropolitan counties that have grown substantially and reached the relevant size threshold are reclassified as metropolitan and, potentially, counties that have downsized are reclassified as nonmetropolitan. Generally, rural counties that are growing in population are doing well economically. This reclassification means high-performing (e.g., high levels of economic growth) rural counties will no longer be counted as nonmetropolitan and instead be reclassified as metropolitan. As a result, the counties that remain in the nonmetropolitan category are those that have not grown, or at least not grown enough to move up into the metro category. And, the counties that are classified as metro are all of those that are growing or have grown in the past to substantial size.

This system almost necessarily implies that the metropolitan counties are going to systematically outperform nonmetropolitan counties across several measures of economic performance. That is to say the observation that rural places are "lagging" is at least partly to do with how we classify rural places. Rather than look at the most recent categorization of rural, perhaps a better way to analyze rural economic performance is to look back at historically rural counties and track them over time with particular attention to those counties that grew so well that they moved up into the metropolitan category.

In Figure 1, we use the historic rural classification from 1970 to examine the population growth of four types of counties. We show the population growth of counties classified as metro in 1970 that have stayed metro as of the most recent classification (n = 604), counties that flipped from nonmetro in 1970 to metro (n = 524), counties that flipped from metro to nonmetro (n = 21), and last counties that stayed nonmetro during the period (n = 1,929). The high-performing rural counties, those with the most dramatic growth, are the counties that flipped from nonmetro to metro. That is to say, if we were to use their current metro classification, the performance of these once rural counties would be attributed to larger urban areas. Conversely, the counties with the least growth, though not by much, were those that flipped from metro to nonmetro, followed closely by the constant nonmetro counties.

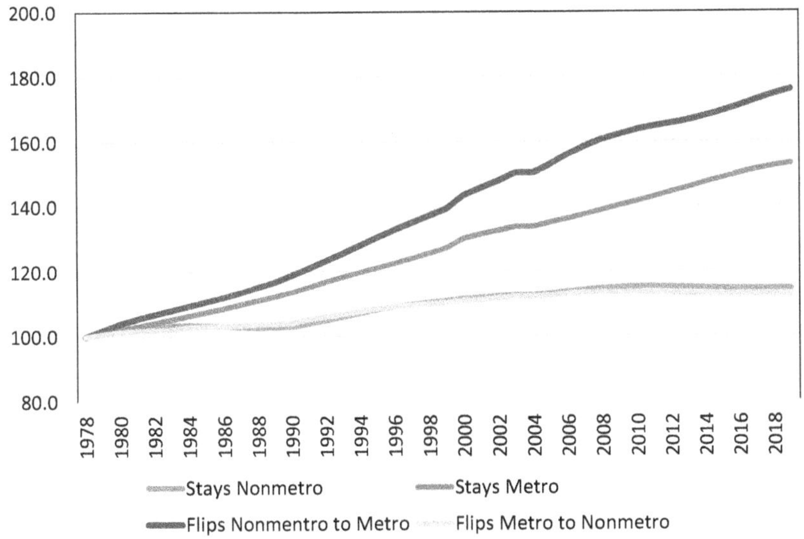

Figure 1: Population Growth Index.
Source: Authors' analysis of data from the U.S. Department of Commerce Bureau of Economic Analysis

Similarly, in Figures 2 and 3, we show employment growth and income growth, respectively, over time for the counties that stayed metro, stayed nonmetro, flipped from non-metro to nonmetro or from nonmetro to metro since 1970. The pattern of performance is the same as for population growth. The counties that flipped from nonmetro to metro perform the best and the constant nonmetro counties and flips from metro to nonmetro had the least growth. With regard to employment, counties that flip from metro to non-metro did rank just slightly better than the constant nonmetro counties which had the least growth. For income, the counties that flipped from metro to nonmetro had the least growth of all four categories just behind the constant nonmetro counties.

Taken together, these results indicate that counties that would be considered metro by today's standard are the best performing rural counties under the 1970s standard. That is, the size-based definition of rural counties, while sensible on face value does systematically categorize the high growth places as metro. An analysis of

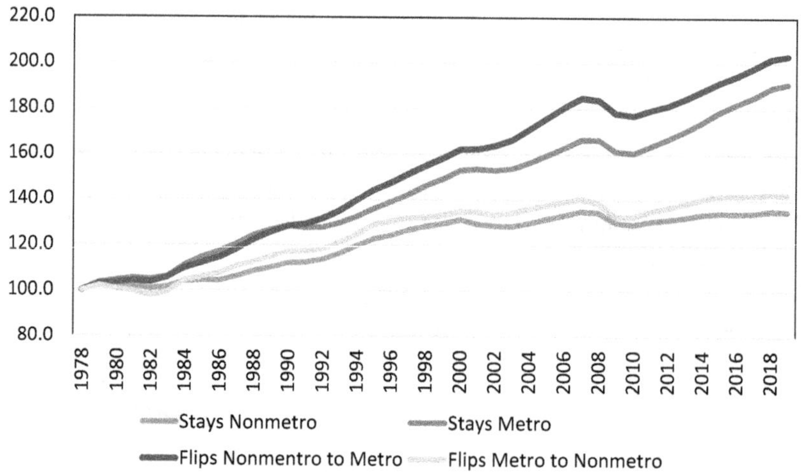

Figure 2: Employment Growth Index.
Source: Authors' analysis of data from the U.S. Department of Commerce Bureau of Economic Analysis

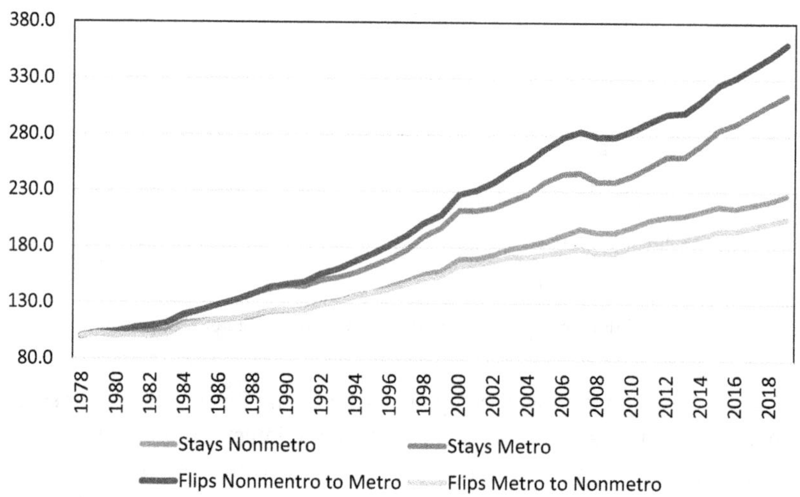

Figure 3: Total Personal Income Growth Index (2012$).
Source: Authors' analysis of data from the U.S. Department of Commerce Bureau of Economic Analysis

rural counties based on their current classification would exclude those rural counties that have performed well economically and grown, perpetuating the perception of underperforming rural counties. This finding is consistent with the work of Isserman (2005) and Schaeffer, Kahsai and Jackson (2013).

Given the importance of the rural classification system in analyzing economic performance across population, employment, and income, it is worth asking if there is a similar pattern for business growth and start-up activity. It could be that when we apply the same framework to entrepreneurial outcomes, we see that the classification system influences the perceived performance of rural places. In Figures 4 and 5, we look at employer and nonemployer establishment growth, respectively. While we discuss the difference between employer and nonemployer businesses in more detail below, the difference can be thought of as a business where an individual is self-employed and has no other paid employees versus a business that has at least one formal paid employee.[1]

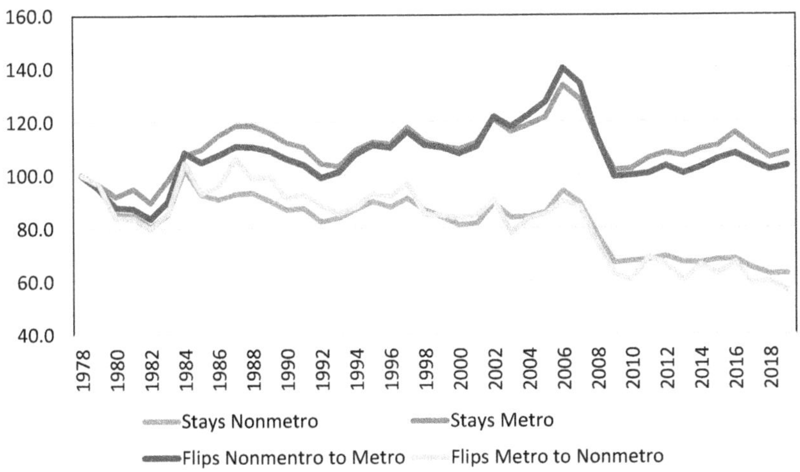

Figure 4: Employer Establishment Growth Index.
Source: Authors' analysis of the U.S. Census County Business Patterns

When looking at the growth trajectory of these two types of businesses, the same general pattern emerges. For employer establishments, those with paid employees, metro counties, and counties that flipped from nonmetro to metro performed the best. In addition to the relatively strong performance of metro counties, there are several trends worth noting. First, there was a large decline in employer firms associated with the Great Recession across all county subsets. In metro counties, the Great Recession eliminated at least two decades worth of growth, putting the number of employer firms near 1980 levels. In nonmetro counties, the Great Recession accelerated the decline of employer firms. In 2010, nonmetro employer establishments were 60–70% of their levels at the beginning of the series in 1978. Since the Great Recession metro employer establishments have grown modestly, while nonmetro have continued to slowly decline in number.

1 There are some "one person shops" that fall under the employer business classification because of the way they structure their businesses. For example, the self-employed person sets the business up as a corporation and they draw a salary. From a purely technical perspective, if the business pays into the federal unemployment insurance program, they are considered employer businesses.

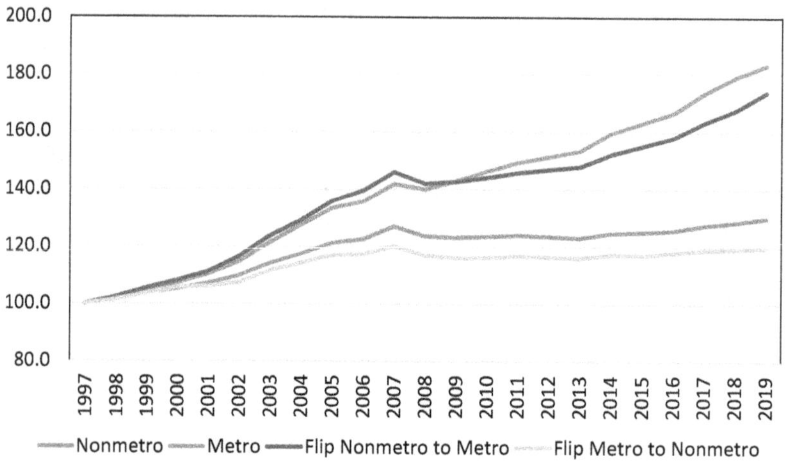

Figure 5: Nonemployer Establishment Growth Index.
Source: Authors' analysis of the U.S. Census Nonemployer Statistics

For nonemployer establishments, we again see that metro counties and counties that flip to metro have the strongest performance. In this case, the constant metro counties do slightly better than the counties that flip but both categories exceed the performance of the nonmetro subsets. Unfortunately, data on nonemployer firms is only available since 1997, a much shorter time period than the other economic indicators considered. The growth of nonemployer establishments, however, during this short time period is remarkable. Nonemployer establishments in metro counties grew by almost 85% in the 22-year period. In counties that flipped from nonmetro to metro, they grew by almost 75%. For constant nonmetro counties, nonemployers grew 30% and 20% in counties that flipped from metro to nonmetro. Combined with the trends in Figure 5, we can conclude that nonemployer establishments are the primary source of growth in the business community—especially in rural areas.

The implication here is that, for rural areas, entrepreneurship tends to be dominated by the self-employed who do not hire formal employees. From the perspective of the community that may be striving to assist new businesses, these self-employer businesses tend to be "hidden" and difficult to observe within the community. They could be home-based businesses that, while vital to the vibrancy of rural communities, can almost be invisible, making it difficult to provide assistance.

In Figure 6, we apply this same analysis to the start-up rate or establishment entry rate. Though not a growth index as in Figures 1–5, the long-run trend downward is remarkably consistent across the different types of counties. It is still the case that metro counties, especially those that flipped from nonmetro to metro, do relatively well in terms of the start-up rate. Somewhat unsurprisingly, counties that flip from metro to nonmetro do relatively poorly, but, in general, the trend is downward for all types of counties. The downward trend in the start-up rate alongside the growth pattern of employer and nonemployer establishments can offer some insight into the state of entrepreneurship in the U.S., especially the rural U.S. Much has been made of the decline in entrepreneurial activity in the U.S., but the growth of nonemployer establishments suggests some types of entrepreneurial activity are increasing. In addition to the classification challenges discussed in this section, this disconnect between declining startup activity and the rapidly growing number very small establishments points to another potential issue in understanding rural entrepreneurship – how we measure startup activity.

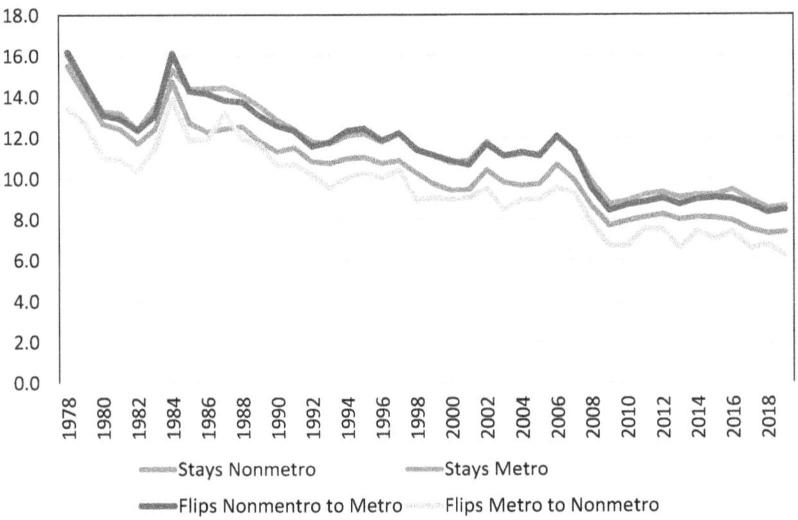

Figure 6: Average Establishment Entry Rate.
Source: Authors' analysis of the U.S. Census Business Dynamic Statistics

4 How we Measure Start-Up Activity

In the U.S., there are few publicly available sources of data on new firms. The best known, such as the Business Dynamic Statistics, come from the U.S. Census Bureau and define an establishment birth based on employment. A new firm is "born" in the year it transitions from zero to positive employment. That is, a new firm is counted when it hires its first employees and files payroll taxes. A new establishment can either be a business that first hires employees after operating for some time with just the owner(s) or it may be a de novo establishment that hires employees at the outset. In the former case, the business is not truly new or a "start-up" in the sense that it opened long before the first employees were hired. In this case, the establishment is counted as a birth not when it first opened but when it hit an important growth stage in moving from employing only the owners to hiring wage-or-salary workers. The actual start of these firms is relatively unaccounted for, at least in terms of a comprehensive publicly available dataset.

As a consequence of data availability, the start-up rate then often reflects only businesses with paid employees. In general, it does not include the vast majority of businesses which have no paid employees most likely because they simply are not tracked as closely. In the U.S., businesses with paid employees represent a small and shrinking share of all businesses. As of 2019, the most recent year available, just 23% of businesses had employees.[2] Twenty years ago in 1999, 30% of businesses had paid employees.[3] Meanwhile nonemployer firms have grown rapidly over the last several decades in rural and urban communities alike, far outpacing the growth of businesses with paid employees. In the U.S., from 1999 to 2019, nonemployer establishments grew by 68% overall whereas employer establishments increased by just 13%. In rural counties, based on the 2013 Rural-Urban Continuum Codes from the USDA, nonemployer growth was much more modest at just 16%. Yet, these businesses were the only source of growth in the business community as employer businesses declined by 8% during the same period.[4] The result is that the composition of businesses in the U.S. is changing – an indicator that the composition of entrepreneurship changing. Small start-ups of nonemployer firms are seemingly becoming more common as new employer businesses stagnate or even recede in many rural places.

Absent the entrepreneurial activity of nonemployer businesses, the start-up rate as typically presented based on employer firms does not tell the full story of entrepreneurship. Broad swaths of entrepreneurial pursuits from sole proprietors and partnerships are missing. It could be that the long-run decline in entrepreneurship represented by the downward trend in start-up activity should more precisely be interpreted as a long-run decline in new employer firms. If we were to track and include the entrepreneurial activity of small nonemployer businesses we might observe a different trend. Currently, this large and growing segment of entrepreneurial activity is largely unseen. The so-labeled "decline of entrepreneurship" may then at least partly reflect a change in the type of entrepreneurship toward poorly-accounted-for small individual proprietors rather than a comprehensive decline in entrepreneurial activity. For rural communities, where nonemployers are a source of growth, accounting for this change may be especially important.

---

2 In 2019, there were 27,104,006 nonemployer businesses and 7,959,103 employer businesses (U.S. Census, 2022).

3 In 1999, there were 16,152, 604 nonemployer businesses (U.S. Census, 2002) and 7,008,444 employer establishments (U.S. Census, 2001).

4 For comparison, in urban counties, nonemployer establishments grew by 78% and employer establishments grew by 18%.

5 The Growth of Nonemployers

Nonemployer businesses make up a large and growing share of the business community. The increasing number of nonemployers may be attributable to the smaller average minimum efficient scale for businesses in the U.S. as the economy shifts more toward providing services. More businesses too are opting to contract specialty skills and business services rather than have those skills in-house. For example, a small firm may simply hire a self-employed accountant to do its payroll and taxes rather than hire an accountant within the company. The same may be true of legal services, or even marketing and branding. As a result, firms have become smaller but there are more opportunities for self-employed individuals to work as independent contractors. To some extent, this may reflect the growing gig or share-economy wherein freelance and short-term "gigs" or jobs are becoming more common. There is also some evidence that the increase is linked to diverse populations (McDermott & Conroy, 2021). Perhaps because of challenges in the conventional wage-and-salary labor market, people of color are more likely to pursue self-employment or perhaps this partly reflects the high entrepreneurial propensity for immigrants in the U.S. and abroad which has been highlighted in other research (e.g. Xavier et al., 2012).

The Federal Reserve Banks (2018) classify nonemployers by (1) those doing supplemental work, (2) those doing contract work, (3) stable nonemployers, (4) early-stage potential employers, and (5) late-stage potential employers. Roughly one in four nonemployer firms are supplemental-work firms – those that offer a secondary source of income for the owner with no growth intentions for the future. One in five nonemployer firms are contract workers for whom the business is their primary source of income, but the owner has no plans to expand. Stable nonemployers make up 25% of all nonemployers. They are firms that are not independent contractors but are the primary source of income for the owner(s), though there are no plans to hire employees. The early- and late-stage potential employers are those that intend to hire employees and represent the remaining 25–30% of nonemployers. So, while these nonemployer businesses do not have employees, and the majority do not intend to hire wage and salaried employees, there are some that may eventually hire employees and a handful could become a significant employer in the community. Perhaps more important, most of these nonemployer businesses are the primary source of income for the owner, making them an important segment of the business community and an entrepreneurial seedbed for future employer firms. Indeed, a more robust market for nonemployer businesses can feed into a stronger entrepreneurial ecosystem for the community.

With the pandemic, nonemployers seem to have only become more prevalent. There were many reasons to be worried about entrepreneurship in the pandemic. Business owners struggled as caution and restrictions limited consumer activities. Businesses saw demand fall for many goods and services alongside increased costs and new expectations for sanitation and distancing. Supply chains were crippled and businesses struggled to source some inputs. In this new environment, self-employment decreased dramatically as business owners exited in the early months of the pandemic, especially among people of color (Fairlie, 2020). New business activity also slowed as entrepreneurs likely perceived greater risk and additional challenges.

The decline in entrepreneurship only lasted a few months, however. By the end of the summer in 2020, self-employment began to recover and business applications began to accelerate. Business applications are an indicator of entrepreneurial intent. Business owners must apply for an employer identification number (EIN) early in the process of forming their business. The EIN is essential for filing payroll taxes once a business hires employees, but it will likely be necessary for other business functions such as licensing or opening a business bank account. In July of 2020, business applications reached the highest level on record at over half a million nationwide, a 96% increase from the previous year.

Many of these business applications will result in nonemployer businesses. Only a small share, between 10% and 15% will go on to actually hire their first employees within two years of their application, and this share of business applications that result in fully formed businesses has been declining over time (Julien et al., 2022). The remaining business applications may result in nonemployers businesses or businesses that may never go on to operate at all. The pandemic may ultimately be characterized as a time with a much higher level of business applications but a lower rate of resulting employer business formations. Research suggests that instead a larger and larger share of business applications represent nonemployer businesses (O'Donnell et al., 2021).

The high level of entrepreneurial intent measured by business applications and the compositional shift may be an opportunity for rural communities. Nonemployer businesses have dominated growth in the rural business community at least since the Great Recession and the pandemic may prove to only exacerbate that trend. With a crop of budding entrepreneurs, it is important to consider how rural communities can be supportive and realize the economic benefits of increased entrepreneurial activity.

6 Implications for Rural Development and Policy

Policy has long prioritized jobs as a key outcome. As a result, it is common for entrepreneurship policies to support firms that have paid employees or those very small businesses that are growing quickly and will soon hire more employees or even those that will soon hire their first employees. The firms without paid employees, nonemployers, appear to receive far less attention and resources. The fact that nonemployer firms do provide at least one job – a job for the owner him or herself seems to be largely overlooked. In fact, nonemployer firms employ 17% of the workforce (Federal Reserve Banks, 2018). These jobs are even more important in rural communities where job growth has been modest at best. Importantly, a considerable share of these businesses intend to hire employees in the future as well and may only need the right kind of support to reach their goals.

This bias toward employer firms may effectively exclude an important segment of rural business activity from beneficial policies and programs. Most growth of employer firms has occurred in urban settings as shown by our analysis. As a result, urban areas are likely in a position to disproportionately benefit from entrepreneurial support programs focused primarily job creation. Conversely, in rural counties, business growth has been dominated by nonemployer firms which are less often the target of support programs. The result of more resources going to businesses in regions that are already larger on average could be a growing gap in economic performance between urban and rural places. Policies focused explicitly on nonemployer businesses, or, better, rural nonemployer businesses, may be essential to achieving equitable entrepreneurial support.

Nonemployer businesses may also receive less attention simply because they are harder to see and find. The nature of being a small business with just an owner or owners, may mean the business is more likely to be home-based, less likely to have a store front, and/or operate exclusively online. Without the same kind of physical presence and visibility as traditional downtown businesses or large manufacturers, these types of firms are difficult to identify and track. As a consequence, policymakers and local leaders may be less aware of these types of businesses in their communities, let alone be able to identify their needs and respond with policy. Further, relatively large shares of women-owned businesses as well as those owned by people of color are nonemployer businesses. The historical challenges to representation and long-standing business networks that exclude these often-marginalized groups may make it even less likely that they are the focus of policy conversations and resource allocation.

The opportunity going forward is to try to identify inclusive entrepreneurial support programs that help nonemployers and, by extension, the rural communities where they live. Programs like incubators and accelerators may be a poor fit for supporting rural entrepreneurs as they seem to rely on critical mass that is hard to achieve in sparse rural settings. Further, these can have an orientation toward growth – *rapid growth* – in a way that is not consistent with the reality of rural nonemployer businesses, many of which do not have ambitions to expand.

Investing in broadband infrastructure is one strategy that is well-suited to rural entrepreneurs and inclusive of even the smallest firms. Both Conroy and Low (2022) and Deller, Whitacre and Conroy (2022) find that the startup rate is higher in places with better access to broadband and that impact is larger for small nonemployer-type firms in the most remote rural regions. With the COVID-19 pandemic, broadband has become only more important in all facets of society. For many businesses, connectivity was central to their ability to pivot to new strategies. Among new business applications during the pandemic, the largest number of was in online retail indicating a rapidly accelerating industry that relies on the internet. Broadband may also be important for reaching nonemployer businesses with support programs via online networks. As many of these businesses do not have a store front and many are owned by women of people of color who face challenges to joining mainstream business networks, conventional business associations and in-person events may not reach these nonemployer-entrepreneurs. It may be possible to leverage online professional networks to reach nonemployer business owners and build virtual spaces for gathering, learning, and information sharing.

While investments in the physical broadband infrastructure are necessary for building a stronger rural entrepreneurial ecosystem, it is not sufficient. Policies and development strategies aimed at fostering entrepreneurship must also address adoption of broadband and how to effectively utilize broadband internet. New rural businesses owners and managers need assistance in how best to take advantage of these new investments in the physical infrastructure. For example, how to best use the internet for marketing and sales, building viable input supply chains, and taking advantage of the business services available via the internet.

Childcare can also be an important entrepreneurial support program. Much like broadband, childcare is a service that much of the workforce, not just entrepreneurs, require to be successful. Having adequate affordable quality childcare can support the growth goals of entrepreneurs, in that it affords the space and time they need to dedicate to their businesses. Further, childcare providers are entrepreneur-business owners themselves that are integral to rural communities where childcare can be particularly limited.

Small business support programs may also need to be tailored to businesses without employees and modest to stable growth intentions, which may mean considering the needs of home-based businesses specifically. Access to small loan amounts, expanded technical assistance for online marketing, sales, and customer acquisition may also be beneficial. Keeping in mind that nonemployer businesses are also more common among diverse business owners, support materials may need to be offered in a variety of languages and a range of platforms. Ethnic and diverse business chambers and community development financial institutions may be important partners to reach these relatively underserved audiences.

Perhaps the greatest challenge for rural communities is building a supportive network among local businesses and particularly nascent entrepreneurs. As we have discussed, in rural areas many entrepreneurs are "one person shops" without visible storefronts and identifying them within the community can be a challenge. But being part of a supportive network of local businesses will better position these small businesses to thrive and grow. The phrase "it's not what you know, but who you know" underpins the importance of these networks. For some communities the institution through which these networks connect is a chamber of commerce or business association. These groups must not only be open to all businesses within the community but also actively seek out new members, particularly women and people of color. A welcoming environment can send a strong signal to the strength of the local entrepreneurial ecosystem. These institutions must also provide professional development opportunities to help existing and new businesses be more effective in operating their businesses. Examples include workshops with local business loan officers on how to present business ideas and needs to financial institutions, or how to effectively use social media for marketing and customer relations, how to take advantage of the latest changes in business tax codes, or how to effectively work with employees, among others. Often local business owners, particularly nonemployer businesses, are very good at providing the good or service that they offer, but need assistance in the actual running of the business. This is particularly true of nascent entrepreneurs who struggle with how to structure and operate the business. As we have seen, a supportive entrepreneurial ecosystem is necessary for economically vibrant local economies and the broader well-being of the community.

References

Acs, Z.J., Audretsch, D.B., & Evans, D. (1994). Why does the self-employment rate vary across countries and over time? No. 871. London: Center for Economic and Policy Research.

Birch, D.G.W. (1981). Who creates jobs? The Public Interest, 65, 3–14.

Birch, D.G.W. (1987). Job creation in America: How our smallest companies put the most people to work. University of Illinois at Urbana-Champaign's Academy for Entrepreneurial Leadership Historical Research Reference in Entrepreneurship.

Blau, D.M. (1987). A time-series analysis of self-employment in the United States. Journal of Political Economy, 95(3), 445–467.

Center on Rural Innovation. (2019). Exploring definitions of "Rural". Hartland, Vermont. https://ruralinnovation.us/resources/mapping-and-data-analytics/data-for-action-map-2/.

Cloke, P. (2006). Conceptualizing rurality. In P. Cloke, T. Mardsen, & P.H. Mooney (Eds.), Handbook of rural studies. London, UK: Sage.

Cloke, P., & Little, J. (2005). Introduction: Other countrysides. In P. Cloke, & J. Little (Eds.), Contested countryside cultures. New York: Rutledge.

Conroy, T., & Low, S.A. (2022). Entrepreneurship, broadband, and gender: Evidence from establishment births in rural America. International Regional Science Review, 45(1), 3–35. https://doi.org/10.1177/01600176211018749.

Cromartie, J., Dobis, E.A., Krumel, T.P., McGranahan, D., & Pender, J. (2020). Rural America at a glance, 2020 Edition. United States Department of Agriculture. https://www.ers.usda.gov/webdocs/publications/100089/eib-221.pdf?v=9894.

Deller, S.C. (2010). Spatial variations in the role of microenterprises in economic growth. Review of Regional Studies, 40(1), 71–79.

Deller, S.C. (2021). Are we in the 4th wave of economic development? Southern regional science fellows address. Review of Regional Studies, 51(2), 233–245.

Deller, S.C. (2014). Strategies for rural wealth creation: A progression of thinking through ideas and concepts. In J.L. Pender, B.A. Weber, T.G. Johnson, & J.M. Fannin (Eds.), Rural wealth creation. London and New York: Routledge.

Deller, S.C., & Conroy, T. (2023). Regional economic trends across the rural-urban divide. In N. Walzer, & C. Merrett (Eds.), Rural areas in transition: Meeting challenges & making opportunities. London: Routledge Publishing.

Deller, S.C., & Conroy, T. (2017). Business survival rates across the urban–rural divide. Community Development, 48(1), 67–85. doi: 10.1080/15575330.2016.1246459.
Deller, S.C., & Conroy, T.. (2016). Survival rates of rural businesses: What the evidence tells us. Choices. Quarter 4. https://www.choicesmagazine.org/choices-magazine/submitted-articles/survival-rates-of-rural-businesses-what-the-evidence-tells-us.
Deller, S.C., & Goetz, S. (2009). Historical description of economic development policy. In S. Goetz, S. Deller, & T. Harris (Eds.), Targeting regional economic development. London: Routledge Publishing.
Deller, S., Whitacre, B., & Conroy, T. (2022). Rural broadband speeds and business startup rates. American Journal of Agricultural Economics, 104(3), 999–1025.
Dissart, J.C. (2003). Regional economic diversity and regional economic stability: Research results and agenda. International Regional Science Review, 26(4), 423–446.
Dobis, E., Krumel, T.P. Jr., Cromartie, J., Conely, K.L., Sanders, A., & Ortiz, R. (2021). Rural America at a glance, 2021 Edition. United States Department of Agriculture. https://www.ers.usda.gov/webdocs/publications/102576/eib-230.pdf?v=3045.5.
Eisinger, P.K. (1998). The rise of the entrepreneurial state: State and local economic development policy in the United States. Madison, WI: Univ of Wisconsin Press.
Fairlie, R.W. (2020, July 6). The impact of covid-19 on small business owners: The first three months after social-distancing restrictions. NBER. Retrieved January 12, 2022, from https://www.nber.org/papers/w27462.
Federal Reserve Banks of New York, Cleveland, and Richmond. (2018). Small Business Credit Survey: Report on Nonemployer Firms. https://www.fedsmallbusiness.org/medialibrary/fedsmallbusiness/files/2018/sbcs-nonemployer-firms-report.pdf.
Haltiwanger, J., Jarmin, R.S., & Miranda, J. (2016). Who creates jobs? Small versus large versus young. The Review of Economics and Statistics, XCV(2), 347–361.
Hathaway, I., & Litan, R.E. (2014). What's driving the decline in the firm formation rate? A Partial Explanation. Report. Brookings Institution. https://www.brookings.edu/wp-content/uploads/2016/06/driving_decline_firm_formation_rate_hathaway_litan.pdf.
Isserman, A. (2005). In the National interest: Defining rural correctly for research and policy. International Regional Science Review, 28(4), 465–499.
Julian, H., Callon, T., & Conroy, T. (2022). The rise of entrepreneurship during the pandemic. WIndicators, 5(1), University of Wisconsin-Madison, Division of Extension. https://economicdevelopment.extension.wisc.edu/articles/windicators-volume-5-number-1-the-rise-of-entrepreneurship-during-the-pandemic/.
Kulcsár, L.J. (2019). The demography of rural America. A House Divided: Geographic Disparities in 21st Century America Conference. Boston. https://www.bostonfed.org/-/media/Images/research-conference-2019/papers/Session-5-Kulcsar.pdf.
Little, J. (1999). Otherness, representation and the cultural construction of rurality. Progress in Human Geography, 23, 437–442.
Loveridge, S., & Smith, T.R. (1992). Factors related to success in business retention and expansion programs. Community Development, 23(2), 66–78.
Loveridge, S., Smith, T.R., & Morse, G.W. (1991). What does it take to run a local business retention and expansion program? A six state survey. Economic Development Review, 9(1), 12.
McDermott, M., & Conroy, T. (2021). Nonemployer businesses & diversity. WIndicators, 4(1), University of Wisconsin-Madison, Division of Extension. https://economicdevelopment.extension.wisc.edu/articles/windicators-volume-4-number-2-nonemployer-businesses-diversity/.
O'Donnell, J., Newman, D., & Fikri, K.. (2021, February 8). The startup surge? Unpacking 2020 trends in business formation. Economic Innovation Group. Retrieved January 11, 2022, from https://eig.org/news/the-startup-surge-business-formation-trends-in-2020.

Olberding, J.C. (2002). Diving into the "Third Waves" of regional governance and economic development strategies: A study of regional partnerships for economic development in US metropolitan areas. Economic Development Quarterly, 16(3), 251–272.

Pender, J., Hertz, T., Cromartie, J., & Farrigan, T. (2019). Rural America at a glance, 2019 Edition. United States Department of Agriculture. https://www.ers.usda.gov/publications/pub-details/?pubid=95340.

Porter, M.E. (1998). Clusters and the new economics of competition. Harvard Business Review, 76(6).

Porter, M.E. (2000). Location, competition, and economic development: Local clusters in a global economy. Economic Development Quarterly, 14(1), 15–34.

Rupasingha, A., & Goetz, S.I. (2011). Self-employment and local economic performance: Evidence from US counties. Papers in Regional Science, 92(1), 141–161. https://doi.org/10.1111/j.1435-5957.2011.00396.x.

Salgado, S.. (2020). Technical change and entrepreneurship. The Wharton School, University of Pennsylvania. SRN: https://ssrn.com/abstract=3616568 or http://dx.doi.org/10.2139/ssrn.3616568.

Schaeffer, P.V., Kahsai, M.S., & Jackson, R.W. (2013). Beyond the rural– urban dichotomy: Essay in honor of professor AM Isserman. International Regional Science Review, 36(1), 81–96.

Si, S., Ahlstrom, D., Wei, J., & Cullen, J. (2020). Business, entrepreneurship and innovation toward poverty reduction. Entrepreneurship & Regional Development, 32(1–2), 1–20.

Thiede, B.C., Lichter, D.T., & Slack, T. (2018). Working, but poor: The good life in rural America? Journal of Rural Studies, 59, 183–193. https://doi.org/10.1016/j.jrurstud.2016.02.007.

United States Department of Agriculture. (2020). Rural-Urban Continuum Codes: Documentation. https://www.ers.usda.gov/data-products/rural-urban-continuum-codes/documentation.aspx.

United States Census Bureau. (2022). 2019 CBP and NES Combined Report. https://www.census.gov/data/tables/2019/econ/nonemployer-statistics/2019-combined-report.html.

United States Census Bureau. (2002). Nonemployer Statistics: 1999. https://www2.census.gov/programs-surveys/nonemployer-statistics/tables/1999/ns-99/ns-99.pdf.

United States Census Bureau. (2001). United State County Business Patterns: 1999. https://www2.census.gov/programs-surveys/cbp/tables/1999/cbp99-1.pdf.

Verheul, I., Van Stel, A., & Thurik, A.R. (2006). Explaining female and male entrepreneurship at the country level. Entrepreneurship and Regional Development, 18(2), 151–183.

Wagner, J.E., & Deller, S.C. (1998). Measuring the effects of economic diversity on growth and stability. Land Economics, 74(4), 541–556.

Watson, P., & Deller, S. (2017). Economic diversity, unemployment and the great recession. The Quarterly Review of Economics and Finance, 64, 1–11.

Wennekers, S., van Wennekers, A., Thurik, R., & Reynolds, P. (2005). Nascent entrepreneurship and the level of economic development. Small Business Economics, 24(3), 293–309.

Wojan, T.R., & Pulver, G.C. (1995). Location patterns of high growth industries in rural counties. Growth and Change, 26(1), 3–22.

Xavier, S.R., Kelley, D., Kew, J., Herrignton, M., & Vorderwülbecke, A.. (2012). Global Entrepreneurship Monitor. 2012 Global Report. https://www.gemconsortium.org/file/open?fileId=48545.

Michael W-P Fortunato and Theodore R. Alter

Energizing Rural and Non-traditional Entrepreneurial Ecosystems Using the Sociological Imagination and Theories of the Middle Range

Abstract: This chapter presents two bodies of work from sociology – C. Wright Mills' *The Sociological Imagination* and Robert Merton's *Theories of the Middle Range* – as promising theoretical approaches for improving theory creation within the entrepreneurial ecosystems literature. This approach seeks to bridge the general and the specific in entrepreneurial ecosystem research, creating a body of middle-range theory that views entrepreneurial ecosystems as heterogeneous and diverse social systems intended to support entrepreneurship. It further provides room for rural and non-traditional ecosystems that may be effective, emergent, or nascent according to a different set of value propositions than those suggested by mainstream literature. The chapter presents suggestions for both research and practice that can inform, and be informed by, a more pluralistic and inclusive approach to theory building, as well as describing the pitfalls of applying mainstream techniques to areas with poor model fit to those techniques.

Keywords: entrepreneurship development, entrepreneurial ecosystem, grassroots, middle-range theory, non-traditional, proto-ecosystems, rural, sociological imagination, urban bias

1 On the Plurality of Entrepreneurial Ecosystems

This chapter presents a discussion about rural entrepreneurial ecosystems, and why current research struggles to address rural and non-traditional ecosystems in ways that can profoundly benefit entrepreneurship development in those places. We then propose some alternative ways of thinking about such ecosystems in terms of integrated research and practice, connecting to different disciplinary traditions that receive less attention in the entrepreneurship literature. In the pages that follow, we aim to continue a conversa-

Funding: Alter's work on this chapter was supported by the USDA National Institute of Food and Agriculture and Multistate/Regional Research Appropriations under Project #PEN04802 and Accession #7003365.

Michael W-P Fortunato, Creative Insight Community Development
Theodore R. Alter, The Pennsylvania State University (Retired)

https://doi.org/10.1515/9783110791396-003

tion that we have been advancing as scholars and practitioners in both our research and our daily practice as community and economic development professionals. In that conversation, we have been advocating – through writing, editing, applied research, teaching, and outreach work – for a more robust and nuanced explanation of *the entrepreneurial ecosystem* that considers the capacity of rural areas and non-traditional ecosystems to develop, thrive, and – unlike in the literature – to be recognized as functional and/or emergent ecosystems in the first place.

Ecosystem literature *is* much like entrepreneurship literature *was* about two decades ago – focused either explicitly or tacitly on the cultivation of urban entrepreneurs, or on entrepreneurship as a fundamentally urban phenomenon.[1] While not always stated explicitly, there has been a long urban bias in entrepreneurship development. Cities are, after all, the kinds of places with a dense customer base, talent pool, and the supporting resources necessary to launch a business (including both business support and funding). Cities are historically places of business, trade, and economic development as we understand it today, a perspective that few will likely challenge. The literature on agglomeration economies is large and robust (classics include Puga, 2010; Duranton & Puga, 2004; Rosenthal & Strange, 2004; Porter, 1996), and it is easy to understand why modern entrepreneurs want to be "in the middle of it all." Furthermore, we are very excited by emerging insights about building systems for entrepreneurship in cities across the world as vehicles for distributing economic power to new entrepreneurs with great ideas that hold promise for contributing to well-being and economic growth.

Despite a firestorm of interest in entrepreneurial ecosystems since around 2010, one of our frustrations has been the limited usefulness of the research literature in supporting *rural* and *small-town* ecosystem development, our specialty. Isenberg posits the emergence of one "runaway success" business for every 50,000 to 150,000 population (2011a; 9). However, most of the communities in which we work possess what the literature would likely consider a very weak infrastructure for supporting entrepreneurship. Many of these communities are remote and small, with an economic base centered on a mix of traditional primary and secondary industries, and somewhat basic service-based industries. Government investment or the presence of a county seat can play an outsized role in employing the local population base. The cost of doing business is low, but often so are profit margins. There are few formal support

1 Dabson (2001) chronicled the obstacles facing rural entrepreneurs and why so many entrepreneurs are drawn to urban locations. Entrepreneurship, while not often directly mentioned, is bound up with the fundamentals and mechanisms of economic growth (see Acs and Szerb, 2007; Baumol and Strom, 2007), which by transference can be related to the growth of cities, mega-regions, and clusters in urban locations (see Harrison and Hoyler, 2015; Delgado, Porter, and Stern, 2010). Especially when research institutions are involved (see Feld, 2012; Audretsch and Lehmann, 2005), cities are often considered to have steep competitive advantages in terms of their capability to generate full ecosystems of entrepreneurial action (Isenberg 2011a; 2011b; 2010).

systems, nearby institutions of research or higher education, or an in-migrating talent pool. Agglomeration economies tend to be small and limited in scope; these communities are far enough from population centers to limit the cultivation of a dense, local customer base; and travel can irritatingly long for commuters in either direction. The presence of venture capital is virtually non-existent, and angel investment is small by urban standards, and typically locally focused. Virtual and remote work may not be possible in areas where broadband access is constrained and technical literacy underdeveloped. Tourism increasingly plays a role in building the local export base, but this can be seasonal, cyclical, and unpredictable. When any of these limiting factors for ecosystem development are *not* present in communities, the scale of local advantage is still quite small in comparison to larger areas (i.e., having not one but *two* casket manufacturing companies in one place is hardly an "agglomeration economy" or "cluster" by just about anyone's standards).

As scholar-practitioners in rural areas and small towns, we have watched the evolution of the entrepreneurial ecosystem become more globally connected, more focused on highly specific social and economic contexts, and with few exceptions, more urban and large scale. Yet, we have utilized our own practice to cultivate what might be called *proto-ecosystem* or *nascent ecosystem development* in the communities where we work. We define these as smaller collectives, communities, and peer groups that fulfill many of the functions of an ecosystem in much the same manner that a general store provides goods and sundries in a very small town. The general store is small, not very elaborate, and contains a wide range of very basic offerings. It focuses on scope over scale, perhaps offering one or two quality options for most of life's bare essentials. It is housed under one roof instead of being housed across many storefronts and retail locations, the latter having a higher degree of both variety and specialization. It is unpretentious and lacks modern flare but is still commonly viewed by locals as a lifeline, a gathering place, and a place where information (and gossip, which is underrated in terms of understanding local culture and opportunities) are exchanged. Next to an urban big-box store or an online service like amazon.com, the general store may seem anachronistic and laughably uncompetitive. To rural residents, even those who make prodigious use of online retailers and the occasional trip to the "big town" to visit a big box store or major grocery chain, the general store remains an iconic and culturally relevant establishment where connection centered on local relationships is still alive and well. It is *their* "third place," their gathering spot (Oldenburg, 1997) – even if the general store in question takes the form of a coffee shop, a local diner, or a well-worn retail establishment. It is the kind of place that makes rural *community* possible.

In our view, the same is true for rural entrepreneurial ecosystems, even if they are nascent, small, or seemingly anachronistic and basic compared to most of the urban ecosystems featured in modern literature. The story of rural ecosystems is like the general store: the story of fewer people and organizations doing more to support the basic functions of a thriving entrepreneurial environment within a specific cultural and spatial context. In stark contrast to the origins of the ecosystem literature (Isenberg, 2010; Cohen, 2006), the ecosystem's goal may be less focused on traditional capitalist growth and more focused on lifestyle and interpersonal networks (Jones, Ratten & Hayduk, 2020; Neumeyer et al., 2019) and on connection to place (Kibler et al., 2015), not to mention cherished traditions that are more suited to the local population than a larger, urban center (Dabson, 2001; Mitchell, 1998). The current literature may view this pessimistically, as researchers' eyes are more keenly focused on "large established ecosystems," primarily in developed markets, and use the study of these ecosystems to identify key components of entrepreneurial ecosystems more generally (Roundy, 2017: 242); along with issues like patent development (Audretsch et al., 2019). We advance a counterargument that makes space for ecosystem alternatives centered on a different set of values that incorporate a plurality of *qualities* of life and cultural values that evade monocultural thinking about how to best build a thriving entrepreneurial ecosystem.

A main reason that we are optimistic about rural ecosystem development is that many ecosystem development ideas are not new at all, having seen much of their advancement prior to the mainstreaming of the term *ecosystem* in the entrepreneurship literature. When ecosystems are viewed in terms of tangible "stuff," a laundry list of assets, framework conditions, and organizations a community must possess to support entrepreneurship development, then yes, the idea of a shift in focus from entrepreneurship as an individualistic endeavor toward a structural and environmental phenomenon is relatively new. We have witnessed many of these findings translate into policy that supports a great deal of building new support systems in the fashion of other cities that have been successful, in the hopes that a greater investment in support systems and entrepreneurship-focused infrastructure will translate into more impressive economic growth, still the gold standard for success in urban ecosystems.[2]

However, when ecosystems are viewed more broadly as *evolutionary social systems*, the doors open to entire fields of literature from sociology, organizational behavior, social psychology, community development, politics, institutional and behavioral economics, and other disciplines that have examined the relational dynamics of heterogeneous groups with insights dating back over 150 years. The terms used are different, such as

2 Examples of this abound. On the literature side, see Stam and Van de Ven (2021) for a distillation of such ideas. Isenberg (2011b) is a classic example of a systems/components approach to ecosystem thinking that influenced the field, along with Feld's (2012) focus on what goes into a healthy ecosystem – although he similarly focuses on strategies for energizing that system. Stam (2015) clearly recognizes the impact of culture and networks but treats them more as ingredients rather than dynamic processes. For a critique of the systems-based, components-oriented approach, see Malecki (2018). The Federal Reserve Bank system is also increasingly recognizing the importance of local culture and relationship networks in building effective ecosystems (Gines, 2021), although we again advocate for a greater focus on the *process* of building such culture and networks and not simply viewing them as ingredients – a position with which the Fed and other ecosystem builders with experience would likely agree.

entrepreneurial communities and *entrepreneurial social infrastructure* in the community development literature (Lichtenstein, Lyons & Kutzhanova, 2004; Flora & Flora, 1993), *human ecology, role structure,* and *opportunity structures* in the sociology literature (Ruef, 2010; Carroll & Khessina, 2005; Thornton, 1999; Reynolds, 1992; Merton, 1959), and *transformational leadership* in the management and social psychology literature (Engelen et al., 2015; Paladan, 2015; Yitshaki, 2012). This is not to say that elements – even explicit citations – of these ideas are totally absent in the entrepreneurship literature. What seems to be lacking is a more concrete connection to the idea that entrepreneurial ecosystems are *social* entities first and foremost, that behind every ecosystem is a web of dynamic and adaptive relationships that function well or function poorly, are strategic and focused or random and unfocused, and that entrepreneurship is itself a bounded social (and deviant from the norm) behavior with contextual determinants that are highly significant. On these fronts, the literature on what makes a strong and healthy rural community in an era of increased urbanization has been alive and well for decades. We propose that these insights can help the field of ecosystem development, especially in rural areas, leapfrog ahead in terms of the efficacy of both ecosystem building and research-driven understanding. It can also create space for a *plurality* of ecosystem approaches facilitating a diverse range of styles of ecosystems to emerge that enable rural ecosystems to retain their culture and identity without becoming more like a city.[3]

If we are to use the term *ecosystem* in earnest, we must recognize the danger of using a unilateral set of "best practices[4]" for ecosystem development, or creating an "ideal" ecosystem for entrepreneurship, as though the term *ecosystem* is an ideal typology from zero to excellent. It is as dangerous as saying that the only valuable kind of natural ecosystem is a redwood forest – which says nothing of thriving desert, wetland, high mountain, low valley, coastal, inland, plains, tundra, tropical, permafrost, rainforest, chaparral, and island ecosystems that function just as effectively under a very different set of rules, arrangements, interdependencies, realities, and contexts. Such is equally true for a plurality of regions and cultures, including communities spanning the rural-urban continuum. What is good for the redwood forest is likely not good for the desert, unless one takes the redwood forest to be inherently superior to the desert. Implementing this latter perspective will almost certainly lead to failure in the desert due to dynamic uncertainty and poor model fit.

We fully acknowledge that we are pointing to general trends in research, policy, and practice, and there are certainly approaches that openly embrace rural realties as a starting point for effective ecosystem development that diverge from urban approaches. But we indeed seek to challenge conventional thinking by laying out new ways of thinking about rural communities, entrepreneurship, and business and community development

3 While anecdotal, in our practice, this is a common concern of rural residents who live in their community precisely because it is not urban.
4 We will use the term "best practices" in quotes in this chapter, as we will later make the point that such practices may have limited use in a wide heterogeneity of contexts.

by spilling intellectual silos and echo chambers where they can be identified, overturning path dependency, crossing intellectual boundaries where those boundaries serve little purpose, and incisively challenging the status quo. Conventional thinking about the terms rural, entrepreneurship, and rural entrepreneurship runs the risk of perpetuating itself in real time and over time in a circular, growing, never-evolving circle, sometimes called an *esoteric circle* (Fleck, 1980). Such circles are not about change in an ever-changing world; they can become bereft of non-redundant information, they represent intellectual monocultures, spinning in place, intellectually, and conceptually. Thought in any domain, including rural and entrepreneurship, can become exposed to the esoteric circle phenomenon by remaining too narrowly focused on one set of parameters for examining the efficacy of ecosystems. It is difficult to know when one is on the spinning wheel like a hamster, and it is scary to step or fall off the spinning wheel. It is also difficult to foster non-marginal change and progress if one does not fall off the wheel. Our aim here is merely to raise a reflexive lens to the goals, framing, and context of ecosystem development in a rural setting, and to open the field to a greater degree of imagination, creativity, and cross-cultural understanding that may diverge from conventional thinking. Instead of viewing such shifts as deviant from established norms, a pluralistic approach that accounts for the heterogeneity and dynamic evolution of social systems and their functioning may create a system that works *with* community dynamics instead of imposing pre-established scientific findings atop a cultural and historical milieu that is quite different from the focus of much of the mainstream literature.

Integrating entire disciplines around rural entrepreneurship is a herculean task. Where to begin? In the remainder of this chapter, we begin by examining two helpful writings from Sociology that enabled the field to move past the *status quo* and toward a more holistic theoretical integration in a meaningful way: C. Wright Mills' *The Sociological Imagination* (1959) and Robert K. Merton's "On Sociological Theories of the Middle Range" (1949). We then outline some specific research, theory, and practice points for utilizing these insights as a way to open the field in new ways that incorporate the fundamental importance of rural ecosystems. We conclude with a set of specific insights on the future of rural entrepreneurial ecosystem research and practice.

2 The Sociological Imagination

If there has ever been a good time to revisit the classic Sociology work, *The Sociological Imagination* by C. Wright Mills,[5] now may be the moment. Mills' best-remembered work is a manifesto on the current state of Sociology with an eye to both its promise and its perils. The book is full of heterodox (for the time) insights on how modern

5 All references to Mills in this section draw from this work, Mills (1959), unless otherwise noted. Specific quotes will contain page numbers as part of the citation.

inquiry in the social sciences had lost its way, while remaining bullish on the eventual promise of Sociology to mature and evolve as a discipline. Mills embraced the role of *agent provocateur* – a thinker parallel to the academy, able to walk amongst academics while flaunting an authentic "street cred" and connection to the common man.[6]

By the 1950s, sociology seemed stuck to Mills. It was unable to create general theories that effectively explained human action, nor specific applications that were anything more than abstractions. The field had trended inadvertently in two directions that seemed disconnected from each other and from social reality more broadly. In one direction, much of the theory guiding sociological inquiry had become dominated by "grand theorists" such as Talcott Parsons in his books, *The Social System* (1951) and *Toward a General Theory of Action* (Parsons & Shils, 1951); and "abstracted empiricists" like Paul Lazarsfeld across his highly varied body of work. Grand theories were intended to summarily describe human social action in nearly every situation. Mills criticized such theories as being overly broad and disconnected from lower-order social systems and incapable of explaining heterogeneous populations that had still evolved into functional societies. Recognizing that humans take on different roles in different situations (i.e., people wear more than one hat), Mills examined how grand theory homogenized human action without accounting for a more nuanced examination of subordinate social systems and the roles people play within them. People can be a business executive during the day, but also a parent at night, an amateur athlete on the weekend, a board member for a local arts organization, event organizer for a local social club, and part of a community of avid science fiction readers.[7]

Contrasting from Parsons, Mills insists upon an understanding of social systems that is not grounded in a common ethic, but that seeks to know *how* and *why* people develop their value and belief systems, even when they are minorities or social pariahs. Since each social system is defined and bounded differently, diverse human behavior slides through the cracks of generalized theories based on a grand social system that structures and orders human action. Human values, beliefs, and behaviors are highly variable. While striving to parse out generalized patterns can be useful at one level, inferring from the general to the specific is likely to misinterpret the variability of local perspectives regarding reality and what is possible in a situational context. Inferring from the specific to the general will also likely be misleading. Navigating this ecological fallacy requires acceptance of this variability as fundamental and inherent in social systems so as not to lose the insights provided by such situational variability.

6 It should be noted that Mills' work predates most feminist literature, and thus focuses on the social problems and gendered language of "man" instead of a more nuanced examination of issues spanning genders and other identity groups.

7 See Long (1958) for an examination of the community as an "ecology of games" bounded by "structures, goals, roles, strategies, tactics, and publics (p. 251)." Different players play different roles in a variety of community spaces, with interlocking social systems creating a web of complex social relations and outcomes.

Mills noted that the foil to grand theory was a penetrating focus on the extremely specific, a tendency he called *abstract empiricism.* Mills noted a crescendoing tendency of scholars (like prominent Columbia sociologist Paul Lazarsfeld) to become rapt with highly technical applications of the social sciences befitting very specific situations – i.e., social phenomenon at very specific points in time and very specific contexts and bounded by somewhat uniform social roles. At the time, his primary concern was a focus on polling and attitudinal studies as a primary feature of sociological literature. While such studies produced insights on the values and attitudes of social groups in a variety of situations, the problem with such studies was three-fold. First, such studies examined *what* people thought was important, with only scant detail as to *why* they felt that way. A focus on resultant attitudes without a focus on process was, to Mills' mind, much like examining the nature of the built environment with no attention given to construction, zoning, permitting, legal battles, and the business motivations that led to the construction of that environment in the first place. He similarly critiques too narrow a focus on the technical tools of social science inquiry, choosing research methods that demonstrate methodological elegance while saying very little about human behavior in an applied sense.[8]

Second, abstract empirical studies were often only loosely connected to general theories of society, hence their abstraction. They focused too narrowly on highly specific questions that – while technically consistent with the general theory – are so remote in scope that supporting or rejecting a specific hypothesis could scarcely support or reject the broader general theory. Included in this critique is the sense that general theory assumes a generalized set of values and behaviors, while heterogeneous values (i.e., dissenting groups) and diverse role sets (i.e., employing different social knowledge while at work compared to at home or when off the clock) are endemic to all social systems. Surely, the long persistence of this heterogeneity within otherwise consistent social systems must be theoretically important.

Finally, abstract empirical studies were criticized by Mills as being too distant from practical, everyday life, creating findings that may have limited use for the average person. Too often conceived in the academy, issues that are of interest to academics based on the evolution of current theory may employ a completely different set of reasoning – and may even focus on completely different issues – than those discussed at the corner store or local diner. Compounding such understandings (which fundamentally have their basis in the culture of *institutions*) with elegant tools for analysis may create studies and highlight results that are divorced from the realities of everyday life or make little sense to the average person, even if they are internally consistent and may contain important kernels of insight.

8 This issue has been raised repeatedly in methodological circles, even in economics, and is the basis of the term *spurious precision* (see Irsova, Bom, Havranek and Rachinger, 2023; Nelson, 2018; Kamarck, 2016; Colander et al., 2009).

One clear example of abstract empiricism can be found in very narrow applications of entrepreneurship theories in very specific circumstances that explain only a very small subset of entrepreneurial behavior. An example might be examining the decision-making behaviors of minority-owned firms less than 5 years old under a set of very specific framework conditions, with most of the study participants being in or recently graduated from an MBA program in one region of the world – using a more general social theory to frame the issue. The argument here is not that such examinations are useless – they are often quite interesting – but rather that the research question and framing of the issue is itself highly abstracted from a more general theory to a highly specific application, making it difficult to effectively use inductive reasoning to either support or refute the theory. It is somewhat rare to see academic works integrating across a very wide range of such studies to understand their parameters and to directly compare them to current general theories (or "best practices") to evaluate and examine their usefulness.

A second example of abstract empiricism in the modern age is the ascendance of certain technical tools that are of limited use in understanding research problems. For example, there has been a growing use of structural equation modeling (SEM) in the research literature on entrepreneurship. SEM is a powerful and useful tool, but it is designed primarily for investigating the relationship between latent constructs (via factor analysis) derived from observed variables, and [a] dependent variable[s] of interest (Boateng, 2018). Too often, research is structured in a way that utilizes SEM without specifying the potential of finding latent variables or variable sets, or SEM is applied to relatively simple models where old-fashioned Ordinary Least Squares (OLS) or logistic regression are perfectly suitable. An example might be examining the relationship between the professional backgrounds of the founding team and short-term profitability and growth. We may have a good working hypothesis regarding this relationship, and a data set that spans rural, small town, suburban, and urban areas. A range of behaviors related to culture in those areas may be important inputs – and this would be an excellent application of SEM to examine for latent cultural and locational variables that are likely to emerge, but we may not quite know what they look like *ex ante* or how they interact with the primary variables of interest (including antecedent or mediating variables). When the question is more straight-forward, with well-defined variable sets and little expectation of latency or complexity, ordinary multivariate OLS will do. We have observed the tendency of finding significance in complex models to be interpreted as "highly important" research findings, when effect sizes may actually be quite small: tight precision around a very mild result.

There is a risk of the over-utilization of tools that are currently *en vogue* and a demonstration of technical prowess that does not necessarily answer research questions in a simple and straight-forward way. Epistemologically, it represents a privileging of what Connell (1987) might call theoretical and methodological zeitgeist – and technical elegance – over methodological fit, ensuring that the right tools are used for the job.[9] If you have ever heard the term "using a bazooka to eliminate a fruit fly," this is simply another version of abstract empiricism that uses overly sophisticated tools that are abstracted from the kinds of specific applications they are intended to address, at best. At worst, such approaches can be seen as an epistemic power play privileging technological elegance over simple (but useful) explanations, demonstrating one's own quantitative prowess in a competitive academic environment, or hiding underwhelming findings or sloppy thinking and research design behind a veneer of sophisticated modeling.

The *abstraction* described here is, in Mills' thinking, an isolation or abstraction from broader questions of theory, research design, or practical application. A modern example of practical abstraction would be the relative dearth and limited usefulness of research findings that, while perhaps easy to measure or fitting for a particular tool of inquiry, do not account for either complexity or for a plurality of social systems under their own dynamic equilibrium. To the person on the street, such findings may seem overly specific, academic, or do not match reality. They also do not account for the deep knowledge embedded in different social systems – a point raised by Nassim Taleb in his book *Antifragile* (2012). The persistence of certain cultural values, even when they seem counterintuitive to the researcher or outsider, have evolved over time to form a sort of equilibrium that works under that specific context. They might represent a separate social system that may operate under a different set of cultural assumptions, rules, and norms, but contain embedded knowledge that functions under those assumptions quite well over time – even if they differ ecologically from findings in the mainstream research.

In our view, the situation that faced sociology in the late 1950s bears some similarities to the state of current research in entrepreneurial ecosystems and around entrepreneurial development more broadly. There is a large body of macro-oriented research around best practices for ecosystem development, specifying ecosystem models demonstrating the features and functions of ideal ecosystems. Examples of popular research particularly in the earlier days of ecosystem research, include Gnyawali and Fogel (1994), Van de Ven (1993), Bhidé (2000), and Isenberg (2011b). This *structural-functional* approach has a flavor much like the Sociology of Parsons, seeing ecosystems almost as well-functioning machines in dynamic equilibrium with an explicit focus on the roles of each part, role-sets, interactions between parts of the machine, and missing roles to be filled. Any study or policy paper that reads like an ingredient list of what is needed to make an ecosystem better, whether it be in terms of people, organizations, policy (which structures and guides role sets), or "stuff," falls into this category. There is a strong focus on ecosystem structure over process, examining

9 The literature on *spurious precision*, especially Kamarck (2016), is especially helpful in understanding how technical elegance can produce answers that are, as H.L. Mencken once quipped, "clear, simple, and wrong."

well-functioning ecosystems and the structures and roles that, when properly arranged, comprise its success. Process-oriented ecosystem literature is harder to find, and for a good reason: not much time has passed since the emergence of the ecosystem literature to examine how ecosystems evolve and change over time. Historical studies may fall prey to hindsight bias (Hawkins & Hastie, 1990), presenting a rosier and problem-free picture of how ecosystems evolve, or looking beyond failures that were critically important in their development. Many of the micro-oriented studies we point to, such as those examining decision-making processes in a specific context (Shepherd, Williams, and Patzelt (2015) offer a useful compilation of studies), or the evolution of dynamic leader/feeder relationships over time (see Fortunato and Clevenger (2022), Feld and Hathaway (2020), and Zahra and Nambisian (2011) who synthesize these ideas), or the psychological dynamics of life in an ecosystem (Norris Krueger's work has always been instructive, such as Krueger (2017) – and emergent integrations like Roundy and Bayer (2019)) are very useful. Useful, that is, if they can be connected to more general theories that are still flexible enough to account for the massive heterogeneity found in a wide range of ecosystems.

What is needed to enhance current efforts is a commitment to connecting the general and the specific, the structural-functional and the process/evolution-oriented, in ways that provide useful insights to ecosystem builders and entrepreneurship researchers in any environment, including rural and declining places. The following section proposes a bridge that has been in existence for nearly 75 years, but that, to our knowledge, has not been discussed in the context of entrepreneurial ecosystems.

3 Theories of the Middle Range

About a decade before Mills' writing, a critique of modern sociological research and practice emerged from the great Harvard sociologist Robert C. Merton.[10] Presaging Mills' message, Merton was similarly concerned that sociology, as a still-growing social science, was slowly drifting away from research that could make a positive contribution to humankind. His reasoning was similar – attempts at creating grand theories about a total social system linking all of humanity (much like physics describes the universal behavior of physical phenomena across the universe) were incapable of describing the heterogeneity of outcomes one sees plainly in everyday social life. Grand theories were intended to mimic the universality of the physical sciences, and the quest for an explanation of the total "social system" writ large mimicked similar efforts to explain univer-

10 References to Merton in this section refer to his well-known essay, "On Sociological Theories of the Middle Range" (1949) unless otherwise noted.

sal truths through studies of chemistry, biology, physics, mathematics, and ecology.[11] For this reason, Merton was similarly critical of Parsons, but also of Marxist theory, functionalism, and Sorokin's integral sociology in *Society, Culture, and Personality: Their Structure and Dynamics, A System of General Sociology* (1947).

Despite these criticisms, giving up on Sociology was, to Merton's mind, akin to giving up on the study of medicine due to its growing pains. Merton makes a reference to medical practitioners of the seventeenth century, arguing that losing faith in early medicine – with all its bloodletting and miasmas and amputations – would have never allowed the medical sciences to evolve into life-saving modern medicine with the capability to lengthen and enhance human lives. Indeed, medicine may still have some way to go in this regard, but the point was that sociology was an even *younger* science, still somewhat nascent and ham-handed in its approaches. Strategic decision makers of the day criticized the social sciences too harshly for failing to solve urgent problems, even though the development of any science and full realization of its benefits can take centuries. It is necessary for enough time (read "observations") to pass that social science theories can evolve inductively, subjected to continuous refinement, thus creating a more accurate picture of social action in heterogeneous contexts.

To achieve its fullest potential, Merton proposed a middle path between the general and abstract: theories of the middle range. Middle-range theories are:

> . . . theories that lie between the minor but necessary working hypotheses that evolve in abundance during day-to-day research and the all-inclusive systematic efforts to develop a unified theory that will explain all the observed uniformities of social behavior, social organization, and social change. Middle-range theory is principally used in sociology to guide empirical inquiry. It is intermediate to general theories of social systems which are too remote from particular classes of social behavior, organization, and change to account for what is observed and to those detailed orderly descriptions of particulars that are not generalized at all. Middle-range theory involves abstractions, of course, but they are close enough to observed data to be incorporated in propositions that permit empirical testing. Middle-range theories deal with delimited aspects of social phenomena, as is indicated by their labels. (p. 448)

Stated more simply, middle-range theories are generalized propositions about more specific situations that identify patterns in social action but make room for a heterogeneity of different experiences and manifestations of such action from ground-up observation. They do not identify "outliers," abstracted from general theory viewed as "residuals;" but rather see such residual patterns as important, unexplained variation

11 The roots of such thinking can be traced all the way back to Auguste Compte, considered to be the first Western Sociologist, who believed that a science of the social could be developed that could explain universal truths of human social behavior across time and space. In later efforts, the impact of Charles Darwin cannot be understated, as the social sciences trended toward more mainstream scientific topics with Weber's advances in methodology (see Calhoun, 2002) and the advent of R.E. Park's urban ecology focus at the University of Chicago (see Park, 1952).

that may be the result of nuance and plurality within the broader social system. They are the link between the broad and the general, explaining, for example, why capital availability to entrepreneurs or to university-level talent may be a critical component in urban ecosystems, while rural ecosystems can function well with very different capital and workforce structures – while still upholding a commitment to launching new businesses. The goal of middle-range theories is to discover how such a plurality of mechanisms evolves in the first place to make a functioning system, or why they fail to function or emerge across diverse contexts.

Different groupings of ecosystems may thus represent different modalities of ecosystem evolution that are themselves important and fully functioning. As Merton states, ". . . middle-range theory is not concerned with the historical generalization that a degree of social order or conflict prevails in society but with the analytical problem of identifying the social mechanisms which produce a greater degree of order or less conflict than would obtain if these mechanisms were not called into play (p. 452)." The weakness of general theories of social behavior is that researchers and decision makers alike often expect such theories to be "broad enough to encompass the vast ranges of precisely observed details of social behavior, organization, and change and fruitful enough to direct the attention of research workers to a flow of problems for empirical research (p. 453)." To Merton, this is premature and apocalyptic – the state of social systems science is simply not fully developed enough to derive such specificity from such general propositions of social behavior. To the ecosystem scientist, it means that the brute-force application of ecosystem theories and models to places that do not support such models can create deleterious or unsatisfying outcomes due to poor fit. This does not mean that such ill-fitted ecosystems are somehow "outliers" any more than a person is "ill-proportioned" because off-the-rack clothing does not fit them well.

Merton equally warns against the temptation to hammer explanations of more idiosyncratic social behavior into too general a theory, which eventually led to disagreement and confusion in Sociology:

> . . . almost all the pioneers in sociology tried to fashion his own system. The multiplicity of systems, each claiming to be the genuine sociology, led naturally enough to the formation of schools, each with its cluster of masters, disciples and epigoni. Sociology not only became differentiated with other disciples, but it became internally differentiated. This differentiation, however, was not in terms of specialization, as in the sciences, but rather, as in philosophy, in terms of total systems, typically held to be mutually exclusive and largely at odds. (p. 454)

This is an important warning for both researchers and practitioners in the field who seek to develop a set of specific "best practices" from theories that are too generalized, or who seek specific guidance or research questions from findings that are ill-fitting for the context. The field of entrepreneurship research could too quickly devolve into camps that are quick to discount alternative understandings that are well-suited to different kinds of social systems. A general theory approach might be to ask, "why haven't we seen the kind of job and income growth in Ecosystem X that we have seen in greater Austin, and what can be done to remedy that situation?" Instead, we might take a middle-range approach and ask questions[12] like:

> Questions: Sure, income and job growth are slow in Ecosystem X by urban standards, but are entrepreneurs satisfied with their progress?
>
> KPIs: Entrepreneur business/life satisfaction, longitudinal entrepreneurial achievement self-assessment, local business creation (irrespective of growth rate), self-employment *and* income growth among the self-employed
>
> Questions: What is the nature of the social and economic support system in Ecosystem X, and do local entrepreneurs view this to be sufficient? Where do they need the most help? What is already working?
>
> KPIs: Longitudinal asset mapping, growth in offerings/programs/capital, growth in local investors/investment, relationship development/structural hole identification through longitudinal social network analysis, entrepreneurial achievement self-assessment, longitudinal "wins" of local ecosystem stakeholders and cross-checking with entrepreneurs
>
> Questions: Do entrepreneurs in Ecosystem X sense local barriers or advantages to reaching their own key performance indicators?
>
> KPIs: Entrepreneur self-assessment of barriers and advantages
>
> Questions: What other kinds of value are being created in Ecosystem X beyond income, job, and revenue growth that benefit the entrepreneur and the local society? How is this value measured and perceived?
>
> KPIs: Value measures across economic/social/environmental domains, growth in value measures, open-ended questions about how entrepreneurs measure "success" and progress along those metrics

If this sounds atomistic, the cultivation of middle-range theory occurs when we look across ecosystems that may have similar properties but collectively evade standard ecosystem explanations. Such middle-range theories, taken collectively, can produce a more nuanced "general theory" of healthy ecosystem functioning, but only if they are viewed as meaningful contributions to total system functioning instead of being treated as outliers. In this sense, an ecosystem that emerges in the wild among unemployed and under-employed people and at-risk youth starting scrappy businesses out of a small-town coffee shop (read "incubator") and their support systems ("feeders" in

---

12 We include some example KPIs for measurement of alternative constructs here, with the caveat that one must not fall into the measurement mindset and trap. KPIs should be those that emerge organically in context, guided by reflexive analysis of who chooses the KPIs, and whose KPIs should count. Appropriate KPIs will be variable, emerging from the local situation and dialectic.

Brad Feld's (2012) terminology) may evade classic explanations of ecosystem formations and sustainability requirements. Many scholars and decision makers may see such evolutions as not being true ecosystems, or not an unsuitable model for development. Such a view is akin to criticizing the wetland pond as somehow not worthy of examination because it does not produce redwood trees, or whatever is deemed to be most socially valuable. However, such a pond may contain primordial answers to the self-organization of human behavior that, in fact, supports and enriches our collective understanding of ecosystem dynamics at a more basic and relational level.[13] Middle-range theories thus create space for a greater degree of imagination and appreciation of diversity across social systems. Outliers are no longer seen as accidents or failures, or even as existing beyond the realm of the properly functioning system. In fact, the residual is where the new answers are, providing a more complete understanding of the evolution of human behavior in a range of contexts, and solutions that privilege a more customized set of outcomes and practices.

4 Challenging Current Entrepreneurial Ecosystem Research Efforts

One could make the argument that middle-range theory development with respect to entrepreneurial ecosystems is already happening, and that is not entirely incorrect. There is plenty of room for alternative explanations of entrepreneurial behavior rooted in place across entrepreneurial literature. There is no shortage of examinations of entrepreneurial behavior in specialized groups (i.e., women, people of color, and sports entrepreneurs), or case studies of specific locations outside more mainstream markets (i.e., the global South), as well as the use of theories from allied disciplines like social psychology and organizational behavior to examine entrepreneurial phenomena through different lenses (i.e., motivation, cognition, and theory of planned behavior). Deductive reasoning and middle-range theory testing and use are healthy in the field. Where we observe a disconnect is in the actual *theory building* stages of entrepreneurship research – the inductive steps taken to bring such findings back to a theoretical level that comprehends entrepreneurial ecosystems as a class of related social systems linked by the common intent to support and accelerate entrepreneurship. To return to Merton's medical example, this is the equivalent of seeing "cancer" as *a* disease instead of what it really is – a class of diseases that produce common outcomes, but which are highly nuanced in their development and treatment (American Cancer Society, 2023). Such understandings are currently producing

13 Our thanks to a reviewer who pointed out that a wetland pond is different from a puddle, devoid of any real potential for development.

better treatments that are suited to the specific disease and the nuanced biology of each patient. Similar outcomes could be hoped for as the entrepreneurial ecosystem literature continues to develop, as middle-range theories provide a bridge between atomistic observations and generalized understandings with greater flexibility. Entrepreneurial ecosystems may share common outcomes, often highly general and fuzzy themselves, like "supporting entrepreneurship development." But this is likely to look very different across different contextual and environmental groupings.

Spilling Silos and Shattering Esoteric Circles. Theory development becomes especially powerful when different sub-fields within the entrepreneurship literature – from behaviorists to economists to policy analysts to entrepreneurs themselves – begin to share information, spilling intellectual silos and shattering esoteric circles. We speak of knowledge silos or esoteric circles that are too narrowly focused on the historical evolution of their own discipline, field, or community or region. Spilling silos is a reflexive practice that must be cultivated over time. It is reflexive because it begins with an understanding of the limits of one's own knowledge and knowledge circles. It is deliberate because it takes effort and occasionally discomfort to move beyond the boundaries of one's own area of expertise to open one's mind to new perspectives that may challenge or rearrange one's own thinking. There may be a personal hesitation on the part of the learner to do this because many experts in the field derive a sense of esteem and self-worth from their finely cultivated fund of knowledge. Imagine moving beyond that comfort zone to find that entire fields have been working in your subject area, bringing different perspectives and terminologies to bear on your thinking! It happens to us, regularly. Far from an affront to one's own knowledge or achievements, such discoveries present a very new opportunity for both researchers and practitioners – the opportunity to be a *pontifex*, a bridge builder, and an integrator and synthesizer of disciplines with the capability to bring together formerly discrete actors into productive and integrative conversation by speaking multiple "languages." In the realm of ecosystem building, the necessary diversity involved in any ecosystem at any stage of its evolution necessitates such capabilities which can lay the groundwork for the formation of common insights from the ground up.

Diversity writ broadly is a major topic of conversation within both academic and practitioner circles in the current era. Diversity conversations have largely focused on the inclusion of systemically disadvantaged groups in order to foster a more fair and balanced democracy that empowers voices that are normally suppressed or ignored. This is itself an encouraging sign of positive transformation toward a more equitable future with greater opportunities for empowerment across disadvantaged groups. A lesser focus has been the important cultural and social knowledge of such groups in shaping entrepreneurial ecosystems within diverse contexts and how it pertains to ecosystem theory. Diverse approaches can open the door to disciplinary and experiential diversity, including reconciliation across more traditionally focused ecosystem builders in cities with more developmentally focused ecosystem builders in disadvantaged areas. It can lead to the incorporation of a wide diversity of theoretical insights from across social science and business literatures. Furthermore, it can encourage the study and support of a more diverse sample set, seeing non-traditional entrepreneurs (i.e., disadvantaged people, informal workers, ethnic enclaves) as fundamentally *part* of the broader ecosystem story, not a special case *within* the ecosystem's story. Thinking imaginatively, opening the door to greater human, ideological, and disciplinary diversity should, via middle-range theory development, lead to an opening-up of what may be considered a successful and thriving ecosystem reflecting a diversity of different ecosystem models that are seen as equally viable, useful, and sustainable for supporting entrepreneurial activity whose outcomes may take many forms. Within this conversation is a much-needed debate about what constitutes "high-value" entrepreneurship, whose values are privileged, and what kinds of ecosystem dynamics support those values. Within a pluralistic value system, the values and norms of rural ecosystems can emerge as viable (rather than undesirable or heterodox) alternatives.

Helping Theory to Evolve. Good theories evolve over time as sufficient observations become available that either support, reject, or modify hypothetical propositions derived from that theory. In the case of a more generalized theory of entrepreneurial ecosystems, it is possible to observe outliers that do not follow the hypothesized model. Are these outliers due to idiosyncratic behavior? Or do they represent latent patterns? When examining the potential of grouped residuals to explain nuanced social behavior, we *now* have an excellent case for empirical tools like SEM and latent class analysis that can provide a sense of order to patterns that may seem disorganized under the structure of a more generalized theory. When interpreted inductively, these diverse observations can help ecosystem theories to flourish and expand within the middle range, showing how ecosystems may evolve differently in rural places, or how disadvantaged populations may construct high-functioning ecosystems with limited resources and in the shadow of mainstream ecosystem groups and services. The result is a more nuanced *theory of theories* using the middle range and a greater degree of imagination as bridges to understanding how more generalized theories may look different in localized contexts. On the practice side, this speaks equally to the creation of a bigger toolkit with different strategies better adapted to different contexts. The "fit" of any particular strategy gains strength when it is co-created with locals and with local knowledge, particularly when spilling silos and encouraging diverse viewpoints across backgrounds, educations, areas of expertise, ethnicities, genders, and so on.

Using the middle range and the sociological imagination to help theories to evolve begins with recognizing cross-sectional approaches often using large samples – common in the current literature – for what they are. These are snapshots in time. In large, undifferentiated samples, diverse voices are often relegated to the residuals. In small samples, especially those using business school students as a convenience sample,[14] questions can be raised regarding the external validity of the findings when extrapolated to entrepreneurs working "in the wild." Some simple ways around this problem include increasing the number of *longitudinal* studies with diverse populations to understand how different ecosystems evolve over time, supporting evaluation research for ecosystem building programs, and more studies on non-traditional ecosystems and proto/archetypical/nascent ecosystems that are beginning to emerge – the primordial soup of an entrepreneurial ecosystem, which can occur anywhere. Examining the full life cycle of an entrepreneurial ecosystem presents the field with an opportunity to understand how a variety of healthy ecosystems appear, thrive, and eventually mature, wither, and die. Which ecosystems go the distance, which fade into obsolescence? The factors at play are likely to be both social and socio-environmental, and highly dependent on local cultural, political, spatial, and historical contexts. Greater incorporation of non-traditional ecosystems involving a momentum of players beyond the Silicon Valley set, no matter how far from the Bay Area, can provide clues about healthy ecosystem functioning and a more effective set of building tools beyond those seen in the most advanced, high-growth economies.

Breaking Up with Over-Engineering. A major issue of abstract empiricism is the tendency toward the extremely specific. Even entrepreneurs can appreciate the discovery of a good niche that can be profitable. In scholarship and applied practice, however, too myopic a focus on very specific problems within ecosystems can lead to a sense of *over-engineering* ecosystems down to the nitty-gritty. That is not to say that specific problems within ecosystems are not interesting. But left disconnected from broader middle-range theories and applications, such efforts can give a sense of creating a highly detailed map of a land that is always changing and fraught with uncertainty. This is a simplistic way of stating the dangers of choosing highly sophisticated, specific tools intended for narrow-tailed problems and applying them to complex, uncertain, messy, multidimensional, fat-tail situations with many important alternative phenomena in the residual.

Another way to examine this danger is by looking at two approaches: the machinist and the gardener.[15] The goal of the machinist is to create a better-functioning ma-

14 In full disclosure, this is one of our pet peeves, if only because it is so common. Business school students, even in entrepreneurial programs, are so radically different from the "average entrepreneur" as to make such studies highly questionable based on their internal sampling validity. For a roasting of the literature circa the late 2000's on this topic, see Shane (2008) for what "real entrepreneurs" look like. Similar problems arose in the social psychology literature, with graduate students being a favorite sample for early researchers in the field, despite their vastly different characteristics from the average person and any instrumental biases that may arise due to the power differential between student and professor, a critique going all the way back to Smart (1966).

15 Also see Taleb (2012) for the difference between cats and washing machines, and Krumme (2023) for a discussion of the fallacy of optimization. In practice, Taleb urges us to identify that class of things that can be predictable, engineered, designed *ex ante* and linear – versus those that seem chaotic, but

chine, which requires continuous problem-solving, engineering new solutions, and seeking constant feedback about improvement. This is a highly appropriate direction when discussing simple, straight-forward, less-complex tasks like building a better washing machine. However, it is important to recognize that entrepreneurial ecosystems are very much social systems embedded within a broader *society*, complete with culture, norms, mores, diverse peoples, conflict, politics, and history. A similar complex environment is the garden, which not only contains a wide variety of complex organisms, each with their own specific preferences (not to mention heterogeneity across individuals), but also changing precipitation, water, soil, and nutrient requirements and conditions within the environment. The gardener does not engineer a garden but rather creates a supportive environment rich in water and nutrients, gives extra care to organisms that are struggling, and leaves things alone that are working well. We would not be surprised if the machinist were a poor gardener, as engineering specific outcomes in a context of constant change and internally evolving organisms evade a blueprint. If we take an entrepreneurial ecosystem to be more like a garden than a machine, with all its internal social, political, environmental, and economic complexity, then we open the door to understanding complex socio-economic environments that have been the focus of the social sciences for decades. This open door (and all its literature that is unused by the entrepreneurship field) provides immense opportunities for new insights drawn from parallel situations including community, social deviance, political conflict, behavioral science, institutional strategy, governance, inequality, diversity, conflict, and cooperation. This is a far more broad and rich area of inquiry than studies that seek to elucidate micro-elements of ecosys-

---

also adaptable and stochastic, learning and evolving quickly from any failure or setback. Complex, adaptive systems have so many intervening variables that it is challenging to find any sort of "optimum" at any time based exclusively on the performance of other systems deemed to be similar. There may be clues for helping to make such environments more successful out there, and there may be "better" (not "best") practices derived from other examples. But imposing even carefully engineered and well-researched schema *ex ante* into any system experiencing complex, stochastic change is much like measuring the volume of the ocean with a ruler, even if it makes scientists and economists feel good because it makes sense in the aggregate.

By contrast, the gardener approach first examines what is already working. We do not need to know all the answers as to why one patch of watermelons is growing madly – whatever it is, the watermelons are doing something that works, while the sweet corn is looking a little dry and frail this year. Any good gardener will likely find clues as to why the watermelons seem to like that patch of land so well, and may gauge the soil moisture, acidity, and fertilizer level under the sweet corn. They will water and fertilize the sweet corn (and maybe check in on the beans next to it) even if the seed package directions do not specify such excesses. They will engage directly, not assuming an *ex ante* optimum, but learning from and cheerleading those doing well and tending to the needs of those who are not. The answers may not be known in advance, and opaque without engagement. The seed package directions – a schematic after all – are devoid of local knowledge and resilience capability within the complex garden environment that the good gardener has already identified as essential ingredients through constant engagement.

tems grounded in a narrow conception and understanding of those systems that may be highly idiosyncratic and difficult to replicate.

Getting More Creative and Shedding Path Dependency. In what may seem like commonplace advice, another advancement in the field is a greater focus on *creativity* and allowing the scholar-practitioner imagination to fly more boldly. While all scholarship requires some degree of creative *and* critical thinking, the tendency to conduct research exclusively along the lines of pre-existing theory without reflexively reimagining the connections between that theory and the research, or how practically the theory fits on-the-ground observation, or seeking middle-range connections of existing theories in new contexts, or integrations of multiple theories at the middle range; all these tendencies run the risk of keeping research overly path-dependent and uncritical of existing theory, which can stifle middle-range theory development. Path-dependent thinking also affects entrepreneurship practice. More traditional stories and descriptions of what it means to be entrepreneurial and an entrepreneur limit imagination, creativity, initiative, and innovation. Exposure to new, different, and non-traditional stories, even from differing contexts, tend to provoke questioning of traditional ways, learning, and inspiration all factors in shedding path dependency and fostering creativity in entrepreneurial practice as well as research (see Johansson, 2004).

Part of the lesson here is that the residual is often more interesting than the explained variance. While tight models can be highly explanatory and are frequently revered for their simple elegance, spurious precision due to the overlay of a thin-tailed tool on a fat-tailed phenomenon (Taleb, 2012; 2007) can provide an illusory sense of simplicity. In terms of ecosystem development, this means privileging certain key practices over others as ideal, while perfectly viable alternatives may be thriving as a latent element in the residual, waiting to be discovered. Too great a focus on idealizing models derived from explained variance may support regression to the mean over time, even as new adaptations beyond the mean become necessary due to changing circumstances. We would be wise not to forget that new trends, innovations, and techniques typically emerge from outside the explained variance, particularly *black swan* events that are difficult if not impossible to predict precisely using statistical prediction and extrapolation (Taleb, 2012). A greater focus on the potential of the residual allows the researcher and practitioner imagination to flourish with possibilities of new and unexpected explanations of ecosystem growth and development, suited to a far greater range of human behavior and contexts than the focus of most current models.

5 Conclusion: What About Rural Areas?

When compared to many of the "great" entrepreneurial ecosystems of the world, rural areas may seem like a distant alternative to firm and job creation. Distant from centralized markets and entrepreneurial support systems, what chance do these areas have to create self-sustaining ecosystems of entrepreneurial action? Some of the confusion may be in how one defines the term *ecosystem* in the first place. If the expectation for an ecosystem is a maelstrom of high-value firm creation with sophisticated, overlapping markets for products and services, for talent, and for partnership with cutting-edge universities and firms, then sure – there is little hope of calling a rural area an entrepreneurial ecosystem. But if the goal is supporting firm creation of any kind, creating momentum behind firms that solve local and regional problems that matter deeply to people, creating self-sustaining economies with traditional industries at their base – and occasionally popping out a high-growth firm with niche importance – then rural ecosystems have been viable for decades. For us as development scholars and practitioners, any social system that supports human well-being and self-sufficiency is a major success, no matter how small. Viewed through the lens of a social system without the trimmings of a modern, urban ecosystem, rural areas have long satisfied the capability of supporting entrepreneurial action as seen by the wide variability in entrepreneurship rates across rural areas (Acs & Armington, 2006) – some rural places clearly harbor more self-employed people and business starts than others. Does this make such places any less valuable to the total ecosystem of the global economy, particularly if they support key agricultural, manufacturing, and related business sectors that form the base of the economic pyramid?

The lesson here is that entrepreneurial ecosystems – taken as beneficial, innovative social systems more broadly – can form anywhere, and are no less valuable when they are small and remote than when they are large and centralized. Much like entrepreneurial businesses themselves, it is difficult to predict where the next exciting ecosystem will arise, as the field tends to research those places that are no longer inchoate and whose vital statistics are far more attuned to global-level investment. Beneath that are thousands of communities with varying degrees of ambient success, broadly defined, whose residents and businesses may have little desire to appear on a list of top entrepreneurial ecosystems. Middle-range theories present an opportunity to account for such places as part of a broader ecosystem of social and economic action, and to understand how such wetlands of economic activity contribute subtly to a broader economic picture. Furthermore, a greater focus on rural ecosystem theory in the literature can open the sociological – and entrepreneurial – imagination to higher levels of understanding, and a greater degree of respect for those things that are small and locally beneficial over a fixation on macro-ecosystems and large-scale trends. There is room for a unique *rural* flavor of ecosystem behavior that would be considered residual in dominant models. Much like Mills' and Merton's explorations, we are at a critical juncture in theory development that runs the risk of elevating grand theories about ideal ecosystem dynamics and highly specific, engineering-focused specificity that misses an important middle ground of human entrepreneurial behavior – one that could equally inform the field of large-scale entrepreneurial ecosystem development and entrepreneurial ecosystem development in general the same way that evolutionary biology has informed the medical sciences about the structure of the modern mind (Jerison, 2012; Roth & Dicke, 2005).

Achieving this requires the recognition that entrepreneurial ecosystems, and the researchers that research them, are themselves a *social milieu* complete with a culture, norms, and mores that produce particular outcomes. This is no different from the time of Merton and Mills, who recognized that the culture of the academy privileged a focus on grand (i.e., "important") theorizing, on totalizing models, and on highly technical applications of very specific, narrow issues. Such perspective limits our individual and collective thinking and imagination as researchers and practitioners as to the variability of entrepreneurial behavior, who is an entrepreneur, and the nature of entrepreneurial ecosystems. It tends to cause us to not recognize, to unintentionally marginalize, practical action grounded in the practical experience, the phronetic wisdom, of rural entrepreneurs and entrepreneurial ecosystems as well as others not fitting the conventional parameters of broad, generalized thinking about entrepreneurs and entrepreneurial ecosystems. For researchers and practitioners interested in rural people and places, embracing middle-range thinking and the phronetic wisdom inherent in the lived experience of rural entrepreneurs and community members is an opportunity to spill silos, shatter esoteric circles, shed path dependency, embrace diversity and complexity, nurture creativity and innovation, build theory, and – most important of all – support others in the work of building socially, culturally, and economically viable and vibrant rural communities.

6 Appendix: An Engineer and a Gardener at Work in an Entrepreneurial Ecosystem

We sincerely hope our readers do not think that we are: (a) simply opposed to any kind of sophisticated statistical models and (b) believe that experts (and proponents of urban-style ecosystems) are somehow overblown and misguided – or worse (c) think the field of ecosystem research has decayed into a hopeless abyss of useless studies or ill-fitting grand theories. Not true. The true elegance of middle-range theory is that such theories seek *pragmatic meaning* within our science, applying the best of our findings differentially and appropriately to a variety of social systems that operate under different histories, paradigms, and social milieu. There may indeed be a great deal of similarity among certain classes of ecosystems, such as rural ecosystems over a wide area (compared to more dense urban ecosystems), or proto-ecosystems in Western nations compared with the rest of the world. Perhaps the best way to find out what kind of ecosystem we are dealing with is through direct engagement. This is best demonstrated through an example, using a music-based entrepreneurial ecosystem.

Situation: Community X has an unusual number of talented musicians in its small, rural community. This situation is historical, as the community has long been a stopping place between larger cities, and a regular stop for entertaining travelers and traders. It is a proto-ecosystem: several businesses and a few nonprofits exist, but they are relatively disconnected from one another. The community agrees, however, that music is their strongest attractor to the community, a placemaking centerpiece, and there is room to grow a connected cluster of music-oriented businesses that serves as an economic cluster.

Problem: How do we connect diverse actors into some semblance of a self-reinforcing ecosystem capable of sectoral growth?

Engineer Approach: Well-established blueprints for growing into a music city already exist. Looking at the stories of Nashville, for example, the community became a hub for country music due to the presence of radio shows like the *Grand Ole Opry*, prominent studios like RCA Studio B, and music publishing companies that could sign new acts. Charismatic producers followed, cultivating legendary acts. Austin, by contrast, focused on venues for country musicians that shied from the Nashville sound, taking a venue-and-festival approach incrementally over time. Both started small and slowly filled in what we now know to be a complete, thriving music ecosystem with entrepreneurial efforts prominent throughout its history.

Engineer Research: An SEM was conducted using categories drawn from the literature, including "music leaders," "music feeders," and "non-music feeders." Results clustered well, and many gaps were found in the local music entrepreneurship ecosystem, especially around funding, and all will require some development. The research is used to inductively support broader theories on ecosystems, particularly those focusing on ecosystem structure.

Engineer Practice: Since Nashville and Austin are ideal music cities and very prosperous, the data suggest that creating a balanced mix of venues, small publishing firms, and modern production facilities for online distribution (the new radio) will lead to increased momentum. Research shows that creating a diverse industry that communicates fluidly (through meetups, conferences, etc.) helps to catalyze ongoing growth. Local arts organizations should focus on pairing investment with local entrepreneurs, driving toward right-sized projects of these types to create the genesis of a music entrepreneurship ecosystem over time. Governments should shift toward musician-friendly policies like Nashville, Austin, and Seattle; whatever that means in a small community.

Gardener Approach: Upon visiting Community X, it is clear that local musicians and venues were visibly sickened by the idea of becoming a "Little Nashville or Austin," and besides, it is unlikely to be reproducible and their efforts will never be taken too seriously next to industry giants. Culturally, this community wishes to remain small but sees promise in selling its rural music culture as a packaged experience complete with artisan retail, great restaurants, and cozy inns to meet its fullest potential. Sustainability and slow growth are preferable over rapid development. They recognize that, while also unpalatable, a reasonable amount of tourism will be required to achieve this dream. Several venues are already very successful, along with several local bands – but retail, restaurants, and inns are largely disconnected from this world, and most are not tourist-focused.

Gardener Research: A grounded approach is taken to understand citizen viewpoints, and to take stock of what is already working well. Social network analysis is chosen as a means of finding gaps in communication and relationship-building across diverse actors. A mix of qualitative and quantitative data are compared with other case studies in non-traditional, smaller cities with music as a leading developmental factor, including Leiper's Fork, TN; Taos, NM; Muscle Shoals, AL; and Denton, TX. Relational dynamics from the research are used to build middle-range theory about non-traditional, grassroots music ecosystems in smaller environments, with a general store approach to understanding the contributions of relationships built across and beyond the music scene.[16] Connections are also made to the mainstream literature, identifying which areas of the entrepreneurial ecosystem literature are most appropriate in this type of non-traditional ecosystem, and which diverge from the middle-range theory.

Gardener Practice: This is not a standard "music city," but can still be very successful when it comes to entrepreneurship with music at the center. The goal is not music output (i.e., getting attention as a place that spawns national acts, or a new entrant in the mainstream music industry), but rather moving from output to creating whole experiences. Music becomes a leading factor in a more holistic tourist environment including retail, inns, and restaurants. Focus should shift toward building bridges to other tourist-focused entities and understanding how to enhance participation behind a common vision. Investment should be grassroots and appropriate to place, and may take the form of new restaurant, retail, and lodging offerings – especially if these can be generated locally among latent entrepreneurs that understand the culture. Fusion with music can take the form of a new downtown organization committed to small business development with music as a theme, incorporating members of the already-strong music scene as leaders along with others in the community. This organization can take leadership on attracting local investment, supporting small business development and education, music education, tourist promotion, and attracting grant funds as appropriate.

16 See Balfour et al. (2018) for an example of middle-range theory building in an arts context.

References

Acs, Z.J., & Armington, C. (2006). Entrepreneurship, geography, and American economic growth. Cambridge University Press.

Acs, Z.J., & Szerb, L. (2007). Entrepreneurship, economic growth and public policy. Small Business Economics, 28, 109–122.

American Cancer Society. (2022). What causes cancer? Accessed March 22, 2023 at https://www.cancer.org/healthy/cancer-causes.html

Audretsch, D.B., & Lehmann, E.E. (2005). Does the knowledge spillover theory of entrepreneurship hold for regions? Research Policy, 34(8), 1191–1202.

Audretsch, D.B., Cunningham, J.A., Kuratko, D.F., Lehmann, E.E., & Menter, M. (2019). Entrepreneurial ecosystems: Economic, technological, and societal impacts. The Journal of Technology Transfer, 44, 313–325.

Balfour, B., Fortunato, M.W., & Alter, T.R. (2018). The creative fire: An interactional framework for rural arts-based development. Journal of Rural Studies, 63, 229–239.

Baumol, W.J., & Strom, R.J. (2007). Entrepreneurship and economic growth. Strategic Entrepreneurship Journal, 1(3-4), 233–237.

Bhidé, A. (2000). The origin and evolution of new businesses. Oxford University Press.

Boateng, S.L. (2018). Structural equation modelling (SEM) made easy. Independent publication.

Calhoun, C. (Ed.). (2002). Dictionary of the social sciences. Oxford University Press.

Carroll, G.R., & Khessina, O.M. (2005). The ecology of entrepreneurship. In Handbook of entrepreneurship research: Interdisciplinary perspectives (pp. 167–200).

Cohen, B. (2006). Sustainable valley entrepreneurial ecosystems. Business Strategy and the Environment, 15(1), 1–14.

Colander, D., Föllmer, H., Haas, A., Goldberg, M.D., Juselius, K., Kirman, A., Lux, T., & Sloth, B. The financial crisis and the systemic failure of academic economics. University of Copenhagen, Department of Economics, Discussion Paper 09–03 (2009).

Connell, J.P. (1987). Structural equation modeling and the study of child development: A question of goodness of fit. Child Development, 167–175.

Dabson, B. (2001). Supporting rural entrepreneurship, Conference article. In M. Drabenstott (Ed.), Exploring policy options for a new rural America (pp. 35–48). The Federal Reserve Bank of Kansas City.

Delgado, M., Porter, M.E., & Stern, S. (2010). Clusters and entrepreneurship. Journal of Economic Geography, 10(4), 495–518.

Duranton, G., & Puga, D. (2004). Micro-foundations of urban agglomeration economies. In Handbook of regional and urban economics (Vol. 4, pp. 2063–2117). Elsevier.

Engelen, A., Gupta, V., Strenger, L., & Brettel, M. (2015). Entrepreneurial orientation, firm performance, and the moderating role of transformational leadership behaviors. Journal of Management, 41(4), 1069–1097.

Feld, B., & Hathaway, I. (2020). The startup community way: Evolving an entrepreneurial ecosystem. John Wiley and Sons.

Feld, B. (2012). Startup communities: Building an entrepreneurial ecosystem in your city. John Wiley and Sons.

Fleck, L. (1980). Entstehung und Entwicklung einer wissenschaftlichen Tatsache: Einführung in die Lehre vom Denkstil und Denkkollektiv. Basel: Benno Schwabe und Co. Lothar Schäfer und Thomas Schnelle (Hrsg. und Vorwort), Frankfurt am Main: Suhrkamp. (Genesis and Development of a Scientific Fact, transl. by Fred Bradley and Thaddeus J. Trenn, Thaddeus J. Trenn and Robert K. Merton (eds.), “Foreword” by Thomas S. Kuhn, Chicago: Chicago University Press 1979).

Flora, C.B., & Flora, J.L. (1993). Entrepreneurial social infrastructure: A necessary ingredient. The Annals of the American Academy of Political and Social Science, 529(1), 48–58.
Fortunato, M.W.P., & Clevenger, M. R. (2022). An introduction to entrepreneurial ecosystems and entrepreneurial communities to empower entrepreneurs. In Empowering Entrepreneurial Communities and Ecosystems (pp. 1–28). Routledge.
Gines, D. (2021). 6 essentials for an effective entrepreneurship ecosystem. Washington: Fed Communities. May 6, 2021. Accessed March 22, 2022 at https://fedcommunities.org/entrepreneurship-ecosystem-essentials/.
Gnyawali, D.R., & Fogel, D.S. (1994). Environments for entrepreneurship development: Key dimensions and research implications. Entrepreneurship Theory and Practice, 18(4), 43–62.
Harrison, J., & Hoyler, M. (2015). Megaregions: Foundations, frailties, futures. In Megaregions (pp. 1–28). Edward Elgar Publishing.
Hawkins, S.A., & Hastie, R. (1990). Hindsight: Biased judgments of past events after the outcomes are known. Psychological Bulletin, 107(3), 311–327.
Isenberg, D. (2011a). The entrepreneurship ecosystem strategy as a new paradigm for economy policy: Principles for cultivating entrepreneurship. Babson entrepreneurship ecosystem project. Babson College.
Isenberg, D. (2011b). Domains of the entrepreneurship ecosystem. Babson entrepreneurship ecosystem project. Babson College.
Isenberg, D.J. (2010). How to start an entrepreneurial revolution. Harvard Business Review, 88(6), 40–50.
Jerison, H. (2012). Evolution of the brain and intelligence. Elsevier.
Johansson, F. (2004). The medici effect. Harvard University Press.
Jones, P., Ratten, V., & Hayduk, T. (2020). Sport, fitness, and lifestyle entrepreneurship. International Entrepreneurship and Management Journal, 16, 783–793.
Kamarck, A.M. (2016). Economics and the real world. University of Pennsylvania Press.
Kibler, E., Fink, M., Lang, R., & Muñoz, P. (2015). Place attachment and social legitimacy: Revisiting the sustainable entrepreneurship journey. Journal of Business Venturing Insights, 3, 24–29.
Krueger, N.F. (2017). Entrepreneurial intentions are dead: Long live entrepreneurial intentions. In M. Brännback, & A. Carsrud (Eds.), Revisiting the entrepreneurial mind: Inside the black box: An expanded edition (pp. 13–34). Springer.
Krumme, C. (2023). Optimal illusions: The false promise of optimization. Riverhead Books.
Irsova, Z., Bom, P.R.D., Havranek, T., & Rachinger, H. (2023). Spurious precision in meta-analysis. Kiel, Germany: ZBW – Leibniz Information Centre for Economics.
Lichtenstein, G.A., Lyons, T.S., & Kutzhanova, N. (2004). Building entrepreneurial communities: The appropriate role of enterprise development activities. Community Development, 35(1), 5–24.
Long, N.E. (1958). The local community as an ecology of games. American Journal of Sociology, 64(3), 251–261.
Malecki, E.J. (2018). Entrepreneurship and entrepreneurial ecosystems. Geography Compass, 12(3), e12359.
Merton, R.K. (1959). Social conformity, deviation, and opportunity structures: A comment on the contributions of Dubin and Cloward. American Sociological Review, 24(2), 177–189.
Merton, R.K. (1949). On sociological theories of the middle range. In Social theory and social structure (pp. 39–53). Glencoe: The Free Press.
Mills, C. (1959). The sociological imagination. Oxford University Press.
Mitchell, C.J. (1998). Entrepreneurialism, commodification and creative destruction: A model of post-modern community development. Journal of Rural Studies, 14(3), 273–286.
Nelson, J.A. (2018). Economics for humans. University of Chicago Press.
Neumeyer, X., Santos, S.C., Caetano, A., & Kalbfleisch, P. (2019). Entrepreneurship ecosystems and women entrepreneurs: A social capital and network approach. Small Business Economics, 53, 475–489.
Oldenburg, R. (1997). Our vanishing third places. Planning Commissioners Journal, 25(4), 6–10.

Paladan, N.N. (2015). Transformational leadership: The emerging leadership style of successful entrepreneurs. Journal of Literature and Art Studies, 5(1), 64–72.
Park, R.E. (1952). Human communities: The city and human ecology. Free Press.
Parsons, T., & Shils, E.A. (1951). Values, motives, and systems of action. Toward a general theory of action (Vol. 33, pp. 247–275).
Porter, M.E. (1996). Competitive advantage, agglomeration economies, and regional policy. International Regional Science Review, 19(1–2), 85–90.
Puga, D. (2010). The magnitude and causes of agglomeration economies. Journal of Regional Science, 50(1), 203–219.
Reynolds, P.D. (1992). Sociology and entrepreneurship: Concepts and contributions. Entrepreneurship Theory and Practice, 16(2), 47–70.
Rosenthal, S.S., & Strange, W.C. (2004). Evidence on the nature and sources of agglomeration economies. In Handbook of regional and urban economics (Vol. 4, pp. 2119–2171). Elsevier.
Roth, G., & Dicke, U. (2005). Evolution of the brain and intelligence. Trends in Cognitive Sciences, 9(5), 250–257.
Roundy, P.T., & Bayer, M.A. (2019). Entrepreneurial ecosystem narratives and the micro-foundations of regional entrepreneurship. The International Journal of Entrepreneurship and Innovation, 20(3), 194–208.
Roundy, P.T., Brockman, B.K., & Bradshaw, M. (2017). The resilience of entrepreneurial ecosystems. Journal of Business Venturing Insights, 8, 99–104.
Ruef, M. (2010). Entrepreneurial groups. In historical foundations of entrepreneurship research. Edward Elgar Publishing.
Shane, S.A. (2008). The illusions of entrepreneurship: The costly myths that entrepreneurs, investors, and policy makers live by. Yale University Press.
Shepherd, D.A., Williams, T.A., & Patzelt, H. (2015). Thinking about entrepreneurial decision making: Review and research agenda. Journal of Management, 41(1), 11–46.
Smart, R.G. (1966). Subject selection bias in psychological research. Canadian Psychologist/Psychologie canadienne, 7(2), 115–121.
Sorokin, P.A. (1947). Society, culture, and personality: Their structure and dynamics. A system of general sociology. Harper and Brothers.
Stam, E. (2015). Entrepreneurial ecosystems and regional policy: A sympathetic critique. European Planning Studies, 23(9), 1759–1769.
Stam, E., & Van de Ven, A. (2021). Entrepreneurial ecosystem elements. Small Business Economics, 56, 809–832.
Taleb, N.N. (2012). Antifragile: Things that gain from disorder. Munich: Random House.
Taleb, N.N. (2007). The black swan: The impact of the highly improbable. Random House.
Thornton, P.H. (1999). The sociology of entrepreneurship. Annual Review of Sociology, 25(1), 19–46.
Van de Ven, H. (1993). The development of an infrastructure for entrepreneurship. Journal of Business Venturing, 8(3), 211–230.
Yitshaki, R. (2012). How do entrepreneurs' emotional intelligence and transformational leadership orientation impact new ventures' growth? Journal of Small Business and Entrepreneurship, 25(3), 357–374.
Zahra, S.A., & Nambisan, S. (2011). Entrepreneurship in global innovation ecosystems. AMS Review, 1, 4–17.

Thomas S. Lyons

What Skills Do Rural Entrepreneurs Need for Success, and How Can They Develop Them?

Abstract: This chapter seeks to answer several questions. What is an entrepreneurship skill? Why are skills relevant? How do we best develop entrepreneurship skills? How do we know which skills need to be developed? Can we measure skills, and can we measure them in a way that can be acted upon? And, most importantly for the purposes of this handbook, how can the concept of entrepreneurship skills be adapted to the rural context and further explored by rural researchers? In answering these questions, the author offers a tool for measuring entrepreneurship skills clinically, that features 30 "essential" skills, and a coaching system for using this measurement to drive skill development. Adaptation to the rural context is then discussed.

Keywords: coaching, entrepreneurship skills, skill development, skill measurement, rural entrepreneurship

1 Introduction

In a chapter in the book *Entrepreneurship and Local Economic Development*, Lyons, Lichtenstein, and Kutzhanova (2007) asserted that what makes an entrepreneur successful is the possession of a skillset, and the reason some entrepreneurs are more successful than others is a matter of differences in the level of mastery of those skills. This work was an extension of an earlier article by two of these authors that held that the most actionable way to segment entrepreneurs for development purposes is by their skill level (Lichtenstein & Lyons, 2001).

This assertion has been carried forward by multiple researchers. Smith et al. (2005) expanded upon the entrepreneurship skills put forward by Lichtenstein and Lyons (2001). Lichtenstein and Lyons (2010) offered an extensive discussion of the differences in the behavior and cognition of entrepreneurs at different skill levels and argued that changes in skill level required a "fundamental reorganization of an individual's previous knowledge as well as the structure of his thinking and behavior" (Lichtenstein & Lyons, 2010: 58). Cooney (2012) added further insights to the nature of entrepreneurship skills, providing a three-category typology of skills: technical, management, and entrepreneurship skills.

These were not the first contentions that skills might underlie entrepreneurship success. Ronstadt (1985) identified skills as the key to successful entrepreneurship and

Thomas S. Lyons, University of Tennessee at Chattanooga, email: Thomas-Lyons@utc.edu

https://doi.org/10.1515/9783110791396-004

advocated skill development in entrepreneurship education, as did Stumpf et al. (1991). In the ensuing years, several scholars added their voices to the growing chorus that attributed success in entrepreneurship to skill development (Viswanathan, Fontenot & Hoffman, 1992; Gorman, Hanlon & King, 1997; Iyigun & Owen, 1998; Baron & Markman, 2000). The research on entrepreneurship skills has only continued to grow. Lyons, Lyons and Jolley (2019); Towers et al. (2020); and Galvao, Marques, and Ferreira (2020) have all argued for the development of entrepreneurship skills.

If we accept these arguments, they raise several important questions: What is a skill? Why are skills relevant? How do we best develop entrepreneurship skills? How do we know which skills need to be developed? Can we measure skills, and can we measure them in a way that can be acted upon? And, most importantly for the purposes of this handbook, how can the concept of entrepreneurship skills be adapted to the rural context and further explored by rural researchers?

2 What is a Skill?

Our understanding of the nature of skills comes largely from the field of psychology. A skill represents "a translation of one's expertise/knowledge into a behavior" (Kutzhanova, Lyons & Lichtenstein, 2009: 194). Another way of stating this is that one's behavior is a reflection of one's skill level. This is an important observation because behavior, alone, does not explain an individual's success in their field. This is because behaviors are context specific. That is, they vary from one place and time to another (Lichtenstein & Lyons, 2010); skills do not change with context, a subject that will be taken up in more detail in the following section.

A key element of all definitions of "skill" is that skills involve the integration of agency and context (Lyons, Lyons & Jolley, 2019). Boyatzis and Kolb (1995) and Mascolo and Fischer (1999) assert that skills involve the application of knowledge in a particular context. Fischer and Bidell (2005) add to this the concept of "organization." Thus, a skill is the capability to organize one's behavior toward the achievement of a goal in a given context. In entrepreneurship, this would be the capability to organize and develop an organization in the business environment. It is important to note that skills are action oriented because they are applied knowledge (Lyons, Lyons & Jolley, 2020).

Discussing entrepreneurship skills, Kutzhanova, Lyons, and Lichtenstein (2009) contend that because skills are applied in a given context, development of those skills must be tailored to that context. This links skill development to behavior and practice. An entrepreneur must practice applying their knowledge in the context in which they will be working if they are to develop their skills. This also implies that entrepreneurs do not begin their journey at full capability. They must build this capability, or skill mastery, over time (Kutzhanova, Lyons & Lichtenstein, 2009).

3 Why are Skills Relevant?

If the goal is to develop successful rural entrepreneurs via skill building, this begs the question: "Why are skills the most appropriate attribute to develop?" In order to answer this question fully, an understanding of what skills are *not*, as well as knowledge of their most important properties, is essential.

Skills are often conflated with two other attributes: behaviors and competencies. However, these elements are not synonymous with skills. As noted in the preceding section of this chapter, behaviors are highly context specific. They vary by place and time. A behavior is a consequence of both applied knowledge (skill) and the context within which the skill is applied (Cook, 2015). As an example, a behavior that is deemed "entrepreneurial" in a developing country may not be considered entrepreneurial in a developed country. A behavior that was thought to be entrepreneurial in the 1950s may not be considered as such today. On the other hand, a skill is reproducible. It can be executed by different entrepreneurs, in varying contexts, at different times and is still the same (Lichtenstein & Lyons, 2010).

A competency is a very broad conception. While it gives general guidance as to a capability(ies) that an entrepreneur must have, it is too vague to be acted upon, either to help an entrepreneur develop it or to use it to advance entrepreneurship practice. For example, if entrepreneurs should develop the competency of "opportunity recognition" (Morris et al., 2013), what exactly should they be developing? Arguably, there are several skills embedded in this capability, with varying approaches to development required for each. Competencies might be thought of as macro-level skills, made up of several meta-level skills and many micro-level skills (Lyons, Lyons & Samson, 2021).

Skills possess four important properties that make them ideal for measurement and development, with an eye to action. This is very much in alignment with the nature of entrepreneurship, which has been characterized as learning by doing (LaFontaine & Shaw, 2016; Colombelli, Panelli & Serraino, 2022). Skills are (Dreyfus & Dreyfus, 1986; Thamhain, 1992; Clarke, 2010; Lichtenstein & Lyons, 2010; Lyons, Lyons & Samson, 2021):

- **Learnable** – They can be acquired through a process that begins with the acquisition of knowledge, then an opportunity to practice that knowledge, while receiving regular feedback on that practice.
- **Actionable** – They are arguably applied knowledge.
- **Reproducible** – They remain the same, no matter who carries them out or in what context.
- **Repeatable** – They can be repetitively executed with consistency.

All of this suggests that skills can be learned and developed and then adapted to the context in which they will be used. In effect, skills are a toolkit that entrepreneurs can bring to any context and adjust to the conditions of that context as needed. A study in the field of urban planning provides a parallel perspective from another professional domain. In a survey of over 200 graduates of accredited university planning programs in North America working overseas, Hinojosa, Lyons and Zinn (1992) found that these planners discovered that the skills they acquired through their education could be readily adapted to the context in which they worked, no matter where in the world that might be. These authors emphasized that the key to making this possible was the inclusion of opportunities for real world practice of the knowledge acquired in the classroom. Hinojosa, Lyons and Zinn (1992) asserted that these planning school graduates became "barefoot planners," capable of taking their skills and adapting them to the realities of any context. Arguably, this would be no different when applied to entrepreneurs. If the latter are properly prepared through the development of their skills, they, too, will be able to apply those skills in any context by adapting them.

4 How Can Skills be Developed?

At this point, we have established what skills are and why they are the appropriate attribute upon which to focus if we want to develop successful rural entrepreneurs. The next logical question is: How does one go about developing skills? What is the process for doing so, and how is that process best carried out?

4.1 The Knowledge-Practice-Feedback Cycle

Skill building, or development, is a process with three major steps: procuring knowledge, practicing that knowledge, and receiving regular feedback on that practice (Lyons, Lyons & Samson, 2021). Each of these steps will now be discussed in more detail.

1. **Procuring Knowledge:** Knowledge is the grist for the mill of skill building. Without knowledge, there is no foundation upon which to build. Knowledge can be acquired through reading, classroom education or training, peer interactions, and counseling or mentoring, among other sources/approaches. However, knowledge, alone, is insufficient to skill building. Merely "telling" entrepreneurs what they should know does not ensure successful entrepreneurship.

2. **Practicing Knowledge:** As was noted in the preceding section, preparing entrepreneurs to successfully adapt their knowledge to the challenges of any context requires practicing that knowledge in *some* context; a concept referred to as "experiential learning" (Neck & Greene, 2011). Practice allows the entrepreneur to experience what happens when they apply their knowledge in a real-world situation. When they reflect on this and use what they learn to help them engage in successful action in different contexts in the future, this is known as "generative learning" (Senge, 1990; Gibb, 1997; Cope, 2005).

In order for it to lead to successful skill building, practice must be robust in its quantity and quality. In other words, it matters both how much an entrepreneur practices *and* how well they practice (Coyle, 2009). Coyle (2009) prescribes 10,000 h of practice and what he calls "deep" practice. While the amount of practice necessary is subject to debate, the concept of deep practice is crucial.[1] In deep practice, one must first be strategic about what they need to practice (Coyle, 2009). This raises an interesting question: How do we know what to practice? Oftentimes, our methods for answering this question are superficial. In some cases, we try to self-diagnose – I'm not very good at this; so, this is what I need to practice. However, we might be wrong in our diagnosis regarding the specific skill(s) required and/or our current level of skill. Sometimes, we rely on others to tell us what we need to practice, but they might be wrong as well. The only way to be truly strategic about what to practice is to be able to objectively measure our skill weaknesses and address those. This concept will be explored later in this chapter.

Coyle (2009) further asserts that deep practice involves pushing oneself out of one's comfort zone. Being willing to take and manage risks is important because, as was noted near the beginning of this chapter, developing a skill requires a complete transformation of the entrepreneur's capability (Lichtenstein & Lyons, 2010), which is not something that can be accomplished without venturing "off the sidewalk." Deep practice must also be intentional and focused (Coyle, 2009). It requires considerable repetition, which takes us back to the 10,000 h of practice (Coyle, 2009). Finally, and perhaps most importantly, if one is engaged in deep practice, one must receive regular feedback on that practice from another party (Coyle, 2009), which brings us to the third, and final, step in the skill-building process.

3. **Receiving Regular Feedback on Practice:** This feedback should force honest reflection (Neck, Neck & Murray, 2018), which can cause the entrepreneur to rethink both how they practice and how they think about what they thought they knew (the knowledge they acquired at the start of the skill-building process) (Lyons, Lyons & Samson, 2021). This brings us back to the quote excerpted from Lichtenstein and Lyons (2010) early in this chapter that explains the reason that skill building is transformational: ". . . moving from one skill level to another isn't an incremental change – it is a major shift, one that involves a fundamental reorganization of an individual's previous knowledge as well as the structure of his thinking and behavior" (58).

While this discussion of the skill-building process makes it seem linear, the actual process is a feedback loop that embeds the given skill. This process is captured in Figure 1.

1 See Gladwell (2008). *Outliers: The story of success.* Little, Brown and Company for a detailed discussion of the volume of practice required for exceptional success. Gladwell argues that what we commonly attribute to genius is actually achieved through at least 10,000 h of practice.

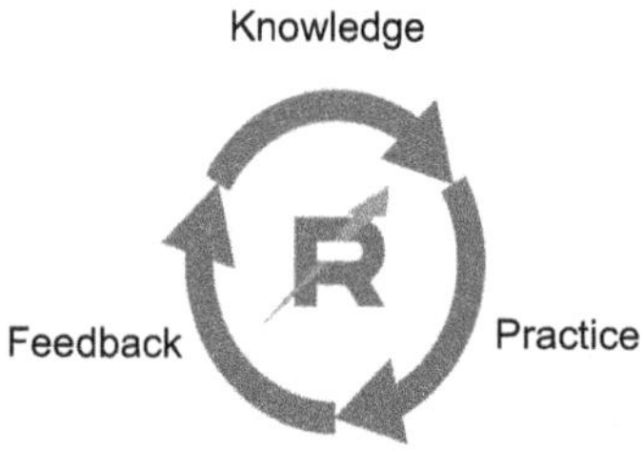

Figure 1: The Skill Development Feedback Loop.
Source: The John Praed Foundation.

4.2 Coaching

If "deep" practice requires regular feedback on one's practice, who should provide this feedback? Extensive field research suggests that a very effective answer to this question is a coach (Kutzhanova et al., 2009; Lichtenstein & Lyons, 2010; Nicholls-Nixon & Maxheimer, 2022; Lyons & Holmes, 2024). This is because of the nature of the coaching approach.

At essence, an entrepreneurship coach is an individual who works with an entrepreneur/team on a long-term basis to help them think through their business challenges and the solutions to those challenges and to guide them in developing their entrepreneurship skills. The end goal is helping the entrepreneur/team to achieve their business goals/objectives. The coach may use a variety of approaches to accomplishing this, including asking thought-provoking questions, assigning "homework," requiring journaling and other forms of self-reflection, leading relevant "field trips," making helpful connections to others with the desired expertise, among others. A coach deals in transformation (deep, lasting change), as opposed to transactions (short-term, arms-length exchanges), which distinguishes the coach from the expert advisor, who primarily dispenses information and knowledge (Lyons & Holmes, 2024).

Because the coach is guiding the entrepreneur in the practice of their knowledge in a context, the coach should be *of* that context. Thus, if an entrepreneur is practicing entrepreneurship in a rural region, the coach should live and work in that region. In this way, the coach knows the culture, economy, values, etc. of the specific context and can help the entrepreneur adapt the skills they are building to these realities of the region. Field research has demonstrated the value of local coaches to the entrepreneurship skills development process (Kutzhanova, Lyons & Lichtenstein, 2009). In the coaching pilot described by Kutzhanova et al. (2009), two types of coaching were employed: personal and peer group. Personal, or one-on-one, coaching pairs the coach with the entrepreneur to create a highly tailored coaching experience. Peer group coaching brings a group of entrepreneurs who are at a similar skill level together to provide mutual support, exchange information, and share differing perspectives, with the coach playing a facilitative role. Kutzhanova et al. (2009) found that when used together these two coaching approaches increased entrepreneurs' self-awareness, opening them to new learning.

5 Which Skills Should be Developed?

All of this begs the question of which skills of entrepreneurship should be developed. Clearly, if one is serious about developing any set of skills, those skills must be actually developable. As discussed earlier in this chapter, the focus cannot be on competencies, or macro-skills, as they are too broad to be acted upon (i.e., developed). Similarly, micro-skills are no more actionable than competencies but for the reason that they are too granular. Parsing skills at this level leads to endless debate about exactly which skills are needed for success in entrepreneurship. While scholars argue over precise skillsets, entrepreneurs miss out on the opportunity to understand and develop the skills that are *essential* to success in entrepreneurship. In addition, micro-skills are often overlapping or repetitive, further confusing and impeding skill development.

In light of this, meta-skills seem to be the "sweet spot" for placing the focus of skill development (Lyons, Lyons & Samson, 2021). These skills each reflect a package of micro-skills that are reinforcing of each other and can be acted upon; and yet, they are not so broad and vague that they cannot be effectively addressed. They permit the identification of a skillset that is manageable for assessment and represents the essential skills necessary for success.

Lyons, Lyons, and Samson (2021) have identified these essential skills for entrepreneurship. They were arrived at through a deep literature review that detected over 150 skills that have been correlated with successful entrepreneurship. Upon further scrutiny, it was found that many of these skills were redundant or overlapping of others, while some were micro-skills that could be combined with others to create meta-skills. In addition, four domains of entrepreneurship skills were identified that were designed to capture the full required skillset for entrepreneurship success, a bow to the value of macro-skillsets when used appropriately. Each domain was populated with just enough individual meta-skills to ensure that domain was adequately represented. When this sorting process was complete, 30 skills remained. These were subsequently tested for their relevance in pilot entrepreneurship coaching programs in the United States. The 30 "essential" skills of entrepreneurship are listed in Table 1, by skill domain.

The domains, themselves, represent forms of management: Business Management, Organizational Process Management, Relationship Management, and Transformation Management. To carry them out effectively, the entrepreneur must possess the skills necessary to manage business structure, business processes, people, and change, respectively. This reflects the fact that successful entrepreneurship is about more than managing a business entity. It is also about managing all of the people relationships outside the company that make it possible for the business to grow and sustain itself as well as the uncertain and ambiguous context in which it operates. To put this another way, successful entrepreneurship requires the skills necessary to build social capital, both bonding and bridging, and to effect lasting change (Lyons, 2022).

Table 1: Skills of the RISE by Domain.

Domain	Individual Skills
Business Management Skills	– Knowledge of field/industry – Knowledge of laws/regulations – Accounting/bookkeeping – Finance – Marketing/communication – Operations management – Technology-enabled business management
Relationship Management Skills	– Networking capacity – Leveraging existing partnerships – Resource leveraging – Building and maintaining reputation – Community involvement and influence – Accountability – Teaming
Organizational Process Management	– Internal communication – Process design – Decision making – Conflict management – Performance and disciplined action
Transformational Management Skills	– Problem solving – Persistence/relentlessness – Passion/charisma – Flexibility and adaptation – Knowledge as a resource – Creativity – Innovation – Leadership – Resilience – Resourcefulness – Self-awareness

Adapted from Lyons, Lyons and Jolley (2019).

6 Actionable Assessment of Skills

If one is to develop skills based on an assessment, then it is crucial that the assessment tool measures skills clinically. This is because clinical assessment permits action. As an example, when an individual is not feeling well, they go to their doctor. The doctor asks about their symptoms and runs some basic tests. Based on this diagnosis, the doctor prescribes a plan of treatment which the patient can act upon – taking medicine, drinking fluids, getting adequate sleep, and so forth. The doctor will then typically follow up to make sure the treatment is addressing the illness effectively. Similarly, a clinical skills assessment tells the entrepreneur where they are weak and permits the development of an action plan for addressing these skill weaknesses. Subsequent skills assessments can be used to determine progress and to revise action plans when they are not working or when the skill weakness has been addressed.

Most skills assessments do not lend themselves to action. This is because their underlying theory of measurement is psychometrics, which is predictive. They are designed to forecast the possession of a skill or whether or not an individual is likely to be a successful entrepreneur. This may be appropriate for someone trying to decide if they should invest in an entrepreneur and their business, but it does not lend itself to developing the pipeline of entrepreneurs and enterprises who can ultimately become attractive to investors (Lichtenstein & Lyons, 2006). In fact, the psychometric theory of measurement has resulted in much entrepreneurship-focused policy that is tantamount to "picking winners," which is arguably inequitable, leaving many would-be entrepreneurs without the help they need (Lyons, 2015).

A relatively new innovation that addresses this problem through its clinical orientation is the communimetric theory of measurement. Communimetrics was, not surprisingly, developed for use in behavioral health environments where sensitivity to the equitability of treatment is high and the approach is clinical (See Lyons, 2009). In this context, measurement that facilitates action is essential. These characteristics lend themselves well to both the measurement and development of entrepreneurship skills for reasons previously discussed. Entrepreneurship is characterized by taking action and learning from it. Any assessment of entrepreneurship skills that purports to facilitate skill development in this arena must be capable of being acted upon.

The communimetric approach also can be applied effectively to coach-based development of entrepreneurs. In collaboration with the entrepreneur, the coach can diagnose the entrepreneur's skill weaknesses in a way that guides the action(s) needed to help the entrepreneur to advance their skills along a continuum of development. Because the measurements generated by the assessment carry meaning, the coach can use them to understand the entrepreneur's skill level on a given individual skill or place the entrepreneur at an overall skill level (Level 1, Level 2, Level 3, Level 4, and Level 5), which facilitates matching the entrepreneur to resources that they are prepared to use effectively.

7 Bringing Skill Definition, Meaningful Measurement, and Development Together

Given the importance of skills to entrepreneurs' success, it is crucial to our ability to support and sustain entrepreneurship as a community economic development activity that we are able to accurately assess these skills in a way that permits their advancement. To do this requires an assessment tool that focuses on the measurement of the essential meta-skills of entrepreneurship and gauges those skills in a clinical way. The Readiness Inventory for Successful Entrepreneurship (RISE) is such a tool.

The RISE is a Web-based assessment tool designed to measure the skills of individual entrepreneurs or entrepreneurial teams. Its measurement system is based on the Communimetric theory of measurement, which gives it a clinical base. As described elsewhere (Lyons, Lyons & Jolley, 2020; Lyons, Lyons & Samson, 2021), the RISE provides a score that, unlike psychometric assessment tools, can be translated into meaning (Blanton & Jaccard, 2006). The RISE scoring creates action levels for each skill, as follows, in a way that permits the user to develop that skill (Lyons, Lyons & Jolley, 2020: 125):

- "0: Lack of skill – requires intensive development.
- 1: Inconsistent skill – requires development.
- 2: Entrepreneur has skill.
- 3: Entrepreneur's skill level is a strength – has exceptional skill."

As Lyons, Lyons, and Jolley (2020: 125) describe this process, "By organizing the assessed skills using the action framework, the coach and entrepreneur both have an immediate understanding of the focus of development for that entrepreneur if he/she wishes to climb the ladder of success. Thus, coaching is individualized to allow for building on strengths and targeting interventions/efforts to enhance areas where skill deficits are understood."

The RISE offers a consensus approach to measurement, where the coach and the entrepreneur are telling a mutually articulated story about the entrepreneur's skill level. This is a story in which the entrepreneur is the hero, the coach is the wise guide, and the quest is entrepreneurship skill mastery (Lyons, Lyons & Samson, unpublished).

8 Why Entrepreneurship Skill Building is Crucial in Rural Areas

To this point, the argument has been made that skill building is important to success in entrepreneurship and, in turn, to entrepreneurship-focused economic development. It is arguably even more important, perhaps even crucial to entrepreneurship success in rural areas. Before delving into the unique aspects of the rural context that make a focus on entrepreneurship skill building imperative, a reminder is in order. Skills are not context specific. So, the 30 "essential" skills of entrepreneurship identified in this chapter are just as relevant to rural entrepreneurship as they are to any other context (i.e., there is no such thing as "rural entrepreneurship skills," merely entrepreneurship skills used in a rural context). Having said this, it should also be remembered that in order for an entrepreneur to be successful, they must effectively adapt these skills of entrepreneurship to the context in which they are working. These observations provide a point of departure for the remainder of this section.

By focusing on rural entrepreneurship, the relevant context has been established. That context must be acknowledged, understood, respected, and adapted to if an entrepreneur is to be successful. It is a source of both opportunities and obstacles. If an entrepreneur is left to their own devices in this context, they will struggle.

Research has consistently shown that business survival rates are higher in rural areas, including very remote rural areas, than they are in urban areas (Renski, 2009; Yu, Orazem & Jolly, 2011; Deller & Conroy, 2016). This could be interpreted as good news for rural communities in the sense that effort put into supporting these businesses is less likely to be wasted. Thus, an investment in entrepreneurship-focused economic development by governments appears to be money well spent.

However, as research by Deller and Conroy (2016) finds, the reasons for higher rural business survival rates may be unanticipated. The three key reasons cited in this research are:

- Because the number of rural business startups is lower in rural areas than in urban, the former lacks the competitive pressures that tend to force unprofitable businesses to close. Thus, rural areas tend to facilitate the survival of more marginal businesses.
- Going hand-in-hand with the first point, opportunity costs for marginal rural businesses are lower because there are fewer alternative business and job opportunities than are found in urban areas, making it more likely that rural operators of unprofitable businesses will continue to pursue their enterprises.
- Because other economic opportunities are less abundant in rural areas, prospective rural entrepreneurs may tend to be more risk averse and may not start businesses that urban entrepreneurs would be more likely to start. Failure carries a greater stigma in rural areas than urban areas. This limits innovation and experimentation by rural entrepreneurs but may result in the creation of enterprises in more traditional/stable, low-growth industries.

As a result, rural entrepreneurs are more likely to attempt to sustain businesses that will not scale and are, therefore, less likely to generate wealth for themselves and their families. This helps to explain the prevalence of "necessity entrepreneurship" – entrepreneurship that emerges as a result of a real or perceived lack of economic options, as defined by the Global Entrepreneurship Monitor (GEM) project (Wong, Ho & Autio, 2005) – in rural areas. This is a form of "subsistence" entrepreneurship that may perpetuate economic survival but is unlikely to advance the rural economy or improve quality of life.

Typical transactional entrepreneurship-focused economic development will not change this situation. This type of economic development is characterized by resources-based approaches that do not truly address human development needs. The assumption is that the entrepreneur merely needs access to resources in order to be successful – financial capital, marketing data, business development expertise, etc. These resources are delivered through arms-length, short-term transactions, which are efficient but not necessarily effective. They presuppose that the entrepreneur is capable of utilizing the resources in question successfully. In most cases, however, entrepreneurs need to be prepared to effectively use resources (Lichtenstein & Lyons, 2010).

This suggests that effective entrepreneurship-focused economic development must be attentive to human development – entrepreneur development – before addressing resource needs. This is not to say that resources are unimportant to entrepreneurship success, only that they must take a second position to the development of the entrepreneur. Entrepreneurs must be sufficiently skilled to employ resources effectively toward the achievement of their goals. This brings the argument in this chapter full circle. The development of an entrepreneur's skills involves a transformation of that entrepreneur's capability. That requires a long-term process, not a short-term transaction. As an entrepreneur develops their skillset, they not only become capable of effectively using the resources available to them, but they are also capable of scaling their business, moving them away from necessity entrepreneurship to what GEM calls "opportunity" entrepreneurship (Wong, Ho & Autio, 2005). This is where wealth building takes place, economies are built, and lives are improved (Lyons, Hamlin & Hamlin, 2018).

There is no shortage of research that supports the idea that rural entrepreneurship is challenging. Rural entrepreneurs work in contexts that tend to have relatively low population densities, limiting available resources, support networks, and markets (Lichtenstein & Lyons, 1996; Dabson, 2001). They are restricted in their ability to innovate by government policy that has traditionally failed to recognize rural economic diversity (Aryal et al., 2018; Lyons, Miller & Mann, 2018) and a culture that overemphasizes the building of bonding social capital (Dabson, 2001). However, these are arguably constraints that can be overcome through the development of an entrepreneurship skillset (Lyons, Lyons & Jolley, 2019, 2020).

Crucial to overcoming these limitations is having the capability to network widely, or to develop bridging social capital (Lyons, Lyons & Jolley, 2020; Lyons, 2022). This allows the rural entrepreneur to reach out to others beyond their rural community or region who can help them acquire needed information, knowledge, and resources. This may involve networking with assistance providers in nearby cities, land grant universities, and/or regional organizations such as Small Business Development Centers (Lyons, Miller & Mann, 2018; Lyons, Lyons & Jolley, 2019). The entrepreneurship skills required to do this are the Relationship Management skills described earlier in this chapter.

Lyons, Lyons, and Jolley (2020) expand upon this by suggesting that building rural entrepreneurial ecosystems driven by skill development can yield both the bonding and bridging social capital essential to successful rural entrepreneurship. Such ecosystems assemble the necessary human, physical, financial, and social capital necessary to sustain support for creating and sustaining enterprises (Isenberg, 2011). However, giving these ecosystems a sustainable form that is transparent to their resident entrepreneurs has proven elusive (Roundy & Lyons, 2022).

Based on the work of Lichtenstein and Lyons, who created and tested pilot entrepreneur coaching programs in rural regions (Kutzhanova, Lyons & Lichtenstein, 2009; Lichtenstein & Lyons, 2010), Lyons and Holmes (2024) prescribe such a coaching system, driven by the RISE skills assessment described earlier in this chapter, as a way to make ecosystems cohesive and transparent. This coaching system begins with the assessment of the skills of the ecosystem's entrepreneurs using the RISE tool. Employing the RISE overall skill level measurement, entrepreneurs can be assigned to coaches from the ecosystem who are capable of coaching at the appropriate skill level (Level 1, Level 2, Level 3, etc.). The coaches can then work with the entrepreneurs in the two modalities previously discussed: personal coaching and/or peer coaching.

As the coach works with the entrepreneur to develop the latter's skills, they can prepare the entrepreneur to use the resources offered by the ecosystem. Using financial capital as an example, an entrepreneur with Level 1 skills is prepared to use FFF (family, friends, and founder), microloans, or crowdfunding, but may not be ready to manage a bank loan or equity capital. These latter resources will require Level 2 or even Level 3 skills. This approach helps to make the ecosystem more transparent to the entrepreneur. Skill level and the action plan created jointly by the coach and the entrepreneur become the guides to where in the ecosystem the entrepreneur needs to be and when. They also help to make it clear when it is time to move on from one resource provider to the next (Lyons & Holmes, 2024).

This benefits the resource providers in the ecosystem as well. It helps them to understand the appropriate role they play in the ecosystem and when it is time to let go of a given client entrepreneur because they have fulfilled that individual's or team's need (Lichtenstein, Lyons & Kutzhanova, 2004; Lyons & Holmes, 2024). The coach becomes the coordinator of the ecosystem for the entrepreneurs they work with. This permits tailoring of assistance to each entrepreneur while at the same time allowing for scaling of the number of entrepreneurs served through the coaching system, via mass customization (Pine & Gilmore, 2011; Lyons, Lyons & Samson, 2022). In this way, the entrepreneurial ecosystem is driven by skill assessment and development through coaching (Lyons & Holmes, 2024).

Rural entrepreneurship coaching systems can help entrepreneurs by coordinating and driving ecosystems in these communities and regions. They can assist rural entrepreneurs to develop the skills they need to overcome the obstacles to successful entrepreneurship presented by the rural context, including the capability to create and sustain essential networks outside of the local environment. This can enable entrepreneurs to get out of the necessity entrepreneurship "quagmire" found in many rural areas by expanding their markets and their bases of resource support.

9 Implications for Research

The scenario sketched out in this chapter offers numerous opportunities for ongoing research to test the concepts presented and to develop frameworks and tools for carrying these ideas forward. It has been argued that the quantity and, more to the point, the quality of rural entrepreneurs can be enhanced through skill development. These skills are measurable in a clinical way and can be developed. A skills assessment tool, the RISE, has been described as the kind of clinical skills measurement instrument needed for this work. Coaching has been advocated as the most effective approach for skill development and for preparing entrepreneurs for the use of the resources offered by the entrepreneurial ecosystem. Coaches can also act as strategic resource "brokers" for the ecosystem.

One question that begs for more exploration has to do with whether or not a skills-focused entrepreneurship support program can be consistently effective in rural areas. This has been tested in a limited fashion through a pilot coaching program using an earlier pencil and paper version of the RISE, which demonstrated some success (Kutzhanova, Lyons & Lichtenstein, 2009). There are also current users of the RISE assessment located in rural communities. However, much more testing of the RISE is needed to fully ascertain its efficacy. It is the goal of the RISE's creators to build a community of RISE users who can share data and experiences (Lyons, Lyons & Samson, 2021). Thus, building a RISE pilot site in a rural area is a ticket to participation in this community.

Such a pilot site would permit testing of the tool with local entrepreneurs. Does it facilitate successful entrepreneurship? If so, how is this best measured? Is entrepreneur coaching guided by the RISE assessment effective in helping entrepreneurs to build their skills, prepare themselves for better use of the resources the ecosystem has to offer, and better understand the ecosystem and their place in it at any given point in time? Can a RISE-driven coaching system help to better organize the entrepreneurial ecosystem by making it clear to resource providers what their role is in relationship to other entrepreneurship support organizations? All of these questions can be tested by the creator of the RISE pilot in their locale.

Engaging the community of RISE users can allow for comparative studies of rural regions and rural vs. urban areas. This facilitates research into questions such as: Is there a difference between skill development in rural areas and urban areas? Is entrepreneurship skill development more effective in some rural regions than others? If so, why? Are there coaching interventions that are more effective in some contexts than others? Are there commonalities in entrepreneurship skill development across contexts?

There is research needed regarding the RISE skills assessment, itself. Are there skills that are more crucial to rural entrepreneurs than they are to entrepreneurs in other contexts? The "essential" skills of the RISE are not static. Over time, conditions and culture change, potentially requiring a reassessment of the skills in the RISE set.

What are the emerging entrepreneurship skills that need to be considered for inclusion in the RISE? Which skills currently in the RISE assessment are in need of modification? Are there emerging entrepreneurship skills specific to the rural context that might improve the RISE or necessitate the creation of a "RISE for Rural Entrepreneurship"?

For researchers interested in the rural entrepreneurial ecosystem concept, RISE-based coaching raises some questions for deeper exploration. Can a RISE coaching system be efficacious in bringing transparency to ecosystems for the entrepreneurs and the resource providers? Might RISE-based coaching effectively address the point-of-entry debate in many ecosystems (e.g., single point-of-entry vs. "no wrong door")? What role could a RISE coaching system play in addressing the ecosystem governance dilemma?

These are just a few of the research opportunities presented by a skills measurement and development model for enhancing rural entrepreneurship. Hopefully, this innovative approach opens doors to new thinking about entrepreneurship-focused rural economic development.

References

Aryal, G., Mann, J., Loveridge, S., & Joshi, S. (2018). Exploring innovative creation across rural and urban firms: Analysis of the national survey of business competitiveness. Journal of Entrepreneurship and Public Policy, 7(4), 357–376.

Baron, R.A., & Markman, G.D. (2000). Beyond social capital: How social skills can enhance entrepreneurs' success. Academy of Management Executive, 14(1), 106–116.

Blanton, H., & Jaccard, J. (2006). Arbitrary metrics in psychology. American Psychologist, 61(1), 27–41.

Boyatzis, R.E., & Kolb, D.A. (1995). From learning styles to learning skills: The executive skills profile. Journal of Management Psychology, 10(5), 3–17.

Clarke, R. (2010). Skilled activity and the causal theory of action. Philosophy and Phenomenological Research, 89(3), 523–550.

Colombelli, A., Panelli, A., & Serraino, F. (2022). A learning-by-doing approach to entrepreneurship education: Evidence from a short intensive online international program. Administrative Science, 12(1), 16.

Cook, E.P. (2015). Behavior is contextual. In E.P. Cook (Ed.), Understanding people in context: The ecological perspective in counseling. American Counseling Association.

Cooney, T.M. (2012, November 28). Entrepreneurship skills for growth-oriented businesses, report for the Workshop on "Skills Development for SMEs and Entrepreneurship". Copenhagen.

Cope, J. (2005). Toward a dynamic learning perspective of entrepreneurship. Entrepreneurship Theory and Practice, 29(4), 373–397.

Coyle, D. (2009). *The talent code.* Bantam.

Dabson, B. (2001). Supporting rural entrepreneurship. In Exploring policy options for a new rural America, Proceedings of a Conference sponsored by Federal Reserve Bank of Kansas City, Center for the Study of Rural America (pp. 35–48).

Deller, S., & Conroy, T. (2016). Survival rates of rural businesses: What the evidence tells us. Choices, 31(4), 1–5.

Dreyfus, H.L., & Dreyfus, S.E. (1986). Mind over machine. Free Press.

Fischer, K.W., & Bidell, T.R. (2005). Dynamic development of action, thought, and emotion. In W. Damon, & R.M. Lerner (Eds.), Theoretical models of human development. Handbook of child psychology, 6th edition (Vol. 1, pp. 313–399). Wiley.

Galvao, A., Marques, C., & Ferreira, J.J. (2020). The role of entrepreneurship education and training programmes in advancing entrepreneurial skills and new ventures. European Journal of Training and Development, 44(6/7), 595–614.

Gibb, A.A. (1997). Small firms' training and competitiveness: Building on the small business as a learning organization. International Small Business Journal, 15(3), 13–29.

Gorman, G., Hanlon, D., & King, W. (1997). Some research perspectives on entrepreneurship education, enterprise education and education for small business management: A ten-year literature review. International Small Business Journal, 15(3), 56–77.

Hinojosa, R.C., Lyons, T.S., & Zinn, F.D. (1992). The relevancy of North American planning education for overseas practice: A survey of graduates. Journal of Planning Education and Research, 12, 32–38.

Isenberg, D. (2011). The entrepreneurship ecosystem as a paradigm for economic policy: Principles for cultivating entrepreneurship (pp. 1–13). Dublin, Ireland: Institute of International and European Affairs, 2 May 2011.

Iyigun, M.F., & Owen, A.L. (1998). Risk, entrepreneurship, and human capital accumulation. The American Economic Review, 88(2), 454–457.

Kutzhanova, N., Lyons, T.S., & Lichtenstein, G.A. (2009). Skill-based development of entrepreneurs and the role of personal and peer group coaching in enterprise development. Economic Development Quarterly, 23(3), 193–210.

LaFontaine, F., & Shaw, K. (2016). Serial entrepreneurship: Learning by doing? Journal of Labor Economics, 34(S2), S217–S254.

Lichtenstein, G.A., & Lyons, T.S. (1996). Incubating new enterprises: A guide to successful practice. The Aspen Institute.

Lichtenstein, G.A., & Lyons, T.S. (2001). The entrepreneurial development system: Transforming business talent and community economies. Economic Development Quarterly, 15(1), 3–20.

Lichtenstein, G.A., & Lyons, T.S. (2006). Managing the community's pipeline of entrepreneurs and enterprises: A new way of thinking about business assets. Economic Development Quarterly, 20(4), 377–386.

Lichtenstein, G.A., & Lyons, T.S. (2010). Investing in entrepreneurs: A strategic approach for strengthening your regional and community economy. Praeger/ABC-CLIO.

Lichtenstein, G.A., Lyons, T.S., & Kutzhanova, N. (2004). Building entrepreneurial communities: The appropriate role of enterprise development activities. Journal of the Community Development Society, 35(1), 1–20.

Lyons, J.S. (2009). Communimetrics: A communication theory of measurement for human services. Springer.

Lyons, T.S. (2015). Entrepreneurship and community development: What matters and why? Community Development, 46(5), 456–460.

Lyons, T.S. (2022). Social capital building for rural innovation. In C. French (Ed.), Building rural community resilience through innovation and entrepreneurship. Routledge.

Lyons, T.S., Hamlin, R.E., & Hamlin, A. (2018). Using entrepreneurship and social innovation to mitigate wealth inequality. DeGruyter.

Lyons, T.S., & Holmes, D. (2024). Making ecosystems sticky: Might skills be the glue? In R. Huggins, F. Kitagawa, D. Prokop, C. Theodoraki, & P. Thompson (Eds.), Entrepreneurial ecosystems in cities and regions: Emergence, evolution and future. Oxford University Press, 479–495.

Lyons, T.S., Lichtenstein, G.A., & Kutzhanova, N. (2007). What makes a successful entrepreneur? In N. Walzer, Entrepreneurship and local economic development. Rowman & Littlefield.

Lyons, T.S., Lyons, J.S., & Jolley, G.J. (2019). The Readiness Inventory for Successful Entrepreneurship (RISE): A tool for university engagement in entrepreneurial learning. Journal of Economic Development in Higher Education, 7(July), 1–7.

Lyons, T.S., Lyons, J.S., & Jolley, G.J. (2020). Entrepreneurial skill-building in rural ecosystems: A framework for applying the Readiness Inventory for Successful Entrepreneurship (RISE). Journal of Entrepreneurship and Public Policy, 9(1), 112–136.

Lyons, T.S., Lyons, J.S., & Samson, J.A. (2021). Entrepreneurship skill building: Focusing entrepreneurship education on skills assessment and development. Springer/Palgrave-Macmillan.

Lyons, T.S., Lyons, J.S., & Samson, J.A. Storytelling for entrepreneurship skills development. Unpublished paper.

Lyons, T.S., Miller, S.R., & Mann, J.T. (2018). A new role for land grant universities in the rural innovation ecosystem? Journal of Regional Analysis and Policy, 48(2), 32–47.

Mascolo, M.F., & Fischer, K.W. (1999). The dynamic co-development of intentionality, self, and social relations. In J. Brandstadter, & R.M. Lerner (Eds.), Action and development: Origins and functions of intentional self-development (pp. 133–166). Sage.

Morris, M.H., Webb, J.W., Fu, J., & Singhal, S. (2013). A competency-based perspective on entrepreneurship: Conceptual and empirical insights. Journal of Small Business Management, 51(3), 352–369.

Neck, H.M., & Greene, P.G. (2011). Entrepreneurship education: Known worlds and new frontiers. Journal of Small Business Management, 49(1), 55–70.

Neck, H.M., Neck, C.P., & Murray, E.L. (2018). *Entrepreneurship: The practice and mindset. Sage.*

Nicholls-Nixon, C.L., & Maxheimer, M.M. (2022). How coaching services help early stage entrepreneurs: An exploration of gender differences. Journal of Small Business and Enterprise Development, 29(5), 742–763.

Pine, B.J. II, & Gilmore, J.H. (2011). The experience economy (updated). Harvard Business Review Press.

Renski, H.C. (2009). New firm entry, survival and growth in the United States. *Journal of the American Planning Association* 75(1), 60–77.

Ronstadt, R. (1985). The educated entrepreneur: A new era of entrepreneurial education is beginning. American Journal of Small Business, 10(1), 7–23.

Senge, P.M. (1990). The fifth discipline: The art and practice of the learning organization. Century Business.

Smith, W.L., Schallenkamp, K., & Eichholz, D.E. (2005). Entrepreneurial skills assessment: An exploratory study. International Journal of Management and Enterprise Development, 2(3), 349–359.

Stumpf, S.S., Dunbar, R.L.M., & Mullen, T.P. (1991). Developing entrepreneurial skills through the use of behavioral simulations. Journal of Management Development, 10(5), 32–45.

Thamhain, H.J. (1992). Developing the skills you need. Research Technology Management, 35(2), 42–47.

Towers, N., Santoso, A.S., Sulkowski, N., & Jameson, J. (2020). Entrepreneurial capacity-building in HEIs for embedding entrepreneurship and enterprise creation – A tripartite approach. International Journal of Retail & Distribution, 48(8), 881–899.

Viswanathan, R., Fontenot, G., & Hoffman, L. (1992). Skill development through Small Business Institute consultations: An exploratory empirical investigation. Journal of Business & Entrepreneurship, 4(2), 1–9.

Wong, P.K., Ho, Y.P., & Autio, E. (2005). Entrepreneurship, innovation and economic growth: Evidence from GEM data. 24, 335–350.

Yu, L., Orazem, P.F., & Jolly, R.W. (2011). Why do rural firms live longer? *American Journal of Agricultural Economics* 93(3), 673–692.

Simona Zollet and Emi Makino

From Entrepreneurship "in" Rural Areas to Entrepreneurship "of" Rural Areas: The Interplay between Entrepreneurship and Place for Rural Community Revitalization

Abstract: This chapter discusses current understandings of rural entrepreneurship and its roles, employing and further developing Korsgaard and Tanvig's (2015) conceptualization of rural entrepreneurship as a place-embedded phenomenon that facilitates community resilience and economies of scope. We exemplify this concept through the case study of a small but innovative family business in rural Italy and its linkages with place and with a multifaceted local entrepreneurial ecosystem. We focus on the process of new value creation through the recombination and codification of the local resource base, and on the importance of synergies and collaboration within local entrepreneurial ecosystems. Through this case study, we also aim to challenge views of entrepreneurship as solely focused on economic outcomes and to show the multiple ways in which rural ventures contribute to rural places and communities not just in quantitative but also qualitative ways, enhancing quality of place and life.

Keywords: embeddedness, bridging, family business, rural entrepreneurial ecosystems, rural revitalization

1 Introduction

Although much has been written about the importance of entrepreneurship for rural economies, particularly in developing country contexts, it is only recently that this topic has started to be placed at the center of research and policy on rural development and revitalization in more affluent countries. This shift has been driven by common trends of progressive socio-economic decline in rural communities, with consequent declines in terms of prosperity and quality of life, and growing rural-urban divides (Gaddefors, 2019; Li et al., 2019; Thiede et al., 2017). Rural areas are generally described as facing significant challenges compared to urban areas due to their social and economic resource constraints and organizational thinness (Figueroa-Armijos et al., 2012; Larsen et al., 2022), often leading to the emergence of "depleted communi-

Simona Zollet, Hiroshima University, Graduate School of Humanities and Social Sciences, School of Integrated Arts and Sciences, Department of Integrated Global Studies (IGS), email: szollet@hiroshima-u.ac.jp
Emi Makino, Hiroshima University, Graduate School of Humanities and Social Sciences, School of Integrated Arts and Sciences, Department of Integrated Global Studies (IGS), email: e-makino@apu.ac.jp

https://doi.org/10.1515/9783110791396-005

ties" (Johnstone & Lionais, 2004). This is especially true in rural areas that are peripheral or remote or that have physical constraints, such as islands or mountainous regions (Qu & Zollet, 2023; Siemens, 2007).

Entrepreneurship is increasingly valued as a strategy for the economic development or revitalization of rural communities because of its capacity to tackle emerging challenges and leverage unique strengths and opportunities to create new economic, social, and environmental value (Anderson & Lent, 2017; Barber et al., 2021; Fortunato, 2014). However, there is relatively little knowledge about how entrepreneurship processes unfold in rural contexts. If rural entrepreneurship is understood as an area of entrepreneurship research and practice with distinctive elements, approaches developed in urban environments may not be suited to the social and economic conditions of rural areas and the characteristics of rural entrepreneurs (Fortunato, 2014). There is also the need for a deeper understanding of the impact of localized, place-based entrepreneurial processes on local development from various dimensions, beyond the economic one (Stathopoulou et al., 2004).

Recent works on rural entrepreneurship have also emphasized the importance of examining the interplay between entrepreneurs and their context, particularly regarding how rural contexts shape and are shaped by entrepreneurial processes. This chapter extends this line of inquiry, connecting previous work on entrepreneurial contexts (Welter, 2011; Welter et al., 2019; Welter & Baker, 2021) with research on the role of place embeddedness and bridging on rural entrepreneurship and community development (Korsgaard et al., 2022; Korsgaard & Tanvig, 2015; Müller & Korsgaard, 2018).

This chapter focuses on (1) the centrality of place for opportunity recognition and value creation; (2) the interplay between rural entrepreneurs' individual motivations and strategies and the community and entrepreneurial ecosystem-level outcomes; and (3) rural businesses' different levels of embeddedness in multiple contexts and their capacity to bridge across contexts. We examine these aspects through the case study of Centro Studi Italiani, an Italian language and culture school founded and run as a family business by the Pasotto family in the small rural town of Urbania in Central Italy. The view of rural entrepreneurship as an embedded phenomenon – potentially leading to new value creation not only for the entrepreneur but also for the place and community – responds to calls for more nuanced articulations of the interaction between context, community, and entrepreneurial processes (Fortunato & Alter, 2015; Lyons et al., 2012; Welter et al., 2017). This interaction needs to be understood as double-sided, thus considering how businesses rooted in a place are not only influenced by their context but can also influence it.

2 Entrepreneurship in Rural Areas and the Centrality of "Place"

A common question raised in rural entrepreneurship research is the extent to which the attributes and characteristics of rural contexts are important in shaping the entrepreneurial process. Although studies comparing rural and urban entrepreneurs are scarce, previous research suggests that there may not be significant differences between the psychological traits of rural and urban founders (Babb & Babb, 1992). This implies that context shapes the forms that (rural) entrepreneurship takes, as well as our understanding of entrepreneurship itself (Fortunato, 2014; Pato & Teixeira, 2019). Local socioeconomic, cultural, environmental, and institutional dynamics, therefore, influence the characteristics of entrepreneurship and entrepreneurial ecosystems in rural areas and small towns, in ways that differ from larger urban areas (Johnstone & Lionais, 2004; Fortunato, 2014; Gaddefors & Anderson, 2019; Mayer & Motoyama, 2020; Newbery et al., 2017; Phillipson et al., 2019; Roundy, 2019).

Despite the tendency to lump "rural areas" into a homogenous category, Table 1 shows that there is in fact a high variability *within* rural areas in terms of environmental features and natural resources, demographic, social, and institutional characteristics, economic structure, and degree of remoteness and isolation from markets and necessary services. These aspects translate into uneven development outcomes, with some places appearing more successful than others in fostering entrepreneurship. Rural areas are generally more industrially diverse. A variety of overlapping growth mechanisms, social capital, and support organizations enable access to different types of resources and knowledge, and locally based entrepreneurs (Li et al., 2019; Shrivastava & Kumar Dwivedi, 2020). Social norms supportive of risk-taking, favorable demographics, and an attractive community environment (Conroy & Low, 2022; Figueroa-Armijos et al., 2012; Welter & Baker, 2021) are also important.

Growth mechanisms do not hold constant over time, however. Even formerly prosperous areas can decline (Johnstone & Lionais, 2004), underscoring the importance of entrepreneurship as a mechanism to create new value and socio-economic revitalization (Lackéus, 2018). That said, the emphasis on easily quantifiable features such as most of those described in Table 1 contributes to creating "overarching narratives of entrepreneurial places that [. . .] emphasize normative homogeneity and "recipes" for success, at the expense of the variety and differences that can be seen through different lenses" (Welter & Baker, 2021:5).

In addition, the specificities of each rural area or community likely matter more to entrepreneurs on the ground than regional or national statistics. As suggested by Drakopoulou-Dodd (2014), "place matters, as the social site of entrepreneurship, the relational and material geography that shapes practice, and is shaped by it in turn," and "which both has and creates a distinct culture and identity" (Johnstone & Lionais, 2004:219). Place is also a key element to consider when interest lies in how entrepre-

Table 1: Author's elaboration based on a review of the rural entrepreneurship literature (Fortunato, 2014; Korsgaard & Tanvig, 2015; Larsen et al., 2022; Liedtke et al., 2021; Pato & Teixeira, 2014; Stathopoulou et al., 2004).

Location: degree of remoteness and isolation (peripherality)	**Natural resources, climate, and topography, physical landscape**	**Population size, density and dynamics (demographics), socioeconomic characteristics**	**Economic structure (e.g. Prevalence of single industries vs. diversified structure)**	**Social and Institutional factors (Social capital, governance, culture)**
Access to: markets firm support services; networks, information and information diversity; institutional support mechanisms; financing options	Resource availability for entrepreneurial activities Amenities Nature and landscape	Skills and attitudes of potential entrepreneurs Human resources and diversified labor pool Market size, characteristics, and diversity	Levels of sector-specific risk Diversity of growth mechanisms Power dynamics in economic production	Values and norms supporting cooperation and civic activity Capacity to develop unified strategies and partnerships to support local interests Culture and narratives

neurs engage with specific (rural) locations and contribute to shaping their community and entrepreneurial ecosystems (Korsgaard & Tanvig, 2015; Larsen et al., 2022).

Centering place as a contextual element highlights the importance of less quantifiable aspects, such as local identities and narratives, and how they translate the perception of entrepreneurship into capacity for entrepreneurial action – or lack thereof (Welter & Baker, 2021). Place becomes crucial when focusing on the everyday activities of entrepreneurs, which unfold through sociocultural processes that are to a large extent place-based (Drakopoulou-Dodd, 2014). This perspective also helps to shed light on many of the motivations driving extant or potential entrepreneurs to create new ventures in rural areas, some of which are overlooked in entrepreneurship research, such as lifestyle (Yachin, 2017; Zollet & Qu, 2023), social or community engagement (Johnstone & Lionais, 2004), and culture (Prince et al., 2021).

Finally, rural areas also possess specific place-based characteristics (such as natural, cultural, and social heritage and amenities) that may help to attract or retain entrepreneurs and sustain attachment to place (Korsgaard & Tanvig, 2015; Naldi et al., 2021). The importance of these elements is demonstrated by the growing literature on rural newcomers starting entrepreneurial ventures in rural areas (Bosworth & Atterton, 2012; Herslund, 2012; Qu et al., 2020; Zollet & Maharjan, 2021). In addition, such characteristics can be seen as resources that offer opportunities for the creation of new entrepreneurial activities building upon the unique mix of resources of rural contexts (Fortunato, 2014; Korsgaard et al., 2022; Stathopoulou et al., 2004).

3 Context and Entrepreneurship

Context can be broadly defined as the "circumstances, conditions, situations, or environments that are external to the respective phenomenon and enable or constrain it" (Welter, 2011:167). In his seminal paper, Whetten (1989) describes, among others, the "where," "who," and "when" dimensions that define a phenomenon; in our case, "where" represents the contexts where entrepreneurship occurs, which can be of different nature – e.g. spatial, business, social, and institutional. Contexts in turn affect (and are affected by) "who" becomes an entrepreneur and what kind of enterprises are created. The temporal and historical dimensions (the "when") describe how contexts change over time and consequently influence the characteristics of local entrepreneurship (Welter, 2011) (Figure 1).

Although it has been long recognized that economic behavior needs to be understood within its social, institutional, spatial, and temporal contexts, entrepreneurship research often underplays the influence of external factors in favor of highlighting personal traits of successful entrepreneurs (Welter, 2011). Focusing solely on the "who," however, can lead to overlooking the interrelation between the environment (where, when) and the entrepreneurial process (Fortunato, 2014; Stathopoulou et al., 2004).

A central concept that defines the relationship between context and entrepreneur is embeddedness. Embeddedness describes the characteristics, depth, and extent of an individual or an organization's ties to a specific place, community, society, or system of institutions (Korsgaard et al., 2015; McKeever et al., 2014). The concept was originally introduced by social theorists to describe the role played by social networks and relationships in determining economic action and outcomes (Granovetter, 1985; Uzzi, 1997).

In relation to context, being "embedded" can be defined as being situated in a context that enables and/or constrains one's activities (Larsen et al., 2022). Embeddedness (or lack thereof) therefore hinders or supports entrepreneurs' capacity to access key resources, identify or create opportunities, and take risks (Welter, 2011). This concept helps to explain why individual entrepreneurs succeed or fail (beyond their individual traits), and how entrepreneurial processes are enabled and/or constrained by their immediate context or "place" (Korsgaard & Tanvig, 2015; Larsen et al., 2022; Wigren-Kristoferson et al., 2022).

Embeddedness is a useful concept for contextualized entrepreneurship research because it represents a bridge between micro and macro levels, the interface where individual agency and structure (context) interact (Kalantaridis and Bika, 2006). This concept is especially relevant for rural entrepreneurship because research disproportionately points to the centrality of embeddedness in rural communities (Akgün et al., 2010; Greenberg et al., 2018; Korsgaard et al., 2015; Larsen et al., 2022; Zollet & Qu, 2023).

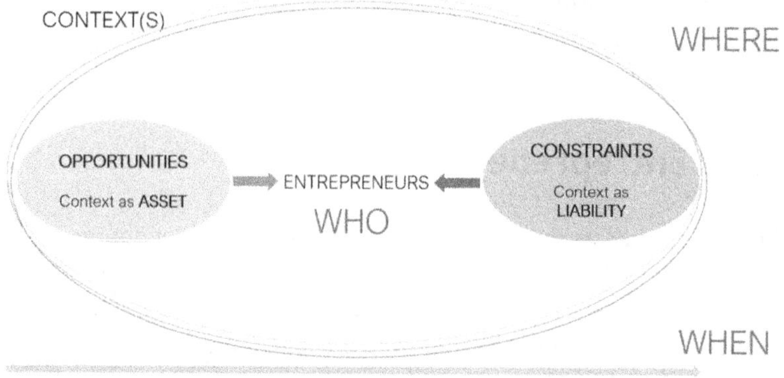

Figure 1: Author's elaboration based on Whetten, 1989 and Welter, 2011.

Embeddedness has been examined in relation to different types of contexts, although the most common are social and institutional ones (Welter, 2011). Embeddedness in spatial contexts (place embeddedness), on the other hand, has so far received less attention, despite the relevance of place for rural entrepreneurship, in both its social and material aspects (such as cultural identities, social interaction and engagement, community networks and institutions, but also the built environment, infrastructure, economic base, and natural features of a place) (Korsgaard et al., 2015; Vlasov et al., 2018). Theorizations of the role of place embeddedness in rural entrepreneurship have been mainly developed in the European context, likely in response to the European Union's focus on rural development policies that build on the specificity of rural areas for economic diversification (see for example the literature on the cultural and quality "turns" (Korsgaard & Tanvig, 2015; Shucksmith, 2010; Stathopoulou et al., 2004; Verdini, 2020)). In general, however, entrepreneurship literature tends to neglect the role of place as a key element of entrepreneurial opportunity creation, likely because forms of entrepreneurship that "count" are often disconnected from the materiality of a location (e.g. technology-based entrepreneurship). This explains why spatial embeddedness is more commonly researched in agriculture and rural tourism entrepreneurship literatures, as they concern economic activities that engage directly with the materiality of place.

4 Place Embeddedness and Bridging in Rural Entrepreneurship

The term place (or spatial) embeddedness (Korsgaard et al., 2015: 586) describes rural entrepreneurs' "intimate knowledge and use of the physical, cultural and historical landscapes [. . .] and the concern shown for the well-being of the places," a definition that implies a two-way relationship between entrepreneurs and place. To discuss how entrepreneurial opportunity creation is both shaped by and shapes the local spatial context and community, it is useful to introduce the two archetypes developed by Korsgaard and Tanvig (2015), "entrepreneurship in the rural" versus "rural entrepreneurship" (Table 2). Their characteristics are based on (1) how entrepreneurial ventures engage with their rural location, and (2) how differences in terms of engagement (embeddedness) influence rural community development and resilience.

"Rural entrepreneurship" refers to entrepreneurial activities with strong connections to the characteristics of a rural place and deeply embedded in its material and social reality. Such activities leverage unique local resources to create value for both the entrepreneur and the community. "Entrepreneurship in the rural," on the other hand, describes enterprises for whom the rural context simply represents the physical location of business activities, rather than a key resource. These two archetypes allow us to explore in more detail the diversity of entrepreneurial ventures in rural areas in terms of their **motivations**, **strategies**, and **outcomes,** and to understand the role of "place" in the entrepreneurial process. Furthermore, the archetypes highlight the diversity of local-level processes of value creation that might not be visible if we examine rural entrepreneurship through conventional lenses.

Table 2: Key differences between "entrepreneurship in the rural" and "rural entrepreneurship." Authors' elaboration based on Korsgaard and Tanvig (2015).

ENTREPRENEURSHIP IN THE RURAL	RURAL ENTREPRENEURSHIP
Motivations	
Primarily monetary incentives and profit creation	Combination of economic and non-economic motivations (e.g. individual and family's economic stability and quality of life, community development, place attachment)
Strategies	
No emphasis on utilizing place-based or localized resources other than for instrumental reasons (e.g. cheap land or labor, existing economic incentives) Choices (e.g. suppliers, markets) driven by competitive advantages for the business Similar to strategies adopted by entrepreneurs in non-rural locations Operating on global markets	Leveraging local resources (natural, cultural, historical, human, social. . .); Place-dependent; value proposition of the business is dependent on or connected to place; Engaging with and supporting local markets and community (e.g., buying at least partly from local businesses and suppliers); Often operating in more localized markets, but not necessarily Engaging others within the business and community ecosystem; learning, innovating, and co-creating

Table 2 (continued)

ENTREPRENEURSHIP IN THE RURAL	RURAL ENTREPRENEURSHIP
Outcomes	
Ventures characterized by fast economic growth	Ventures characterized by slower growth as they are bound by place-based resources
Increased job creation, tax revenue, in-migration	Decreased influence of global market fluctuations
Vulnerable to competition from other localities and to changes in global markets; formation of enclave economies;	Possibility to extract more economic and social value from the optimized use and recombination of local resources
Often disconnected from the long-term development and well-being of the area	Less likely to relocate, especially if their competitive advantage depends upon the characteristics of or linkages to the area
	Support long-term development and resilience; new combinations of place-based resources but also non-material outcomes such as relationship building, place development, quality of life

Embeddedness tends to be described as a static concept, with entrepreneurs being either embedded or disembedded in a specific context, and their level of embeddedness not changing over time. Research, however, shows that an important aspect of entrepreneurial embeddedness is its dynamic nature. Larsen et al. (2022), for example, show that (1) embeddedness can increase or decrease over time; and (2) that ventures can have varying degrees of embeddedness and disembeddedness in different contexts at the same time (Korsgaard et al., 2015; Larsen et al., 2022; Welter, 2011).

Greenberg et al. (2018), for example, describe the "double-layered embeddedness" in both local and extra-local networks of enterprises located in remote rural areas, which helps increase their competitiveness by enlarging their customer base. Korsgaard et al. (2015) similarly found that rural entrepreneurs use both local and extra-local networks, but that extra-local networks tend to be more important for strategic purposes. Other authors have used terms such as translocal embeddedness (Dubois, 2016, 2019) and the concepts of vertical and horizontal networks (Kneafsey et al., 2001), where horizontal networks refer to relationships with local actors, while vertical networks describe alliances with extra-local ones (Stathopoulou et al., 2004).

Finally, the capacity of entrepreneurs to establish ties outside of a specific context is often called bridging. Bridging is important to overcome some of the shortcomings of rural locations because it grants access to new resources (e.g., larger markets, information, and support (Korsgaard et al., 2015; Stathopoulou et al., 2004), and creates stronger rural-urban connections (Mayer et al., 2016), facilitating the development of new ideas and the capacity to leverage opportunities. To understand how rural entrepreneurship occurs, there is therefore the need to simultaneously consider how entrepreneurial activities are enabled/constrained by entrepreneurs' place embeddedness (or disembeddedness) but also by their ability to bridge across local and non-local contexts.

5 Rural Entrepreneurship and the Value Creation Process

Although the definition of "entrepreneurship" remains debated, an increasingly common approach is to see it as a process of new value creation (Lackéus, 2018). As such, it becomes crucial to interrogate the meaning associated with the term "value," especially since rural contexts are often dominated by allegedly "less valuable" forms of entrepreneurship (low-tech, low-growth, small-sized, lifestyle-oriented), which shapes the mainstream outlook toward rural entrepreneurship. For example, it is commonly believed that entrepreneurial activity in rural areas is lower compared to urban areas (Korsgaard & Tanvig, 2015), although there is evidence that self-employment rates in rural areas can be higher (Deller & Conroy, 2017; Thiede et al., 2017).

It has also been said that rural areas "find it more difficult to produce *high-value* entrepreneurs" (Low et al., 2005:62), (*authors' emphasis*), and that rural areas have limited rates of new firm formation in more "valuable" sectors such as professional services or finance (Anderson, 2000). It has been suggested, however, that the issues faced by rural areas are best addressed by enabling the formation of a broad range of entrepreneurial activities, including those that do not conform to the economic logic of profit maximization (Stathopoulou et al., 2004). The aim is to develop "economies of scope" (de Roest et al., 2018) able to create value for a place or a community beyond simplistic and quantifiable outcomes such as revenue and employment generation. These ideas connect to the capacity of a community's socio-economic system to absorb shocks and disruptions and recover from them, in other words its resilience. It has been suggested that in an entrepreneurial context the concept of antifragility (Taleb, 2012) may be more appropriate than resilience, as it refers to a system or organization's ability not just to withstand adversity, uncertainty, and shocks, but also to improve and thrive through them. This notion, however, also partly overlaps with that of "transformative" resilience, which refers to the systems' ability to reconfigure, re-organize, and reinvent itself in response to disruptions (Ramezani & Camarinha-Matos, 2020).

"Rural entrepreneurship" as conceptualized by Korsgaard and Tanvig (2015) can increase the transformative resilience (or antifragility) of community entrepreneurial ecosystems by engendering a virtuous cycle of social and economic development rooted into the community, its resources, and its needs. The first dynamic of this cycle consists of a simultaneous process of *recombination* and *codification*: entrepreneurs extract value from place by recombining existing local resources. This process of recombination often takes the form of bricolage, meaning "making do" with locally available resources regardless of their perceived adequacy or sufficiency (Baker &

Nelson, 2005). Furthermore, it is influenced by entrepreneurs' capacity to create synergies and leverage underutilized resources, which in turn depends on the extent of both embeddedness and bridging (Müller & Korsgaard, 2018).

In addition to recombination, value creation also involves a process of codification, which often entails the active (re)interpretation of the non-material elements or attributes of place and local resources. Through codification, local resources become "transferable and comprehensible in non-local markets and/or settings" (Korsgaard & Tanvig, 2015:15). Importantly, this process does not automatically imply the creation of economic value. Codification may result in other forms of value, (social, cultural, environmental) that can directly or indirectly benefit the entrepreneur and the rural community; examples include higher community engagement and improved visibility of a location.

Contemporary economic trends have also capitalized upon this process: examples include the culture and quality "turns" that are shaping rural development trends in the twenty-first century, especially in rural Europe (Černevičiūtė et al., 2019; Stathopoulou et al., 2004) and Japan (Prince et al., 2021; Qu & Zollet, 2023). Culture (in a broad sense) has emerged as a key pillar of rural entrepreneurial development (Fortunato, 2014; Ray, 1998; Stathopoulou et al., 2004) and underpins the capacity to leverage new societal trends, such as niche markets connected to post-modern consumption (characterized by being experiential, recreational, educational, sustainability-oriented, etc., rather than purely material) (Jenkins, 2000; Mitchell, 2013).

A stronger focus on the positive attributes and values associated with rural areas, often in connection with quality of life and sustainability issues, also reflects this codification process (Qu & Zollet, 2023; Zollet & Qu, 2023). The COVID-19 pandemic has brought renewed attention to these attributes, giving rise to new opportunities that might support the regeneration and resilience of rural communities through new and decentralized ways of working (Bosworth et al., 2021), trends of urban-to-rural migration (Dal Bello et al., 2021; Qu & Zollet, 2023) and counter urbanization (Bosworth, 2010; Dilley et al., 2022; Herslund, 2012).

Recombination and codification, in addition to creating new value for the entrepreneur, can also create value for the community in various ways: beyond possible outcomes of job and wealth creation, value creation may include increased pride and attachment to place, sense of belonging and identity; the enrichment of the local resource base, which can be further employed for the establishment of new activities and ventures (leading to diversification processes and the existence of multiple "growth sources"); and the capacity to attract and/or retain residents and entrepreneurs by increasing quality of life and creating a more attractive community and entrepreneurial ecosystem (Herslund, 2012). Through this conceptualization of rural entrepreneurship, based on place embeddedness and entailing a dialectic relationship between entrepreneur and place, we can more easily recognize emerging processes of value formation at the local level. Although research on how context influences entrepreneurship is expanding, however, there has been considerably less focus on how entrepreneurship impacts its local context and affects change.

6 Methodology

The elements of rural entrepreneurship described above are discussed through the example of the Centro Studi Italiani (CSI), a family-run Italian language and culture school. The information presented here was obtained through primary and secondary data collection. Primary data were collected through an in-depth interview conducted in July 2022 with the CSI founder's son, Giovanni Pasotto, who works as the commercial director of the business. The interview lasted for 2 hours and was recorded and transcribed. Further information was collected through informal interviews and visits to the CSI and some of the businesses the CSI is collaborating with, which form part of its entrepreneurial ecosystem. Primary data was supplemented with data from publicly available secondary sources such as the company's website, to close information gaps about the company's history, mission, and activities, and triangulate the interview data (Creswell, 2017).

We employed thematic analysis to code the data based on the themes identified through the literature review (Braun & Clarke, 2021, Flyvberg, 2012). We examine the motivations to start a rural business, the strategies employed (the ways to extract value from place), and the outcomes (with a focus on how rural enterprises can create value for the place in which they are embedded). We use these elements to discuss the embeddedness and bridging aspect of the business described in the case study and its role in creating a local entrepreneurial ecosystem. By examining these themes, we aim to uncover the role that rural places play in shaping the entrepreneurial process, as well as the influence of entrepreneurial enterprises on place.

7 Background of the Business: Centro Studi Italiani

Centro Studi Italiani (CSI) is a family-run language school founded in 1985 that specializes in teaching Italian language and culture to international students. The school was founded in 1985 by Carlo Amedeo Pasotto and his wife (a British citizen) in Urbania, a small rural town in the central Italian Marche region. CSI is currently run by the second generation of the Pasotto family, with five out of six siblings being involved with different aspects of the school's management.

The small town of Urbania (6829 inhabitants as of 2022), flourished during the Renaissance period as a center of art and culture. It is the birthplace of the Casteldurante ceramic school, renowned in the sixteenth and seventeenth centuries, and boasts an important music tradition. Girolamo Crescentini (1762–1846), a famous opera singer, was born there, and the town has a historical opera house (Teatro Bramante) which now hosts, among other events, the CSI's Opera Festival. Urbania is nestled between Tuscany and the sea resort towns of the Adriatic Sea, in the picturesque scenery of the Montefeltro hills, and is close to Urbino, a UNESCO World Heritage Site.

Despite being relatively close to major tourist destinations including Florence, Perugia, Assisi, and Ravenna, Urbania itself is outside the mainstream tourism circuit and is mostly unknown to international tourists.

In addition to its Urbania headquarters, the historic and main location of the school, CSI has two additional branches: one in Milan, opened in 2011 to give students the possibility to choose a more urban setting for their language studies; and one in Genoa, which was opened in 2018 with the acquisition of "Scuola tricolore," a preexisting Italian school for foreigners. All three branches are managed by members of the Pasotto family. Soon after the beginning of the COVID-19 pandemic, CSI also started offering online courses through a virtual platform.

During its 37 years of activity, CSI has hosted more than 16,000 students from all over the world, thanks to a network of partnerships at the national and international level built over the years. The business currently organizes both academic and non-academic programs in collaboration with Italian institutions, international universities, colleges, fine arts academies, and music conservatories worldwide. CSI offers general Italian language courses for different levels, but also dedicated language and singing programs specifically targeted at opera singers. The founders recognized early on the potential of opera singers and music students as a target market segment for Italian language classes.

The school is active year-round, but during the summer it hosts the Opera Festival, which was created to offer the opera singers studying at the school the opportunity to practice the interpretation of Italian opera repertoire and perform in a historical Italian theater. In addition, CSI offers a variety of specific thematic tracks for students interested in deepening the study of specific aspects of Italian culture (food, art, design, art history, etc.) in connection with the study of the language. Some of these activities are offered in partnership with local small enterprises, especially in the food and rural agritourism business. Examples include cooking classes, cheese-making and pasta-making workshops, wine tastings, and food-wine pairing classes, designed so that students can experience regional Italian cuisine and locally sourced specialty products while learning about Italy's enogastronomic culture. CSI also offers art and ceramics classes with local artists, building upon the long-standing local artistic ceramic tradition.

8 The CSI as an Example of Rural Entrepreneurship

8.1 Motivations

Before establishing CSI, the founders were university professors living in Milan teaching Italian literature and English respectively. The initial spark for establishing their own private language school was the desire to move out of a large city like Milan and into a more rural area. Giovanni's parents wished to raise a large family, which was difficult in a place like Milan, but also wanted to seek out new opportunities to start their own business in the field of education by making use of their knowledge and international experience. Moving to a rural area was a priority, and eventually the Pasotto family discovered the Marche region, which was less popular than neighboring Tuscany and considerably less expensive. They ended up falling in love with the area around Urbino (which had a university and therefore could offer a backup employment option) and eventually purchased an abandoned building in Urbania. This eventually became CSI's first language school and main headquarters.

The business started out very simply, with a flyer. The Pasotto family used it to reach out to a few universities and, as Giovanni says, "believe it or not, four students actually responded to that sort of open call." Everything was done in a very simple way: "we hosted students at our own house, the first group of four students, my mom cooked for them." For the first few years, the business remained a two-person operation, with Giovanni's father responsible for the management and teaching, and his mother for the students' meals and board. From the second year onward, the couple started marketing their school more widely by joining the Dante Alighieri society, an institution that provides support for people interested in learning Italian language and culture. Over the next two years, the CSI grew exponentially to 350 students.

Giovanni attributes this success to the fact that his parents had a clear vision of the kind of business they wanted to establish, one that was based on their skills but also their passion for language, culture, and rural living. They were also outsiders to the Urbania community and had a multicultural background, a factor to which Giovanni ascribes their capacity to create a new and innovative business. "Maybe they had new energy, new ideas. Maybe because they were in Milan, they were part of the international community there, that they thought, okay, well, this could work. But if you're not exposed to things, then you just tend to continue with everything that is already there." This attitude has carried over to the next generation: Giovanni attributes his involvement in the business to feeling of connected to the rest of the world, which in turn helps him with his current role as commercial director and the de facto "face" of the CSI.

The first turning point for the business was the creation of CSI's opera program. The founders realized that opera singers were a key market segment for Italian language classes. They pitched a pilot opera program to professors from Ohio's Oberlin Conservatory, and the pitch was successful enough to encourage them to continue. CSI is now recognized as one of the most prominent centers for Italian language study connected to opera singing. A second turning point was the onset of the internet and e-commerce. This was a difficult adjustment period, because the founders found it hard to adapt to the rapid technological change. This is when the family's younger generation decided to step in and support the business with their better understanding of new technological needs.

Although not all second-generation members of the family are involved to the same degree in CSI's activities, most of them feel a strong sense of responsibility toward ensuring the continuation of the business. The COVID pandemic, and the complete stop to the arrival of students in Urbania, put this into stark perspective, as the Pasotto family felt the double pressure not only to uphold the school's long history, but also to meet community expectations. At the same time, knowing the role that the business plays in the community became an important motivator to ensure CSI would stay afloat: "we did feel that we needed to do something . . . and that we needed to work even harder because there was an expectation from the community."

8.2 Strategies

In addition to the founders' individual motivations, skills, and abilities, the success of CSI has strong roots in the characteristics of the place where it was established. When CSI was founded, most Italian language schools were in places such as Milan, Florence, Rome. There was little to no competition for schools in rural Italy, mostly because of the perceived constraints of rural locations. Even now for example, there is no train station in Urbania; buses are the only form of public transportation available. Despite these apparent disadvantages, the CSI founders chose to focus on the concept of "small (language) courses in a small town," which became the motto of the school and its source of competitive advantage. They reasoned that in small towns it is much easier to connect with the local community. This is particularly evident in Urbania. The selling point of the school is that "you come here, you're part of a small community. You're connecting with them. And that's how you're going to learn not only the language, but also the cultural aspect. [. . .] You really start learning about a culture once you start getting to know the people and getting to know them more and more."

The atmosphere of hospitality that characterizes rural areas and smaller communities also was identified as added value. To facilitate immersion in and connection with the community, CSI developed a homestay system, where students are hosted by local families. The small size of the town allows the staff to vet host families personally and to provide accommodation within walking distance of the school and other essential services. Finally, the Urbania branch of the school is marketed as offering a "peaceful and relaxing stay." Its small-town setting and relative isolation are appreciated by many students – especially adult learners of Italian language and culture – who seek a quiet rural setting, but also by overseas schools seeking to send students to a safe environment.

At the same time, the town is not too isolated, allowing participants to visit some of Italy's most popular tourist attractions. The rural setting facilitates the organization of a wide variety of experiences for participants, such as traditional cooking workshops, guided nature excursions, food and wine tours, outdoor activities (e.g. canoeing, sailing, trekking), and arts and ceramics courses. These experiences are designed to make the most of the historical, cultural, naturalistic, and gastronomic heritage of the area. Although CSI did switch to online classes during COVID to stay afloat, much of the value proposition of the school rests on this immersive experience. The cultural aspect is perceived not as a plus but rather as necessary for CSI’s customers. Giovanni reflects that ultimately “a lot of students want to learn Italian specifically because they want to be connected with Italy. English, you learn it because it’s a necessity. So no matter where, no matter how, you can do everything in front of a computer. But when you learn such a beautiful language like ours, you really want to be connected with Italy and everything that Italy brings. [. . .]. All these things are really hard to do through a computer in a very dry way.”

As such, promoting Urbania has become a key aspect of CSI’s promotional activities. As Giovanni says, “whenever I go and talk about our products, I begin with the city of Urbania. Because it’s so isolated, so unknown [. . .] we do so much promotion of Urbania, the territory, the country, the region and everything.” This aspect is crucial to overcome persistent negative images associated with rural areas or preconceived ideas of rural ventures as not being on par with their urban counterparts. Giovanni reflects that every time he pitches the CSI in Urbania, it is essential to show to potential customers that “Urbania has got so much more, that maybe it’s worth considering. And then when they come here, they’re always impressed, and they go, oh, I thought this was going to be much more campy and much more rural. This is nice. Okay, we’ll consider it. But they have to come here and see it.”

There are, however, instances in which the “rural” character of the school does prove to be a disadvantage. One of the reasons behind the creation of the Milan branch of the CSI was the desire to capture the Chinese market. CSI was losing Chinese students to the competition because of the perception of rural areas held by urban, educated Chinese: “If you’re coming from Shanghai, you’re coming from a rich family, Urbania looks very small. . . in certain cultures rural means not so good. [. . .] Maybe the education there is not good. If you show them a nice building in the city center of Milano, they automatically think, well, if you’re in Milano, then you’re good. [. . .] It means prestige, it means quality.” Consequently, the Pasotto family decided that rather than losing students to the competition, they would create a satellite school in Milan and let students choose whether to go to a small town or a large city. The decision was proven right. Currently nearly all Chinese students choose the Milan school. In general though, students who want to come to Italy “want picturesque, ‘the sweet life’.” Having different locations fulfills different market niches.

8.3 Outcomes

Over the years, the school has become a significant source of revenue for Urbania. Before the new branches were opened and before COVID, the school hosted about 500 students per year (in a community of fewer than 7,000 people), who stayed for an average of four weeks. The amount of money spent in supermarkets, restaurants, bars, cafes, and accommodations is quite significant. Giovanni stresses that it is not only the tangible financial impact, but also the cultural impact a business like CSI can have in a small rural community in terms of cultural liveliness.

He also reflects that the town has come to realize the impact of the school only since the onset of the pandemic, which stopped the flow of students. "I think COVID changed everything. We had people saying, please don't quit, don't give up. This is beautiful. The local people now feel a sense of ownership [. . .]. So there is the economic impact, but also that sense of pride, of ownership which I think the people are now starting to feel and that is such a relief for us. And at the same time, we feel like that there is a team behind the school," he said. Over the years, the local community has helped CSI in various ways, from providing accommodation to returning lost wallets, to showing their hospitality and making sure students feel like they are part of the community. This attitude, however, is the result of a process that did not happen overnight: "It took about 40 years to get everybody on board, to get everybody to agree that this is something unique and it's not just them (CSI) getting all the benefits out of this, that it's the entire community."

Much time and effort have been spent in building and maintaining this positive relationship with the community. The founders themselves were not locals. According to Giovanni, his mother was the first "foreigner" to live in Urbania in the 1980s. Getting local people to become used to interacting with people from different countries, cultures, and backgrounds took a long time. Giovanni mentions the challenge of nurturing this kind of open attitude while maintaining a balance between the town's lifestyle and "this big international community that kind of like invades the town, in a way." This process requires a willingness to engage with and commit to the community for a long time, through constant engagement with residents, businesses, and the local government.

Over its almost four decades of existence, CSI has supported the formation of a vibrant community atmosphere, which also translates into the presence of more businesses that cater, at least partly, to the school's students, pioneering tourism in a town that was originally not a tourism destination: "I think we [. . .] put the idea into the local government people that tourism here is possible. So we were kind of like pioneers, with a very specific focus in that we wanted cultural tourism and language-based tourism. But in fact, that started to spin that wheel, that tourism is possible and that you need to get it organized, and that if people come here, they need to have the support, the system. Restaurants and museums need to be open, you need to organize tours."

The evolution of the entrepreneurial ecosystem in Urbania – and the atmosphere of the town itself – has been influenced by CSI and by how the school chooses which local businesses to collaborate with. Beyond practical considerations (type of goods or services offered, being able to meet certain quality standards, having the needed spaces or capacity to host groups of certain sizes. . .) CSI considers it crucial to try to involve as many businesses as possible, to make all of them "feel like they are part of the magic." This helps CSI to develop a more diversified offer for students. It encourages healthy competition among the businesses, which not only works to CSI’s advantage but also helps the businesses themselves to tailor and diversify their offerings.

Many local businesses have significantly improved what they offer and customer service levels because of CSI’s presence and the type of customers it attracts. For example, the fare served at local restaurants and bars has become more diversified and sophisticated. As Giovanni explains, “If you start having more money and more people coming in, and people ask, ‘do you have a bottle of wine of a certain level’, ‘no, we just have the house wine’. Okay, well, maybe we should start providing [that] because customers are asking. And if I don’t provide it, well, then I’m going to start getting isolated from the whole system. I think we brought a level of sophistication into the town that was definitely not there.” Other examples include cafes starting to offer free Wi-Fi, and the local hotel being fully renovated with the addition of a spa.

Over the years, CSI has formed lasting collaborations with many local businesses and has encouraged the development of an entrepreneurial mindset among them. Openness to new ideas and willingness to take some risks are traits that CSI looks for in local partners. Giovanni makes the example of “a new café in town [. . .] the guy came over to the school and said hi, I would like to introduce myself. [. . .] he came up with a plan about doing international dinners. [. . .] He had this idea of cultures coming together. And I was like, you know what? This is good, [. . .] we’re going to reward this guy. I like what he brought to the table.”

9 Discussion

As the case study shows, rural entrepreneurs and ventures do not operate in a vacuum. They are embedded in a variety of contexts that affect their activities in multiple ways (Korsgaard & Tanvig, 2015; Welter & Baker, 2021). The rural context of Urbania displays traits that can either constrain or enable entrepreneurship; the outcomes are determined by the interaction between entrepreneurs (with their background, knowledge, and skills), their level of embeddedness in the locale, and their capacity to bridge across contexts. As “outsiders” with a specific background and skillset, the Pasotto family was uniquely positioned to recognize the opportunity to create a venture such as CSI; however, it is Urbania’s unique mix of resources that determined and shaped much of CSI’s business model.

CSI’s entrepreneurial outcomes in turn, acted as a driving force for changing some of the characteristics of the town environment and strengthened its entrepreneurial ecosystem. Beyond the relationship with other businesses, what is striking about the case is the change in the attitude of the community toward CSI and the increased support of local people and the local government. The progressive recognition of the role of CSI in the sociocultural and economic fabric of Urbania is the result of a process of progressive embedding: the Pasotto family went from being disembedded "outsiders" to becoming prominent embedded members of the community, while maintaining their capacity for bridging between the local and global context which ensures their capacity to access various kind of resources and remain innovative. The success of CSI also stems from the fact that innovation often occurs at the intersection of diverse ideas, people, and backgrounds; diversity, while often bringing conflict, also acts as a catalyst for innovation by fostering learning, creativity, and entrepreneurial activity (Johansson, 2006). The new knowledge and experiences that the Pasotto family brought to rural Urbania, and the new information and opportunities the rural context offered to the Pasotto family, came together to facilitate the development of an innovative business like CSI.

This case study also highlights the importance of non-economic motivations in the creation of rural ventures. The original aim of the CSI founders was to move to a rural location, improve their quality of life, and engage in activities that would allow them to pursue their passions and skills. Over time however, a sense of responsibility toward the community has become another source of motivation. Indeed, the opportunity to do something for a community and "make a difference" is a common trait among rural entrepreneurs, as evidenced by previous literature (e.g. Zollet & Qu, 2023).

In terms of strategies, CSI exemplifies the process of extracting value from place through the creative recombination of local resources and their codification to make them appealing to a wider audience. CSI was able to turn Urbania's rural character and isolation – typical contextual elements usually considered detrimental to rural entrepreneurship – into a strength and a point of differentiation from similar businesses. Urbania's rural location offers students an authentic experience through direct immersion in the Italian culture and lifestyle, upholding CSI's commitment to a "100% Italian experience."

In the same vein, the three locations of the school show the centrality of place and the uniqueness of rural settings. Although CSI's different branches fulfill different market niches, the rural remains a central aspect of the business' value proposition, a value proposition that is effectively "rooted in place." The opera program is another example: the combination of the town's location, history, and the presence of a historic theatre, together with the CSI offering Italian language classes, opened the possibility to start a dedicated opera program and opera festival. Local resources and an entrepreneurial attitude, therefore, work together to recombine and codify existing resources to create new value.

Looking at the outcomes, and particularly at how the business creates value for the rural location, the influence of entrepreneurship on the community and the local entrepreneurial ecosystem appears clear. Beyond its direct economic impact, CSI's presence brought a series of indirect benefits. Indeed, the local community now prides itself on having an international school in the town. This has motivated the community to develop a sense of ownership and responsibility toward the business, leading to a process of co-creation of the local environment in a way that is conducive to the success of CSI and of the various businesses connected to it. CSI has also played an important role in developing the local entrepreneurial ecosystem, underscoring the importance of synergies and collaboration over pure competition and the importance of making the community – as a whole – more entrepreneurial (Larsen et al., 2022). This also implies the need for a functioning support system that goes beyond the local community and private businesses and involves the local government and local organizations.

A potential limitation of using the concept of place embeddedness to examine rural entrepreneurship pertains to the choice of boundaries for the context, which in turn goes back to the choice of definition of rural areas. For example, Baumgartner et al. (2013) question the extent to which the "local milieu" can be considered the main source of opportunities for entrepreneurship, especially when focusing on small rural communities. However, as this case study demonstrates, the capacity to bridge local and extra-local contexts makes the boundaries fuzzy and suggests the importance of thinking in terms of relational and networked ruralities (Woods et al., 2021; Young, 2010).

10 Conclusions

The discussion has highlighted three important aspects: first, how entrepreneurial opportunity creation is influenced by the spatial context, in a dialectic relationship with the individual entrepreneurs' traits and characteristics (Korsgaard et al., 2015; Korsgaard & Tanvig, 2015); second, how place-embedded firms, in turn, influence the local community and entrepreneurial ecosystem; and third, how successful rural entrepreneurs can bridge and span across contexts (Korsgaard et al., 2022), connecting the local with the global, as rural entrepreneurship in the twenty-first century generally "involves interaction in globalized flows of products, capital, and people, which connect and constitute locations" (Korsgaard et al., 2015: 575).

The CSI case study also shows that the viability of a rural venture is often determined or influenced by the unique qualities of a place and the combination of its spatial, social, and economic contexts with the individuality of the entrepreneur. Even more crucially, an important feature of rural entrepreneurship is the capacity to address the challenges of rural locations by embracing them and turning them into opportunities, rather than simply "bypassing" them, an approach that connects with the notions of transformative resilience and antifragility. Furthermore, rather than just discussing rural entrepreneurship as a phenomenon rooted in place, we also interrogated what rural entrepreneurship is *for* vis-à-vis different notions of "value" and how it is created. The aim is ultimately to reflect on how entrepreneurship in rural areas is conceptualized, challenging common assumptions and perspectives on rural entrepreneurship and opening new venues for research and education (Dodd et al., 2021). This is an invitation to researchers and practitioners to explore the intersection of rural entrepreneurship with individual quality of life, community development, and more sustainable and resilient/antifragile local economies.

The Authors have no conflicts of interest to disclose related to the company described here.

This research was funded in part by the Japan Society for the Promotion of Science (JSPS) Grant No. 21K20068.

References

Akgün, A.A., Nijkamp, P., Baycan, T., & Brons, M. (2010). Embeddedness of entrepreneurs in rural areas: A comparative rough set data analysis. Tijdschrift Voor Economische En Sociale Geografie, 101(5), 538–553. https://doi.org/10.1111/j.1467-9663.2010.00630.x.

Anderson, A.R. (2000). Paradox in the periphery: An entrepreneurial reconstruction? Entrepreneurship and Regional Development, 12(2), 91–109. https://doi.org/10.1080/089856200283027.

Anderson, A.R., & Lent, M.D. (2017). Enterprising the rural; creating a social value chain. Journal of Rural Studies. https://doi.org/10.1016/j.jrurstud.2017.08.020.

Babb, E.M., & Babb, S.V. (1992). Psychological traits of rural entrepreneurs. Journal of Socio-Economics, 21(4), 353–362. https://doi.org/10.1016/1053-5357(92)90004-Q.

Baker, Ted, and Reed E. Nelson. 2005. "Creating Something from Nothing: Resource Construction through Entrepreneurial Bricolage." Administrative Science Quarterly 50:329–66.

Barber, D., Harris, M.L., & Jones, J. (2021). An overview of rural entrepreneurship and future directions. Journal of Small Business Strategy, 31(4), 1–4. https://doi.org/10.53703/001C.29468.

Baumgartner, D., Schulz, T., & Seidl, I. (2013). Quantifying entrepreneurship and its impact on local economic performance: A spatial assessment in rural Switzerland. Entrepreneurship and Regional Development, 25(3–4), 222–250. https://doi.org/10.1080/08985626.2012.710266.

Bosworth, G. (2010). Commercial counterurbanisation: An emerging force in rural economic development. Environment and Planning A, 42(4), 966–981. https://doi.org/10.1068/a42206.

Bosworth, G., & Atterton, J. (2012). Entrepreneurial In-migration and neoendogenous rural development. Rural Sociology, 77(2), 254–279. https://doi.org/10.1111/j.1549-0831.2012.00079.x.

Bosworth, G., Whalley, J., Fuzi, A., & Merrell, I. (2021). Rural coworking: It's becoming contagious. Regions. https://doi.org/10.1080/13673882.2021.00001096.

Clarke, V., & Braun, V. (2021). Thematic analysis: A practical guide. London: Sage.

Černevičiūtė, J., Strazdas, R., Kregždaitė, R., & Tvaronavičienė, M. (2019). Cultural and creative industries for sustainable postindustrial regional development: The case of Lithuania. Journal of International Studies, 12(2), 285–298. https://doi.org/10.14254/2071-8330.2019/12-2/18.

Conroy, T., & Low, S.A. (2022). Entrepreneurship, broadband, and gender: Evidence from establishment births in rural America. International Regional Science Review, 45(1), 3–35. https://doi.org/10.1177/01600176211018749.

Creswell, J.W. (2017). Research design: Qualitative, quantitative, and mixed methods approaches. Sage publications.

Dal Bello, U.B., Marques, C., Sacramento, O., & Galvão, A. (2021). Neo-rural small entrepreneurs' motivations and challenges in Portugal's low density regions. Journal of Enterprising Communities. https://doi.org/10.1108/JEC-04-2021-0047.

de Roest, K., Ferrari, P., & Knickel, K. (2018). Specialisation and economies of scale or diversification and economies of scope? Assessing different agricultural development pathways. Journal of Rural Studies, 59, 222–231. https://doi.org/10.1016/j.jrurstud.2017.04.013.

Deller, S.C., & Conroy, T. (2017). Business survival rates across the urban–rural divide. Community Development, 48(1), 67–85. https://doi.org/10.1080/15575330.2016.1246459.
Dilley, L., Gkartzios, M., & Odagiri, T. (2022). Developing counterurbanisation: Making sense of rural mobility and governance in Japan. Habitat International, 125, 102595. https://doi.org/10.1016/j.habitatint.2022.102595.
Dodd, S., Wilson, J., Karampela, M., & Danson, M. (2021). Crafting growth together. Entrepreneurship and Regional Development, 33(9–10), 789–815. https://doi.org/10.1080/08985626.2021.1914741.
Drakopoulou-Dodd, S.L. (2014). Roots radical – place, power and practice in punk entrepreneurship. Entrepreneurship and Regional Development, 26(1–2), 165–205. https://doi.org/10.1080/08985626.2013.877986.
Dubois, A. (2016). Transnationalising entrepreneurship in a peripheral region – The translocal embeddedness paradigm. Journal of Rural Studies, 46, 1–11. https://doi.org/10.1016/j.jrurstud.2016.05.003.
Dubois, A. (2019). Translocal practices and proximities in short quality food chains at the periphery: The case of North Swedish farmers. Agriculture and Human Values, 36(4), 763–778. https://doi.org/10.1007/s10460-019-09953-y.
Figueroa-Armijos, M., Dabson, B., & Johnson, T.G. (2012). Rural entrepreneurship in a time of recession. Entrepreneurship Research Journal, 2(1). https://doi.org/10.2202/2157-5665.1044.
Flyvbjerg, B. (2012). Making social science matter: Why social science inquiry fails and how it can succeed again. Cambridge, UK: Cambridge University Press. https://doi.org/10.1017/CBO9780511810503.
Fortunato, M.W.P. (2014). Supporting rural entrepreneurship: A review of conceptual developments from research to practice. Community Development, 45(4), 387–408. https://doi.org/10.1080/15575330.2014.935795.
Fortunato, M.W.P., & Alter, T. (2015). Community entrepreneurship development: An introduction. Community Development, 46(5), 444–455. https://doi.org/10.1080/15575330.2015.1080742.
Gaddefors, Johan, and Alistair R. Anderson. 2019. "Romancing the Rural: Reconceptualizing Rural Entrepreneurship as Engagement with Context(S)." International Journal of Entrepreneurship and Innovation 20(3):159–69. doi: 10.1177/1465750318785545.
Granovetter, M. (1985). Economic action and social structure: the problem of embeddedness. American Journal of Sociology 91 (3) pp. 481–510.
Greenberg, Z., Farja, Y., & Gimmon, E. (2018). Embeddedness and growth of small businesses in rural regions. Journal of Rural Studies, 62, 174–182. https://doi.org/10.1016/j.jrurstud.2018.07.016.
Herslund, L. (2012). The rural creative class: Counterurbanisation and entrepreneurship in the Danish countryside. Sociologia Ruralis, 52(2), 235–255. https://doi.org/10.1111/j.1467-9523.2011.00560.x.
Jenkins, T.N. (2000). Putting postmodernity into practice: Endogenous development and the role of traditional cultures in the rural development of marginal regions. Ecological Economics, 34(3), 301–314. https://doi.org/10.1016/S0921-8009(00)00191-9.
Johansson, F. (2006). The Medici effect: What elephants and epidemics can teach us about innovation. Harvard Business School Press.
Johnstone, H., & Lionais, D. (2004). Depleted communities and community business entrepreneurship: Revaluing space through place. Entrepreneurship and Regional Development, 16(3), 217–233. https://doi.org/10.1080/0898562042000197117.
Kalantaridis, Christos, and Zografia Bika. 2006. "In-Migrant Entrepreneurship in Rural England: Beyond Local Embeddedness." Entrepreneurship and Regional Development 18(2):109–31. doi: 10.1080/08985620500510174.
Kneafsey, M., Ilbery, B., & Jenkins, T. (2001). Exploring the dimensions of culture economies in rural West Wales. Sociologia Ruralis, 41(3), 296–310. https://doi.org/10.1111/1467-9523.00184.

Korsgaard, S., Ferguson, R., & Gaddefors, J. (2015). The best of both worlds: How rural entrepreneurs use placial embeddedness and strategic networks to create opportunities. Entrepreneurship and Regional Development, 27(9–10), 574–598. https://doi.org/10.1080/08985626.2015.1085100.

Korsgaard, S., & Tanvig, H.W. (2015). Rural entrepreneurship or entrepreneurship in the rural – Between place and space. International Journal of Entrepreneurial Behaviour and Research, 21(1), 5–26. https://doi.org/10.1108/IJEBR-11-2013-0205.

Korsgaard, S., Wigren-Kristoferson, C., Brundin, E., Hellerstedt, K., Alsos, G.A., & Grande, J. (2022). Entrepreneurship and embeddedness: Process, context and theoretical foundations. Entrepreneurship & Regional Development, 34(3–4), 1–12. https://doi.org/10.1080/08985626.2022.2055152.

Lackéus, M. (2018). "What is value?" – A framework for analyzing and facilitating entrepreneurial value creation. Uniped, 41(1), 10–28. https://doi.org/10.18261/issn.1893-8981-2018-01-02.

Larsen, J.S.K., Lauvås, T., & Sørheim, R. (2022). In the same boat? The dynamics of embedded firms in peripheral regions. Entrepreneurship & Regional Development, 34(3–4), 1–22. https://doi.org/10.1080/08985626.2022.2055151.

Li, Y., Westlund, H., & Liu, Y. (2019). Why some rural areas decline while some others not: An overview of rural evolution in the world. Journal of Rural Studies, 68(March), 135–143. https://doi.org/10.1016/j.jrurstud.2019.03.003.

Liedtke, M., Asghari, R., & Spengler, T. (2021). Fostering entrepreneurial ecosystems and the choice of location for new companies in rural areas – The case of Germany. Journal of Small Business Strategy, 31(4), 76–87. https://doi.org/10.53703/001c.29480.

Lyons, T.S., Alter, T.R., Audretsch, D., & Augustine, D. (2012). Entrepreneurship and community: The next frontier of entrepreneurship inquiry. Entrepreneurship Research Journal, 2(1). https://doi.org/10.2202/2157-5665.1064.

Low, S., Henderson, J., & Weiler, S. (2005). Gauging a region's entrepreneurial potential. Economic Review – Federal Reserve Bank of Kansas City, 90(3), 61–89. http://search.proquest.com/docview/218425038?accountid=14541%5Cnhttp://pc6bf4sj5m.search.serialssolutions.com/?ctx_ver=Z39.88-2004&ctx_enc=info:ofi/enc:UTF-8&rfr_id=info:sid/ProQ:abiglobal&rft_val_fmt=info:ofi/fmt:kev:mtx:journal&rft.genre=article&rft.jti.

Mayer, H., Habersetzer, A., & Meili, R. (2016). Rural-urban linkages and sustainable regional development: The role of entrepreneurs in linking peripheries and centers. Sustainability (Switzerland), 8(8). https://doi.org/10.3390/su8080745.

Mayer, Heike, and Yasuyuki Motoyama. 2020. "Entrepreneurship in Small and Medium-Sized Towns." Entrepreneurship and Regional Development 32(7–8):467–72. doi: 10.1080/08985626.2020.1798556.

McKeever, E., Anderson, A., & Jack, S. (2014). Entrepreneurship and mutuality: Social capital in processes and practices. Entrepreneurship and Regional Development, 26(5–6), 453–477. https://doi.org/10.1080/08985626.2014.939536.

Mitchell, C.J.A. (2013). Creative destruction or creative enhancement? Underastanding the transformation of rural spaces. Journal of Rural Studies, 32, 375–387. https://doi.org/10.1016/j.jrurstud.2013.09.005.

Müller, S., & Korsgaard, S. (2018). Resources and bridging: The role of spatial context in rural entrepreneurship. Entrepreneurship and Regional Development, 30(1–2), 224–255. https://doi.org/10.1080/08985626.2017.1402092.

Naldi, L., Nilsson, P., Westlund, H., & Wixe, S. (2021). Amenities and new firm formation in rural areas. Journal of Rural Studies, 85(April 2020), 32–42. https://doi.org/10.1016/j.jrurstud.2021.05.023.

Newbery, Robert, Juliana Siwale, and Andrew Henley. 2017. "Rural Entrepreneurship Theory in the Developing and Developed World." International Journal of Entrepreneurship and Innovation 18(1):3–4. doi: 10.1177/1465750316686232.

Pato, L., & Teixeira, A.A.C. (2014). Twenty years of rural entrepreneurship: A bibliometric survey. Sociologia Ruralis, 56(1), 3–28. https://doi.org/10.1111/soru.12058.

Pato, L., & Teixeira, A.A.C. (2019). Are new rural ventures different from new urban ones? An exploratory analysis of businesses located in Portuguese incubators and science parks. Journal of Entrepreneurship and Public Policy, 8(4), 470–482. https://doi.org/10.1108/JEPP-08-2019-113.

Phillipson, Jeremy, Pattanapong Tiwasing, Matthew Gorton, Sara Maioli, Robert Newbery, and Roger Turner. 2019. "Shining a Spotlight on Small Rural Businesses: How Does Their Performance Compare with Urban?" Journal of Rural Studies 68(May 2019):230–39. doi: 10.1016/j.jrurstud.2018.09.017.

Prince, S., Qu, M., & Zollet, S. (2021). The making of art islands: A comparative analysis of translocal assemblages of contemporary art and tourism. Island Studies Journal, 16(2), 235–264. https://doi.org/10.24043/isj.175.

Qu, M., Mccormick, A.D., & Funck, C. (2020). Community resourcefulness and partnerships in rural tourism. Journal of Sustainable Tourism, 1–20. https://doi.org/10.1080/09669582.2020.1849233.

Qu, M., & Zollet, S. (2023). Neo-endogenous revitalisation: Enhancing community resilience through art tourism and rural entrepreneurship. Journal of Rural Studies, 97(November 2022), 105–114. https://doi.org/10.1016/j.jrurstud.2022.11.016.

Ramezani, J., & Camarinha-Matos, L.M. (2020). Approaches for resilience and antifragility in collaborative business ecosystems. Technological Forecasting and Social Change, 151(March 2019), 119846. https://doi.org/10.1016/j.techfore.2019.119846.

Ray, C. (1998). Culture, intellectual property and territorial rural development. Sociologia Ruralis, 38(1), 3–20.

Roundy, Philip T. 2019. "'It Takes a Village' to Support Entrepreneurship: Intersecting Economic and Community Dynamics in Small Town Entrepreneurial Ecosystems." International Entrepreneurship and Management Journal 15(4):1443–75. doi: 10.1007/s11365-018-0537-0.

Shrivastava, U., & Kumar Dwivedi, A. (2020). Manifestations of rural entrepreneurship: The journey so far and future pathways. Management Review Quarterly, 0123456789. https://doi.org/10.1007/s11301-020-00199-1.

Shucksmith, M. (2010). Disintegrated rural development? Neo-endogenous rural development, planning and place-shaping in diffused power contexts. Sociologia Ruralis, 50(1), 1–14. https://doi.org/10.1111/j.1467-9523.2009.00497.x.

Siemens, L. (2007). Challenges faced by rural/remote tourism businesses on Vancouver Island: An exploratory study. Journal of Enterprising Communities, 1(4), 308–320. https://doi.org/10.1108/17506200710833818.

Stathopoulou, S., Psaltopoulos, D., & Skuras, D. (2004). Rural entrepreneurship in Europe: A research framework and agenda. International Journal of Entrepreneurial Behaviour & Research, 10(6), 404–425. https://doi.org/10.1108/13552550410564725.

Taleb, N. N. (2012). Antifragile: Things that gain from disorder. Random House.

Thiede, B., Greiman, L., Weiler, S., Beda, S., & Conroy, T. (2017). 6 charts that illustrate the divide between rural and urban America. PBS NewsHour: The Rundown, 1–8. https://www.pbs.org/newshour/nation/six-charts-illustrate-divide-rural-urban-america.

Uzzi, B. (1997) Social structure and competition in inter-firm networks: the paradox ofembed- dedness. Administrative Science Quarterly 42 pp. 37–67.

Verdini, G. (2020). Creative-led strategies for peripheral settlements and the uneasy transition towards sustainability. International Planning Studies, June. https://doi.org/10.1080/13563475.2020.1779043.

Vlasov, M., Bonnedahl, K.J., & Vincze, Z. (2018). Entrepreneurship for resilience: Embeddedness in place and in trans-local grassroots networks. Journal of Enterprising Communities, 12(3), 374–394. https://doi.org/10.1108/JEC-12-2017-0100.

Welter, F. (2011). Contextualizing entrepreneurship – Conceptual challenges and ways forward. Entrepreneurship: Theory and Practice, 35(1), 165–184. https://doi.org/10.1111/j.1540-6520.2010.00427.x.

Welter, F., & Baker, T. (2021). Moving contexts onto new roads: Clues from other disciplines. Entrepreneurship: Theory and Practice, 45(5), 1154–1175. https://doi.org/10.1177/1042258720930996.

Welter, F., Baker, T., Audretsch, D.B., & Gartner, W.B. (2017). Everyday entrepreneurship – A call for entrepreneurship research to embrace entrepreneurial diversity. Entrepreneurship: Theory and Practice, 41(3), 311–321. https://doi.org/10.1111/etap.12258.

Welter, F., Baker, T., & Wirsching, K. (2019). Three waves and counting: The rising tide of contextualization in entrepreneurship research. Small Business Economics, 52(2), 319–330. https://doi.org/10.1007/s11187-018-0094-5.

Whetten, D.A. (1989). What constitutes a theoretical contribution. Academy of Management Review, 14(4), 490–495.

Wigren-Kristoferson, C., Brundin, E., Hellerstedt, K., Stevenson, A., & Aggestam, M. (2022). Rethinking embeddedness: A review and research agenda. Entrepreneurship and Regional Development, 34(1–2), 32–56. https://doi.org/10.1080/08985626.2021.2021298.

Woods, M., Fois, F., Heley, J., Jones, L., Onyeahialam, A., Saville, S., & Welsh, M. (2021). Assemblage, place and globalisation. Transactions of the Institute of British Geographers, 46(2), 284–298. https://doi.org/10.1111/tran.12430.

Yachin, J.M. (2017). The entrepreneur–opportunity nexus: Discovering the forces that promote product innovations in rural micro-tourism firms. Scandinavian Journal of Hospitality and Tourism, 19(1), 47–65. https://doi.org/10.1080/15022250.2017.1383936.

Young, N. (2010). Globalization from the edge: A framework for understanding how small and medium-sized firms in the periphery "go global. Environment and Planning A, 42(4), 838–855. https://doi.org/10.1068/a42315.

Zollet, S., & Maharjan, K.L. (2021). Overcoming the barriers to entry of newcomer sustainable farmers: Insights from the emergence of organic clusters in Japan. Sustainability (Switzerland), 13(2), 1–24. https://doi.org/10.3390/su13020866.

Zollet, S., & Qu, M. (2023). Urban-to-rural lifestyle migrants in peripheral Japanese island communities: Balancing quality of life expectations with reality. In P.H. Johansen, A. Tietjen, E.B. Iversen, H.L. Lolle, & J.K. Fisker (Eds.), Rural quality of life, 1st ed. Manchester University Press.

Kelly Cowan

How Technology Roadmapping for Smart Grid Could Be Applied to the Agriculture Sector

Abstract: This research discusses the use of technology roadmapping together with business model development to describe how to develop new products that better meet challenges in the technological, regulatory, and business-market landscapes. The research was originally applied to the smart grid industry and the specific application of electric vehicle charging. However, the research has broad applicability to other industries as well, including the agricultural sector. While agriculture has not been traditionally considered a high technology-based industry, it nonetheless relies heavily on a great deal of advanced technology nowadays to maximize yields, conserve resources, and optimize overall profitability. This chapter will describe previous research on technology roadmapping with the goal of showing the types of analysis that would be needed for a similar roadmap in an agriculture-related industry. We propose calling any future roadmaps that are developed in this area smart agriculture roadmaps (SMRs). One particular SMR with high similarity to previous research on smart grid research is the area of agrivoltaics. Agrivoltaics combine the use of photovoltaic (PV) panels, which generate electricity from exposure to sunlight with certain types of agriculture, like grape cultivation, which benefit from a certain amount of shade that can be provided by the PV panels. Likewise, the PV panels benefit from cooling that is provided to the underside of the panels as the grapes transpire moisture. This makes the panels produce electricity more efficiently and the grapes grow more efficiently, similar to symbiotic relationships that occur in nature. Agrivoltaics could then be directly integrated to the types of smart grid electrical systems discussed in this previous research. So, to understand how a smart roadmap for agriculture could be developed, we need to first look at research on smart grid roadmaps.

The "smart grid" has been described as the "Energy Internet: Where ET (Energy Technology) meets IT (Information Technology)." The incorporation of such technology into existing utility infrastructures offers many advantages, including possibilities for new smart appliances, energy management systems, better integration of renewable energy, value added services, and new business models, both for supply- and demand-side management. Smart grid also replaces aging utility technologies that are becoming increasingly unreliable, as the average ages for many critical components in utility systems now exceed their original design lives. However, while smart grid offers the promise of revolutionizing utility delivery systems, many questions remain about how such systems can be rolled out at the state, regional, and national levels. Many unique regulatory and market structure challenges exist, which makes it criti-

Kelly Cowan, University of New Mexico, email: kcowan@unm.edu

https://doi.org/10.1515/9783110791396-006

cal to pick the right technology for the right situation and to employ it in the right manner. Technology roadmapping may be a valuable approach for helping to understand factors that could affect smart grid technology and product development, as well as key business, policy and regulatory drivers. As emerging smart grid technologies are developed and the nascent industry matures, a critical issue will be understanding how the combination of industry drivers impact one another, what barriers exist to achieving the benefits of smart grid technologies, and how to prioritize R&D and acquisition efforts. Since the planning of power grids often relies on regional factors, it will also be important investigate linkages between smart grid deployment and regional planning goals. This can be used to develop strategies for overcoming barriers and achieving the benefits of this promising new technology. This research builds upon existing roadmapping processes by considering an integrated set of factors, including policy issues, which are specifically tuned to the needs of smart grids and have not generally been considered in other types of roadmapping efforts.

Keywords: technology, smart grid, smart agriculture roadmap, photovoltaic

1 Introduction

This research discusses the use of technology roadmapping, together with business model development to describe how to develop new products that better meet challenges in the technological, regulatory, and business-market landscapes. The research was originally applied to the smart grid industry and the specific application of electric vehicle charging. However, the research has broad applicability to other industries as well, including the agricultural sector. While agriculture has not been traditionally considered a high technology-based industry, it nonetheless relies heavily on a great deal of advanced technology nowadays to maximize yields, conserve resources, and optimize overall profitability. This chapter will describe previous research with the goal of showing the types of analysis that would be needed for a similar roadmap in an agriculture-related industry. We propose calling any future roadmaps that are developed in this area SMRs. One particular SMR with high similarity to previous research on smart grid research is the area of agrivoltaics. Agrivoltaics combine the use of photovoltaic (PV) panels, which generate electricity from exposure to sunlight with certain types of agriculture, like grape cultivation, which benefit from a certain amount of shade that can be provided by the PV panels. Likewise, the PV panels benefit from cooling that is provided to the underside of the panels as the grapes transpire moisture. This makes the panels produce electricity more efficiently and the grapes grow more efficiently, similar to symbiotic relationships that occur in nature. Agrivoltaics could then be directly integrated to the types of smart grid electrical systems discussed in this previous research. So, to understand how a smart roadmap for agriculture could be developed, we need to first look at research on smart grid roadmaps in general.

2 Investigating the Problem of Smart Grids

Electrical utility systems are part of a large and important industry in the US, with nearly $400 billion in revenues in 2016 (EEI, 2017; EIA, 2020). Smart grid technologies offer many promising benefits for the modernization of electrical power delivery systems. The following are just a few of the benefits offered by smart grid: (1) Improvement in operating efficiencies of electricity grids at all levels of the system; (2) Improvement of communications and controls within the power system for all actors, including generators, transmitters, system operators, distributors, and end-users; (3) Opportunities for new value-added services related to control and management of energy; (4) and increased system reliability by replacing obsolete hardware that is nearing the end of its useful service life (Hammerstrom & Gephart, 2006). With the average age of electrical transformers in the US power grid now at 42 years, out of a maximum design life of 40 years, critical elements of the power system are now at risk, and there is a strong need to modernize aging infrastructure for the power grid (Rouse & Kelly, 2011; Hussler, Tang & Picard, 2010).

Current power grids, especially in the United States, are being used well past their designed lifetime. Updates to these systems are important to address energy inefficiency, reliability, and security vulnerabilities of the twenty-first century (Coombs, Saviotti & Walsh, 1987). It is possible to use the emerging technology smart grid technology product platform (Smith & Kern, 2009) on many types of utility systems, including gas, water, and electricity delivery systems, but this research will focus only on smart electricity grids.

Power grid modernization offers the opportunity to implement technologies with new capabilities that may have been difficult or impossible in the past. From remotely operated energy management systems, self-monitoring and self-healing systems, to smart electric vehicles, smart grid can open a myriad of new opportunities for businesses, consumers, and decision makers (Fox-Penner, 2009; Stimmel, 2015). Therefore, it is critical to examine how smart grid is likely to develop in the future, what its effects may be, and to create a detailed roadmap showing how this vision might occur.

The next section will describe the smart grid industry and related technologies in greater detail. The need for development of roadmaps to guide the deployment of smart grid technologies will then be discussed, including current efforts in Oregon and the US Pacific Northwest. This field is very broad, so only a limited number of technologies and the capabilities they provide will be described, with an emphasis on technologies that are currently being introduced and seen as important in the region. In particular, this research will focus on how smart grid technologies can be used to meet key regional goals, such as enabling the integration of renewable energy, which according to recently enacted legislation, must now provide 25% of the energy mix in Oregon by 2025 (Jenkins, Bauman & Bissonette, 2007; EPRI, 2010). Thus, the following questions will be specifically explored.

What factors are most significant in motivating the adoption of smart grid technologies? How can important emerging smart technologies, like electric vehicles, be used to integrate renewable energy into the power system? What policies can encourage businesses and individuals to participate in such systems?

3 Research Problem Description

The topic described above raises a number of interesting questions that are important to explore both in the industry practitioner literature and the academic research literature. However, to aid in the analysis of these general questions, we will explore how specific frameworks, like technology roadmapping could be used to help address them in more detail. So, first, how can a tool such as technology roadmapping be extended to include a policy layer, business services model layer, and an expanded product market needs layer, which includes the ability to consider appropriate technology performance metrics. The research further raises the question of the interaction between technology push versus market pull. It then extends these concepts by considering how they might be affected by policy and business model push-pull dynamics. After exploring the broad research questions, we examine some initial research objectives that can address specific aspects of those questions.

4 Initial Research Objectives

1. How can technology roadmapping be used to improve regional smart grid planning?
2. How can technology roadmapping be extended to better integrate technology planning, business model development, and regulatory and policy considerations for smart grid?
3. What are the best ways to encourage the adoption of emerging smart grid technologies that meet critical regional needs, such as the use of electric vehicles to help with the integration of renewable energy?
4. How could the previous technology roadmap frameworks developed for industries like smart grid be used to develop similar frameworks in the agriculture sector.

5 Significance of the Research

This research can provide insights to help planners understand which factors are most likely to promote diffusion and adoption of smart grid technologies and their use for the integration of renewable energy, as well as their applications to the agriculture sector. It offers valuable extensions to the concept of technology roadmapping by integrating consideration of regulatory and policy issues, business model development, and technology research and development. It explores the interactions between traditional technology push and market pull dynamics by adding consideration of the policy and business model push-pull relationships. It then helps to build an understanding about how these factors inform one another to improve chances of successful deployment of technology.

6 History of Smart Grid Development

The alternating current power grid used in the United States evolved primarily from technologies developed in the 1880's by industry pioneers, such as Edison, Tesla, Ansull, and Westinghouse (Shively & Ferrare, 2010). Many of the core concepts used for developing early local grids, such as centralized unidirectional electric power transmission, are still common today.

Smart grid differs from the traditional grid in a number of ways. Some of this distinction depends upon the definition of smart grid. At the most fundamental level, smart grid is a term for the application of modern technology components and design architectures to the power grid, mainly in the form of digital information and communication technologies (Fox-Penner, 2010).

Recent government policy has begun to recognize the importance of smart grid. According to Title XIII of the Energy Independence and Security Act of 2007, the United States Department of Energy identifies the following as key elements that collectively characterize smart grid (DOE, 2007):

7 Elements of Smart Grid

1) Increased use of digital information and controls technology to improve reliability, security, and efficiency of the electric grid.
2) Dynamic optimization of grid operations and resources, with full cyber-security.
3) Deployment and integration of distributed resources and generation, including renewable resources.
4) Development and incorporation of demand response, demand-side resources, and energy-efficiency resources.
5) Deployment of "smart" technologies (real-time, automated, interactive technologies that optimize the physical operation of appliances and consumer devices) for metering, communications concerning grid operations and status, and distribution automation.
6) Integration of "smart" appliances and consumer devices.

7) Deployment and integration of advanced electricity storage and peak-shaving technologies, including plug-in electric and hybrid electric vehicles, and thermal-storage air conditioning.
8) Provision to consumers of timely information and control options.
9) Development of standards for communication and interoperability of appliances and equipment connected to the electric grid, including the infrastructure serving the grid.
10) Identification and lowering of unreasonable or unnecessary barriers to adoption of smart grid technologies, practices, and services.

8 Definitions of Smart Grid

While these attributes are useful for describing what smart grid does, there is no commonly agree upon definition of what smart grid is. Many definitions are possible from the point of view of different stakeholders who are interested in a different aspect of smart grid systems.

From the point of view of utility companies, a critical distinction between the smart grid and traditional electricity systems is that while the traditional grid is a one-way system between the utility companies and end-users, smart grid allows an interactive two-way communication system. This is shown in Figure 1.

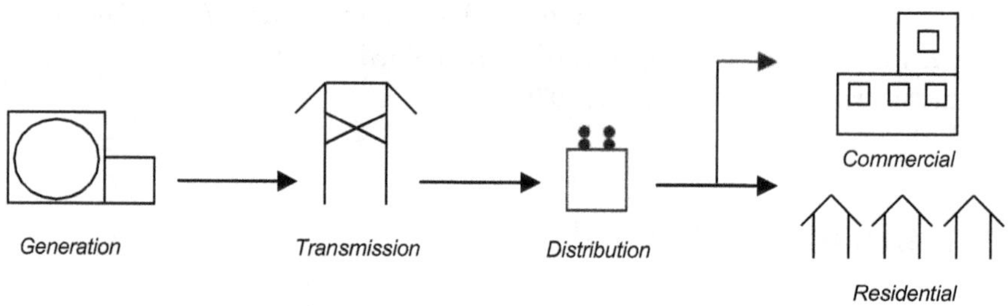

Figure 1: Traditional Electric Utility Structure – One-way System.
Source: Derived from (EPRI, 2010)

Smart grid provides two-way communication among the components of the utility system. This is shown in Figure 2.

Two-way communication helps with the three key aspects of electrical utility systems: (1) Power Production (Generation); (2) Power Transport (Transmission); and (3) the Power Delivery to serve loads, or needs of end users (Distribution) (Shively & Ferrare, 2010). It can also enable end-users to manage their energy use and participate in how the utility system operates. This leads to three different functional views of communication in utility systems, which are shown in Figure 3.

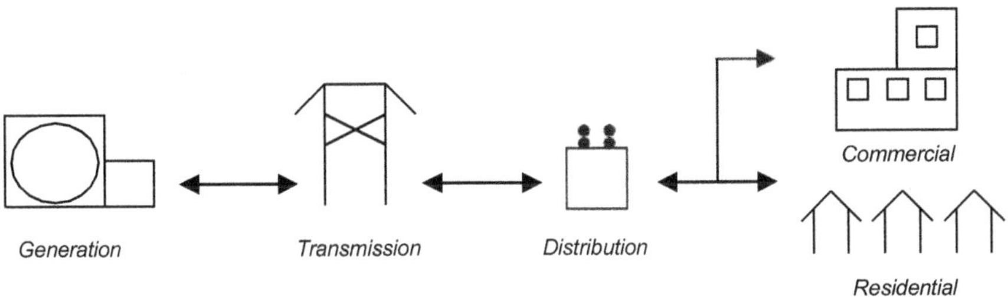

Figure 2: Smart Grid Electric Structure – Two-Way System.
Source: Derived from (EPRI, 2010)

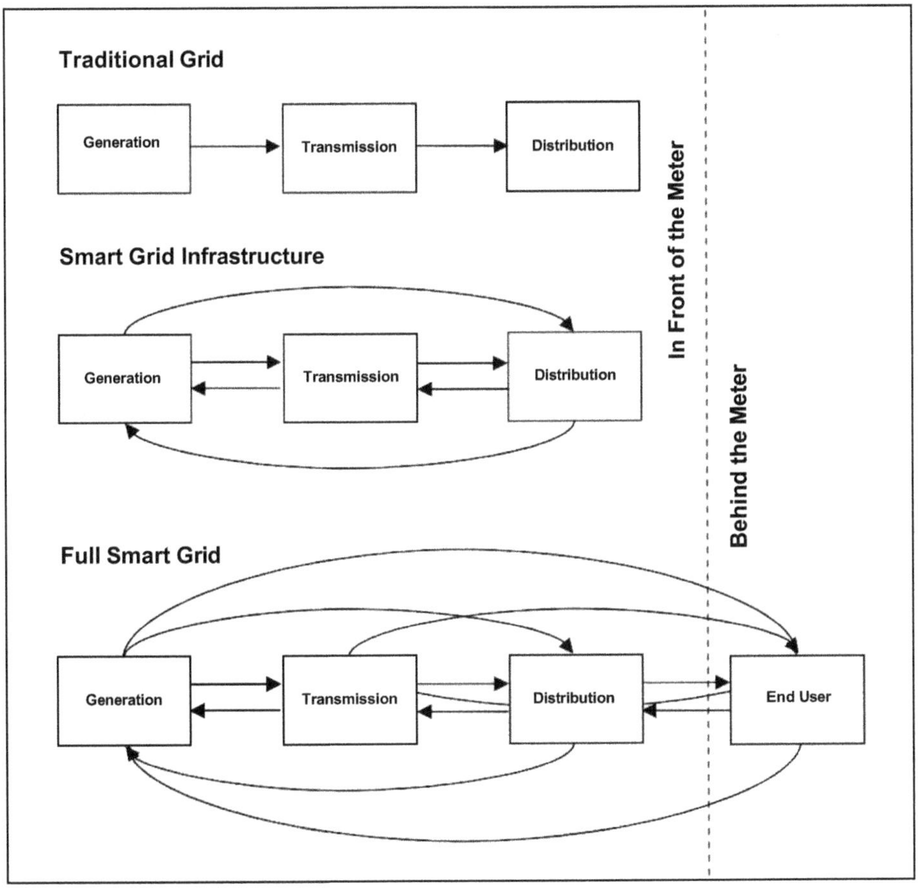

Figure 3: Functional Views of Smart Grid Communication Channels.
Source: Derived from (Shively & Ferrare, 2010) and (Warkentin-Glenn, 2006)

The replacement of one-way communication enables a more robust and efficient utility system, or *smart grid infrastructure*. However, both the traditional grid and the new smart infrastructures enabled by two-way communication have generally focused only on delivery of electricity to the end-user's utility meter (Shively & Ferrare, 2010). Anything the end-user does with the electricity after it has been delivered by the utility company is considered, in common industry parlance, to be "behind the meter," while utility companies have traditionally seen their role as providing the service "in front of the meter" *(Warkentin-Glenn, 2006)*. However, smart grid allows a new paradigm where customer energy management can affect the operations of the utility system as a whole, allowing generation, transmission, and distribution to be adjusted based on real time usage levels. Based on this viewpoint, realization of *full smart grid* requires an ability to address issues both in front and behind the meter. Thus, several different definitions of smart grid are possible based on the viewpoints of those involved.

Smart grid allows better coordination between the key components of the utility system, enabling better utilization of resources, and lower costs. Thus, it can be seen as a form of system level energy efficiency. System operators provide an additional function of managing the interactions between generation, transmission, and load serving entities in the utility system, as well as coordinating with regional transmission operators in the four major electrical interconnection systems in North America. Traditionally, many utilities have had vertically integrated structures, providing all of the generation, transmission, distribution, and system operation functions within their control areas (Fox-Penner, 2010). Under a smart grid framework, the overall system can be operated by Independent System Operators (ISOs) at state or regional levels, as well as through power pools or traditional vertically integrated utilities.

Based on a utility systems viewpoint, the Electric Power Research Institute (EPRI) has offered the following definition of smart grid (EPRI, 2009):

> *The overlaying of a unified communications and control system on the existing power delivery infrastructure to provide the right information to the right entity.*

However, from the point of view of electricity end-users, smart grid is not all about infrastructure, and it does not stop with the delivery of power to their homes or businesses. It may also involve smart appliances that are part of Home Area Networks, which can manage energy usage based on time-of-use prices and minimize utility costs for consumers (Proctor, 2011). It may also include intelligent dashboards, or monitoring devices, which can keep track of and control energy usage. Some devices can even remotely control or schedule the operations of smart appliances across the Internet, or through mobile devices, like smartphones.

While utility companies can play a role in supporting such systems for consumers, from their point of view, a smart grid can exist regardless of whether end-users attach smart devices to it or not. But, from the end-user point of view, little difference would be seen between a smart grid and a traditional grid unless these end-use devices are present.

Thus, author Thomas Friedman offers a more general, consumer-oriented definition of the smart grid as "The Energy Internet: Where IT meets ET." The terms "IT" and "ET" here refer to "Information Technology" and "Energy Technology" (Friedman, 2008).

With these two concepts in mind regarding a consumer-oriented smart grid definition, versus an industry-oriented smart grid, what are the key benefits of smart grid? What are the costs of such a system, and who will bear them? These costs and benefits are summarized in Table 1.

Table 1: Estimated Costs and Benefits of US Smart Grid Deployment.

	20 Year Total (billion $US)
Net Investment Required	338–476
Net Benefit	1,294–2,028
Benefit to Cost Ratio	2.7–6.0

Source: Derived from (EPRI, 2011).

According to the above estimates, the cost to deploy smart grid technology in US utility control centers and connect them to consumers' homes could range between "$338 billion and $476 billion over the next 20 years" (EPRI, 2011). However, the study projects "$1.3 trillion to $2 trillion in benefits over that period." Such benefits will include greater grid reliability, integration of renewable energy, plug-in vehicles, reductions in electricity demand, and stronger cybersecurity. Overall, benefits would be expected to outweigh costs by a factor of 2.7 to 6.0.

EPRI expects costs to fall most heavily on utility distribution systems that deliver power to retail customers. The breakdown of these costs is summarized in Figure 4. Just over 71% of the expenses for the higher-cost estimate in this study would go toward upgrades of substations, lines, poles, meters, and retail billing and communication systems. Nearly 19% of total costs would go to upgrading high-voltage transmission, including installation of sensors to monitor potential failures in the system. Almost 10% of costs would go toward components that would be installed directly in the homes of residential consumers. The breakdown of these costs is summarized in Figure 4.

Given the potential benefits of smart grid, it is important to plan for future deployment of such technology. Smart grid technologies present enormous opportunities, but also challenges. Thus, the section below will explore what has currently been found in the literature regarding smart grid roadmapping efforts. However, first it is important to examine what is and is not included in smart grid.

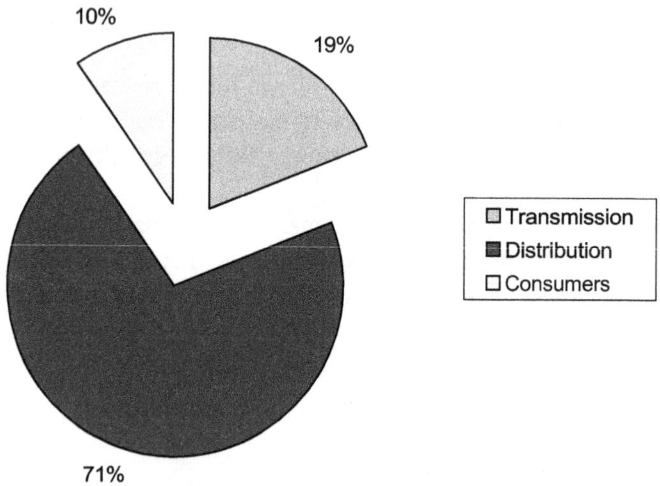

Figure 4: Investment Required for a Fully Functioning Smart Grid.
Source: Derived from (EPRI, 2011)

9 What Technologies Are Included in Smart Grid?

While the term “smart grid” has been in widespread use since at least 2005, it has not always been consistently used (Amin & Wollenberg, 2006). Smart grid is not a single thing, or an exact end state. It is a process of gaining more and more capabilities to improve upon the features that the electric utility industry has traditionally been able to offer for over a century. Figure 5 shows some of the key technologies that comprise smart grid, where they fit in the general smart landscape, and the main drivers affecting smart grid.

Smart grid technologies cover a wide range of functions, so it would be difficult to describe all the technologies that comprise it in detail. However, its main categories and functional areas are shown in Figure 5 and selected key terms are further defined in the glossary in Appendix B. The figure also shows key policy, market, business model and technology drivers that are influencing the evolution of the industry. The next section further explores these drivers to help understand why an integrated approach is needed for constructing smart grid roadmaps. An Integrated Approach to Smart Grid Roadmapping

Now that we have explored the definitions of smart grid, looked at what technology types it includes and what those technologies do, this gives us a more complete picture regarding this rapidly evolving industry. We have identified many different elements and drivers for smart grid, but more explanation is needed regarding the type of integrated approach that will be necessary to construct comprehensive smart grid roadmaps. Table 2 shows examples of some of the factors to be considered in creating such an integrated approach.

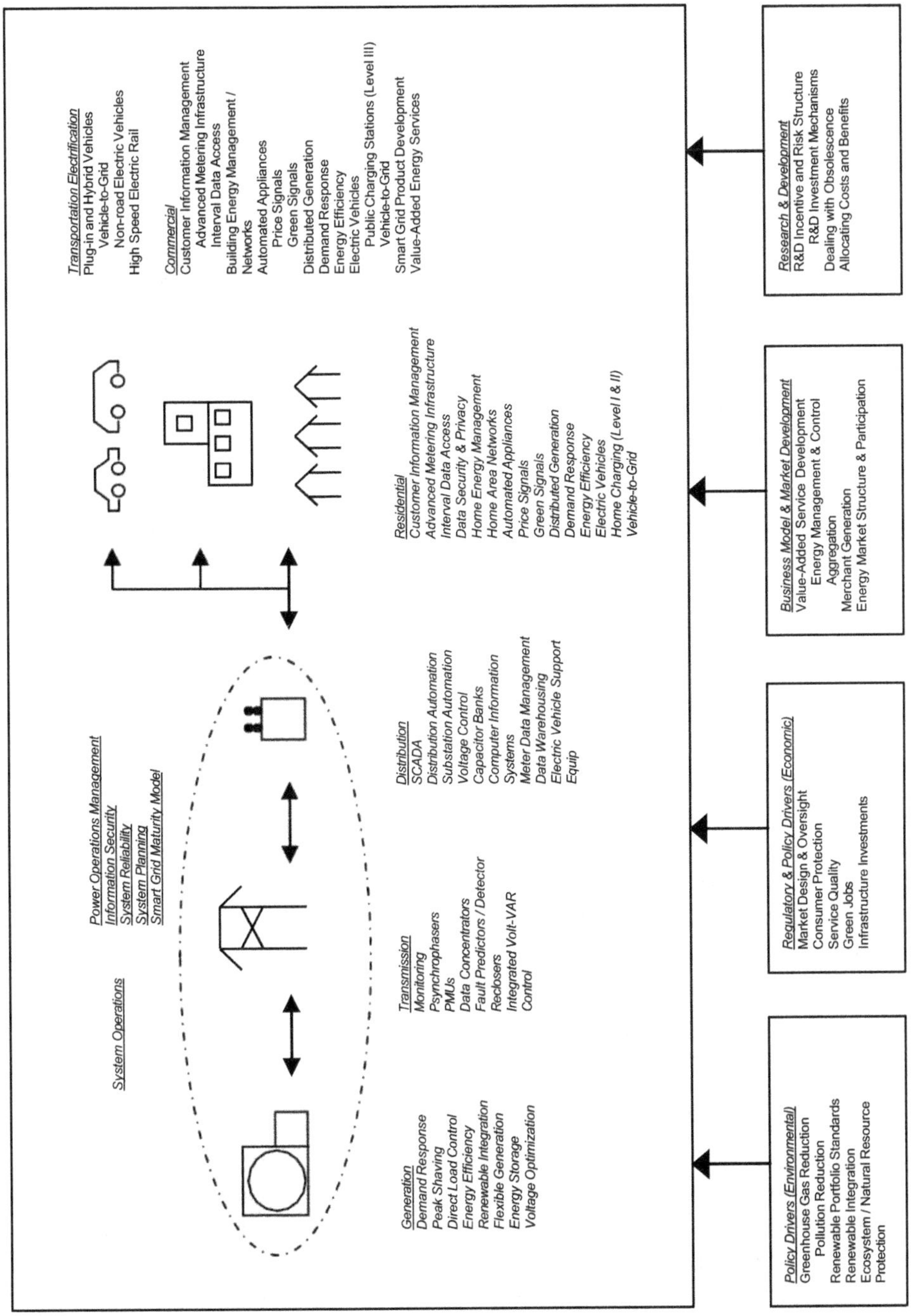

Figure 5: Key Elements and Drivers Contributing to Smart Grid.
Source: Derived from (EPRI, 2010)

Table 2: Why an Integrated Approach to Smart Grid Roadmapping Is Needed.

Industry Characteristics	**Regulatory & Policy Structure**
Capital Intensity (B)	Partially or Fully Regulated Monopoly (M)
Economies of Scale (B) Network Effects (B)	Regulated Profit or Rate of Return (B)(M)
Tendency toward Natural Monopoly (M)	Protect Customers from Lack of Competition (M)
Business & Market Development Process	Provide Investors with Stable Returns (B)
Develop Value-Added Services (B)	Provide Vital Quality of Life Services (P)
Avoiding Product Commoditization (B)	Provide Key Economic Development Functions (P)
Need for Standards and Interoperability (P)(T)	Provide Strategic and National Security Functions (P)
Dealing with Built-in Obsolescence (T)(B)	Planning Method: Least Cost Least Risk (P)(B)
Capturing Rapid Technological Improvements (T)(B)	Minimize Risks to Customers (M)(P)
Market Structures for End User Service Delivery (M)	Cost Recovery only for Prudently Incurred Risks (B)
Retail Competition (B)(P)	**Research & Development Process**
Wholesale Competition (B)(P)	Technology Intensive Industry (T)
Incentivizing Customer Participation (P)(B)	Low Incentives to Innovate (P)(M)
Energy Efficiency (T)(P)(B)	0.25% of Revenues Spent on R&D (B)(M)
Distributed Generation (T)(P)(B)	High R&D Needs (T)
Demand Response (T)(P)(B)	Increase Energy Efficiency (T)(B)
Electric Vehicles / Vehicle-to-Grid (T)(P)(B)	Reduce Operations & Maintenance Costs (T)(B)
	Support Renewable Energy (T)(P)
	Support Environmental Policies (T)(P)
	Support Economic Development Policies (T)(P)(B)

Unlike many other technology intensive industries, such as the Internet, the electric power industry has been highly regulated almost since its inception, when Thomas Edison opened the first commercial power station in lower Manhattan in 1882 (Cramer, 2001). With high barriers to entry, high capital requirements, and generally positive economies of scale in production, the industry has many key characteristics of natural monopolies (Filippini, 1998). It benefits from network effects, making it cheaper to serve customers when they are all part of the largest possible network of interconnections (Fox-Penner, 2010). Once the health, safety, environmental, and economic benefits of electrification became widely known, states began establishing regulatory compacts to extend the benefits of electric power to all citizens (Fox-Penner, 2010). This was generally done by creating monopoly services territories with utilities agreeing to an "obligation to serve" under regulated rates. Early industry pioneers, like Samuel Ansull, felt the industry could benefit from the stability and protection of a regulated monopoly structure, thus setting a tone that has remained to the present day (Insull & Keily, 1915).

Although the electricity industry has many key characteristics of natural monopolies, there are also some significant disadvantages to the regulated monopoly structure. It can be argued that highly regulated industries lack the normal incentive to innovate, since they are primarily beholden to regulatory bodies rather than responding to the more market-driven forces that drive innovation in other industries. In fact, the percentage of R&D expenditures in the utility industry is only 0.25%, one of the lowest of all major technology-based industries (NSF, 2010). Maximum profits are set by regulators and costs can only be recovered for investments carefully described and approved ahead of time. This strongly discourages uncertainty in favor of simple, predictable operating efficiency. Thus, the incentive to take risks and try unproven new ideas can often be neglected. While efforts to "deregulate" or "restructure" the industry offer some potential to realign incentives for more innovation and competition, early failures, like the collapse of Enron in 2001, have caused many to move very cautiously (Fox, 2003). Despite a historical aversion to risk, and methodological biases toward "least cost" and "least risk" planning, the electrical utility industry is being forced to innovate. Intermittent sources of renewable energy, like wind power and solar, are being added to the grid, along with legal requirements to generate power from renewable sources and reduce greenhouse gases; Electric Vehicles and Plug-in Hybrid Electric Vehicles are being developed which have the potential to both improve and exacerbate issues with peak demand. At the same time, businesses and consumers alike are demanding more information and control over the management of their electricity use, as well as protection of their critical financial and personal data. But, these new demands can only be met if the proper regulatory and market structures can be put in place that enable the right technologies and business models to be developed to meet these needs.

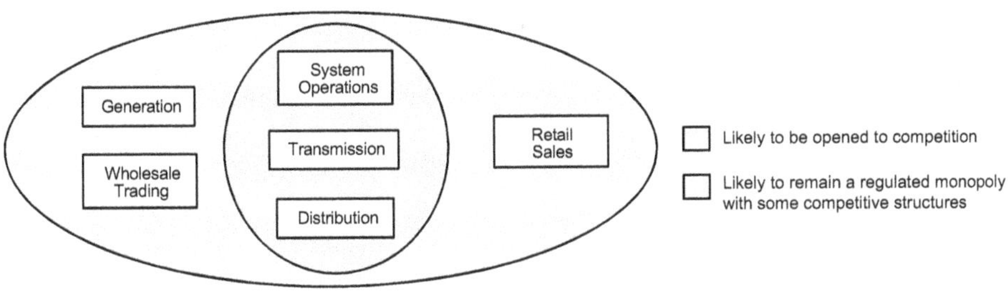

Figure 6: Electric Market Restructuring.
Source: Derived from (Shively & Ferrare, 2010)

Figure 6 shows elements of US electric power industry that are generally considered likely or unlikely to have some form of competitive market restructuring in the near future (Casazza, 2010).

Thus, the portions of the electric power industry which have historically worked best as regulated monopolies are likely to continue operating in this manner. However, the portions of industry that are most amenable to market development would then begin a restructuring process. This is summed up on the market maturation diagram (Figure 7).

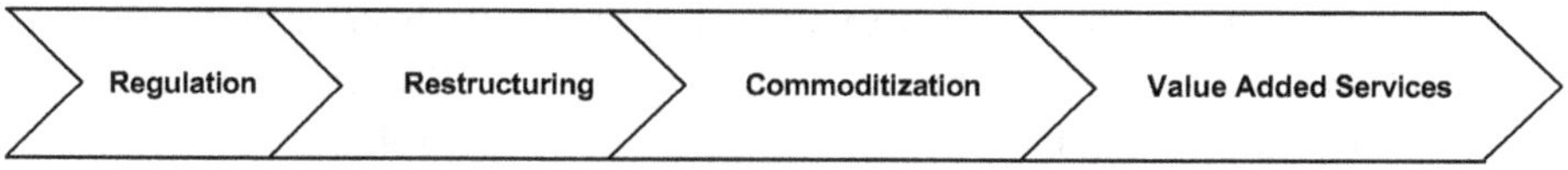

Figure 7: Market Maturation Process.
Source: Adapted from (Shively & Ferrare, 2010)

Each of the sectors previously proposed for restructuring is likely to develop at a different pace through the market maturation process. The breakup of the AT&T monopoly in the US telecommunications industry provides an example of this that may be illustrative (Coll, 1986). Although the breakup initially led to only a few more choices for basic services, over the intervening decades, a wide range of new service offerings have emerged. Thus, if proper oversight is exercised, the electric power industry, and the smart grid sector in particular, may be able to benefit from some similar processes that have led to the creation of new value-added services and business models in other industries.

10 Roadmapping and Key Driving Factors

Roadmapping is a term used in many industries, but it is not always interpreted in the same way. For the purposes of this research, the technology roadmapping process pioneered by Motorola in the 1980's is the main concept that will be extended (Willyard & McClees, 1987). Second-generation roadmaps for disruptive technologies were developed by Walsh (Walsh, 2004). The concept was further refined in the 1990's (Bray & Garcia, 1997) and a standard approach, known as the T-Plan was developed in early 2000 (Phaal, Farrukh & Probert, 2001, 2004). In addition, a process known as an S-Plan was developed to provide an overview of the strategic landscape for a potential technology product. Such roadmaps are useful for identifying key technologies and gaps that exist in a strategic and technology planning processes (Holmes & Ferrill, 2005).

Roadmaps show key possibilities for relationships between technologies and products over time. Most successful roadmaps attempt to integrate the perspectives of "technology push" and the "market pull" (Nauda & Hall, 1991). In the case of the development of smart grid roadmaps, integration of these perspectives is critical. While the Shumpeterian view that essential change within an industry depends strongly on the type and quality of technology developed in that new industry (Schumpeter & Opie, 1934), it also must meet important and well-defined market needs, as described by Schmookler (Coombs et al., 1987). Additionally, the history of strong regulation in the electric utility industry requires an understanding of the policy and regulatory perspectives. As the industry looks at possible regulatory restructuring, the development of new market structures and business models will also be key perspectives to incorporate. Several forms of analysis are used to examines these perspectives, including interpretative flexibility of policy storylines, which have been applied in the energy sector in relation to the transition of institutional priorities (Smith & Kern, 2009). Figure 8 provides visual representation of the integrated approach that this research proposes in balancing the various roadmap perspectives.

Regulatory and policy factors can exert both a push and a pull on traditional technology push and market pull perspectives. At times, policy may combine with technology push to create a sort of "policy push," which nudges technology to do more to meet an important policy goal, such as increased fuel efficiency vehicles or zero emission vehicles, for example. It is possible that this may cause technologies to fall out of alignment with market pull demands of consumers, such as with those who prefer larger but less fuel-efficient vehicle for other reasons, such as horsepower and cargo capacity. At other times, policymaking takes the form of a pull, attempting to get technology more aligned with market preferences than it otherwise might be given new technological capabilities that have been developed. An example of this might include privacy and information security requirements for customer data from devices like smart wireless utility meters. While the requirements for protecting this data do present some significant challenges, they provide an important protection to consumer and thus serve a significant policy purpose. This would be an equal and opposite case to the previous policy-push example, so it could be termed a "policy pull." For the purposes of this research, as we consider the possible role of policy in balancing the technology push and market pull perspectives, it is useful to consider a "policy push-pull" dynamic that would be able to act back and forth on these other two perspectives.

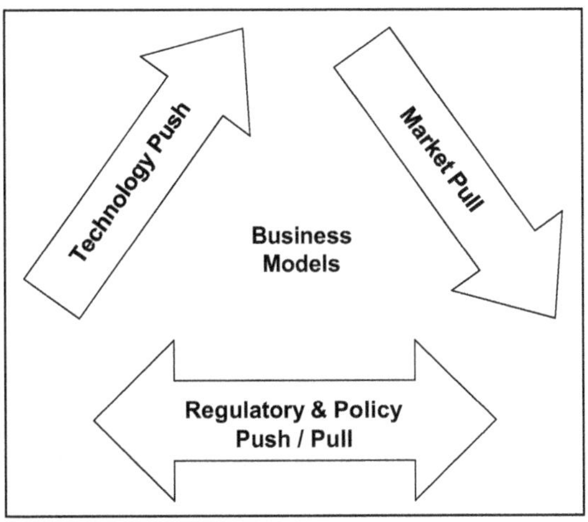

Figure 8: Balancing Planning Perspectives in Regulated Industries.
Source: Created by author

Figure 8 illustrates the regulatory and policy push/pull factors focusing on balancing perspectives for planning in the utility industry.

Business models are shown occupying the central space in the above diagram, as they are reliant on technology, market, and policy factors. They can be seen as a means for implementing successful combinations of these factors. The exact combination of factors can be visualized as a shape, if you will, that represents the space made available by the dynamic action of the other three factors. For the purposes of this research, this visual metaphor is essential for understanding the central importance of business models and the essential nature of an integrated approach for understanding successful technological innovation. Furthermore, while these points are likely applicable to a wide range of industries, the central role of regulation and policy on the utility industry, and the impact it exerts on shaping business models are seen as a reason why it may be particularly important for this research.

11 Conclusion

This chapter has examined the technology, market, policy, and business development issues associated with smart grid. Taking an integrated approach to addressing these issues can help provide a more complete picture of how to construct comprehensive smart grid roadmaps. More information on specific techniques regarding the technology roadmapping as well as the specific factors within the agriculture sector and the proposed area of agrivoltaics would be needed in order to construct a full roadmap on agrivoltaics. The goal of this chapter was to show the initial types of analysis that would be necessary for beginning the construction of a smart grid roadmap. Based on that, researchers interested in constructing a smart grid agriculture roadmap for an application area like photovoltaics could then see the types of information needed in order to begin that roadmapping process. However, this effort would undoubtedly be valuable, as this technique is a perfect fit for a nascent industry like agrivoltaics and could offer many benefits in term of attracting investment in this area of rural entrepreneurship. It would be an excellent tool to visualize all the key considerations regarding the adoption of such new technology in a sector that is not traditionally associated with high technology. Without such a vision, the development of new technologies and supporting industries can take longer and be more chaotic and uncertain. But, by highlighting and discussing market, policy, and business implications associated with this new field, it would provide a clear, concise vision for potential technology adopters and investors to refer to in analyzing the various factors that could determine future success in this area as well as identifying potential new opportunities and figuring out how to overcome barriers.

References

Amin, S.M., & Wollenberg, B.F. (2006). Toward a smart grid. IEEE Power & Energy, 4, 66.
Bray, O.H., & Garcia, M.L. (1997). Technology roadmapping: The integration of strategic and technology planning for competitiveness. Paper presented at the PICMET (Portland International Conference for Management of Engineering and Technology). Portland, OR.
Casazza, J. (2010). Understanding electric power systems: An overview of the technology, the marketplace, and government regulation. John Wiley & Sons.
Coll, S. (1986). The deal of the century: The break up of AT&T. New York: Atheneum.
Coombs, R., Saviotti, P., & Walsh, V. (1987). Economics and technological change. Totowa, N.J: Rowman & Littlefield.
Cramer, C. (2001). Thomas Edison. San Diego, CA: Greenhaven Press.
DOE. (2007). Energy Independence and Security Act of 2007. Retrieved from Washington, D.C.
Edison Electric Institute (2017). Industry Data: Statistical Highlights. Retrieved from: https://www.eei.org/en/resources-and-media/industry-data
EIA. (2020). What is U.S. electricity generation by energy source? Retrieved from https://www.eia.gov/tools/faqs/faq.php?id=427&t=3.
Electric Power Research Institute (2009). The Green Grid: Energy Savings and Carbon Emissions Reductions Enabled by a Smart Grid. Retrieved from: http://large.stanford.edu/courses/2015/ph240/xu1/docs/epri-1016905.pdf
Electric Power Research Institute (2010). Smart Grid Demonstration Two-Year Update. Retrieved from: https://smartgrid.epri.com/doc/EPRI%20Smart%20Grid%20Demonstration%202-Year%20Update_final.pdf
EPRI. (2011). Estimating the Costs and Benefits of the Smart Grid: A Preliminary Estimate of the Investment Requirements and the Resultant Benefits of a Fully Functioning Smart Grid. Retrieved from Palo Alto, CA.
Filippini, M. (1998). Are municipal electricity distribution utilities natural monopolies? Annals of Public and Cooperative Economics, 69, 157.
Fox-Penner, P. (2009). Fix utilities before they need a rescue. Harvard Business Review, 87.
Fox-Penner, P.S. (2010). Smart power: Climate change, the smart grid, and the future of electric utilities. Washington: Island Press.
Fox, L. (2003). Enron: The rise and fall. Hoboken, NJ: Wiley.
Friedman, T.L. (2008). Hot, flat, and crowded: Why we need a green revolution – And how it can renew America. New York: Farrar, Straus and Giroux.
Hammerstrom, D.J., & Gephart, J.M. (2006). Smart technology brings power to the people. Power Engineering International, 14(10), 45–46.
Holmes, C., & Ferrill, M. (2005). The application of operation and technology roadmapping to aid Singaporean SMEs identify and select emerging technologies. Technological Forecasting and Social Change, 72, 349–357.
Hussler, C., Tang, M., & Picard, F. (2010). Taking the ivory from the tower to coat the economic world: Regional strategies to make science useful. Technovation, 30, 508–518.
Insull, S., & Keily, W.F. (1915). Central station electric service: Its commercial development and economic significance. Chicago.
Jenkins, J. Bauman, J., and Bissonette, J. (2007). Renewable Energy Standard. Retrieved from: http://www.poweringoregonsfuture.org/PoweringOregonsFuture/PDFs/RES_FAQ_07Oct10.pdf
Nauda, A., & Hall, D.L. (1991). Strategic technology planning–developing roadmaps for competitive advantage. Paper presented at the Portland, OR.

National Science Foundations (2010). Funds for Industrial R&D as a Percent of Net Sales of Companies Performing Industrial R&D in the United States. Washington, D.C. Retrieved from: https://ncses.nsf.gov/pubs/nsb20225/u-s-business-r-d

Phaal, R., Farrukh, C., & Probert, D. (2001). T-plan: The fast-start to technology roadmapping – Planning your route to success. Cambridge, UK: University of Cambridge, Institute for Manufacturing.

Phaal, R., Farrukh, C., & Probert, D. (2004). Technology roadmapping – A planning framework for evolution and revolution. Technological Forecasting and Social Change, 71, 5.

Proctor, R.J. (2011). Smart Grid Inventory: A Report to the Oregon Public Utility Commission. Retrieved from Salem, OR.

Rouse, G., & Kelly, J. (2011). Electricity reliability: Problems progress and policy solutions. Galvin Electricity Initiative.

Schumpeter, J.A., & Opie, R. (1934). The theory of economic development: An inquiry into profits, capital, credit, interest, and the business cycle. Cambridge, MA: Harvard University Press.

Shively, B., & Ferrare, J. (2010). Understanding today's electricity business. Laporte, CO: Enerdynamics.

Smith, A., & Kern, F. (2009). The transitions storyline in Dutch environmental policy. The Transitions Storyline in Dutch Environmental Policy, 18.

Stimmel, C.L. (2015). Big data analytics strategies for the smart grid.

Walsh, S.T. (2004). Roadmapping a disruptive technology: A case study. Technological Forecasting and Social Change, 71, 161–185.

Warkentin-Glenn, D. (2006). Electric power industry in nontechnical language. Tulsa, OK: PennWell Corporation.

Willyard, C.H., & McClees, C.W. (1987). Motorola's technology roadmap process. Research Management, 13–19.

Christina Theodoraki, Karim Messeghem and Elias G. Carayannis

Entrepreneurial Ecosystem and Quadruple Helix: A Sub-ecosystem Approach

Abstract: While the concept entrepreneurial ecosystem is rapidly evolving, the academic literature highlights the lack of theoretical and methodological frameworks. This chapter aims to address these shortfalls by proposing a dynamic model of the ecosystem in the form of sub-ecosystems. This approach broadens the theoretical spectrum of the concept and highlights a new perspective of understanding. Building on the literature on the Quadruple Helix model,[1] a conceptual framework is developed to revisit the regional entrepreneurial ecosystem by highlighting five structuring sub-ecosystems. Our exploratory empirical study shows how the sub-ecosystems and their interactions have contributed to the dynamics of entrepreneurship in the South of France. This chapter thus strengthens the theorization of the ecosystem and provides useful recommendations for policymakers in designing entrepreneurship strategy.

Keywords: entrepreneurial ecosystem, modelling, sub-ecosystem, Quadruple Helix

1 Introduction

Many regions and cities around the world are striving to foster entrepreneurial activities by drawing inspiration from emblematic success stories such as Silicon Valley. To achieve this goal, public authorities offer incentives and mechanisms to facilitate the emergence and development of entrepreneurial ecosystems. However, while in the field of entrepreneurship, it is still unclear why some places "flourish" more than others (e.g., Silicon Valley, Route 128 in Boston, the Research Triangle in North Carolina, or Sophia Antipolis near Nice) (Cohen, 2006; Neck et al., 2004), some authors have suggested that it is essential to consider the regional context when examining entrepreneurial activity (Audretsch & Belitski, 2020).

Likewise, there is broad interest in structuring ecosystems by highlighting their characteristics (Isenberg, 2011; Spigel, 2017; Stam & Van de Ven, 2021). This reading is of great interest in understanding the constituent elements of ecosystems and how they

1 This study is funded by LabEx Entreprendre: government-funded through the National Research Agency as part of the "Invest in the Future" program reference: ANR-10-LABX-11–01.

Christina Theodoraki, IAE Aix-Marseille University, email: christina.theodoraki@iae-aix.com
Karim Messeghem, University of Montpellier, email: karim.messeghem@umontpelier.fr
Elias G. Carayannis, George Washington School of Business, email: caraye@gwu.edu

https://doi.org/10.1515/9783110791396-007

interact and influence entrepreneurial dynamics (Spigel, 2017). However, this reading remains relatively analytical (Stam & Van de Ven, 2021) and does not allow us to grasp the emergence and transformation of ecosystems (Roundy et al., 2018). To fill this gap, several authors (Roundy et al., 2018; Stam & Van de Ven, 2021) suggest returning to the foundations of the systemic approach, which proposes a reading that considers subsystems. An emerging stream of research represents ecosystems in the form of sub-ecosystems (Dubina et al., 2017; Harrington, 2017; Malecki, 2018; Theodoraki & Messeghem, 2017; Theodoraki & Catanzaro, 2022). A sub-ecosystem can be defined as a subset of the entrepreneurial ecosystem characterized by an identity and a logic of action. Structuring sub-ecosystems create the conditions for the dynamics of entrepreneurship, and specialized sub-ecosystems are 'tailored to specific industries, technologies, or interest areas' (Harrington, 2017: 13). Therefore, we formulate the following research question: *What are the structuring sub-ecosystems that enable the dynamics of entrepreneurship?* The objective of this chapter is to propose a dynamic model of the entrepreneurial ecosystem in the form of structuring sub-ecosystems.

To highlight the structuring sub-ecosystems, we use the Quadruple Helix model (Carayannis & Campbell, 2009; Carayannis et al., 2018a, 2018b, 2019; Dubina et al., 2017). This framework allows us to appreciate the dynamics of entrepreneurship in a region (Scaringella & Radziwon, 2018). More precisely, this model, inspired by the Triple Helix (Etzkowitz & Leydesdorff, 2000), considers that the dynamics of entrepreneurship are the result of interactions between universities, industry, government, and civil society. We argue that each of these four helices contributes to the emergence of a sub-ecosystem (Dubina et al., 2017; Harrington, 2017; Malecki, 2018) and that the interaction between the helices gives rise to the entrepreneurial support sub-ecosystem (Cloitre et al., 2023; Theodoraki & Messeghem, 2017). The latter includes actors and hybrid organizations (Etzkowitz et al., 2005) such as incubators, accelerators (Shankar & Shepherd, 2019), as well as funders like business angels or venture capital. It can be seen as a facilitating sub-system for the emergence and development of new firms. The dynamics of innovation require strong interaction between these sub-ecosystems and coordination that can be shared or assumed by a specific actor, such as the State in a *top-down* logic or entrepreneurs in a *bottom-up* logic (Etzkowitz et al., 2005; Feld, 2020). To illustrate this model, we rely on an exploratory case study conducted in the Montpellier area (South of France). While this ecosystem contributes to the emergence of innovative companies, these companies lack high-growth strategies and make limited contributions to regional development.

Hence, this conceptualization offers valuable insights into the crucial adaptations required to foster the dynamics of entrepreneurship. First, we propose developing a representation of the entrepreneurial ecosystem in the form of sub-ecosystems based on the Quadruple Helix model. Next, we introduce our exploratory qualitative methodology, which seeks to examine the "what" aspect by focusing on sub-ecosystems and the "how" aspect by emphasizing modes of interaction. Third, we detail the results of the study by showing how each helix contributes to the emergence of a sub-ecosystem that participates in the dynamics of entrepreneurship in the region. Finally, we conclude the study by discussing its results, its limitations, and prospects for future research.

2 Ecosystem Modelling in the Form of Sub-ecosystems

Recent work acknowledged the lack of a holistic and dynamic understanding of the entrepreneurial ecosystem (Theodoraki et al., 2022). After highlighting the need for such an understanding, we propose a model in the form of sub-ecosystems in connection with the Quadruple Helix (Cloitre et al., 2023).

2.1 From a Structural to a Dynamic Understanding

The literature on entrepreneurial ecosystems has been interested in the structuring of these ecosystems, focusing on two perspectives. One dominant perspective focuses on factors (elements, components, attributes, or domains) (Isenberg, 2011; Spigel, 2017; Stam & Van de Ven, 2021, see Table 1), while another emerging perspective focuses on sub-ecosystems (Harrington, 2017; Malecki, 2018; Theodoraki & Messeghem, 2017; Messeghem et al., 2023).

This representation of the ecosystem in the form of factors is useful for highlighting the salient elements, but it has an analytical character (Stam & Van de Ven, 2021) that can be contrasted with the dynamic and systemic understanding of the entrepreneurial ecosystem concept (Mack & Mayer, 2016; Roundy et al., 2018). As emphasized by Roundy et al. (2018), simply creating lists of attributes is inadequate and propose the adoption of a systemic approach as a more effective to comprehend the emergence of entrepreneurial ecosystems. This suggestion opens the way to a model in the form of sub-ecosystems.

This emerging line of research is reflected in work that aims to analyze the ecosystem in the form of subsystems (Dubina et al., 2017) or sub-ecosystems (Harrington, 2017; Malecki, 2018; Theodoraki & Messeghem, 2017). This approach is useful for demonstrating that the evolutionary dynamics of the system are linked to those of its subsets and their interactions. Harrington (2017, p. 10) defines sub-ecosystems as "ecosystems within the ecosystem that are tailored to specific industries, technologies, or interest areas." To illustrate, Harrington (2017) uses Kansas City as an example and highlights five sub-ecosystems: "art, commercialization of universities, business growth, education, and women." These sub-ecosystems are the result of the ecosystem's trajectory of evolution and specialization and take the form of clusters or networks of entrepreneurs (Harrington, 2017). Malecki (2018) shares this representation,

Table 1: Characterizations of Entrepreneurial Ecosystems.

Perspectives	Definition	Constituent elements	Authors
Components	This framework, [. . .], adopts the interorganizational community or field as the unit of analysis, and focuses on the core activities necessary to develop and commercialize a technological innovation. (p. 214)	Informal and formal Networks? university; government; professional and support services; capital services; talent pool.	Cohen (2006)
Domains	This entrepreneurship ecosystem consists of a dozen or so elements (which we consolidate into six domains for convenience sake; see the diagram) that, although they are idiosyncratic because they interact in very complex ways, are always present if entrepreneurship is self-sustaining. (p. 6)	Policy (leadership, government), finance, culture (success stories, societal norms), support (non-governmental institutions, support occupations, infrastructure), human capital (educational institutions, laboratories), markets (networks, clients).	Isenberg (2011)
Elements	The ten elements are operational constructs of the broader concepts of institutions and resources of an entrepreneurial ecosystem (Stam & Van de Ven, 2021, p. 813).	Framework conditions (formal institution, culture, physical infrastructure, demand), systemic conditions (entrepreneurial networks, leadership, finance, talent, knowledge, and support services).	Stam (2015); Stam and Van de Ven (2021)
Attributes	These attributes should be understood as the major factors that help create supportive environments for entrepreneurial activity and provide external resources that increase the competitiveness of new ventures. (p. 56)	Cultural (supportive culture, entrepreneurial stories) social (networks, talent pool, mentors, investment capital), material (policies, universities, infrastructure, open markets, support services).	Spigel (2017)

which favors a logic of specialization. In other words, certain sub-ecosystems have a structuring character and condition the dynamics of the ecosystem. The literature has tended to focus on two structuring sub-ecosystems (Clarysse et al., 2014; Dubina et al., 2017): the knowledge ecosystem and the business ecosystem. While they play a central role (Malecki, 2018), these two sub-ecosystems reveal only part of the structure of the entrepreneurial ecosystem (Spigel, 2017).

We propose a broader definition that considers the structuring and specialized sub-ecosystems. A sub-ecosystem can be defined as a localized subsystem that is open and interacts with other constituent sub-ecosystems of the entrepreneurial ecosystem, carried by, or linked to a player or a group of players contributing to the dynamics of entrepreneurship (Theodoraki & Catanzaro, 2022; Messeghem et al., 2023). The structuring sub-ecosystems create the conditions for the dynamics, and the specialized sub-ecosystems are "tailored to specific industries, technologies or interest areas" (Harrington, 2017: 13). What are the structuring sub-ecosystems? What framework should be used to characterize them? We suggest an understanding based on helices.[2]

2.2 A Model of Sub-ecosystems Based on the Quadruple Helix

In this study, we propose a model of the entrepreneurial ecosystem in the form of structuring sub-ecosystems. We propose articulating these sub-ecosystems in relation to the Quadruple Helix model. This model refers to families of players around which dynamics of co-opetition, co-specialization, and co-evolution (3C) are created (Carayannis et al., 2018a, 2018b, 2018c, 2019). Scaringella and Radziwon (2018), in their critical study of ecosystems, underline the value of using the Quadruple Helix model to understand the dynamics of the entrepreneurial ecosystem. Within the literature on ecosystems, a stream has developed around the Quadruple Helix model (Carayannis et al., 2018a, 2018b), which is an extension of the Triple Helix model developed by Etzkowitz and Leydesdorff (2000). These authors propose a better understanding of the dynamics within an innovation system. This systemic understanding emphasizes networked university-industry-government[3] relationships and the importance of hybrid organizations in supporting the firm creation process (Etzkowitz et al., 2005). In this model, universities are key players (Malecki, 2018). They are involved in a wide range of activities, commitments, collaborations, and knowledge transfer to other organizations, including industry and government (Etzkowitz & Leydesdorff, 2000). While Etzkowitz and Leydesdorff (2000) stress the important role of the university-industry-government triptych and its foothold in a societal context, they do not examine the interactions between these three helices and existing networks within civil society (Carayannis & Campbell, 2009). The Quadruple Helix model, anchored in systems theory, makes it possible to explore the relationships between systems and networks or clusters (Carayannis & Campbell, 2009) and thus to envisage an ecosystem model in the form of sub-ecosystems (Cloitre et al., 2023). While the Triple Helix was initially

2 This metaphor – derived from biology and, more precisely, from the structure of DNA.

3 University-industry-government terminology is generic and dependent on the institutional context (Etzkowitz et al., 2005). By universities, we refer to the academic world, which includes universities in the strict sense and other higher-education institutions as well as private and public research centers that contribute to the production of knowledge. By industry, we refer to companies (regardless of their size and maturity) and to business networks. By state or government, we refer to policymakers at the national, international, or local levels that have the capacity to lead public policies on entrepreneurship and innovation.

used to better understand the innovation process and is mainly applied to linear models, the Quadruple Helix allows us to understand more complex models. The initial model is extended to include a fourth helix based on media and public culture (summarized as civil society) (Carayannis & Campbell, 2009). The civil society helix refers to values, lifestyle, and culture. According to Carayannis and Campbell (2009: 206), "This fourth helix associates with 'media', 'creative industries', 'culture', 'values', 'life styles', and perhaps also the notion of the 'creative class' (a term, coined by Richard Florida, 2004). Plausibility for the explanatory potential of such a fourth helix are that culture and values, on the one hand, and the way how 'public reality' is being constructed and communicated by the media, on the other hand, influence every national innovation system."

However, research related to the Quadruple Helix has tended to focus on a limited number of subsystems. For example, Dubina et al. (2017) put forward an original model by focusing on two subsystems: the innovation subsystem and the entrepreneurial subsystem. This typology is in line with research linking the knowledge ecosystem and the business ecosystem (Clarysse et al., 2014). While these two subsystems play a structuring role, they are not sufficient to understand the dynamics of entrepreneurship. For example, Clarysse et al. (2014) suggest adding a third helix, a financial support network, although the empirical results are not conclusive.

The four helices and their interaction are likely to generate five sub-ecosystems. Based on the literature on sub-ecosystems and on the Quadruple Helix, we thus formulate two proposals. First, it is possible to associate each helix with a sub-ecosystem that conditions the dynamics of entrepreneurship in a region. Second, at the crossing of the helices emerges a sub-ecosystem made up of organizations that Etzkowitz et al. (2005) describe as hybrids, such as incubators, accelerators or even competitiveness clusters that can be described as an entrepreneurial support sub-ecosystem (Theodoraki & Messeghem, 2017).

The **institutional sub-ecosystem** plays a decisive role in facilitating or constraining the dynamics of entrepreneurship (Etzkowitz & Leydesdorff, 2000; Guerrero & Urbano, 2017). National and regional research and innovation strategies for smart specialization have been designed to create the conditions for collaboration between ecosystem players in a logic of vertical specialization (Foray, 2015). Political decision-makers, through their modes of governance and their incentive systems, play a catalytic role. They create the necessary conditions by generating infrastructures that are indispensable for the creation and dissemination of new knowledge and the development of new economic activities with growth potential.

The **knowledge sub-ecosystem** refers to organizations that contribute to the development of knowledge through training that fosters the research and development (R&D) of human capital. Dubina et al. (2017) refer to subsystems of innovation or research or R&D. According to Clarysse et al. (2014: 1165), universities and public research organizations play a decisive role in the dynamics of entrepreneurship: "Both linkages among firms and with universities and public research organizations as well as intense labor mobility across different players facilitate collective learning and increase the speed of innovation diffusion." Beyond universities and public research organizations, other players, such as start-ups and established companies, have a decisive role.

The **business sub-ecosystem** refers to the players and activities deployed to create or co-create value (Jacobides et al., 2018; Moore, 1993). According to Scaringella and Radziwon (2018), the creation and appropriation of value through innovation are the main objectives of this ecosystem. It is a network of firms characterized by proximity. Other research focuses on co-opetition relationships between firms (Moore, 1993; Theodoraki, 2020; Theodoraki et al., 2022). For Clarysse et al. (2014), the business ecosystem differs from the innovation ecosystem in terms of the direction given to markets and opportunities. Certain focal companies, called "hub" or "keystone" companies, play a central role by contributing to the mobility of knowledge, the appropriability of innovation, the stability of networks and the pursuit of new business opportunities (Clarysse et al., 2014).

The **socio-cultural sub-ecosystem** indicates the degree of openness and the capacity to generate innovations. Norms, values, and beliefs play a decisive role in fostering innovation and entrepreneurship in a region (Carayannis et al., 2018a, 2018b, 2019). For example, Scaringella and Radziwon (2018: 63) evoke the role of the base of the pyramid in the context of emerging or developing countries. Other authors take a more elitist view. Florida (2002) defends the thesis that certain social groups contribute to the dynamics of entrepreneurship in regions because of their creative potential. This "creative class" plays a driving role in a context marked by tolerance and openness to diversity (Audretsch & Belitski, 2020). More broadly, the cultural and artistic vitality in a region encourages the development of new ideas and pollination between different fields. This sub-ecosystem refers to values conducive to the dynamics of entrepreneurship. Spigel (2017) insists on the existence of an entrepreneurial culture forged by entrepreneurial successes in a region. The portrayal of innovation and entrepreneurship by the media contributes to the reinforcement of this culture.

At the crossroads of the four helices, a structuring sub-ecosystem – the **entrepreneurial support sub-ecosystem** – takes shape. Theodoraki and Messeghem (2017) define this sub-ecosystem as a system comprising players who support companies in the emergence or development phase. This subsystem is characterized by a high degree of hybridization. Etzkowitz et al. (2005: 413) refer to this hybridization phenomenon within the Triple Helix model: 'Changes in triple helix relations allow us to track the emergence of innovation mechanisms. Hybrid organizations are created by synthesizing elements of different institutional spheres. The incubator is one of several triple helix hybrids such as the technology transfer office and the venture capital firm. McAdam et al. (2016), in their multi-level model, also defend this idea of hybridization. Initiatives can be driven by the academic world (academic incubators, transfer structures, etc.), by public authorities (incubators, competitiveness clusters, etc.), by large companies (accelerators) or even by civil society (social innovation platforms). Interactions between these players are essential and often take the form of co-opetitive relationships (Theodoraki, 2020). Competitive relationships can be observed in the selection of projects. The credibility of these players resides in their capacity to select and support promising projects (Theodoraki et al., 2022). These players may also have an interest in collaborating to facilitate their access to resources and networks (Theodoraki & Catanzaro, 2022). Public authorities can encourage the implementation of coordination actions.

Figure 1 proposes a model in the form of sub-ecosystems. The dynamics of entrepreneurship appear at the heart of the model as the result of the interactions between the five sub-ecosystems.

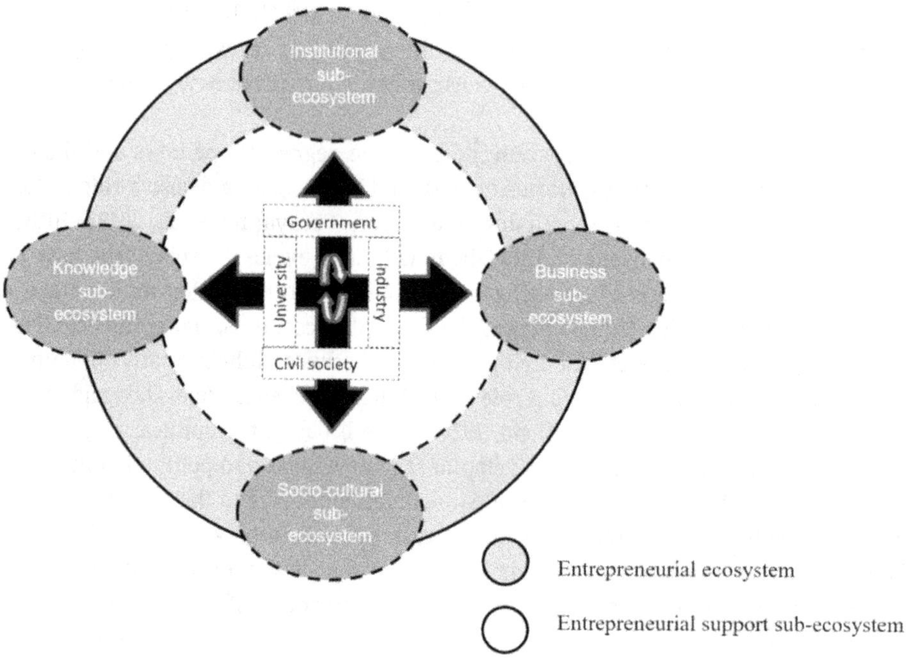

Figure 1: Model of the Ecosystem in the Form of Sub-ecosystems, adapted by Messeghem et al. (2023).

3 Method

This research employs a qualitative research design through an in-depth examination of an exploratory case study. This method is particularly suited for analyzing concepts that are emerging, non-linear, or have received limited attention in existing literature (Miles & Huberman, 1994; Yin, 2018). By adopting this approach, our aim is to comprehensively investigate the ecosystem as a whole, taking into account its dynamic and complex nature (Yin, 2018). Instead of delving into the intricate dynamic relationships within each sub-ecosystem, our objective is to illustrate and explore the "what" aspect by highlighting various types of sub-ecosystems, and the "how" aspect by emphasizing their dynamics, drawing upon the Quadruple Helix model (Carayannis et al., 2018a, 2018b, 2019).

3.1 Case Study

Our illustrative case study draws on the Montpellier metropolitan area, as outlined in Table 2. The selection of this area is justified by the presence of numerous actors and factors, as well as the emergence of original initiatives (Cohen, 2006). Montpellier, the seventh-largest city in France, encompasses a total population of 607,896 inhabitants (with 281,613 inhabitants residing within the city limits). The area is characterized by significant population growth, with an average annual growth rate of 1.3% according to INSEE. Moreover, Montpellier has a predominantly young population, with individuals under the age of 30 comprising 43% of the total population. The city combines a vibrant entrepreneurial ecosystem with a challenging economic situation, marked by a notably high unemployment rate of 21.5%. It is recognized as the fifth-largest research site in France, housing 7,500 researchers, 70,000 students, eight competitiveness clusters, and several R&D centers. Over the past three decades, the region has implemented ambitious policies to foster innovation and entrepreneurship. In 1987, the metropolitan government established an innovation incubator that achieved the distinction of being ranked the world's second-leading start-up incubator in 2018. Since 2014, Montpellier's ecosystem has been awarded the FrenchTech label by the French government, recognizing it as one of the most dynamic entrepreneurial ecosystems in France in terms of entrepreneur mobilization, fundraising, and the number of rapidly growing start-ups.

Table 2: Socio-demographics of Montpellier.

	Montpellier	France
Population in 2014	281 613	66 361 587
Population change: average annual rate between 2011 and 2016, in %	1.3	0.4
Share of tax-paying households taxed in 2016, in %	46	52
Median disposable income per unit of consumption in 2016, in euros	17 814	20 340
Poverty rate in 2016, in %	26	14.02
Unemployment rate of 15- to 64-year-olds in 2016, in %	21.5	14.1

Source: *INSEE.*

3.2 Data Collection

The data collection was based on 48 semi-directive interviews with major players in the entrepreneurial ecosystem of the metropolitan area (including institutions, academic organizations, funding agencies, entrepreneurial support providers, and entrepreneurs). Respondents were selected based on their location in the Montpellier metropolitan area, their belonging to the local entrepreneurial ecosystem or their close collaboration with a regional player.

The historical observation of regional entrepreneurial activity was deepened by the semi-directive interviews, which were conducted face-to-face between June 2013 and November 2014[4] with the help of a guide outlining the organizational characteristics of the interviewee (services, specificities, strategy, etc.) and of the entrepreneurial ecosystem (composition, interaction with other players, types of relationships, etc.). The interviews were fully recorded (with an average duration of 82 min), transcribed and coded using NVivo12 software (Bazeley & Jackson, 2013). In addition, supplementary secondary data were collected to enable data triangulation (site visits; participant and non-participant observations in meetings, events and working groups within the ecosystem; secondary sources; and documents such as brochures, annual reports, press releases, and archives). This approach allowed us to further validate the results of our research (Jick, 1979).

3.3 Data Analysis

The data collected underwent thematic content analysis that structures the text based on interviews, extracts key themes, and identifies recurring patterns within the entire dataset (Miles & Huberman, 1994). The data analysis process involved two stages: primary coding focused on the theme of the entrepreneurial ecosystem, encompassing its structure, interactions, and overall representation. In the secondary coding stage, the analysis incorporated the Quadruple Helix model (consisting of universities, industry, government, and civil society) and explored ecosystem dynamics such as co-opetition, co-specialization, and co-evolution (Carayannis et al., 2018a, 2018b, 2018c, 2019).

During the phase of decontextualization, nodes were established using open coding, which allowed for the identification and grouping of emerging concepts. This process involved analyzing the data without specific contextual constraints. In the subsequent phase of recontextualization, axial coding was employed to categorize, group, and reorganize the codes by identifying similarities or differences among them, ultimately creating overarching themes. At the same time, representative verbatim

4 The law on regional boundaries was passed on January 16, 2015 (law no. 2015-29), giving birth to the Occitania Region, the result of a merger between Midi-Pyrénées and Languedoc-Roussillon.

quotes were cross-tabulated using the query wizard feature in NVivo12 software to facilitate the synthesis of key codes and enable the presentation of results in a structured manner.

4 Presentation of Results

After showing how helices and their interactions contribute to the emergence and development of sub-ecosystems, we will highlight the dynamics of the ecosystem.

4.1 Demonstrating the Sub-ecosystems and Their Interactions

From Government to the Institutional Sub-Ecosystem

The institutional sub-ecosystem[5] comprises policymakers, administrations, agencies and other structures that contribute to the definition and implementation of the innovation and entrepreneurship policy. Under the impetus of Georges Frêche, Mayor of Montpellier from 1977 to 2004 and then President of the Languedoc-Roussillon Region from 2004 to 2010, an innovation and entrepreneurship policy was conducted proactively and consistently. According to most interviewees, local political decision-makers are in charge of steering the ecosystem. Their objective is to encourage the creation of innovative companies through various mechanisms. The region[6] is mobilizing resources, particularly European resources, within the framework of the *Smart Specialization Strategy*, with entrepreneurship and innovation as the strategic line of action. An official in charge of the region's economic development confirms that "we are going to take on the role of coordinator, facilitator, but obviously this cannot be done without the partners. It's the very idea of a leader or conductor [. . .]. In the entrepreneurial ecosystem, public policies can be seen, for example, as being at the origin of the creation of an environment favorable to entrepreneurship." This orchestration at the regional level is not without its problems. Over the period 2014 to 2020, tensions emerged between the region and the metropolitan area.

---

5 In the French context, it is difficult to circumscribe the institutional sub-ecosystem at the local level insofar as institutional arrangements are designed at both the national and local levels.
6 The NOTRe law (New Territorial Organization of the Republic) of August 7, 2015, has strengthened the economic competence of the region.

From Universities to the Knowledge Sub-ecosystem

The knowledge sub-ecosystem is made up of universities, schools, and research organizations, which contribute to the creation and development of new knowledge and aim to implement actions to promote knowledge dissemination. The Montpellier metropolitan area benefits from a highly dynamic knowledge ecosystem with a university campus and the presence of the main research centers such as INRA and the CNRS. The aim of this sub-ecosystem is to raise awareness regarding and provide training in entrepreneurship and innovation; to provide students with pre-support; to transfer and harness scientific knowledge; and to market technologies. It is characterized by a diversity of players and strong coordination promoted through structures such as PEPITE and SATT.

The creation of the PEPITE scheme has encouraged students to embark on the entrepreneurial adventure. The head of an academic organization states, "Our missions are at the same time information about entrepreneurship, it is entrepreneurship awareness, it is entrepreneurship training, and it is pre-support." Beyond raising awareness, the university components (e.g., IAE, Faculty of Medicine, and Polytech) play a crucial role in training students in entrepreneurship by offering courses, hosting events (e.g., start-up weekends) and providing tools (e.g., serious games).

Since 2013, with the emergence of the SATTs,[7] we have seen strengthened incentives to market academic innovations. The number of patents is an indicator of the capacity for invention and commercialization. Over the last 5 years, Montpellier has registered 139 patents. Moreover, the creation of incubators within higher-education institutions also contributes to the innovation dynamic. As the head of the academic incubator explains, "There are a lot of specific characteristics around the cultures and themes of each institution, so there is a network of partners around the institutions, there is research in most of these institutions, there is a pool of students who must also be made aware of innovative entrepreneurship. These ecosystems lend themselves particularly well to this, and it can even be a vector of pedagogical innovation with project modes that can be triggered from the incubators, with a direct influence on the teaching that is carried out."

From Industry to the Business Sub-Ecosystem

The business sub-ecosystem brings together all economic players and all actions implemented by companies to develop common projects supporting growth, innovation, and sector development. It is worth noting the presence of major players, particularly in the high-tech field. As early as 1965, IBM chose to set up in Montpellier. Dell, in the 1990s, and Alstom Grid, more recently, consolidated the digital transformation of the Montpellier region. However, relations between large companies and start-ups re-

7 SATT: Technology Transfer Accelerator Offices (*Société d'Accélération de Transfert Technologique*).

main relatively underdeveloped. In response, initiatives have been launched to foster these relationships; for example, *Bigup For Startup* was created in 2015 as part of the *FrenchTech* in Montpellier. The diversity of the business ecosystem offers many opportunities for entrepreneurs to collaborate. One entrepreneur who benefited from support in the sub-ecosystem details these collaborations and contacts: "There were hundreds of outsourced players who were involved in the project as external services (lawyers, accountants, consulting firms, specialists in the healthcare field to define the strategy, more specialized service providers in relation to IT development, the creation of the website, a secure database including the CNIL, etc.)." The business sub-ecosystem can be illustrated by various business networks, such as the *FrenchTech* label awarded to the Montpellier metropolitan area, which brings together players in the digital sector and associates public authorities, industry members, the media, and universities.

From Civil Society to the Socio-cultural Sub-ecosystem

The socio-cultural life[8] is dynamic with related entrepreneurial activity. One entity, *Context'Art*, specializes in art-related projects. This dynamism has helped attract companies such as Ubisoft. Players in the ecosystem, particularly political decision-makers, are highly committed to regional marketing that aims to strengthen the region's attractiveness to companies, entrepreneurs, and investors. This is reflected in a massive effort in communication with a strong presence in the media and on social networks. The media also contributes to regional attractiveness and the dissemination of an entrepreneurial culture. These communication efforts are essential to the sustainability of the ecosystem by promoting the opening of the region. The dynamism of the ecosystem is linked to the many events that help spread an entrepreneurial culture, such as the event "A Tramway Named Startup." Organized every year by the Montpellier metropolitan area, this event brings together the main players in the ecosystem and aims to make the entrepreneurial adventure accessible to all citizens in the region.

The entrepreneurial culture is created and disseminated with the help of the media coverage of success stories such as the *MedTech*[9] company, while certain failures, such as the 2019 bankruptcy of the very promising company Care Labs,[10] are left in the shadows. However, there is a growing gap between the "start-up city" and the

---

8 The associative world is highly dynamic, with 2600 associations active in the socio-cultural universe. This importance can be put into perspective with the weight of the Social and Solidarity Economy, which represents 15% of employment in Montpellier compared to 10.5% in Toulouse.

9 MedTech was created by Bertin Nahum, ranked fourth-best technology entrepreneur in the world (in 2012 by Discovery Series) behind only Americans Steve Jobs, Mark Zuckerberg and James Cameron.

10 Care Labs was a start-up created in June 2014 by Vincent Daffourd, issuer of the Chèque Santé (healthcare voucher) (€7.2 million in funds raised and less than €20,000 in revenue).

rest of the Montpellier region. We may wonder about the impact and sustainability of these efforts to build an entrepreneurial culture. Public authorities are sensitive to this lack of inclusion and are developing and supporting entrepreneurial actions in working-class neighborhoods.

Entrepreneurial Support: A Cross-functional Sub-Ecosystem

Organizations involved in support are linked to the four other structuring sub-ecosystems. Each sub-ecosystem has contributed to the emergence of hybrid structures to foster the dynamics of entrepreneurship.[11] This sub-ecosystem is linked to the will of the players in the ecosystem to create an environment favorable to the creation and development of new companies. This common will has given rise to several initiatives and, in particular, the creation of support networks that help structure and unite players involved in entrepreneurial support. These players have a decisive role in strengthening networking, access to human and financial resources and learning dynamics. The mobilization of these different players is essential to the development and success of an innovative project in a logic of collective innovation. The Synersud[12] network is a good illustration of this collaborative dynamic.

4.2 The Dynamics of the Entrepreneurial Ecosystem

This section highlights the dynamics of the ecosystem through three modes (3C). The first mode concerns the **dynamics of co-opetition**, or simultaneous cooperation and competition. The dynamics of cooperation are present in the region, as noted by the director of a technology transfer company: "People work in good intelligence, even set up common actions." In parallel to these actions that showcase the characteristics and assets of the region, there is competition between the players mainly due to the lack of financial resources, according to the manager of a rural support structure: "And then of course there is competition because today we have the same amount of cake, except that there are more of us. And so, we have a cake, 'the subsidies', and this cake, it gets smaller or even stays the same, while there are more people who

11 Knowledge sub-ecosystem: Languedoc-Roussillon Incubation, an academic incubator, which has been integrated in the SATT AxLR. Institutional sub-ecosystem: Business & Innovation Center – BIC of Montpellier (Montpellier metropolitan area) or REALIS cluster (region). Business sub-ecosystem: Leader network that unites companies with growth potential or corporate incubators, such as the Village by CA. Socio-cultural sub-ecosystem: Alter'Incub.

12 The Synersud network of incubators and business centres, created in 1999 (which represented the former Languedoc-Roussillon), was merged with the Rezopep network (which represented the former Midi-Pyrénées) to create the network of incubators and business centres in Occitanie, RésO IP+, in December 2018. This network has united 21 support structures at the regional level and created 2200 companies and more than 8000 engineering jobs, according to a Synersud network 2013 report.

come to eat it, and so of course the slices are smaller." Competition is expressed within the ecosystem but also between regions. It is competition in terms of image that is accentuated by the adoption of the same strategy by several regions. A consultant specializing in social networks observes that

> most regions in France and even in Europe have the same policy as Languedoc-Roussillon. This is what I call competition in terms of image. That is to say that all of them, well, I mean me, I'm relaying articles from Montpellier Unlimited and the LR Region that talk about the initiatives carried out in Languedoc and their successes, but on the same day I'm going to have other articles from Midi-Pyrénées, from start-ups in Toulouse, in Paris.

The second mode corresponds to the **dynamics of co-specialization**, which is reflected in a concomitant specialization of the players and sectors of activity and reinforces the adaptability of the ecosystem. The *Smart Specialization Strategy* was an opportunity for the region to start considering the sectors at the heart of its competitiveness. All players were mobilized to build a common strategy. Representatives of the knowledge, business, and entrepreneurial support sub-ecosystem have been very active in the working groups. This region has chosen to retain seven major areas of innovation, including entrepreneurship and innovation. This line of focus has been considered "a cross-functional area that surrounds the other areas and allows the mobilization of European credits for the benefit of companies and structures implementing social innovation, marketing, etc."[13]

Montpellier's ecosystem has been built up in connection with several sectors, such as healthcare and digital technology, and has contributed to the emergence of specialized subsystems, such as *FrenchSouth.digital*, which has been renamed *Digital 113*, and *Montpellier Capital Santé*, in connection with the *FrenchTech* label. The logic of specialization is highly visible in the social and solidarity economy. This sub-ecosystem contributed to the emergence of the first social innovation incubator, Alter-Incub, in 2007. Business leaders contribute to the creation of numerous business networks, such as *Leader*. All players have to find their place and contribute to creating value for the region. One entrepreneur confirms the importance of finding one's place in order to co-exist with the other players by adopting a collaborative approach that creates value within the ecosystem: "We know this environment very well, the operations behind the scenes, the practices, methods, and goals, which helped us find our place in this ecosystem, that we can really bring the added value of our ways of doing things, and it was essentially to make the link between communities, citizens, and industry, through participatory processes."

---

13 Seven areas of innovation: (1) H2O: large and small water cycle; (2) industrial and energy transition; (3) innovative and targeted therapies – diagnosis; (4) data acquisition, data processing and visualization of digital data; (5) innovative and sustainable production and processing of Mediterranean and tropical cultures; (6) coastal economy; (7) entrepreneurship and innovation. Source: www.3s-en-lr.com

The third mode refers to the **dynamics of co-evolution** of the players and their interactions over time. This mode contributes to the creation of a collective competence within the region and a converging long-term vision, according to an innovation facilitator: If we go back to the local ecosystem, the former mayor of Montpellier, Georges Frêche, made the observation when he took over the town hall that we don't have any major accounts [. . .] So, he turned the corner 30 years ago so that everything must be done for innovation. Why did he do it? Because here we have the grey matter, we have a lot of research labs in a lot of fields, and we have to exploit that and make it an economic asset of the region.

This dynamic accentuates the need for a complementary structuring of players to avoid the "millefeuille" effect. According to the coordinator of the support network, The danger, what we really need to avoid is the "millefeuille", which is totally counterproductive [. . .] however, in an entrepreneurial support ecosystem there have to be areas of intersection [. . .] what is needed is the overall philosophy which has to be in the spirit of open innovation and collaborative work. We have to succeed in working together, and we have to do it in good intelligence. In other words, you can't add on extra layers and do the same job six times because that would cost the community a fortune.

All three modes highlight the dynamic and complex nature of the ecosystem. These modes concern both sub-ecosystems and the ecosystem as a whole. They can thus intervene at all levels and at any phase of the ecosystem's life cycle.

5 Discussion

In this chapter, we aimed to represent the entrepreneurial ecosystem by advancing a renewed understanding in the form of sub-ecosystems based on the Quadruple Helix. This new model underlines the importance of the logics of co-opetition, co-specialization, and co-evolution implemented in a region (Carayannis et al., 2018b; Carayannis & Rakhmatullin, 2014; Theodoraki, 2020; Theodoraki et al., 2022). We have highlighted five structuring sub-ecosystems that create the necessary conditions for the dynamics of entrepreneurship in a region. The ecosystemic approach led us to take into account both the sub-ecosystems and the interactions between them. The case of Montpellier has proved particularly relevant to highlight the co-construction process that took place over 30 years and the complexity of an ecosystem characterized by dynamism in terms of business creation and real difficulties in terms of development.

This research has theoretical and managerial implications. From a theoretical point of view, this research revisits the concept of ecosystem. We go beyond the structural understanding in the form of attributes (Spigel, 2017). Drawing on the contributions of Roundy et al. (2018), we show that the ecosystem has an analytical character and is not sufficiently dynamic (Stam & Van de Ven, 2021). As suggested by several authors, we propose a representation in the form of sub-ecosystems (Dubina et al., 2017; Harrington, 2017; Malecki, 2018; Theodoraki & Messeghem, 2017). This reading offers interesting perspectives for understanding the evolution of an ecosystem (Harrington, 2017; Mack & Mayer, 2016). We have defined sub-ecosystems in greater depth and proposed differentiating them according to whether they have a structuring character or are the result of a dynamic of specialization. We chose to focus on the structuring sub-ecosystems that can be highlighted using the Quadruple Helix. More precisely, we selected five structuring sub-ecosystems, four directly linked to each helix and one resulting from interaction and hybridization (Etzkowitz et al., 2005). The institutional, knowledge, business, and socio-cultural sub-ecosystems are necessary but not sufficient. Their interactions create the conditions for the emergence of the entrepreneurial support sub-ecosystem. The approach focusing on sub-ecosystems offers promising research perspectives, particularly for understanding ecosystem evolution and trajectories (Mack & Mayer, 2016; Radinger-Peer et al., 2018). Indeed, as Harrington (2017) points out, the multiplication of sub-ecosystems reflects an indicator of the degree of maturity of ecosystems. It would be interesting to extend these research avenues by showing how the evolution of sub-ecosystems and interactions influence ecosystem trajectories and enable their evaluation and outcomes.

Another perspective is emerging around evaluation, to understand how these different sub-ecosystems impact innovation dynamics. It seems possible to evaluate the ecosystem through the achievements of its sub-ecosystems (Oh et al., 2016). Guerrero and Urbano (2017) proposed to measure the impact of agents in the triple helix model on performance in terms of entrepreneurial innovations in an emerging country. Similarly, Carayannis et al. (2018a) constructed a composite index based on the Quadruple Helix model. These approaches are at a national level and are more difficult to apply at a regional level. Other authors have built models for assessing the entrepreneurial ecosystem at the local level. Stam (2015) suggests some fifteen indicators to measure the ten characteristics of the entrepreneurial ecosystem (entrepreneurial culture, networks, formal institutions, etc.). Re-organizing these elements, Vedula and Kim (2019) design the regional entrepreneurial ecosystem quality index. This index is built upon five key characteristics: (i) supportive entrepreneurial culture, (ii) access to finance, (iii) availability of human capital, (iv) innovation capacity, and (v) formal support organizations. Stangler and Bell-Masterson (2015) also propose around ten indicators grouped around four dimensions: density, fluidity, connectivity and diversity. Drawing on these works and our own study, we can propose five types of indicators linked to the structuring sub-ecosystems of the innovation and entrepreneurship ecosystem and their objectives (see Table 3).

This research also presents managerial contributions, especially for policymakers who wish to create or develop entrepreneurial ecosystems in their region. The replication of emblematic successes is only an illusion (Isenberg, 2011). The challenge is to take into account the specific characteristics of each region. Analysis focusing on sub-

Table 3: Ecosystem Measurements.

Sub-ecosystems / Helix	Aim	Indicators
Institutional / Government	Offering quality infrastructures and promoting and supporting the dynamics of entrepreneurship and innovation in a region	– Infrastructure quality – Amount of aid devoted to innovation and entrepreneurship – Regional competitiveness index
Knowledge / University	Promote the creation and dissemination of knowledge in the form of technology transfer and academic spin-offs	– Number of researchers – Number of patents – Number of scientific publications
Business / Industry	Develop joint initiatives to promote growth, innovation and industry development	– Number of innovative companies created – Number of jobs created
Sociocultural / Civil society	Promoting tolerance, openness and an entrepreneurial culture	– Share of foreign population – Share of university graduates in the population – Percentage of gay marriages – Number of events/ participants
Entrepreneurial support	Providing support for businesses	– Number of support programs – Amount of funds raised

ecosystems demonstrates the conditions of the dynamics of entrepreneurship based on a holistic and idiosyncratic understanding. The success of the ecosystem relies as much on each sub-ecosystem as on their interactions. The proposed model allows us to map the ecosystem and can foster debate on the strengths and weaknesses of a region. Within an intelligent specialization strategy (Foray, 2015), it could be used to identify the most promising specialized sub-ecosystems in terms of innovation.

This research has limitations that offer promising research avenues. We focused on a single region to assess the relevance of our model in the form of sub-ecosystems. It would be interesting to conduct a study comparing ecosystems of equivalent sizes in France and abroad to better understand the roles of each sub-ecosystem and interactions. Last, we did not test the relationship between the characteristics of the sub-ecosystems and ecosystem performance. Drawing in particular on the work of Stam and Van de Ven (2021), a promising research program is emerging to assess sub-ecosystems and their influences on the dynamics of entrepreneurship.

References

Audretsch, D.B., & Belitski, M. (2020). Towards an entrepreneurial ecosystem typology for regional economic development: The role of creative class and entrepreneurship. Regional Studies, 1–22.

Bazeley, P., & Jackson, K. (2013). Qualitative data analysis with NVivo. New York, NY: Sage Publications Limited.

Carayannis, E., & Campbell, D. (2009). 'Mode 3' and 'Quadruple Helix': Toward a 21st century fractal innovation ecosystem. International Journal of Technology Management, 3(4), 201–234.

Carayannis, E.G., Goletsis, Y., & Grigoroudis, E. (2018a). Composite innovation metrics: MCDA and the quadruple innovation helix framework. Technological Forecasting and Social Change, 131, 4–17.

Carayannis, E.G., Grigoroudis, E., Campbell, D.F., Meissner, D., & Stamati, D. (2018b). The ecosystem as helix: An exploratory theory-building study of regional co-opetitive entrepreneurial ecosystems as Quadruple/Quintuple Helix Innovation Models. R&D Management, 48, 148–162.

Carayannis, E.G., Grigoroudis, E., Campbell, D.F., Meissner, D., & Stamati, D. (2018c). 'Mode 3'universities and academic firms: Thinking beyond the box trans-disciplinarity and nonlinear innovation dynamics within coopetitive entrepreneurial ecosystems. International Journal of Technology Management, 77, 145–185.

Carayannis, E.G., Grigoroudis, E., Stamati, D., & Valvi, T. (2019). Social business model innovation: A quadruple/quintuple helix-based social innovation ecosystem. IEEE Transactions on Engineering Management, 68(1), 235–248.

Carayannis, E.G., & Rakhmatullin, R. (2014). The quadruple/quintuple innovation helixes and smart specialisation strategies for sustainable and inclusive growth in Europe and beyond. Journal of the Knowledge Economy, 5, 212–239.

Clarysse, B., Wright, M., Bruneel, J., & Mahajan, A. (2014). Creating value in ecosystems: Crossing the chasm between knowledge and business ecosystems. Research Policy, 43, 1164–1176.

Cloitre, A., Dos Santos Paulino, V., & Theodoraki, C. (2023). The quadruple/quintuple helix model in entrepreneurial ecosystems: an institutional perspective on the space case study. R&D Management, 53(4), 675–694.

Cohen, B. (2006). Sustainable valley entrepreneurial ecosystems. Business Strategy and the Environment, 15, 1–4.

Dubina, I.N., Campbell, D.F., Carayannis, E.G., Chub, A.A., Grigoroudis, E., & Kozhevina, O.V. (2017). The balanced development of the spatial innovation and entrepreneurial ecosystem based on principles of the systems compromise: A conceptual framework. Journal of the Knowledge Economy, 8, 438–455.

Etzkowitz, H., de Mello, J.M.C., & Almeida, M. (2005). Towards "meta-innovation" in Brazil: The evolution of the incubator and the emergence of a triple helix. Research Policy, 34, 411–424.

Etzkowitz, H., & Leydesdorff, L. (2000). The dynamics of innovation: From National Systems and "Mode 2" to a Triple Helix of university–industry–government relations. Research Policy, 29, 109–123.

Feld, B. (2020). Startup communities: Building an entrepreneurial ecosystem in your city. John Wiley & Sons.

Florida, R. (2002). The rise of the creative class. Washington Monthly, Washington, DC.

Foray, D. (2015). Smart specialisation: Opportunities and challenges for regional innovation policy. Abingdon, UK: Routledge.

Guerrero, M., & Urbano, D. (2017). The impact of Triple Helix agents on entrepreneurial innovations' performance: An inside look at enterprises located in an emerging economy. Technological Forecasting and Social Change, 119, 294–309.

Harrington, K. (2017). Entrepreneurial ecosystem momentum and maturity the important role of entrepreneur development organizations and their activities. SSRN Electronic Journal, 1–30.

Isenberg, D. (2011). The entrepreneurship ecosystem strategy as a new paradigm for economic policy: Principles for cultivating entrepreneurship. Dublin, Ireland: Institute of International European Affairs.
Jacobides, M.G., Cennamo, C., & Gawer, A. (2018). Towards a theory of ecosystems. Strategic Management Journal, 39, 2255–2276.
Jick, T.D. (1979). Mixing qualitative and quantitative methods: Triangulation in action. Administrative Science Quarterly, 24, 602–611.
Mack, E., & Mayer, H. (2016). The evolutionary dynamics of entrepreneurial ecosystems. Urban Studies, 53, 2118–2133.
Malecki, E.J. (2018). Entrepreneurship and entrepreneurial ecosystems. Geography Compass, 12, e12359.
McAdam, M., Miller, K., & McAdam, R. (2016). Situated regional university incubation: A multi-level stakeholder perspective. Technovation, 50–51, 69–78.
Messeghem, K., Theodoraki, C., & Carayannis, E.G. (2023). Pour une modélisation de l'écosystème entrepreneurial sous forme de sous-écosystèmes: Apport de l'approche des systèmes complexes adaptatifs. Management International, 27(2), 93–104.
Miles, M.B., & Huberman, A.M. (1994). Qualitative data analysis: An expanded sourcebook. New York, NY: Sage.
Moore, J. (1993). Predators and prey: A new ecology of competition. Harvard Business Review, 71, 75–86.
Neck, H.M., Meyer, G.D., Cohen, B., & Corbett, A.C. (2004). An entrepreneurial system view of new venture creation. Journal of Small Business Management, 42, 190–208.
Oh, D.S., Phillips, F., Park, S., & Lee, E. (2016). Innovation ecosystems: A critical examination. Technovation, 54, 1–6.
Radinger-Peer, V., Sedlacek, S., & Goldstein, H. (2018). The path-dependent evolution of the entrepreneurial ecosystem (EE) – Dynamics and region-specific assets of the case of Vienna (Austria). European Planning Studies, 26, 1499–1518.
Roundy, P.T., Bradshaw, M., & Brockman, B.K. (2018). The emergence of entrepreneurial ecosystems: A complex adaptive systems approach. Journal of Business Research, 86, 1–10.
Scaringella, L., & Radziwon, A. (2018). Innovation, entrepreneurial, knowledge, and business ecosystems: Old wine in new bottles? Technological Forecasting and Social Change, 136, 59–87.
Shankar, R.K., & Shepherd, D.A. (2019). Accelerating strategic fit or venture emergence: Different paths adopted by corporate accelerators. Journal of Business Venturing, 34(5), 105886.
Spigel, B. (2017). The relational organization of entrepreneurial ecosystems. Entrepreneurship Theory and Practice, 41, 49–72.
Stam, E. (2015). Entrepreneurial ecosystems and regional policy: A sympathetic critique. European Planning Studies, 23, 1759–1769.
Stam, E., & Van de Ven, A. (2021). Entrepreneurial ecosystem elements. Small Business Economics, 56, 809–832.
Stangler, D., & Bell-Masterson, J. (2015). Measuring an entrepreneurial ecosystem. Ewing Marion Kauffman Foundation.
Theodoraki, C. (2020). A holistic approach to incubator strategies in the entrepreneurial support ecosystem. M@n@gement, 23, 13–27.
Theodoraki, C., & Catanzaro, A. (2022). Widening the borders of entrepreneurial ecosystem through the international lens. The Journal of Technology Transfer, 47(2), 383–406.
Theodoraki, C., & Messeghem, K. (2017). Exploring the entrepreneurial ecosystem in the field of entrepreneurial support: A multi-level approach. International Journal of Entrepreneurship and Small Business, 31, 47–66.

Theodoraki, C., Messeghem, K., & Audretsch, D.B. (2022). The effectiveness of incubators' co-opetition strategy in the entrepreneurial ecosystem: Empirical evidence from France. IEEE Transactions on Engineering Management, 69(4), 1781–1794.
Vedula, S., & Kim, P.H. (2019). Gimme shelter or fade away: The impact of regional entrepreneurial ecosystem quality on venture survival. Industrial and Corporate Change, 28(4), 827–854.
Yin, R.K. (2018). Case study research: Design and methods. Thousand Oaks, CA: SAGE Publications.

Dax Jacobson

Rural Everyday Entrepreneurial Ecosystems and Higher Education

Abstract: The entrepreneurial ecosystem concept still has more to give us – as researchers, policymakers, and entrepreneurs. Entrepreneurship and entrepreneurial ecosystems in all contexts, but especially in rural contexts, require multiple types of financing, human capital, infrastructure, favorable policies, and ecosystem builders. In this chapter I suggest we consider this combination of factors as critical to *rural everyday entrepreneurial ecosystems* and suggest that higher education institutions remain an understudied and underutilized provider of these factors and members of these ecosystems. I define and briefly review the research on *entrepreneurial ecosystems, everyday* entrepreneurs, and the *rural* context before reviewing some of the roles role higher education institutions are (and are not) playing in these ecosystems.

Keywords: rural everyday entrepreneurial ecosystems, higher education

1 Entrepreneurial Ecosystems

Entrepreneurship does not happen in a vacuum. In addition to the innovative minds and actions of entrepreneurs, access to different kinds of financing, technology, employees, the impact of policies and regulations and more can make it easier or harder for entrepreneurs to start, sustain, and stop businesses (and then do it all over again). In both researchers' and policymakers' quest to find the secret sauce, to make it easier for entrepreneurs and for entrepreneurship (and local, regional, and national economies) to thrive, we have all jumped on the "ecosystem" metaphor bandwagon (cf. Kuckertz, 2019). It is understandable. For one, we all understand that we live in and are part of ecosystems in the natural world. And that understanding and lived experience, combined with perhaps a continued naïveté about how we can manipulate the natural world, has led researchers and policymakers alike to embrace the entrepreneurial ecosystem concept.

At this point, the concept has become shorthand and the various stakeholders all have their own definitions but reviewing some of the most common definitions, and the concepts they share, is useful to set the stage for the approach I aim to take in this chapter. Ecosystems – as metaphor or theoretical construct – have a rather long history at this point. Rocha and Audretsch (2022) linked this history to similar histories (and trajectories) of regional clusters and industrial districts and asked whether all

Dax Jacobson, Westminster University, email: djacobson@westminsteru.edu

https://doi.org/10.1515/9783110791396-008

three are "different phenomena producing historical transformations or just rhetorical devices" (p. 2). Acs and colleagues (2017), citing the "rapidly growing interest" in ecosystems, traced their history back to two distinct research lineages – strategy and regional development, highlighting that "both lineages share common roots in ecological system thinking, focusing on the interdependence of actors in a particular community to create new value" (p. 2).

Stam and Spigel (2016) noted how the ecosystem concept developed in the 1980s and 1990s as entrepreneurship researchers moved from "individualistic, personality-based research towards a broader perspective that incorporated the role of social, cultural, and economic forces in the entrepreneurship process" (p. 1). Not quite called an "ecosystem" yet, researchers during this era, including Pennings (1982), Dubini (1989), Van de Den (1993) and Bahrami and Evans (1995), were focusing on an entrepreneurial "environment" to try and understand and explain the impact of social and regional factors on entrepreneurship.

For some researchers this became a call to action to understand the importance and influence of what can more broadly be called the context (cf. Welter, 2011) in which entrepreneurship takes place. For many others, "ecosystem" became the "conceptual umbrella for the benefits and resources produced by a cohesive, typically regional community of entrepreneurs and their supporters" (Spigel & Harrison, 2018, p. 152). And while there are many other definitions that have and continue to be developed for the entrepreneurial ecosystem concept, the Spigel and Harrison definition is both clear enough and broad enough to illustrate why the ecosystem concept is so appealing, used, and potentially useful. That definition also highlights why the ecosystem concept has almost become overused, or at least often cited but not always properly understood or applied in research or policy (*disruption* is another example of a concept with the same promise and pitfalls). This is an important point because the ecosystem concept has indeed moved from research to policy with governments around the word – in both developed and developing economies – turning to it as a way to "create jobs, boost innovation, and in turn, generate economic prosperity" (Spigel et al., 2020, p. 482).

The aim of this chapter, in a book on rural entrepreneurship, is not to disparage the entrepreneurial ecosystem concept or contribute to its relegation to buzzword or fad status. Rather, it is to reclaim the concept by pointing out how it might be more fruitfully applied to the understudied context of rural entrepreneurship. The idea behind the *rural everyday entrepreneurial ecosystem* concept is as a way to both highlight the importance of the rural context but also to highlight some of the gaps and opportunities that remain in our understanding of entrepreneurial ecosystems as it relates to the role(s) of higher education in *rural everyday entrepreneurial ecosystems.*

2 Everyday Entrepreneurs

Just like every big new idea in the last decade was going to disrupt an industry, most entrepreneurial ecosystems in dynamic and innovative regions in the last decade were given a name and touted as the next Silicon Valley. Silicon Valley, was, and is, of course, a very unique ecosystem with a special mix of people, time, and place. Its specific context cannot be replicated (Etzkowitz, 2022 is a nice, brief overview of the history of that ecosystem), but that hasn't stopped entrepreneurs, policymakers, and marketers from creating Silicon Beach (Southern California), Silicon Alley (New York City), Silicon Desert (Phoenix, Arizona), Silicon Forest (Portland, Oregon), Silicon Hills (Austin, Texas) Silicon Slopes (Salt Lake City, Utah), and Silicon Prairie (multiple parts of the Midwestern region of the U.S.) to name just a few in the United States alone.

And just like Silicon Valley was the ecosystem that launched and help grow some extremely large and valuable global companies (Intel, Apple, Google/Alphabet to name just a very few), the new Silicon ecosystems hope to be the place where the next gazelle (high growth startup), unicorn (privately held startup with a valuation over $1 billion), or maybe even decacorn (privately held startup with a valuation over $10 billion) start. Some of these Silicon ecosystems are seeing tremendous success. The one I am most familiar with, Silicon Slopes, made up of the Provo, Salt Lake City, Ogden region of the state of Utah in the U.S. is currently the home to 13 unicorns (and that is up from just 2 in 2019) (Utah Business, 2023) and the focus on unicorns is clear from state government down to university incubators.

Unicorns are amazing creatures. And still rare. As Aldrich and Ruef (2020) recently noted, the "level of interest doesn't match the reality of these high-capitalization events." In the world of startups, unlike real life, unicorns do exist. There is no doubt the likes of Apple and Google have an outsize impact on the lives of billions of people and the stock market but they still only make up a very small part of the global economy. Globally, small-and medium-size businesses in a typical year make up well over 90% of all businesses and 50% of all employment. As Kuratko and Audretsch (2021) recently noted, "in developed countries, small firms are the economy"; the unicorns are "proliferating at a breathtaking pace yet, the true heartbeat of a vibrant economy is the growth of small- and medium-sized ventures." They go on to argue that that the small- and medium-sized businesses are the heartbeat in some very important ways, for example, by stabilizing local economies through local employment, they become the economic backbone in many cities and towns; serving local market segments, which may be too small or insufficiently profitable to be served by aggressive growth or large companies; producing incremental innovations that can become product or process innovations; enabling the poor and lower middle classes to meaningful improve their economic lot through the launch of the smaller ventures; and contributing to the fabric of communities by actively engaging with community groups and organizations, supporting local causes.

Unfortunately, these small- and medium-sized businesses not only get less attention in our stock portfolios, from the press, and from the policymakers, they get less attention from entrepreneurship researchers. Using a metaphor I can understand and appreciate having grown up in rural Idaho, Welter et al. (2017), stated that with the continued obsession with unicorns and other fanciful creatures and the "neglect of the majority, that is, the cows and horses of entrepreneurship, both our theory development and the practical relevance of our work remain stunted" (p. 313).

The cows and the horses – those *everyday* (not mythical) creatures – are seldom the reason the next "Silicon" ecosystem is created in a new area and are rarely the focus of our research, or our policies, or our attention. Indeed, for many the everyday are simply the other, the entrepreneurs *not* trying to start gazelles or achieve unicorn status. Even for those researchers, like Welter and colleagues (2017), calling for research on everyday entrepreneurs, the everyday is defined as the "vast bulk and diversity" of the majority of entrepreneurship and not the "outliers" that typically get all of the attention (p. 313). Or as Kuratko and Audretsch (2021) put it, is the future of entrepreneurship about the few or the many? But who are the many? A first step in understanding the vast bulk and diversity of the many would be to know who makes up that diverse majority. And to do that we likely need to look at the individual everyday entrepreneurs and their everyday businesses.

A key question, then, as Roundy and Lyons (2023) recently suggested is, where are the entrepreneurs? Their important question was more about where are the actual entrepreneurs in our research and policies but I do not believe it is a stretch to say the question can also mean, where are the entrepreneurs physically located?

3 The Rural Entrepreneurship Context

As American writer, farmer, and environmental activist Wendell Berry stated, when asked about his lifelong personal and professional commitment to his rural Kentucky home, "The context – the circumstances, the place, knowing your place – is all-important."

While we still debate the precise definition, conceptualization, measurement, and impact of context in entrepreneurship research (Wurth et al., 2021) we seem to agree that context does indeed matter for entrepreneurs (cf. Theodoraki et al., 2023). That has been made clear by Welter and colleagues (cf. Welter, 2011; Welter, Baker & Wirsching, 2019). Welter (2011), citing Gartner (1995) and Baumol (1990), noted that researchers (and I would add policymakers) tend to overestimate the influence of personal factors and underestimate the influence of external factors and forget that circumstances for entrepreneurs change from place to place and over time (Theodoraki et al., 2023). Put another way, Welter (2011) went on to argue that "context simultaneously provides individuals with entrepreneurial opportunities and sets boundaries for their actions; in other words, individuals may experience it as asset and liability" (p. 165–6). And even more succinctly, Welter (2011) suggested that "context is important for understanding when, how, and why entrepreneurship happens and who becomes involved."

Korsgaard and colleagues (2015) went a step further, suggesting two categories of contexts – social and institutional, and spatial. Social and institutional contexts have helped researchers "explore on the one hand how economic rationality and optimization is often compromised by social and institutional embeddedness and on the other hand how this enables entrepreneurial activities for individuals with privileged positions in networks and institutions" (p. 8). The spatial context is where entrepreneurial action takes place. More formally the "intersection of topographical, geographical, environmental, and infrastructural materiality and the socialized meanings and experiences attached to those materialities" (p. 9).

This is not a chapter on the history, debates, typologies, and suggestions for the path forward for research on entrepreneurial context (see Welter et al., 2019 as one of several good primers) but this overview is included to emphasize, in solidarity with many of my fellow researchers around the world, that context matters and that the theoretical and methodological challenges associated with making context a fundamental part of any entrepreneurial research should not keep us from trying. There is so much more meaningful and impactful work to be done. Researchers should take context more seriously, "not just as something to be 'controlled for' but rather as a theoretical and methodological lens" (Welter et al., 2019, p. 323).

In a longitudinal ethnography of a rural small town in Northern Sweden, Gaddefors and Anderson (2018) described how context mattered for them – "It may be no more than a container of entrepreneurship; it can be an arena where entrepreneurship is enacted. In some cases, context is the very stuff from which entrepreneurship is wrought." Context matters for all entrepreneurs, of course, but perhaps even more so for rural everyday entrepreneurs like those in the rural town in Northern Sweden studied over time by Gaddefors and Anderson. There is a significant regional and local component (context) to understanding entrepreneurship (Fritsch & Schmude, 2007), a significance enhanced in rural settings (Fortunato, 2014). For while every entrepreneur is different, every entrepreneurial ecosystem is different, every rural context is different, a good place to start for understanding the context for many rural entrepreneurs comes from Fortunato (2014):

> Remoteness, lack of diversity, gaps in financial and human capital, and lopsided power relationships that strip local citizens of their sense of control, have all been defining features of some rural communities, and they all pose threats to entrepreneurship. When one understands the importance of the local culture and context of entrepreneurship in general, the effects of these challenges seem particularly daunting for a social phenomenon empowered by human interaction, a thriving marketplace, diversity of ideas, appropriate capitalization outlets, and relatively flat power structures that support small business. (p. 394)

That is a start but what is rural entrepreneurship? There was some debate about whether rural entrepreneurship is any different than urban or suburban entrepreneurship (Fortunato, 2014) but the general agreement that context matters has meant an understanding that the context for entrepreneurs in a rural place matters in ways that are different than in urban spaces. Rural entrepreneurship has been defined as "all forms of entrepreneurship that are located in areas characterized by large open spaces and small population relative to the national context" (Korsgaard et al., 2015, p. 5). Korsgaard et al. (2015) did note this definition does not adequately capture the link between the spatial context and entrepreneurial activities and highlighted that rural entrepreneurship research in general has focused more on the social, economic, and institutional contexts rather than the spatial or on how the spatial interacts with the other three. Hunt et al. (2021) classified research on rural entrepreneurship into "structural and environmental approaches," "economic theory," "individual approaches," and "cultural approaches" and noted (and cautioned against) a fragmenting of the research. What is interesting here (but not highlighted in their paper) is that despite the fragmentation, a, if not the, fundamental concern is about, whether, and how, rural entrepreneurs identify, connect to, and use resources. For example, as Hunt et al. (2021) suggested, there may be concerns with geographic distances ("structural and environmental approaches"), "limited access to finite inputs" ("economic theory"), lack of education, formal training, or skills ("individual approaches"), a lack of rural entrepreneurship role models leading to limited views or imagination of entrepreneurial opportunities ("cultural approaches").

It quickly becomes clear that we are back where we started (and can get caught in a loop) and that we cannot get very deep into the definitions of, or the research on, rural entrepreneurship before we see context become the critical factor. It also becomes clear that rural entrepreneurship is conceptually underdeveloped (2018). Muller and Korsgaard (2018) suggested rural entrepreneurs are "enabled and constrained by their immediate local spatial context" (p. 215) and highlighted two themes related to this enablement and constraint for rural entrepreneurs – local embeddedness and non-local connections. Local embeddedness can enable rural entrepreneurs in spite of resource constraints by making use of "specifically rural resources available in the local area" (p. 220) and access to these resources through local networks and their local community. Non-local connections are those connections rural entrepreneurs use to extend from their own local place to access resources and markets – "the study of spatial context is an important research gap in entrepreneurship, especially at the local spatial level, and notably contextual differences are likely to be important as different spatial contexts influence entrepreneurial processes in different ways" (p. 221).

Rural entrepreneurship is about context. Context is in part about resources. To properly understand rural entrepreneurship is to understand how entrepreneurs connect to (or don't) these resources in their context(s). "Each context has different resources, so understanding rural entrepreneurship entails relating actions and practices to the enactment of these resources. Understanding entrepreneurship is about understanding *the engagements with contexts*, rather than simply with context" (Gaddefors & Anderson, 2019, p. 10). That engagement, the connecting, the knowledge of and access to multiple types of financing, human capital, infrastructure, favorable policies, access to is often (or should be) through education.

4 Higher Education

Any discussion on rural entrepreneurship and rural higher education should start with discussing the rural "brain drain." The size, scope, and impact of the rural brain drain continues to be debated but the phenomenon – where a disproportionate number of rural youth leave for college and never return to rural communities – does exist (Estes et al., 2016). And even when researchers or policymakers do not find a "hemorrhaging," they more often than not do find a brain drain and in small, rural communities, any significant loss is felt. I lived it. Not everyone left. But the majority of friends and family from my rural small town did leave after high school and did not return (including me).

Brain drain is not felt the same across rural communities and it is complicated (there is some in-migration in many rural locations) but among the many reasons any loss is felt, Dabson and colleagues (2003) found that while people in rural areas without a college degree are often self-employed, they are much less likely to create rural jobs for others than entrepreneurs with a college degree. In another study, counties with a highly education population were found to generate more income and value of output per dollar of investment than counties with a lower educated population (Henderson et al., 2007), a problem that rural counties frequently find themselves dealing with.

The attention and debate surrounding the rural brain drain is important and should continue. It is important to note, however, that the narrow definition that includes "leaving for college" does not capture the full complexity of the problem. Some (like me) do leave for college and opportunity and do not return. Others leave simple for opportunity (i.e., employment) and never return. And some stay and get some form of an education and then leave. Or they may leave, get an education, and return, only to leave again – a segment of the workforce and the brain drain phenomenon where young, educated professionals leave rural areas for urban locals for better pay or opportunities – leaving a mismatch between the skills of those left behind and the jobs available (Goetz & Rupasingha, 2006). This is a gap and weakness in the ecosystem. It is important to have people stay, be creative, and start and run businesses because in all communities but especially in rural communities where there simply fewer entrepreneurs and businesses "the presence of entrepreneurial energy serves to invigorate others" (Gaddefors & Anderson, 2018, p. 63). Indeed, research has indicated that having a "creative class" in rural communities leads to more entrepreneurial activity (McGranahan et al., 2011).

Artz (2003) highlighted another dimension to the brain drain phenomenon, suggesting

> the current debate over brain drain overlooks the possibility that individuals' reasons for moving and their preferences for certain locations may change with age. Younger people move to take advantage of school and job opportunities. However, as people marry, have children, and acquire job experience, they may choose to relocate for "quality of life" reasons. There is little information about the motivations and choices of "reverse" migrants opting to relocate in mid-life. Policy makers should be concerned about the supply of all educated workers not just young, educated workers. (p. 14)

The rural brain drain is especially sad when we consider that some data suggested that the rural students who are the highest-achieving are those with strongest attachment to their community (Petrin et al., 2014). Whatever the reason, and whenever or however it happens, the rural brain drain continues to have a damaging impact on rural communities. As Carr and Kefalas (2009) thoughtfully argued – "What is happening in many small towns – the devastating loss of educated and talented young people, the aging of the population, and the erosion of the local economy – has repercussions far beyond their boundaries. Put simply, the health of the small towns that are dotted across the Heartland matters because, without them, the country couldn't function, in the same way that a body cannot functions without a heart" (preface).

For those who do stay, or return, too few rural communities are able to provide the education needed for the entrepreneurial opportunities that do or may exist with some exploration. And the small- and medium-sized businesses that rural entrepreneurs do start and sustain need "more entrepreneurial education programming" (Cowell et al., 2018). Industry associations, seeing the current promise of rural innovation and entrepreneurship, are finding there are real challenges, chief among them not only the rural brain drain but limited access to educational advancement opportunities (cf. Association of Managers (2023) – Addressing the Rural Workforce Challenge).

Researchers have pointed out not only the need for understanding and addressing educational access and advancement opportunities but also the role of higher education in the entrepreneurial process of rural regions. As Brekke (2021) put it, we have a need for better understanding how higher education institutions' "absorptive capacities to disseminate, utilize, and share" knowledge needed for entrepreneurship can be embedded in rural regions. Of course, just having an institution of higher education nearby (itself a problem in many rural areas) is not enough. Too often there is a mismatch of courses, programs, degrees, and degree levels leading to a waste of resources in rural areas – a problem that will require these institutions to acquire some skills they too often lack, the ability to serve not just in an education role but also to help develop policy and serve as an intermediary (Hill, 2022).

5 Workforce Development

In the current political and economic climate in the U.S., the value of higher education is in question, adding another layer of complexity to this issue. For example, will rural residents even take advantage of educational opportunities if they are accessible? There is more work for colleges and universities to do to demonstrate the value of a degree while they are helping with policy and serving as intermediators. However, traditional higher education institutions are not the only place to get the training entrepreneurs need to start and sustain new businesses. Workforce development, often the realm of local, state, and the federal government but increasingly the role of business themselves is a growing area and area of concern for rural entrepreneurship.

Workforce development can have a range of meanings, from specific skill training to certificates to up-skilling and more. Former U.S. Federal Reserve Chairman Janet Yellen defined it as "a catchall phrase to encompass different types of initiatives that help prepare people for jobs by providing them with training, placement assistance, and other support" (Yellen, 2017). A previous federal study of the workforce development system in the U.S. suggested it as a patch-work quilt of programs, organizations, policies, and activities that help workers access skills and supports that get workers into jobs (Good & Strong, 2015).

Starting at the federal level, the United States Department of Agriculture (USDA), the leading agency for all things not only agricultural but rural in the United States, recently issued a report with a plan to help the rural U.S. "build back better" coming out of COVID. The agency is organizing programing and funding in four key areas and tellingly, "workforce development planning" is # 1. The other three are key to the discussion in the chapter and book and are (2) Infrastructure and equipment financing; (3) Industry and employer engagement, entrepreneurship and local business development; and (4) Education, training, and apprenticeship.

Whatever it is called or whichever part of the system we highlight, workforce development is clearly top of mind for government officials and agencies at all levels. It is also a concern repeatedly highlighted by think tanks and consulting companies. Even the consulting giant McKinsey is getting in on the action, proposing recently in "Rural rising: Economic development strategies for America's heartland" that workforce development has to be part of any strategy for rural economic development.

The relationship between higher education and workforce development is complicated. Part of the challenge is that despite an understanding of the importance of workforce development, the broad definition of, and the various entities seeking to provide it, have created an ecosystem in its own right (from traditional education to reskilling to health care, housing, and transportation). The "patchwork quilt of workforce development is seen as one singular system or entity by its job-seeker and business consumers, but there remain opportunities to improve the operations of the many disparate entities in the quilt" (Andreason, 2021).

Workforce development has not yet become a significant part of rural entrepreneurship research nor has it been consistently considered as part of entrepreneurial ecosystems. This must change. Not only workforce development as a critical element but the patchwork of stakeholders providing it, including higher education. As Lyons and colleagues argued, "defining, measuring and developing skills are crucial to successful entrepreneurship and that being able to do so can help to build strong rural entrepreneurial ecosystems" (Lyons et al., 2020).

In the next section, I review two higher education-related entities that should be key players in what I call rural everyday entrepreneurial ecosystems (placing both a neglected type of entrepreneur (everyday) and an underexamined place (rural) in the entrepreneurial ecosystem concept) – but who are not yet realizing their potential as rural everyday entrepreneurial ecosystem leaders. This is followed by a section with three examples of institutions trying to get it right.

6 Land-Grant Universities

A land-grant university or college is a higher-education institution that has been designated by Congress to receive the benefits of the Morrill Acts (originally 1862 and subsequently 1890 and 1994). The original mission of land-grant institutions was to "teach agriculture, military tactics, and the mechanic arts as all as classical studies so members of the working classes could obtain a liberal, practical education" (APLU). The goal was to educate all and integrate the "toil and practice in everyday life with a liberal education" (Flanagan et al., 2013, p. 248). The teaching mission was expanded with the Hatch Act of 1887 and the Smith-Level Act of 1914 to include three pillars: teaching, research, and extension (King, 2021).

It is the extension mission that is most critical to the rural everyday entrepreneurial ecosystem discussion. Land-grant extension offices are meant to be "a partnership between county, state, and federal governments to share scientific knowledge from universities and research stations with the public" (Rasmussen, 2002). Many in the U.S. think of extension as the place to go to learn about agricultural innovation, future farmers, and for landscape advice but there is much more – at least much more potential – for extension offices to do and be for rural entrepreneurship, innovation, and rural economic equality (Lyons et al., 2018).

There are examples of successes. The University of Nebraska Extension Service has played a critical role in the entrepreneurial culture of Nebraska and the development of entrepreneurs in Nebraska (Weigle et al., 2022) and North Carolina State (a land-grant university) has been key to the development of a remarkable environment for entrepreneurship in the Research Triangle Park region of North Carolina (Choi & Markham, 2019), to just two of many. Yet there are also concerns and areas for improvement. Interestingly, given how this chapter has highlighted the rural brain drain, Estes et al. (2016), noted, “Land grant universities should play a key role in enhancing economic, social and educational opportunities in rural communities. Yet, by their very natures, land grant universities are part of the mechanism whereby the most academically capable rural youth are enabled to leave rural communities, with potentially negative consequences for these communities” (p. 9).

The rural drain aside, land grants could be leading the creation and cultivation of rural everyday entrepreneurial ecosystems because, as Lyons and colleagues (2018) suggested, “land-grants are uniquely positioned to play a leading role in the effort to create and sustain rural wealth through innovation.” The authors finish that sentence by asking, “but are they playing that role as fully and effectively as they could be?” The answer is no. As Lyons and colleagues highlighted, there are problems with higher education bureaucracy and inefficiency and a lack of focus on the customer. Extension is also too often the place knowledge sharing and collaboration stop.

The land-grant university, if it steps up as the key player it should be, can be at the center not only of education and skill development but of matching funding with opportunity, facilitate information and technology transfer, and in general serving as hub of the ecosystem (Lyons et al., 2018). The work of Lyons and colleagues (2018) serves as the best call yet for what land-grants are not doing but can and should be as part of a rural everyday entrepreneurial ecosystem. They offer the following important suggestions for land-grants to consider to increase their support of rural entrepreneurship:

1. Geographically diffuse university spending to reach isolated rural areas;
2. Encourage economic specialization in rural regions (e.g., forestry products in forested areas);
3. Move beyond agriculture to encourage innovation in a diversity of industries;
4. Think in terms of entire industry value chains and the possibilities for innovation at every stage of the chain and of opportunities for the university to play the role of coordinator of those value chains (Lyons, 2015);
5. Utilize the connections of Extension to import knowledge created by the university into rural areas, with a focus on utilizing experts and industry to spread that knowledge, as well as to build urban-rural knowledge linkages;
6. Acknowledge that, today, industry rivals the public sector in its support of agricultural research (Amanor-Boadu & Zereyesus, 2007) and work with industry to meet its needs;
7. Work with community colleges to create labor force experiences that facilitate the development of tacit and codified knowledge;
8. Utilize Extension and experiment stations for technology transfer and rural entrepreneurship support, including assistance with opportunity recognition/creation, marketing and creative financing;
9. Build rural regional networks of industry, educational institutions, entrepreneurship support organizations, economic development organizations and others to recreate the agglomeration effects enjoyed by urban areas;

10. Utilize the latest communications technology in support of these networks; and
11. Network with land grant universities across state boundaries to foster innovation and entrepreneurship on a larger scale. (p. 43)

Interestingly, Lyons et al. (2018) note that extension offices are unlikely to do some of the practical things expected of an entrepreneurial support organization, for example running the actual marketing or capital campaigns that entrepreneurs need. Yet extension offices can be part of the network of those organizations that can. In what sounds like a very good description of the role extension offices can play in rural everyday entrepreneurial ecosystems, the authors state that they see the primary role of extension offices as that of "building the networks with centers of innovation, industry stakeholders and business service providers to facilitate the exchange of services and knowledge that place rural areas on more equitable footing with urban areas" (Lyons et al., 2018, p. 42).

7 Small Business Development Centers (SBDCs)

Small Business Development Centers (SBDCs) in the U.S. have a long and interesting history, one that is linked to university-based business extension efforts in the 1940s and the formation of the Small Business Administration (SBA) in the 1950s. There was a recognition nearly 80 years ago that not only were small businesses vital to the American economy but that these small businesses needed support from the federal government to be successful (Irvin et al., 2021). There are currently over 60 SBDC service centers in the United States, the District of Columbia, Puerto Rico, the U.S. Virgin Islands, and American Samoa.

According to research from the U.S. Congress, the mission of SBDC centers is to aid entrepreneurs and small businesses in areas of marketing and business strategy, finance, engineering, management, and other areas at no cost (Congressional Research Service, 2017). In addition, a primary service offered by SBDCs is access to their network of lenders (Dunne & McBrayer, 2019). SBDCs are only partially funded by the U.S. Congress and are hosted by academic institutions. The idea is that with a college and university as a partner, SBDCs will offers small businesses in their region support in areas that are taught as subjects by the host college or university – to help small businesses from initial startup to growth strategies (Irvin et al., 2021). The aim is for SBDCs to serve as a connector of support and services from higher education, small business, and government. They are having an impact. According to a report by Chrisman (2019) in 2017–18, SBDCs reported helping entrepreneurs get access to over $5.6 billion in financing with a return of $123.5 million in federal or state revenues. SBDCs also helped create over 99,000 new jobs during 2017–18.

However, SBDCs are also not necessarily having the impact they could or should be having, particularly across all regions and types of businesses they are supposed to be serving. That includes rural regions and rural entrepreneurs – or, as Dunne et al. (2021) stated, SBDC programs and services "are not having the same impact in rural settings as they are having closer to urban centers." This despite of the fact that by statute, the SBA requires SBDCs to do the following:

- Assist "small businesses in rural areas in an effort to increase their participation in exporting, government procurement, tourism, access to credit, incubators, innovation and technology and other small business programs, in cooperation with the U.S. Department of Commerce (DOC) and other relevant Federal Agencies"
- Provide "counseling and training to rural entrepreneurs and small business owners"
- Must make a full range of business development and technical assistance services available to small businesses located in rural areas. These services will be designed to increase rural small business "participation in exporting, government procurement, tourism, access to credit, incubators, innovation and technology and other small business programs." (U.S. Small Business Administration Office of Small Business Development Centers, 2019)

The unevenness in impact is a significant problem when in some states rural entrepreneurship can make up two-thirds of all business in the state (Cicero, 2018). The state I work and live in – Utah – is such a state. Although, as mentioned, the Silicon Slopes' gazelles and unicorns get all of the attention, 27 of the 29 counties are rural and rural entrepreneurs and small business remain the backbone of the state's economy. The current governor, Spencer Cox, is proudly from rural Utah, attended the state's land-grant university (Utah State University), and has made "One Utah" a hallmark of his administration, elevating rural issues and making it a point to focus on the economic wellness of the everyday folks in rural Utah. The following are examples of higher education institutions taking the lead in rural everyday entrepreneur ecosystems and highlight what is possible.

8 Women's Business Centers

In 1998, the US Congress passed the Women's Business Ownership Act to provide seed funding for Women's Business Centers (WBCs) through the SBA. WBCs were tasked with providing free technical and other assistance for women entrepreneurs and women who wanted to grow or expand their small business owners, particularly for women both socially and economically disadvantaged. There are critiques and question – are WBCs "reproducing gendered stereotypes of women entrepreneurs," neglecting class and ethnicity, or restricting access to wider networks and to other sources of capital and training (Arhsed et al., 2022)?

Yet WBCs can make strategic use of "spatial contexts" and allow women entrepreneurs to legitimize their entrepreneurial identify in what can sometimes be challenging environments (Müller & Korsgaard, 2018). WBCs have been tremendously successful and that success can be attributed to WBCs' focused mission to build relationships, develop social capital, and to tailored educational programs to women based on their individual needs – no matter the size of the company, the capital requirements, or the geographical location (Langowitz et al., 2006). There is also this – women's entrepreneurship continues to be a growing area of focus for researchers and policymakers alike.

In Utah, WBC Utah was founded in 1997 as a 501(c)(3) nonprofit organization with a cooperative agreement with the US SBA and the Salt Lake Chamber of Commerce. In 2016, WBC Utah sought out strategic partnerships with rural Chambers of Commerce across the state resulting in rural-focused programming in every one of Utah's 29 counties (the majority of which are rural). The rural focus was in so much demand – and so successful – that in 2019 WBC Utah secured an additional grant from the SBA to open a second office in Cedar City, Utah, to better serve women entrepreneurs in rural Southern and Eastern Utah, far from the population center and economic hub of the Wasatch Front in Northern Utah (WBC Utah – Our Story).

9 Utah Rural Leadership Academy

The Utah Rural Leadership Academy is a partnership between the Utah Association of Counties (UAC), Utah's Governor's Office, and Southern Utah University (SUU) with funding from the Utah legislature. The aim of the program is to provide professional development and leadership training for Utah's rural county elected and appointed officials (in those 27 of Utah's 29 counties designated as a rural) The program includes learning modules (virtual and in-person) on intergovernmental relations and partnerships, public budgeting and finance, and concludes with a rural government entrepreneurship incubator.

The program, now in its third year, runs once per year. Rural county elected and appointed officials apply for the program and every rural county is represented. The cohort-based program is one year long and includes not only the modules listed above but also virtual and in-person guest lectures from senior state officials, a "day on the hill" for rural students in the program to meet with their elected officials in Salt Lake City, and a graduation ceremony at Governor Cox's annual One Utah Summit. In addition to a certificate of completion awarded through the university, a significant added benefit (and innovation) to participants are six Professional Development credits awarded through SUU that may be applied to undergraduate or graduate degrees at SUU.

10 Banking on Women

A partnership between Synchrony Bank, the Utah Microloan Fund, and Westminster University, Banking on Women has since 2010 provided Utah women entrepreneurs and business owners with financial literary classes, business plan development training, mentoring, and an opportunity to apply for a microenterprise loan, which is significant itself given research highlighting that women entrepreneurs (especially rural women entrepreneurs) are still in need to direct access to financing and financial services (Fletschner & Kenney, 2014). In that time, the program has had 18 in-person cohorts that included over 240 participants. Thirty-five percent of the women have businesses that are currently operating and generating revenue. Over 152 jobs are currently in existence due to the businesses these women created and operate. The estimated annual sales revenue for the businesses exceeds $15,000,000. Twenty-three women have received loans from the Utah Microloan Fund totaling over $700,000. Perhaps most importantly given the mission of the program, at least 70% of participants have household incomes that fall below the low to moderate income (LMI) parameters and approximately 15% of participants are women of color including, Native American, Asian, Black, and Hispanic.

During the core years of the COVID pandemic (2020 and 2021), virtual courses were run for the cohorts. Given the success of the virtual programming and the need of women entrepreneurs in rural Utah, Westminster College, in partnership with the WBC Utah office in rural Cedar City, Utah, proposed a second cohort for 2023 – a virtual cohort for rural Utah. Given the vast geographical distances in rural Utah, this virtual programming will include weekly virtual classes but keep the mentoring component and add a competency-based model (which Westminster already does well) for financial literacy and business plan development. The ultimate goal, with Westminster leading, will be to deepen the level of financial and entrepreneurship literacy for women entrepreneurs in all of Utah and developing pathways for additional training and education at Westminster and beyond.

11 Conclusion

Over 20 years ago, Lyons (2002) argued that rural entrepreneurs faced major challenges including access to business services, information, and social capital. Recently Lyons (2022) made a very similar argument, noting that rural entrepreneurs still face the significant challenges of “acquiring the financial, human, and physical capital they require to start, grow, and sustain their businesses” and called for the creation and sustaining of networks to overcome these challenges. Cleary, the challenges remain and there is much work to be done. I suggest such networks already exist. Rural everyday entrepreneurial ecosystems should be providing the solutions and higher education institutions can and should be the ecosystem leaders or at least key members, something that has begun to be highlighted in other entrepreneurial ecosystem contexts in Europe (cf. Bischoff et al., 2018; Lehmann et al., 2020; Delanoë-Gueguen and Theodoraki (2021). I also suggest, with Fortunato (2014), that we need not only additional research but especially community-based research to develop new strategies for "catalyzing entrepreneurship in rural areas" (p. 401). Higher education institutions, and the researchers and students with ties to and interest in rural communities, are ideally situated to work with and lead the development of these strategies, these "new forms of learning, connecting and bridging knowledge gaps" to combine rural entrepreneurship with rural community development (p. 401).

References

Acs, Z. J., Stam, E., Audretsch, D. B., & O'Connor, A. (2017). The lineages of the entrepreneurial ecosystem approach. Small Business Economics, 49(1), 1–10. https://doi.org/10.1007/s11187-017-9864-8.

Addressing the Rural Workforce Challenge. (2023, March 31). https://www.aem.org/news/addressing-the-rural-workforce-challenge.

Aguilar, E.C. (2021). Rural entrepreneurial ecosystems: A systematic literature review for advancing conceptualisation. Entrepreneurial Business and Economics Review, 9(4), 101–114.

Aldrich, H.E., & Ruef, M. (2020). Scholars should study everyday entrepreneurs, not gazelles. Entrepreneur & Innovation Exchange. https://eiexchange.com/content/Scholars-should-study-everyday-entrepreneurs-not-gazelles.

Alsever, J. (2023, April 7). Unicorn companies with IPO dreams might be in trouble. Utah Business. https://www.utahbusiness.com/unicorn-companies-with-ipo-dreams-might-be-in-trouble/.

Alvedalen, J., & Boschma, R. (2017). A critical review of entrepreneurial ecosystems research: Towards a future research agenda. European Planning Studies, 25(6), 887–903.

Amanor-Boadu, V., & Zereyesus, Y. A. (2007). Producers as Investors in Agricultural Research: Searching for Alternative Funding Strategies in Land-Grant Universities. https://ageconsearch.umn.edu/record/9756/.

Andreason, S. (2021). Coordinating regional workforce development resources. Investing in America's Workforce, 353.

Arshed, N., Martin, G., & Knox, S. (2022). Ties that bind or blind? The role of identity and place in understanding women entrepreneurs' support needs. Entrepreneurship Theory and Practice, 10422587221134786. https://doi.org/10.1177/10422587221134786.

Artz, G. (2003). Rural area brain drain: Is it a reality? Choices, 18(4), 11–15.

Atherton, A., & Hannon, P.D. (2006). Localised strategies for supporting incubation: Strategies arising from a case of rural enterprise development. Journal of Small Business and Enterprise Development, 13(1), 48–61. https://doi.org/10.1108/14626000610645306.

Athiyaman, A., Dabson, B., Hamm, G.F., Henderson, J., Holley, J., Hustedde, R., Kayne, J., Kutzhanova, N., Lichtenstein, G.A., & Loveridge, S. (2007). Entrepreneurship and local economic development. Lexington Books.

Bahrami, H., & Evans, S. (1995). Flexible Re-Cycling and High-Technology Entrepreneurship. California Management Review, 37(3), 62–89. https://doi.org/10.2307/41165799.

Baumol, W. J. (1993). Formal entrepreneurship theory in economics: Existence and bounds. Journal of Business Venturing, 8(3), 197–210.

Bischoff, K., Volkmann, C.K., & Audretsch, D.B. (2018). Stakeholder collaboration in entrepreneurship education: An analysis of the entrepreneurial ecosystems of European higher educational institutions. The Journal of Technology Transfer, 43, 20–46.
Brekke, T. (2021). What do we know about the university contribution to regional economic development? A conceptual framework. International Regional Science Review, 44(2), 229–261. https://doi.org/10.1177/0160017620909538.
Caillouet, O.C. (2022). A qualitative study of Cooperative Extension's use of a systems approach leveraging land-grant universities to address complex issues [PhD Thesis]. University of Florida.
Carr, P.J., & Kefalas, M.J. (2009). Hollowing out the middle: The rural brain drain and what it means for America. Beacon Press.
Choi, J., & Markham, S. (2019). Creating a corporate entrepreneurial ecosystem: The case of entrepreneurship education in the RTP, USA. Journal of Open Innovation: Technology, Market, and Complexity, 5(3), Article 3. https://doi.org/10.3390/joitmc5030062.
Chrisman, J.J., & Katrishen, F. (1994). The economic impact of small business development center counseling activities in the United States: 1990–1991. Journal of Business Venturing, 9(4), 271–280. https://doi.org/10.1016/0883-9026(94)90008-6.
Chrisman: The economic impact of small business development. – Google Scholar. (n.d.). Retrieved June 15, 2023, from https://scholar.google.com/scholar_lookup?title=SBA%3B+and+the+%E2%80%9CEconomic+Impact+of+Small+Business+Development+Center+Counseling+Activities+in+the+United+States%3A+2017-2018.%E2%80%9D&publication_year=2019&author=J.J.+Chrisman.
Cicero. (2018). Idaho Small Business Development Center Rural Small Business Analysis and Awareness Study.
Congressional Research Service. (2017, March 16). Small Business Administration (SBA) Funding: Overview and Recent Trends. https://www.everycrsreport.com/files/20170316_R43846_926d413c939fd7fd2ea0d94c4ea2dde95278c8dd.pdf.
Cowell, M., Lyon-Hill, S., & Tate, S. (2018). It takes all kinds: Understanding diverse entrepreneurial ecosystems. Journal of Enterprising Communities: People and Places in the Global Economy, 12(2), 178–198. https://doi.org/10.1108/JEC-08-2017-0064.
Cresswell, T. (2018, September 2). The Promise of the Experiential Liberal Arts. The Chronicle of Higher Education. At DuckDuckGo. (n.d.). Retrieved August 15, 2022, from https://duckduckgo.com/?q=Cresswell%2C+T.+(2018%2C+September+2).+The+Promise+of+the+Experiential+Liberal+Arts.+The+Chronicle+of+Higher+Education.&t=newext&atb=v278-1&ia=web.
Dabson, B., Malkin, J., Matthews, A., Pate, K., & Stickle, S. (2003). Mapping rural entrepreneurship. Washington, DC: Corp. for Enterprise Development.
Delanoë-Gueguen, S., & Theodoraki, C. (2021). From incubator to full internal entrepreneurship education ecosystem: The example of TBS. In Innovation in global entrepreneurship education (pp. 18–31). Edward Elgar Publishing. https://www.elgaronline.com/abstract/edcoll/9781839104190/9781839104190.00009.xml.
Dubini, P. (1989). The influence of motivations and environment on business start-ups: Some hints for public policies. Journal of Business Venturing, 4(1), 11–26.
Dunne, T. C., & McBrayer, G. A. (2019). In the interest of small business' cost of debt: A matter of CSR disclosure. Journal of Small Business Strategy, 29(2), 58–71.
Dunne, T.C., Toyoshima, K., & Byrd, M. (2021). Small business development centers and rural entrepreneurial development strategies: Are we doing enough for rural America? Journal of Small Business Strategy, 31(4), 57–63. https://doi.org/10.53703/001c.29493.
Erickcek, G.A. (2023). Key research and policy questions in economic development and workforce development. Economic Development Quarterly, 37(1), 5–6. https://doi.org/10.1177/08912424221148563.

Estes, H.K., Estes, S., Johnson, D.M., Edgar, L.D., & Shoulders, C.W. (2016). The rural brain drain and choice of major: Evidence from one land grant university. NACTA Journal, 60.
Etzkowitz, H. (2022). Entrepreneurial university icon: Stanford and Silicon Valley as innovation and natural ecosystem. Industry and Higher Education, 36(4), 361–380. https://doi.org/10.1177/09504222221109504.
Flanagan, C., Faust, V., & Pykett, A. (2013). Educating the public in the spirit of the land-grant university. The Journal of General Education, 62(4), 247–257.
Finley, A. (2021). How college contributes "to" workforce success: Employer views on what matters most. In Association of American Colleges and Universities. https://eric.ed.gov/?q=black+and+white+and+american+and+racial+and+conflict&ff1=dtysince_2021&pg=351&id=ED616977.
Fletschner, D., & Kenney, L. (2014). Rural women's access to financial services: Credit, savings, and insurance. In A.R. Quisumbing, R. Meinzen-Dick, T.L. Raney, A. Croppenstedt, J.A. Behrman, & A. Peterman (Eds.), Gender in agriculture: Closing the knowledge gap (pp. 187–208). Springer Netherlands. https://doi.org/10.1007/978-94-017-8616-4_8.
Fortunato, M.W. (2017). High-and low-entrepreneurial communities: A multiple case study 1. In Toward entrepreneurial community development (pp. 177–235). Routledge.
Fortunato, M.W.-P. (2014). Supporting rural entrepreneurship: A review of conceptual developments from research to practice. Community Development, 45(4), 387–408. https://doi.org/10.1080/15575330.2014.935795.
Fortunato, M.W.-P., & Clevenger, M.R. (2022). Revisiting entrepreneurial communities, entrepreneurial ecosystems, and ecosystem logic. In Entrepreneurial communities and ecosystems. Routledge.
Fritsch, M., & Schmude, J. (2007). Entrepreneurship in the region (Vol. 14). Springer Science & Business Media.
Gaddefors, J., & Anderson, A. (2018). Context matters: Entrepreneurial energy in the revival of place. In Creating entrepreneurial space: Talking through multi-voices, reflections on emerging debates. Emerald Publishing Limited.
Gaddefors, J., & Anderson, A.R. (2019). Romancing the rural: Reconceptualizing rural entrepreneurship as engagement with context (s). The International Journal of Entrepreneurship and Innovation, 20(3), 159–169.
Gaddefors, J., Korsgaard, S., & Ingstrup, M.B. (2020). Regional development through entrepreneurial exaptation: Epistemological displacement, affordances, and collective agency in rural regions. Journal of Rural Studies, 74, 244–256.
Gartner, W. B., & Shane, S. A. (1995). Measuring entrepreneurship over time. Journal of Business Venturing, 10(4), 283–301.
Goetz, S.J., & Rupasingha, A. (2006). Wal-Mart and social capital. American Journal of Agricultural Economics, 88(5), 1304–1310.
Good, L., & Strong, E. (2015). Reimagining workforce policy in the United States. Transforming Workforce Development Policies for the 21st Century, 13–43.
Haase Svendsen, G.L., Kjeldsen, C., & Noe, E. (2010). How do private entrepreneurs transform local social capital into economic capital? Four case studies from rural Denmark. The Journal of Socio-Economics, 39(6), 631–644. https://doi.org/10.1016/j.socec.2010.06.012.
Henderson, J., Low, S., & Weiler, S. (2007). The drivers of regional entrepreneurship in rural and metro areas. Entrepreneurship and Local Economic Development, 81–102.
Hill, C. (2022). Entrepreneurship in Rural Areas: Examining the Influence of Postsecondary Education. Business Administration Dissertations. https://doi.org/10.57709/29012274.
Hunt, R.A., Townsend, D.M., Korsgaard, S., & Naar, A. (2021). Urban farmers and cowboy coders: Reimagining rural venturing in the 21st century. Academy of Management Perspectives, 35(4), 660–681. https://doi.org/10.5465/amp.2017.0157.
Investing in Rural Prosperity Chapter 17. (n.d.).

Irvin, J.A., Minifie, J.R., Runsewe, D., & Thompson, W.G. (2021). Best practices of small business development centers with host institutions. Small Business Institute Journal, 17(1). https://doi.org/10.53703/001c.28167.

Isaksen, A., Kyllingstad, N., Rypestøl, J.O., & Schulze-Krogh, A.C. (2018). Differentiated regional entrepreneurial discovery processes. A conceptual discussion and empirical illustration from three emergent clusters. European Planning Studies, 26(11), 2200–2215. https://doi.org/10.1080/09654313.2018.1530143.

Kalantaridis, C., & Bika, Z. (2006). Local embeddedness and rural entrepreneurship: Case-study evidence from Cumbria, England. Environment and Planning A, 38(8), 1561–1579.

King, A.E. (2021). It's complicated: Exploring the co-creation of land-grant brand identity amongst faculty members at Oklahoma State University [PhD Thesis]. Oklahoma State University.

Korsching, P.F., & Allen, J.C. (2004). Local entrepreneurship: A development model based on community interaction field theory. Community Development, 35(1), 25–43.

Korsgaard, S., Müller, S., & Tanvig, H.W. (2015). Rural entrepreneurship or entrepreneurship in the rural–between place and space. International Journal of Entrepreneurial Behavior & Research, 21(1), 5–26.

Kuckertz, A. (2019). Let's take the entrepreneurial ecosystem metaphor seriously! Journal of Business Venturing Insights, 11, e00124.

Kuratko, D.F., & Audretsch, D.B. (2021). The future of entrepreneurship: The few or the many? Small Business Economics, 1–10.

Kures, M., & Deller, S.C. (2023). Growth in commuting patterns and their impacts on rural workforce and economic development. Economic Development Quarterly, 37(1), 54–63. https://doi.org/10.1177/08912424221145173.

Kusio, T., Kudełko, J., Borges, A., Delic, A., & Stroila, I. (2022). Are there any differences in rural development challenges within European countries? Social and economic contexts from EU rural leaders. International Food and Agribusiness Management Review, 25(5), 737–756. https://doi.org/10.22434/IFAMR2021.0147.

Land-Grant University FAQ. (n.d.). APLU. Retrieved June 15, 2023, from https://www.aplu.org/about-us/history-of-aplu/what-is-a-land-grant-university/.

Lang, R., & Fink, M. (2019). Rural social entrepreneurship: The role of social capital within and across institutional levels. Journal of Rural Studies, 70, 155–168. https://doi.org/10.1016/j.jrurstud.2018.03.012.

Langowitz, N., Sharpe, N., & Godwyn, M. (2006). Women's business centers in the United States: Effective entrepreneurship training and policy implementation. Journal of Small Business & Entrepreneurship, 19(2), 167–182. https://doi.org/10.1080/08276331.2006.10593365.

Leendertse, J., Schrijvers, M., & Stam, E. (2021). Measure twice, cut once: Entrepreneurial ecosystem metrics. Research Policy, 104336. https://doi.org/10.1016/j.respol.2021.104336.

Lehmann, E.E., Meoli, M., Paleari, S., & Stockinger, S.A.E. (2020). The role of higher education for the development of entrepreneurial ecosystems. European Journal of Higher Education, 10(1), 1–9. https://doi.org/10.1080/21568235.2020.1718924.

Leick, B., Gretzinger, S., & Makkonen, T. (2022). The rural enterprise economy. Routledge.

Letaifa, S.B., & Reynoso, J. (2015). Toward a service ecosystem perspective at the base of the pyramid. Journal of Service Management.

Lewis, J.L.W., & Don Macke, B. (2022). Raising entrepreneurial ecosystems: Three Nebraska case studies. In empowering entrepreneurial communities and ecosystems. Routledge.

Lichtenstein, G.A., & Lyons, T.S. (1996). Incubating new enterprises.

Lyons, T.S. (2002). Building social capital for rural enterprise development: Three case studies in the United States. Journal of Developmental Entrepreneurship, 7(2), 193–216.

Lyons, T.S. (2022). Social capital building for rural innovation. In building rural community resilience through innovation and entrepreneurship. Routledge.
Lyons, T.S., Lyons, J.S., & Jolley, G.J. (2020). Entrepreneurial skill-building in rural ecosystems: A framework for applying the Readiness Inventory for Successful Entrepreneurship (RISE). Journal of Entrepreneurship and Public Policy, 9(1), 112–136. https://doi.org/10.1108/JEPP-09-2019-0075.
Lyons, T.S., Miller, S.R., & Mann, J.T. (2018). A new role for land grant universities in the rural innovation ecosystem? Journal of Regional Analysis & Policy, 48(2). https://jrap.scholasticahq.com/article/3775-a-new-role-for-land-grant-universities-in-the-rural-innovation-ecosystem.
Mack, E., & Mayer, H. (2016). The evolutionary dynamics of entrepreneurial ecosystems. Urban Studies, 53(10), 2118–2133.
Malecki, E.J. (2018). Entrepreneurship and entrepreneurial ecosystems. Geography Compass, 12(3), e12359.
Markley, D.M., Lyons, T.S., & Macke, D.W. (2015). Creating entrepreneurial communities: Building community capacity for ecosystem development. Community Development, 46(5), 580–598.
Mason, C., & Brown, R. (2014). Entrepreneurial ecosystems and growth oriented entrepreneurship. Final report to OECD (Vol. 30(1), pp. 77–102). Paris.
McGranahan, D.A., Wojan, T.R., & Lambert, D.M. (2011). The rural growth trifecta: Outdoor amenities, creative class and entrepreneurial context§. Journal of Economic Geography, 11(3), 529–557. https://doi.org/10.1093/jeg/lbq007.
McLaren, P.G., & Durepos, G. (2021). A call to practice context in management and organization studies. Journal of Management Inquiry, 30(1), 74–84.
Miles, M.P., & Morrison, M. (2020). An effectual leadership perspective for developing rural entrepreneurial ecosystems. Small Business Economics, 54(4), 933–949. https://doi.org/10.1007/s11187-018-0128-z.
Miller, D.J., & Acs, Z.J. (2017). The campus as entrepreneurial ecosystem: The University of Chicago. Small Business Economics, 49(1), 75–95. https://doi.org/10.1007/s11187-017-9868-4.
Müller, S., & Korsgaard, S. (2018). Resources and bridging: The role of spatial context in rural entrepreneurship. Entrepreneurship & Regional Development, 30(1–2), 224–255.
Muñoz, P., & Kimmitt, J. (2019). Rural entrepreneurship in place: An integrated framework. Entrepreneurship & Regional Development, 31(9–10), 842–873. https://doi.org/10.1080/08985626.2019.1609593.
North, D., & Smallbone, D. (2000). The innovativeness and growth of rural SMEs during the 1990s. Regional Studies, 34(2), 145–157.
Ondracek, J., Witwer, K., & Kim, J.-H. (2005). State-level entrepreneurship policy and tertiary entrepreneurship education: A study of benchmarks and trends in North Dakota. University of Illinois at Urbana-Champaign's Academy for Entrepreneurial Leadership Historical Research Reference in Entrepreneurship.
Pato, M.L., & Teixeira, A.A. (2016). Twenty years of rural entrepreneurship: A bibliometric survey. Sociologia Ruralis, 56(1), 3–28.
Pennings, J. M. (1982). The Urban Quality of Life and Entrepreneurship. Academy of Management Journal, 25(1), 63–79. https://doi.org/10.5465/256024.
Petrin, R.A., Schafft, K.A., & Meece, J.L. (2014). Educational sorting and residential aspirations among rural high school students: What are the contributions of schools and educators to rural brain drain? American Educational Research Journal, 51(2), 294–326. https://doi.org/10.3102/0002831214527493.
Pocock, L. (2022). Community innovation and entrepreneurial ecosystem development: A case study of startup Tucson. In M.M. Mars, & H.J. Schau (Eds.), How alternative is alternative? The role of entrepreneurial development, form, and function in the emergence of alternative marketscapes (Vol. 29, pp. 149–165). Emerald Publishing Limited. https://doi.org/10.1108/S1048-473620220000029007.

Ramussen, W.D. (2002). Taking the university to the people: Seventy-five years of cooperative extension. Purdue University Press.
Rocha, H., & Audretsch, D. B. (2022). Entrepreneurial ecosystems, regional clusters, and industrial districts: Historical transformations or rhetorical devices? The Journal of Technology Transfer. https://doi.org/10.1007/s10961-022-09920-6.
Roth, M.G., & Morris, R. (2020). Here I come to save the day? Reassessing the efficacy of small business development centers in the Internet Era. Journal of Entrepreneurship and Public Policy, 9(3), 319–328. https://doi.org/10.1108/JEPP-12-2019-0095.
Roundy, P. T., & Lyons, T. S. (2023). Where are the entrepreneurs? A call to theorize the micro-foundations and strategic organization of entrepreneurial ecosystems. Strategic Organization, 21(2), 447–459. https://doi.org/10.1177/14761270211056240.
Roundy, P.T., Brockman, B.K., & Bradshaw, M. (2017). The resilience of entrepreneurial ecosystems. Journal of Business Venturing Insights, 8, 99–104.
Ruiz, S.M.de A., Martens, C.D.P., & da Costa, P.R. (2020). Entrepreneurial university: An exploratory model for higher education. Journal of Management Development, 39(5), 705–722. https://doi.org/10.1108/JMD-08-2019-0363.
Rural economic development strategies for local leaders | McKinsey. (n.d.). Retrieved May 5, 2023, from https://www.mckinsey.com/industries/public-and-social-sector/our-insights/rural-rising-economic-development-strategies-for-americas-heartland.
Spigel, B. (2018). Envisioning a new research agenda for entrepreneurial ecosystems: Top-down and bottom-up approaches. In J.A. Katz, & A.C. Corbett (Eds.), Reflections and extensions on key papers of the first twenty-five years of advances (Vol. 20, pp. 127–147). Emerald Publishing Limited. https://doi.org/10.1108/S1074-754020180000020004.
Spigel, B. (2020). Entrepreneurial ecosystems: Theory, practice and futures. Edward Elgar Publishing.
Spigel, B., & Harrison, R. (2018). Toward a process theory of entrepreneurial ecosystems. Strategic Entrepreneurship Journal, 12(1), 151–168.
Spigel, B., Kitagawa, F., & Mason, C. (2020). A manifesto for researching entrepreneurial ecosystems. Local Economy: The Journal of the Local Economy Policy Unit, 35(5), 482–495. https://doi.org/10.1177/0269094220959052.
Stam, E. (2015). Entrepreneurial ecosystems and regional policy: A sympathetic critique. European Planning Studies, 23(9), 1759–1769.
Stam, E., & van de Ven, A. (2021). Entrepreneurial ecosystem elements. Small Business Economics, 56(2), 809–832. https://doi.org/10.1007/s11187-019-00270-6.
Stam, F.C., & Spigel, B. (2016). Entrepreneurial ecosystems. USE Discussion Paper Series, 16(13).
Team. (n.d.). Women's Business Center of Utah. Retrieved June 15, 2023, from https://wbcutah.org/about.
Theodoraki, C., Audretsch, D.B., & Chabaud, D. (2023). Advances in entrepreneurial ecosystem and places: Time, space and context. Special issue editorial. Revue de l'Entrepreneuriat / Review of Entrepreneurship, Hors Série, 2(HS2), 11–25. https://doi.org/10.3917/entre.hs4.0011.
USDA Launches Resource Guide to Help America's Rural Workforce Build Back Better. (n.d.). Retrieved May 5, 2023, from https://www.usda.gov/media/press-releases/2021/06/10/usda-launches-resource-guide-help-americas-rural-workforce-build.
Van de Ven, H. (1993). The development of an infrastructure for entrepreneurship. Journal of Business Venturing, 8(3), 211–230.
Weigle, J. L., Macke, D., & Lewis, B. (2022). Raising Entrepreneurial Ecosystems: Three Nebraska Case Studies. In Empowering Entrepreneurial Communities and Ecosystems (pp. 112–131).
Welter, F. (2011). Contextualizing entrepreneurship – Conceptual challenges and ways forward. Entrepreneurship Theory and Practice, 35(1), 165–184.
Where are the entrepreneurs? A call to theorize the micro-foundations and strategic organization of entrepreneurial ecosystems – Philip T Roundy, Thomas S Lyons, 2023. (n.d.). Retrieved June 16, 2023,

from https://journals.sagepub.com/doi/full/10.1177/14761270211056240?casa_token=bmorcOXUEjUAAAAA%3ASUHuBOabmoooVP_XNsmBtMOmdmeOXdACcLSEvnPwj6_Xx1JhrIJClknx_GT2Sokwwo5HvdqnRUFVhl4.

Welter, F., Baker, T., & Wirsching, K. (2019). Three waves and counting: The rising tide of contextualization in entrepreneurship research. Small Business Economics, 52(2), 319–330. https://doi.org/10.1007/s11187-018-0094-5.

Welter, F., Baker, T., Audretsch, D. B., & Gartner, W. B. (2017). Everyday entrepreneurship—A call for entrepreneurship research to embrace entrepreneurial diversity. In Entrepreneurship Theory and Practice (Vol. 41, Issue 3, pp. 311–321). SAGE Publications Sage CA: Los Angeles, CA.

Wurth, B., Stam, E., & Spigel, B. (2021). Toward an entrepreneurial ecosystem research program. Entrepreneurship Theory and Practice, 46(3), 729–778. https://doi.org/10.1177/1042258721998948.

Yellen, J. L. (2017). Addressing Workforce Development Challenges in Low-Income Communities: A speech at\backslash" Creating a Just Economy,\backslash" the 2017 annual conference of the National Community Reinvestment Coalition, Washington, DC, March 28, 2017. https://ideas.repec.org/p/fip/fedgsq/943.html.

Bryan Collins and Marcus Taylor

How Alternative Farmers in Southeastern Ontario Mobilize Mission-driven Approaches for Rural Revitalization and Resilience

Abstract: As debates around sustainable development and resilience proliferate, the concept of social entrepreneurship is being applied to rural areas to foreground potential solutions to socioeconomic and sustainability challenges. To help illustrate the concept of social entrepreneurship in rural settings, this chapter outlines an analytical framework based on the tension between value creation and value capture that can guide analysis of farm management strategies. To highlight the diversity of strategies for mission-driven value creation in rural settings, the chapter then applies the framework to four case studies of alternative farms in Southeastern Ontario. Results from these studies demonstrate how farmers mobilize unique business practices to maximize what they consider pathways toward ecological sustainability and community resilience. In comparing these strategies, the chapter concludes by discussing preconditions for success, including the necessity of proactively building and mobilizing social capital to support networks that facilitate social innovation in enterprises where value capture has been deliberately compromised.

Keywords: social entrepreneurship, social enterprise, social capital, resilience, sustainable development, rural revitalization, qualitative research, Ontario, Canada

1 Introduction

As debates around sustainable development proliferate, the concept and practices of social entrepreneurship have been placed at the forefront of scholarly attention.[1] Referred to as mission-driven enterprises, academic work from across disciplines has sought to evaluate the potential of social enterprises as a response toward the numerous critical issues facing society in the twenty-first century (Abu-Saifan, 2012; Lang & Fink, 2019; Saebi et al., 2019). With a focus on rural areas in North America, this chapter traces the origins of social entrepreneurship and outlines an analytical framework

1 We use the terms *social entrepreneurship* and *mission-driven entrepreneurship* interchangeably given the overlapping definitions of each term as suggested in the literature (Santos 2012, Sinthupundaja et al, 2020).

Bryan Collins, SUNY Oneonta, email: bryan.collins@oneonta.edu
Marcus Taylor, Queen's University, email: taylorm@queensu.ca

https://doi.org/10.1515/9783110791396-009

building on Santos (2012) that help to operationalize the concept for applied qualitative research. We then illustrate this framework using case studies of farms in rural southeastern Ontario to show potential links between social entrepreneurship and the building of social capital for community resilience. These case studies explore how farmers harness their enterprise to leverage societal benefits through the pursuit of alternative models of business. While they represent unique examples of the benefits of rural social enterprises in a space where typical profit-motivated businesses predominate, we also point to limitations and tensions. In conclusion, the chapter synthesizes this analysis within a discussion of the preconditions for success for social enterprises for the purpose of developing future research to address issues of rural decline. Specifically, we highlight the necessity of social capital that supports community networks and encourages social innovation and participation.

2 Social Entrepreneurship as a Concept and Practice

Social entrepreneurship is often dated as a unique branch of entrepreneurial operations to the 1950s with the publication of H. Bowen's "The Social Responsibilities of the Businessman" (1953). This led to lively and unresolved debates over the ensuing decades as to whether businesses had any social responsibility beyond the maximization of profits so long as they operated within the law and according to shared social norms (Friedman, 1970). In the 2000s, however, growing tensions over the social legitimacy of corporate activities in the era of globalization led to a strong renewal of these themes and their uptake across diverse academic fields. The core of the subsequent social entrepreneurship literature focused not simply on how businesses could avoid doing harm as per salient models of corporate social responsibility (Shamir, 2008). Rather, and more pointedly, attention shifted toward how the form and functions of an enterprise might be harnessed to solve complex social problems (Abu-Saifan, 2012). This academic literature quickly spread into a practical application, with business schools creating a diversity of social entrepreneurship courses aimed at translating theory into practice (Mair & Marti, 2006).

Within this hybrid field, numerous scholars have posited definitions of mission-driven social entrepreneurship, each of which have considerable overlap (Leadbetter, 1997; Dees, 1998; Zahra et al., 2008; Thompson et al., 2000; Brinckerhoff, 2009). Dacin et al. (2010), for example, compiled a list of 37 definitions of the term. These range from simply emphasizing the role of an entrepreneur as an innovator in their business operations through to those able to enact social change through visionary management. By focusing on what social entrepreneurs do in practice, Abu-Saifan (2012) sought to cut through this analytical clutter by labelling such social entrepreneurs as "mission-driven individuals" who deploy a toolbox of behaviors to deliver a social value to less privileged groups through an "entrepreneurially oriented entity that is financially independent, self-sufficient, or sustainable" (p. 25). On this basis, most definitions speak to the agency that business owners possess in enacting the change they wish to see in society in their respective domain through a suitably reformed and repurposed business model. In this respect, social entrepreneurs have been argued to have harnessed the power of entrepreneurialism to empower woman (Datta & Gailey, 2012), improve poverty rates (Ghauri et al., 2014), and promote inclusive growth within the marketplace (Ansari et al., 2012; Azmat et al., 2015).

While the burden of proof for such claims has sometimes been questioned, in the rural context, studies have sought to demonstrate that social entrepreneurship can serve as a beneficial force in marginalized rural regions particularly when it builds upon shared community norms and goals (McCarthy, 2012; Munoz et al., 2015). In this respect, social entrepreneurship has also been linked with emerging discourses around sustainability and resilience. Here, debates around the environmental crisis within and beyond rural regions seek to tie in sustainability-driven entrepreneurs as a solution to mitigate pressing social-ecological issues (Parrish, 2010; Westley, 2013; Lane, 2014). This is especially appropriate for observing rural farming communities given that agroecosystem change is manifested in the form of coupled social and ecological processes, synergies and tradeoffs. On this basis, the case studies presented in this chapter analyze social entrepreneurship through this dual lens, highlighting that farms that take a mission-driven approach typically do so to leverage simultaneous social benefits across their community as well as building agroecosystem resilience.

3 Analytical Framework

As highlighted above, there is no strong consensus as to what constitutes social entrepreneurship despite significant burgeoning cross-disciplinary literature (Nichols, 2006). This has led some to claim that the term is poorly defined and operates without clear boundaries (Mair & Mart, 2006). Others argue that social entrepreneurship is merely a subfield of entrepreneurship and therein does not require specific analytical theories or concepts (Dacin et al., 2010). In response to these challenges, a number of authors have sought to propose unifying theories of social entrepreneurship as a guide to both analysis of existing case studies and a basis for practical planning. In this vein, Santos (2012) proposes a "positive theory of social entrepreneurship" that seeks to move beyond the notion that social entrepreneurship is manifested when a business has a social component in its business plan. For Santos, the key to understanding a social enterprise is based on how the enterprise conceives of value. To explain what distinguishes a social enterprise from a commercial enterprise, Santos asks the degree to which the enterprise prioritizes value *creation* or value *capture*. Here, value creation is defined as processes to increase value through the creation of products or services that provide a measurable usefulness to people or environment

(Chesbrough et al., 2018; Sjodin et al., 2020). In contrast, value capture occurs when a business appropriates the benefits generated from value creation, typically measured as profits (Chesbrough et al., 2018; Dyer et al., 2018). A higher ratio of value returned to the business increases its value capture, but may be at the expense of value creation, such as an organization that raises product prices to increase revenues. However, if this action decreases total sales, the business will have fewer profits to generate value creation activities, indicating how the two components of creation and capture are tightly correlated and can exist in tension.

While some amount of value capture is necessary to promote business growth necessary for value creation, an enterprise's business strategy dictates the tradeoffs between value and creation. This tradeoff between value creation and capture can become complicated when determining the overall value that an enterprise has to society. At one level, some entrepreneurial endeavors capture more value than they create, such as industries that pollute the environment or become involved in fraudulent business practices. At another, some endeavors create more value than they capture, with a prime example of this being the education sector. Some endeavors, such as public education, do not have the potential for value capture because value spills over to other sectors due to externalities (Santos, 2012). Given this central tension, it is essential to analyze tradeoffs between capture versus creation to better understand how they affect market value and public perception. For example, a business that highlights value capture strategies over value creation strategies tends to see higher share prices. Mizik and Jacobson (2003) note the implausibility of maximizing both value creation and value capture, citing that often ownership tends to prioritize one or the other.

Marketing strategy research also highlights the strong influence that ownership has in determining an appropriate tradeoff between value creation and value capture. Ownership's vision in establishing this tradeoff is central to business identity given that it immediately impacts the scope of activities a business will prioritize. Santos (2012) offers an example of a pharmaceutical company. If this company prioritizes value creation, they might invest in vaccines to help fight and control deadly diseases despite poor potential returns to investments. If the same company prioritized value capture, they would be less likely to invest in these vaccines, given the high potential for marginal returns. In this vein, Seelos and Mair (2005) illustrate a case study in which the nonprofit pharmaceutical company OneWorld Health assisted in developing a new vaccine supply chain in an explicit act of prioritizing value creation with multiple positive externalities.

Santos uses this tension between value creation and value capture to elaborate further an analytical framework for understanding social entrepreneurship. He emphasizes how the tension between value creation and value capture emerges in themes of control versus empowerment. To efficiently capture value, enterprises seek to control as many external forces and variables as possible, such as exerting control over the supply chain. This control allows for a larger percentage of value to be retained rather than diffused into the social environment. On this basis, some theorists relate the idea of control to power (Schoenberger, 1994). In contrast, because social entrepreneurs do not seek value capture to the same degree, they may forego control in favor of promoting empowerment. Empowerment attempts to "remove unjust inequalities in the capacity of an actor to make choices, and any attempt to increase empowerment will involve disrupting the existing status quo and moving from a position of being unable to exercise choice to a position of doing so" (Haugh & Talwar, 2016). On this basis, social entrepreneurs tend to focus more on empowering those outside of the enterprise, including the partnerships, stakeholders and intermediaries involved in the value creation process. By empowering these agents, the intent is to boost innovation and capacity both internally within the social enterprise as well as externally outside of the organization.

These positive qualities associated between value creation and empowerment shape Santos's four propositions for the positive theory of social entrepreneurship.

Table 1: Defining Features of Social Enterprises (A Positive Theory of Social Entrepreneurship, Santos, 2012).

Key Propositions of Social Enterprises	
1	Social entrepreneurship's critical mission is to prioritize value creation involving positive externalities to address neglected societal issues.
2	Social entrepreneurs often act within the space of creating value for marginalized communities or causes.
3	Social entrepreneurs prefer a "sustainable solutions" approach to value diffusion rather than a sustainable advantages approach.
4	Social entrepreneurs tend to prefer methods of empowerment rather than control.

Using this framework, we analyze four alternative agriculture enterprises in eastern Ontario that seek to add a fundamental mission-driven component to their farming enterprise. Notably, while all four enterprises emphasize a common commitment to local community building and environmental sustainability, they work with diverging strategies and manifest distinct approaches to agriculture. This provides a useful basis on which to evaluate social enterprises in the region and to validate the conceptual framework elaborated above (Table 1).

4 Method

This study presents four case studies that represent diverse examples of mission-driven rural entrepreneurship. We briefly explore the unique operations of each case and then identify themes and patterns between the cases to provide an overview of social entrepreneurship qualities and values and how they connect to Santos's positive theory of social entrepreneurship. Prior to introducing the four case studies, we present context on the Ontario farming landscape as whole by describing the overarching policy landscape that frames prevalent agribusiness models. This context will situate the "alternative" farmers into another domain; one that is against the norm and marked by placing values over profits and self-interest. By situating the mission-driven farmer in contrast to the conventional farmer, we can begin to explore potentials and limitations to rural social entrepreneurship serving as a template for maximizing social capital and scaling up societal transformation, such as introduced by Alvord et al. (2004), Morrison et al. (2017), and Daskalopoulou et al. (2023).

Research results were gathered primarily through qualitative methods. Semi-structured in-person interviews with farmers at their farm's location allowed for questioning about their business practices as well as for observation of their farm's layout and design. Such interviews were well suited for this research given that they allowed for a broad structure of relevant topics to be discussed in depth, while equally allowing participants to engage topics that they identified as most relevant, such as the unique values that drive their operations (O'Keefe et al., 2016). Choosing which farms to include in the study required identifying a diversity of "alternative" farms that did not conform to a typical conventional model of a farm that relies on chemical inputs and high mechanization to maximize yield and profit-returns through achieving economies of scale (Therond et al., 2017). In contrast, alternative farms applied a wider purpose of value-maximization to their operations, including techniques they viewed as sustainable such as using organic manure over fertilizer, and favoring polyculture over monoculture to improve biodiversity. They also typically work on a smaller and more localized scale. Interviews with alternative farmers revealed why they are choosing an alternative agriculture livelihood, and how they are enacting these strategies and goals on their farm. When selecting alternative agriculture farms, we sought out a diverse range of farm types, with each farm specializing in a different area; a vegetable farm, an apple orchard, a permaculture farm, and a dairy farm.

5 Ontario Farming Landscape

For farmers in rural southeastern Ontario, to practice mission-driven entrepreneurship rubs against the grain of the dominant policy orientation that has prioritized farm profitability through integration into globalized commodity markets (Andree et al., 2015; Laforge et al., 2018). To this end, the Ontario Ministry of Agriculture, Forestry, and Rural Affairs (OMAFRA) has sponsored recurrent programs designed to induce farms to increase both scale and mechanization and specialize in highly competitive commodity markets that are international in scope. The ripple effects of this policy orientation on the farming landscape have been significant for practices of social entrepreneurship. First, it has directed farming enterprises toward a specific type of farming that is more highly specialized, with corn and soy farms growing rapidly. Soy and corn comprised 11% of the total market share in Ontario in 2011 whilst in 2021 this rose to 27% of market share. Farming activities related to growing corn and soy came at the expense of farmers growing diverse sets of other crops, such as fruits and vegetables. Second, it has reshaped the scale of farming toward larger enterprises managing a more limited set of crops. The overall number of farms in the province dropped by 19% from 2001 to 2021 and the largest percentage of farms lost were small farms (Statistics Canada, Census of Agriculture). Overall, the province has seen less diversity in agricultural production as policies are emphasizing growing a slimmer set of specialized crops that produce higher yields and profits.

This policy approach tends to institutionalize a farm business outlook that emphasizes economic prosperity through upscaling and specialization. This trend is encompassed by OMAFRA's 2021 vision statement to "foster the sustainable economic growth of rural Ontario and of the agri-food sector and its associated value and supply chains" (OMAFRA, 2020). In 2017, the federal government produced an Advisory Council on Economic Growth report, claiming there exists significant further opportunity for Canada's agricultural sector to expand into global markets to assist in feeding growing world populations. OMAFRA's programs reflect this productivist mindset, such as their investment in the Growing Forward 2 framework, which deployed $150 million to help farmers develop their business to participate in global markets. The framework also offered insurance programs to reduce the risk for farmers for extending their business to the world market. The Ontario premier also supported the Canadian Free Trade Agreement that held the Going Global Trade Strategy, which was a program designed to assist small farms to join global trade markets. All told, these programs contributed to Ontario's agricultural exports jumping from $9.4 billion in 2010 to $17.2 billion in 2020 (Statistics Canada, 2021). Arguably, however, these trends have concurrently restricted the creativity necessary for farms to add societal value to their land and community.

6 Rural Decline and Resilience

The focus on a productivist mission of increasing output to maximize profitability has had numerous well charted implications for rural space in advanced industrialized countries. As Li et al. (2019) document, an urban bias coupled to increases in farm mechanization and scale has led to the decline of rural communities as sites for the production and reproduction of social value. Scholars have documented rural decline in the US (Wood, 2008), Australia (Luck et al., 2010), Sweden (Hedlund & Lundholm, 2015), Canada (Markey et al., 2008), and Germany and Japan (Wirth et al., 2016). Marginalized rural areas suffer "brain drain" as skilled youth immigrate to urban areas that offer higher education and greater economic opportunity (Lang & Fink, 2019).

In conjunction with these socioeconomic pressures, the impact of widespread environmental change and crises has furthered stress points within rural communities. In Ontario, for example, there are several environmental stresses that contribute to farm management challenges and food system dislocation including extreme weather events, outbreak of disease and pests, soil degradation, and a noticeable waning of pollinators and biodiversity (Table 2).

Table 2: Selection of Environmental, Socioeconomic, and Intergenerational Short-Term and Long-Term Shocks and Stresses Affecting Rural Communities in Southeastern Ontario (Collins, 2023).

	Environmental	Socioeconomic	Longevity/Intergenerational
Short term shocks	Extreme weather events (droughts, strong rains, hail, floods)	Price volatility of inputs and outputs	Loss of autonomous decision making
	Outbreaks of pests or disease	Decline in availability of laborers	Stress about farm ownership
		Disruptions due to a pandemic	
		Rising land prices	
Long term stresses	Climate change	Liberalized markets introducing new competitors	Lack of generational renewal
	Soil degradation	Increased scarcity of resources	Aging rural population with shortage of upcoming farmers
	Decline of animal life and pollinators	Further separation between farmers	Loss of knowledge and skills
		Shifts to specialization	
		Less government support	

At the same time, socioeconomic issues compound the impacts of environmental stress including restrictions on access to land, declines in labor availability, sharp price volatility within unpredictable markets, increased scarcity of key productive resources such as water, cultural disintegration of rural communities, and less government support. One key detriment contributing to rural decline is the lack of intergenerational continuity on farms. Threats to longevity and intergenerational farms are the result of an aging population and shortage of upcoming farmers, as well as a loss of autonomous decision making, and a decrease in agricultural knowledge. Food deserts are also common in the Canadian countryside, as farms have specialized in cash crops at the expense of providing healthy accessible foods for rural residents (Lebel et al., 2016).

This has left some scholars calling for an urgent need to revitalize the rural sphere, asking whether rural areas can become sites for a prospective "re-coupling" and reconnection of new, more sustainable forms of production and circulation (Marsden et al., 2020). In what follows, we build upon Santos' analytical framework above to provide an initial evaluation of both the prospects and constraints upon social entrepreneurship in providing part of an answer to this core question of rural revitalization.

7 Mission-driven Farms

As highlighted above, Ontario's policy landscape purposefully encourages productivist farming methods predicated on simplification and scale. This in turn tends to strongly orientate farming businesses toward a narrow prioritization on profit margins. However, while much of southeastern Ontario's countryside is now dominated by highly specialized large farms with a limited range of outputs, there are a growing subset of farmers who take an alternative approach to the conventional ways of farming in the area. This chapter will highlight four such cases, where each case highlights how a farm actualizes a particular vision of social and ecological health and places it centrally within their business operation (Table 3). By consciously integrating such broader goals into the management of their business, these farms differ from the productivist business model and fit the general definition of mission-driven entrepreneurship as established in the four propositions outlined by Santos (2012). While each case can be described as an example of social entrepreneurialism, each manifests a diverse set of goals and management strategies to accomplish them. The first

Table 3: Name, Type, and Core Values of Alternative Farms That Represent Social Enterprises in Southeastern Ontario.

Farm Name	Type of Farm	Core Values
Patchwork Gardens	Medium Scale Vegetable Farm	Growing local foods, minimizing environmental impact, maximizing soil quality
Loughborough Heritage Orchard	Small Organic Apple Orchard Family Farm	Providing organic fruits at a low cost to community members
Edible Forest Farms	Small Permaculture Family Farm	Spreading permaculture practices as a method of sustainable agriculture
Sonset Farms	Small Organic Dairy Family Farm	Keeping family farming alive for sound environmental stewardship

case study demonstrates a farm that situates improving and maintaining land health as its primary mission. The second case study demonstrates a farm that serves its local community as its primary mission. The third demonstrates a farm that seeks to install a permaculture cause as its primary mission. And the fourth demonstrates a farm that prioritizes sustainable family farming as a valued cultural heritage of sound environmental stewardship.

8 Case Study 1: Patchwork Gardens

Patchwork Gardens was brought into business 18 years ago by 3 owners without previous farming experience. The farm is about 40 acres and produces vegetables and salad produce that is sold exclusively to the nearest urban hub, Kingston, about 10 miles away. The primary motivation for starting their business was the owners' enthusiasm for creating a farm centered upon ecological and organic principles that ensured their land was as healthy as possible in a farming operation while providing nutritious food for local markets. Contrary to the productivist model, they have no intention of expanding their markets further as they value the notion of localized food systems in which there is a community basis to supply chains as a foundational moment of value creation. They grow a variety of vegetables, including carrots, beets, radishes, tomatoes, potatoes, and leafy greens. Despite the ever-present challenges of growing diverse varieties of crops, warding off pests that target vegetables, and coping with drought, the owners do not use synthetic inputs or pesticides within what they designate to be a sustainable farming system.

Their commitment to improving the farm's natural capital is supported through a cornerstone of strong soil quality. Of the farm's 40 acres, only 20 acres are used at any one time. This rotation replenishes soil nutrients. They also occasionally plant a mix of legumes which are designed to improve soil health in preparation for the next cultivation. Strong soil health also protects against harmful pests that can strongly diminish crop yields. The farm does not use any synthetic fertilizers or pesticides, citing the harmful impact those inputs have on the soil. Because they don't use these inputs, they are maximizing their long-term soil health and saving on input costs. Additionally, because growing vegetables is water intensive, the owners pay great attention to their water supplies. Notably, high quality soil is better able to store water in situ, offering an insurance policy against the increasing number of seasonal droughts occurring throughout the area. This maximizes the efficiency of their primary well and mitigates against a vicious cycle in which dry soil can reduce organic matter, reducing soil productivity and its subsequent ability to hold moisture.

Last, strong soil quality raises the quality of the farming produce, with the owners stating that their vegetables are more nutrient dense and more flavorful than conventionally grown vegetables. In turn, this increases their demand and allows for consistent sales to consumers, particularly the bespoke local restaurant industry. This quote from the farm's website summarizes their mission-driven approach:

> Patchwork Gardens began as an idea that food should be grown locally and sustainably. . . Our mission is to sustainably grow the most nutrient dense, best tasting vegetables. We are able to achieve this by focusing our attention on soil life. Good soil has high organic matter (humus) with lots of living organisms like bacteria and fungi, worms etc. – an ecosystem. When the soil is healthy and full of life your food is healthy – great tasting – and full of life!

In this manner, Patchworks Gardens' primary avenue of value creation is through maximizing ecological health of their land and promoting this idea as a reasonable course of action to business partners and consumers who are prepared to pay a premium in return. They are open to acting as a template for others to follow, recognizing the value their operation brings toward building natural and social capital. A positive externality, recognized by the owners, are the benefits to health due to consumption of nutrient-dense products. One way in which the owners are seeking sustainable solutions rather than a competitive advantage is their mission of staying local. The owners indicated they have the potential to scale up operations to reach a larger geographic area with more demand, this would betray their founding ideas when starting the farm which was to benefit the local community. Patchwork's strong commitment to remaining locally grounded enterprise factors into its emphasis on empowerment. Patchwork stands out compared to the majority of farms in the area in its approach toward managing its labor force. Providing strong training has resulted in a dedicated workforce, with a larger ratio of women being employed compared to most farms in the province.

Notwithstanding the social mission of the farm, Patchwork Gardens must balance this goal with nurturing a profitable enterprise that can cover costs, pay a small but important hired workforce, remunerate the co-owners, and provide enough surplus capital to replace machinery and make new investments. To ensure that they had suitable business skills, prior to launching the farm the co-owners attended workshops, hired consultants, consulted with the economic development office, and took business planning courses. They spent two years building this business acumen, which contrasts with many other alternative agriculture initiatives. In terms of profitability, the farm is reliant entirely on agriculture with no side ventures or sources of income. In some ways, this creates tension between a growing season that is primarily in the summer and fall seasons where profits must be accrued for the remainder of the year. That said, the co-owners emphasize that the social mission of the enterprise predicated on local supply chains helps to minimize economic risk by creating durable embedded relationships across markets. Having nurtured a community across their markets, they argued, helped them throughout the disruptions of the Covid-19 pandemic. In order to further maximize economic resilience, they have started selling value-added products such as pre-made salads. To this end, they have considered expanding by creating a commercial kitchen on site to help prepare more value-added products, but the potential risks mean that they are not ready to make that jump yet.

9 Case Study 2: Loughborough Heritage Orchard

Loughborough Heritage Orchard has been in operation for nine years. Similar to Patchwork Gardens, the owners of the orchard had little farming experience prior to starting the venture. The name of the farm included the word "heritage" due to the uniqueness of the land. The 17 acres of land they bought had an old orchard from the 1940s with many of the original apple trees. Growing organic apples is the primary source of income, but they also sell eggs, maple syrup, seasonal vegetables, homemade bread, and jams and jellies to supplement their income. Despite the agroecological approach the farm takes to maintaining their orchard, the self-identified defining feature of the venture's mission is to serve their local community through building social capital.

In this respect, the owners have a strong connection to their local community, finding that people in their community of Inverary rely on them for provision of nutritious and flavorful goods at a reasonable price without having to drive to supermarkets in the closest urban area. The owners felt this concept was even more critical during the Covid-19 pandemic, when accessing food in rural communities was more of a challenge. While the connection with locals benefits the Inverary community, the owners also find this connection to benefit their business as well. By building this social capital with their neighbors, they feel confident that they will have a long-term market for their products. Selling directly to their community neighbors also buffers against market and supply chain disruptions, such as those presented during the volatility of the pandemic.

The owners have a strong conviction to keep prices lower than comparable products that are sold in grocery stores. They take the position of food being a human right, where no human ought to be priced out of buying nutritious foods. This ethical choice the owners take recognizes that some of their neighbors depend on the orchard's products, summarized by this statement on their website: "Today, a great divide is being created between those who can afford organic and everyone else who cannot. When we price our products, we compare against major grocery store chains and then price our products a bit lower. We feel that prices should be lower when buying directly from the farm as there is not the usual "middleman" to deal with. We truly believe that everyone, regardless of income levels, should be able to afford great food for their family. Products purchased directly at the farm are not only better, but should be more affordable; ours are both!"

The business has also adopted an eco-tourism model, where community members are encouraged to visit, learn about the operation, and roam the grounds. They regularly entertain school field trips and have an annual Heritage Saturday event, where they host a large communal gathering. These eco-tourist events have a dual effect of earning supplemental income while building social capital designed to benefit both the farm and the farm's visitors long term by establishing long term connection.

Heritage Orchard's passion for extending the value they create to its local community is central to their mission. The social issue they care about most, as evidenced in their organizations branding, is to solve the issue of poor access to organic foods in rural areas. They identified the primary barrier to this community goal is high cost. They also identified a marginalized community to assist, whereby they aim to solely help those in need rather than those who don't need help accessing organic products. Because of their centrality in the community, they only sell their products at their farm, which helps reduce costs. The owners specify they've done this to make it easier for nearby patrons to drop in at any time because as the owners say, their primary customers rely on their product or else they wouldn't be able to access organic products at all.

This aspect of only focusing on their immediate surrounding geographic area exemplifies the enterprises match with proposition 3 of the positive theory of social enterprise. The owners are clearly not interested in focusing on value appropriation, as they are forgoing potential profits in two ways. Making their products more accessible to the nearby urban area, only 25 min away, would greatly increase demand. Furthermore, as they mention, they could greatly increase their prices. Instead, they hope to act as a model for other social enterprises to see that it is possible to maintain an organic orchard selling products at lower prices. Part of this is keeping an open farm policy, where everyone is encouraged to tour the grounds and see how they can keep their organic production running while selling at such cheap prices.

That said, to be able to operate in such a fashion requires three fundamental pillars of the enterprise. First, everything is sold in-situ on the farm, as opposed to restaurants and markets. This avoids both the labor needed for transportation and the costs incurred. Second, they rely heavily on volunteer labor, including overseas volunteers through the Worldwide Opportunities on Organic Farms (WWOOF) program that places young volunteers on farms to learn the skills of organic farming. However, it also relies on local community volunteers as well. These volunteers are integral to the operation, as the farm does not have the finances to make use of paid staff, yet the labor demands in peak harvesting season are considerable. Third, expanding eco-tourism is considered very important for the farm's annual income with an emphasis on school tours and local events such as Heritage Saturday that draws people from across the region into the farm. In short, the value creation operation requires considerable community support to allow the farm to make tradeoffs on value appropriation.

10 Case Study 3: Edible Forest Farms

Edible Forest Farms encompasses 76 acres with a substantial tract of land forming a dedicated permaculture farming project. The farm grows over 50 crop varieties, with a particular emphasis on growing a diverse set of trees mixed into edible crops as a form of agroforestry. These crops grown include berries, legumes, and vegetables. Managing this enhanced biodiversity is one of the owners' favorite aspects of farming: by synthesizing complex intercropping patterns at the microscale the farm is designed to extract ecosystem services and benefits throughout the farm that spread into the wider landscape. This approach toward agroecological farming fits within the owner's vision for their farm to serve as an excellent example of permaculture that expands community understandings of what value diverse farms provide.

Edible Forest works within a unique business framework centered around the owner's vision, where a permaculture farm's foremost mission is to balance its inputs and outputs, encapsulating a "living within your means" mindset. Within this neo-subsistence orientation, all the farm's products which are not necessary to put back into the agroecosystem or used within the household are considered excess and are given away to the community for free. Products that are considered necessary are kept for consumption by the owner's family or recycled back into the environment, such as for compost or seeds. For example, in the 2022 growing season, the farm produced many peaches that were far too many for the owners to consume themselves, so the rest were given away. While Edible Forest could sell these peaches on the market for substantial profit, they believe this would violate the true vision of permaculture. The only products that are sold for money are garlic and maple syrup, which are sold to pay for rare instances when new inputs are required, such as new trees.

While the non-profit oriented business model has provided ample products for the owner's family, the farm is also designed to broadcast the benefits of permaculture models to others to carry on the vision to benefit future generations. Exemplified by this are the resources available on their website, such as highlighting several textbooks to help farmers establish permaculture techniques. The farm also holds events and workshops for the community to help spread permaculture principles to those who are interested, ranging from broad farm tours to more specific agroforestry techniques such as mushroom log inoculation.

Whereas the value created by Patchwork Gardens and Heritage Orchard is tangible, through improving ecological health and improving access to healthy food, Edible Forest Farm's primary mode of value is the knowledge that is created and spread to the community. Knowledge ranges from specific farming methods such as which plants grow well next to each other, to broad methods such as the philosophy of permaculture and new conceptions of farming. This value is not targeted to marginalized communities, rather those who are unfamiliar with permaculture or those whose only conception of farming is one of conventional methods and are unaware of more sustainable farming ideas. That said, the farm does collaborate with local indigenous communities with the goal of preserving traditional varieties within the region.

To be able to support this model of permaculture, the farm relies in part on volunteer labor through the WWOOF program. At the same time, the owner has invested his earnings from a previous career as an educator to build up some of the required infrastructure while other household members work outside the farm and provide income for the family. On this basis, for the owner-operator, there is also no reason to gain a competitive advantage to serve value appropriation because the farm does not earn an income.

11 Case Study 4: Sonset Farms

Sonset Farms is a dairy farm located in Inverary, Ontario, that endured a radical shift in the 1990s, when it transitioned from a conventional to a fully organic dairy farm. In addition to the farm's 60 cows, they also have diversified to raising pigs and chickens and grow their own organic soy, buckwheat, and spelt. The shift toward diversification and embracing organic methods was the result of a newfound focus for the farm's owners toward long-term sustainability. The farm has a rich history, with Sonset farm being operated by the same family on the same land for nearly 80 years, covering four generations. The farm's heritage, and commitment to honoring that heritage, underscores the decisions and operations of the farm. The owners recognize the immense challenge of maintaining a multigenerational farm, while also recognizing the profound benefit that operating a multigenerational farm has on both the farm's core family as well as the surrounding rural community.

The transition to relying more on ecosystem services through agroecological techniques was described by the owners as being more difficult to generate reasonable profits, meaning that passion for farming is even more important. They note this passion must come from an understanding of the importance of keeping their farm running, especially considering so many of their farming neighbors have left the business over the years. As a result, the rural space surrounding Sonset Farms has fractured, leading to a perceived shift in farming community vitality. The owners are grateful that their children and grandchildren are taking an interest in the farm given its strong history of co-management, where each family member's opinions are considered when making decisions. Without the integration of younger generations, the farm's immediate and long-term future would be in great jeopardy. The owners report risks of burnout, prompting a movement toward holistic resource management to better manage their personal health and resiliency.

Sonset Farms' primary form of value creation is also more abstract: on the one hand the shift to organic farming is argued by the owners to safeguard on-farm agroecological conditions into the future by building soil health and enhancing natural capital. Equally, the owners emphasize how sustainable farming practices are central to preserving biodiversity across the regions. On the other, the farm is organized to consciously push back on the idea that generational farms are a relic of the past and can't survive unless taking a conventional productivist agriculture approach. They see themselves as a family farm that can act as a model for struggling intergenerational farms to see that Sonset has survived despite all of the turmoil and struggles that so many other family farms in their region have faced. The owners believe that given all of the turmoil, farming has to be a passion as otherwise the farm wouldn't survive. The owners also cite the dystopian reality that could occur if family farms all went out of business at the mercy of large-scale corporate farms. In this way, the enterprise certainly values empowerment and acting as a sort of "role model" figure in their community.

At the same time, unlike the previous two farms, Sonset actively seeks to turn a profit that can underpin the family's material needs and provide a surplus for reinvestment in relatively expensive machinery vital to the operation. Shifting from purely dairy to a more diverse farm – including producing organic soy and cereals – provides a more resilient set of diversified income streams than relying on milk only and is therefore key to reliable value appropriation. The milk is sold to an organic milk wholesaler and enters the mainstream food system. This provides a relatively reliable price for the primary output, although it does mean that the farm has no direct relationship with a consumer base, which partially contrasts with their social mission orientation. That said, other farm products are sold locally, through a more relationship-based set of market exchanges. Such embedded relationships within the locality help to guarantee that they are paid on time and can avoid dockages and hidden fees that the owners claim are rife within the wider market economy.

12 Social Capital, Social Entrepreneurship, Community Resilience in Rural Areas

All four of the above farm enterprises explicitly seek to maximize value creation in a variety of forms, with the promotion of ecological health and community resilience standing as common goals. To pursue these wider social missions, however, each farm is compromising elements of value appropriation that raises key questions about the sustainability of their operations with respect to profitability and the ability to maintain a labor force. In each case study, social capital emerges as a necessary theme that allowed each farmer to bridge the tension between value creation and value capture. As has been well established, social capital measures the strength of connectivity across social networks. Where social capital is strong, it connects an individual, group, or community to wider networks that can provide information, contacts, resources or political voice (Ifejika Speranza, 2013; Tittonell, 2020). In the above examples, building and mobilizing social capital was a foundational requirement for each farm to realize its social mission as it provided access to embedded exchanges of goods and labor that operated outside of a strict market exchange.

For example, the Heritage Orchard business model relies on social capital within their community as a means to build an embedded client base and ensure volunteer labor to underscore the social purpose of the farm. Similarly, the Edible Forest Farms owner's pursuit of community building provided significant benefit when operations on the farm require extra help, as neighboring farmers often would mobilize in times of need. Sonset Farms noted the usefulness of embedded connections with community-based agents who work in the rural supply chain, providing for a mutual and cordial relationship of giving and receiving fair prices when exchanging products. In all these cases, the embedded quality of the social mission farm is pivotal for generating the conditions under which it functions year over year.

In addition to these positives, farm owners argue that building social capital facilitates the creation of transformational change across broader rural society. Rural areas are often contrasted to the urban setting where – as Kipatrick et al. (2015) outline – social enterprises can more readily pursue both horizontal and vertical network connections to open access to important resources that allow the enterprise to fulfill its mission and to build a wider client base. In contrast, rural areas do not readily have these formal strategies and linkages available (Lang & Fink, 2019). In this way, building community is seen by mission-driven farms as pivotal to generalizing the wider goals of sustainable food systems and community resilience. For example, Edible Forest Farm's main mission is to establish permaculture as a viable and necessary farming approach through leading by example to the community to showcase its potential in real time. Building social capital by distributing produce for free is part of attracting attention to the viability of the permaculture model. Similarly, Sonset Farms' mission of keeping intergenerational small family farms alive also requires community connections to act as a showcase, both for other family farms to see that family farming is still viable, as well as for society to see that small family farms still exist and are worth supporting. Finally, given that Heritage Orchard wishes to revolutionize the way society views food, suggesting access to healthy food ought to be a human right, then social networks must be built that connect to Heritage Orchard to a wider network of food system transformation at a larger scale.

Measuring the social capital that exists within each farm's community was outside of the scope of this research but would be an optimal course of study to examine opportunities and barriers to scaling up social enterprises to maximize societal change (Scheuerle & Schmitz, 2016). What the current study does suggest is that alignment with the argument put forward by Hidalgo et al. (2021), social entrepreneurs have agency to create social capital within their network that can be effectively used to mobilize institutions and other community groups within a social mission agenda. At the same time, while social capital drives social enterprise, both help build resilience that can address rural decline by finding ways for communities to cope with change. For example, social engagement has been argued as an important form of resilience building for rural areas that are facing economic decline (McManus et al., 2012). Social engagement improves social capital through the creation of networks that encourage innovation and participation. These social networks are the foundations of not only allowing social enterprises to emerge, but also for them to flourish.

They also allow for social entrepreneurs to identify problems that are most relevant to the target community to boost local resilience.

In this respect, a contrast can be drawn between the types of social networks created by alternative farmers and conventional farmers in Southeastern Ontario. Conventional farms participate within the large-scale agribusiness industry, where most of the decisions they make come from agribusiness networks. Conventional farmers reported working with input dealers to determine optimal crops to grow, which also require chemical inputs and fertilizers advertised by the dealers. They also reported a strong reliance on heavy machinery that is specially equipped to work with the crops recommended to them. Conventional farms grow cash crops which are exported nationally or overseas, as incentivized by the policies outlined in the earlier sections of this chapter. While conventional farmers do maintain social networks with other conventional farmers, these networks were orientated toward how best to maximize farming business within the industrial agribusiness model (i.e. value capture) rather than sharing new ideas outside of this model to help build local resilience (value creation).

In contrast, alternative farms utilized their networks to integrate two key indicators of resilience into their operations. First, they emphasized reflective and shared learning, where they foregrounded collective experimentation in hopes to generate and broadcast successful methods throughout their network. For example, Heritage Orchard experimented incorporating animals into their orchard's agroecosystem using a system of holistic resource management. This improves the health of their agroecosystem allowing them to forego paying for external inputs such as pesticides, which allows them to keep prices low. Edible Forest Farms takes a trial-and-error approach to see which combinations of crop varieties grow best in different assortments. Combinations that are successful are documented for other permaculturists to try under their conditions.

The second key resilience indicator they displayed was integrating local knowledge systems into their business plan. Local knowledge sharing encourages the transfer of knowledge between experts and non-experts, with that knowledge being used to inform decision making about local-scale topics to help solve issues relevant to the community. For example, both Patchwork Gardens and Edible Forest Farms partner with KASSI (Kingston Area Seed Savers Initiative) to grow locally adapted seeds. The ability to grow locally adapted crops is critical to both enterprises' missions in delivering crops that don't require harmful inputs and keeping an emphasis on keeping the scope of their business model local. In this respect, social entrepreneurs exist as a focal point that can turn social capital into rural resilience. The dynamics processes that strengthen resilience also strengthen social innovation within the context of social enterprise (cf. Westley, 2013).

13 Conclusion

This chapter offered a general overview of rural social entrepreneurship by discussing common definitions and applications, introducing an analytical theory framework, showcasing four examples of social enterprises in rural Southeastern Ontario, and evaluating the preconditions needed to scale up social enterprises to maximize social benefit. Drawing upon the theory proposed by Santos (2012), the paper explored how these social enterprises prioritize value creation over value capture by mobilizing diverse strategies aimed at safeguarding environmental health and community revitalization.

The context for this social mission orientation was a long-term policy orientation by the Canadian federal and provincial governments that has promoted a rural business environment that seeks to capture value rather than create value. Rural Southeastern Ontario farming tends to be productivist export-oriented that does little to revitalize rural communities that have experienced significant decline in the age of globalization. Alternative farming businesses that challenge the status quo of productivist agriculture seek to offer a vision of how social enterprises can maximize societal benefit and challenge rural decline. The enterprises we examined explicitly sought to achieve core values such as reducing environmental impact, lowering barriers to healthy food access, spreading permaculture ideals, or promoting small family farms as a fulcrum of community revitalization.

As the chapter indicates, however, each of these enterprises encountered tensions between value creation and value capture, with notable limitations in their ability to ensure profitability, provide adequate labor supply, or to mitigate market volatility. To do so, each social enterprise relied on its capacity to actively build social capital which could feed back into the broader mission of the farm by ensuring a reliable consumer base, providing labor inputs at times of need, or facilitating embedded market relations that helped stabilize supply chains. In so doing, these farms could be argued to help elevate community resilience by creating a more socially embedded food system. These social entrepreneurs were keen to argue that rural areas remain prone to systemic change as markets and demographics continue to shift to urban areas and therefore require the proactive creation of resilience to mitigate further outmigration and declining earnings in the agricultural sector. Inarguably, the foundation for social enterprises to help contribute to community resilience is their ability to foster social capital to allow for social participation and engagement. Future inquiry into how to measure social capital in rural areas can further bridge social enterprise research to broader research themes of rural studies research.

References

Abu-Saifan, S. (2012). Social entrepreneurship: Definition and boundaries. Technology Innovation Management Review, 2(2).

Alvord, S.H., Brown, L.D., & Letts, C.W. (2004). Social entrepreneurship and societal transformation: An exploratory study. The Journal of Applied Behavioral Science, 40(3), 260–282.

Andrée, P., Ballamingie, P., & Sinclair-Waters, B. (2015). Neoliberalism and the making of food politics in Eastern Ontario. Local Environment, 20(12), 1452–1472.

Ansari, S., Munir, K., & Gregg, T. (2012). Impact at the 'bottom of the pyramid': The role of social capital in capability development and community empowerment. Journal of Management Studies, 49(4), 813–842.

Azmat, F., Ferdous, A.S., & Couchman, P. (2015). Understanding the dynamics between social entrepreneurship and inclusive growth in subsistence marketplaces. Journal of Public Policy & Marketing, 34(2), 252–271.

Bowen, H. R. (1953). Social responsibility of the businessman. New York: Harper & Row.

Brinckerhoff, P.C. (2009). Mission-based management: Leading your not-for-profit in the 21st century (Vol. 231). John Wiley & Sons.

Chesbrough, H., Lettl, C., & Ritter, T. (2018). Value creation and value capture in open innovation. Journal of Product Innovation Management, 35(6), 930–938.

Collins, B. (2023). Farm resilience in Southeastern Ontario: A comparative study of alternative and conventional farms. (Doctoral dissertation, Queen's University, School of Environmental Studies).

Dacin, P.A., Dacin, M.T., & Matear, M. (2010). Social entrepreneurship: Why we don't need a new theory and how we move forward from here. Academy of Management Perspectives, 24(3), 37–57.

Daskalopoulou, I., Karakitsiou, A., & Thomakis, Z. (2023). Social entrepreneurship and social capital: A review of impact research. Sustainability, 15(6), 4787.

Datta, P.B., & Gailey, R. (2012). Empowering women through social entrepreneurship: Case study of a women's cooperative in India. Entrepreneurship Theory and Practice, 36(3), 569–587.

Dees, J.G. (1998). The meaning of social entrepreneurship.

Dyer, J.H., Singh, H., & Hesterly, W.S. (2018). The relational view revisited: A dynamic perspective on value creation and value capture. Strategic Management Journal, 39(12), 3140–3162.

Friedman, M. 1970. The social responsibility of business is to increase its profits. New York Times Magazine. September 13.

Ghauri, P., Tasavori, M., & Zaefarian, R. (2014). Internationalisation of service firms through corporate social entrepreneurship and networking. International Marketing Review, 31(6), 576–600.

Haugh, H.M., & Talwar, A. (2016). Linking social entrepreneurship and social change: The mediating role of empowerment. Journal of Business Ethics, 133, 643–658.

Hedlund, M., & Lundholm, E. (2015). Restructuring of rural Sweden–employment transition and out-migration of three cohorts born 1945–1980. Journal of Rural Studies, 42, 123–132.

Hidalgo, G., Monticelli, J.M., & Vargas Bortolaso, I. (2021). Social capital as a driver of social entrepreneurship. Journal of Social Entrepreneurship, 1–24.

Ifejika Speranza, C. (2013). Buffer capacity: Capturing a dimension of resilience to climate change in African smallholder agriculture. Regional Environmental Change, 13, 521–535.

Kilpatrick, S., Johnson, L., King, T.J., Jackson, R., & Jatrana, S. (2015). Making connections in a regional city: Social capital and the primary social contract. Journal of Sociology, 51(2), 207–220.

Laforge, J., Fenton, A., Lavalée-Picard, V., & McLachlan, S. (2018). New farmers and food policies in Canada. Canadian Food Studies/La Revue canadienne des études sur l'alimentation, 5(3), 128–152.

Lang, R., & Fink, M. (2019). Rural social entrepreneurship: The role of social capital within and across institutional levels. Journal of Rural Studies, 70, 155–168.

Lane, M.J. (2014). The mission-driven venture: Business solutions to the world's most vexing social problems. John Wiley & Sons.

Leadbeater, C. (1997). The rise of the social entrepreneur. (No.25). Demos.

Lebel, A., Noreau, D., Tremblay, L., Oberlé, C., Girard-Gadreau, M., Duguay, M., & Block, J.P. (2016). Identifying rural food deserts: Methodological considerations for food environment interventions. Canadian Journal of Public Health, 107, eS21–eS26.

Li, Y., Westlund, H., & Liu, Y. (2019). Why some rural areas decline while some others not: An overview of rural evolution in the world. Journal of Rural Studies, 68, 135–143.

Luck, G.W., Black, R., & Race, D. (2010). Demographic change in rural Australia: Future opportunities and challenges. Demographic Change in Australia's Rural Landscapes: Implications for Society and the Environment, 375–384.

Mair, J., & Marti, I. (2006). Social entrepreneurship research: A source of explanation, prediction, and delight. Journal of World Business, 41(1), 36–44.

Markey, S., Halseth, G., & Manson, D. (2008). Challenging the inevitability of rural decline: Advancing the policy of place in northern British Columbia. Journal of Rural Studies, 24(4), 409–421.

Marsden, T., Lamine, C., & Schneider, S. (2020). A research agenda for global rural development.

McCarthy, B. (2012). From fishing and factories to cultural tourism: The role of social entrepreneurs in the construction of a new institutional field. Entrepreneurship & Regional Development, 24(3–4), 259–282.

McManus, P., Walmsley, J., Argent, N., Baum, S., Bourke, L., Martin, J., . . . Sorensen, T. (2012). Rural community and rural resilience: What is important to farmers in keeping their country towns alive? Journal of Rural Studies, 28(1), 20–29.

Mizik, N., & Jacobson, R. (2003). Trading off between value creation and value appropriation: The financial implications of shifts in strategic emphasis. Journal of Marketing, 67(1), 63–76.

Morrison, C., Ramsey, E., & Bond, D. (2017). The role of social entrepreneurs in developing community resilience in remote areas. Journal of Enterprising Communities: People and Places in the Global Economy, 11(1), 95–112.

Munoz, S.A., Steiner, A., & Farmer, J. (2015). Processes of community-led social enterprise development: Learning from the rural context. Community Development Journal, 50(3), 478–493.

Nichols, A. (2006). Social entrepreneurship: New models for sustainable change.

O'Keeffe, J., Buytaert, W., Mijic, A., Brozović, N., & Sinha, R. (2016). The use of semi-structured interviews for the characterisation of farmer irrigation practices. Hydrology and Earth System Sciences, 20(5), 1911–1924.

Ontario Federation of Agriculture. Our farm environmental agenda. Ontario Federation of Agriculture, 2020.

Parrish, B.D. (2010). Sustainability-driven entrepreneurship: Principles of organization design. Journal of Business Venturing, 25(5), 510–523.

Saebi, T., Foss, N.J., & Linder, S. (2019). Social entrepreneurship research: Past achievements and future promises. Journal of Management, 45(1), 70–95.

Santos, F.M. (2012). A positive theory of social entrepreneurship. Journal of Business Ethics, 111(3), 335–351.

Scheuerle, T., & Schmitz, B. (2016). Inhibiting factors of scaling up the impact of social entrepreneurial organizations–a comprehensive framework and empirical results for Germany. Journal of Social Entrepreneurship, 7(2), 127–161.

Schoenberger, E. (1994). Corporate strategy and corporate strategists: Power, identity, and knowledge within the firm. Environment and Planning A, 26(3), 435–451.

Shamir, R. (2008). The age of responsibilization: On market-embedded morality. Economy and Society, 37(1), 1–19.

Seelos, C., & Mair, J. (2005). Social entrepreneurship: Creating new business models to serve the poor. Business Horizons, 48(3), 241–246.
Sinthupundaja, J., Kohda, Y., & Chiadamrong, N. (2020). Examining capabilities of social entrepreneurship for shared value creation. Journal of Social Entrepreneurship, 11(1), 1–22.
Sjödin, D., Parida, V., Jovanovic, M., & Visnjic, I. (2020). Value creation and value capture alignment in business model innovation: A process view on outcome-based business models. Journal of Product Innovation Management, 37(2), 158–183.
Therond, O., Duru, M., Roger-Estrade, J., & Richard, G. (2017). A new analytical framework of farming system and agriculture model diversities. A review. Agronomy for Sustainable Development, 37, 1–24.
Thompson, J., Alvy, G., & Lees, A. (2000). Social entrepreneurship–a new look at the people and the potential. Management Decision, 38(5), 328–338.
Tittonell, P. (2020). Assessing resilience and adaptability in agroecological transitions. Agricultural Systems, 184, 102862.
Westley, F. (2013). Social innovation and resilience: How one enhances the other. Stanford Social Innovation Review, 11(3), 28–39.
Wirth, P., Elis, V., Müller, B., & Yamamoto, K. (2016). Peripheralisation of small towns in Germany and Japan–Dealing with economic decline and population loss. Journal of Rural Studies, 47, 62–75.
Wood, R.E. (2008). Survival of rural America: Small victories and bitter harvests. University Press of Kansas.
Zahra, S.A., Rawhouser, H.N., Bhawe, N., Neubaum, D.O., & Hayton, J.C. (2008). Globalization of social entrepreneurship opportunities. Strategic Entrepreneurship Journal, 2(2), 117–131.

Chyi-Lyi (Kathleen) Liang and Maria I. Marshall

Examples of Theories and Data Sources in Conducting Research of Rural Entrepreneurship

Abstract: Entrepreneurship is an integrated subject. Many theories and frameworks have been connected with research topics focusing on entrepreneurial behavior, decision-making, enterprise management strategies, and evaluations of consequences. This chapter provides an overview of several theories that scholars have adopted to examine or explore activities and decisions associated with rural entrepreneurship. Some datasets are also included in the discussion to support research related to rural entrepreneurship development. Future research topics are recommended to stimulate new research domains and expand knowledge and applications.

Keywords: entrepreneurship theories, rural entrepreneurship, data sources

1 Background

Researchers have different perspectives about entrepreneurs in rural locations versus rural entrepreneurs (e.g. Fortunato, 2014; Korsgaard, Müller & Tanvig, 2015). Entrepreneurs in rural locations often mobilize resources to conduct business transactions in rural areas because these entrepreneurs live in or work from rural areas, and use resources or labor that are located in other areas to conduct business. Rural entrepreneurs who also live and work in rural communities, based on literature examples, interact and access rural resources to promote business activities and target rural economic development. Given the availability of fast-growing information and communication technology, only few industry sectors would be location-dependent if entrepreneurs could make decisions and engage in day-to-day operations via online platforms and tele-communication channels effectively. However, rural entrepreneurship is unique when it comes to community development, local workforce development, training and education opportunities, and economic mobility directly transforming and affecting the prosperity of rural populations.

Most of the theories in entrepreneurship studies are affiliated with economic growth, economic development, wealth creation, and income generation. Recent studies have

Chyi-Lyi (Kathleen) Liang, North Carolina Agricultural and Technical State University, email: cliang@ncat.edu
Maria I. Marshall, Department of Agricultural Economics, Purdue University, email: mimarsha@purdue.edu

https://doi.org/10.1515/9783110791396-010

broadened the lens of entrepreneurship to investigate entrepreneurs and entrepreneurial decisions from an integrated approach. However, most of the theories related to entrepreneurship do not specify timeframe of decisions made, actions triggered by decisions across time and space, and explicit or implicit impacts associated with decisions on rural communities. Limited discussions exist about rural entrepreneurship theory in high-income countries which have unique settings compared with low-income countries (Newbery, Siwale & Henley, 2017). There are some commonalities shared between rural entrepreneurship in high- and low-income countries, including challenges and barriers of access to resources, capital, and opportunities. However, community characteristics, social capital, network configurations, and access to opportunities and information pose different barriers for rural entrepreneurs in high-income countries versus low-income countries.

Scholars have argued that entrepreneurship is not a singular research domain with well-categorized divisions (e.g., Microeconomics vs Macroeconomics). It has been tricky for scholars to pursue research in rural entrepreneurship due to the nature of academia demanding sounded theoretical framework to generate creative research questions, testable hypotheses, and logical approaches to analyze data. Sometimes scholars do not have a good definition to identify entrepreneurship within existing fields or among integrated fields (e.g., economics, sociology, geography, business management, engineering). This chapter will present some theories and data that have been referenced in studying rural entrepreneurship in developed economies to support scholars expanding the theory domain. Hopefully more scholars from different fields would share the expertise beyond the traditional research domains to stimulate collaboration and innovation to enhance rural wealth.

2 Examples of Theories Related to Research in Rural Entrepreneurship

2.1 Location Theory

Location theory in previous literature has been linked to the theory of regional economic growth in historical context. Earlier economic theories focused on industrialization, productivity, and growth. Pred (1967) argued that previous location theory seemed to emphasize maximizing firms' profit and minimizing transportation costs. Pred (1967) offered additional insight to justify producers' decisions based on both economic and non-economic factors. These non-economic factors would involve entrepreneur's understanding of geographical restrictions, social characteristics, imperfect knowledge or information, and other behavioral variables. Scholars also introduced additional propositions to enhance the linkages between location theory and economic growth theory under certain conditions associated with the development of rural entrepreneurship (North, 1955). For example, North (1955) discussed that new business establishments in a region must identify products that would generate comparative advantage in cost structures including production and transportation. The development of specialized markets, improvement of finance and services, and workforce development also needed to support the enterprises within a reasonable geographic location. This finding echoes the earlier discussions regarding differences between entrepreneurs in rural areas or rural entrepreneurship – geographic location does not limit the entrepreneur's ability to design and implement business decisions, however, effective support of local markets, local workforce development, and local investment strategies would trigger rural economic growth.

Shields (2005) studied rural settings and how they impacted entrepreneurs from two aspects: geo-demographic features and sociocultural features. The natural environment and agricultural working landscape played a key role in rural entrepreneurship, particularly for those businesses that rely on the natural environment for strategies such as tourism. Depending on the scope and purpose of the business, a remote location could be a barrier or opportunity for the business. While employment opportunities might be limited in rural communities, residents who chose to stay in rural communities often had a strong sense of place, tradition, and legacy. Terluin (2003) provided an overview and analysis of theories to discuss differences in economic development in rural regions of developed countries. Terluin summarized that the factors influencing the concentration of labor and capital in a specific location could be related to the existence of a leading or dominating firm, which acted as a primary convener/driver to stimulate economic growth within the region for other industries and businesses. Research in this aspect (agglomeration) could examine the types of leadership among rural communities across different sectors, the investment in education and training to fill the gaps of employment, and the market supply chain configurations to support demand and supply.

Recent studies seemed to follow a similar path to design and develop research in rural entrepreneurship based on the linkages of location theory and economic growth theory. Emerging industries such as tourism and local-oriented niche businesses have grown significantly in rural areas. However, most of these businesses are small and exposed to higher risks being in rural locations. For example, Shields (2005) investigated effects of rural geo-demographic and sociocultural features on a group of small businesses (Shields, 2005). A survey instrument was designed and implemented to gather information from 76 small business owners to test if there were any statistical significance across geo-demographic and sociocultural features such as access to transportation, labor market, gender of the business owners, and other perceived characteristics regarding rural. Findings revealed that rural geo-demographic had negative impacts on marketability of product and service most significantly. Siemens (2010) discussed some factors driving entrepreneurs to stay in rural communities – wanting to control their own business, enjoying a lifestyle being in rural, and creating employment opportunities within the community. Muñoz and Kimmit (2019) introduced an integrated framework to reflect rural entrepreneurship in place via interviews to identify key variables that affect the development of an adequate place for rural entrepreneurship. Interesting findings included four distinct elements of a rural entrepreneurship place that involved material location (i.e. resources), rural locale (i.e. characteristics), rooted enablers, and collaborative places. Main lessons learned discussed the socio-spatial connectivity that reflected rural sensitivity and multi-level connections. These factors are similar to what have been discussed in literature where rural entrepreneurs conduct business based on relationships and trust. Some downsides of rural businesses could be higher transportation costs, longer time and distance to acquire inventory and supplies, lacking connection with a large customer base, and lacking infrastructure and network support. Many new topics still need more research attention such as how rural entrepreneurs reduce the barriers and challenges to form an effective supply chain.

Several scholars shared diverse views of regional and rural development associated with entrepreneurship from multi-theory reviews. For example, Kačar, Curić and Ikić (2016) offered a detailed analysis of some principals in the theory of economic development and revealed historical contexts of rural/local development associated with specific community factors such as technological change. Rural communities not too far from metropolitan areas with good community factors such as labor and investment would be able to adapt and thus benefit from technological change; while other communities might fall behind due to lack of infrastructure (e.g., rural communities may not have quality broadband access). Káposzta and Nagy (2022) introduced a series of studies to examine rural/local economic growth and applied spatial concepts to synthesize the strategies of resource-based bottom-up development expected to (1) generate new development triggers to stimulate new innovations, and (2) identify new development directions while integrating into broader spatial sociocultural traditions. Such studies involving location theories and spatial analysis recognized the complexity of factors in rural development and recommended designing a multifactor and system-wide framework to examine the interactions among social, economic, and environmental factors beyond a singular factor approach (e.g., labor profile and distribution, categories and priorities of local investment, local technical infrastructure, geographical characteristics, market, and transportation). Some suggested topics following this trend could explore types of social/economic/environmental triggers that stimulate or hinder certain categories of rural enterprises and to what extent. Other research topics could examine time values of investment in rural enterprises and workforce development, versus investment in stock markets or other interest-bearing strategies to compare present and future returns on investment.

2.2 Social Network Theories

Social network concepts have been widely applied to many disciplines such as community development, workforce development, grower-buyer connections, education stimulation, and health and food security. Early discussions of social networks could be traced to the late 1890s when scholars identified social groups that linked individuals or groups who shared value and belief. Freeman (1996, 2003, 2004), for example, described components, activities, and consequences given various types of social networks. A social network consists of individuals (actors) and the relationships among them. Common examples could be a family, an organization (e.g., a faith-based group, a school or a school district, a clinic or a hospital, a business or an industry). Rural entrepreneurship is an ideal setting to design, create, and grow a social network at a defined rural area (e.g., a town, a county). Many scholars have examined or explored entrepreneurial performance, challenges, barriers, and opportunities from a social network analysis aspect. For example, Pinho and Sampaio de Sa (2013) examined the pattern of networks between low, moderate, and high entrepreneurial performance of new ventures among 73 businesses. A survey was designed and implemented to gather information about the relationships of these businesses with different stakeholders (e.g., customers, suppliers, financial institution, relatives, and friends and colleagues). Findings revealed that close relatives, friends, and colleagues were most important to the businesses in early stage of business formation. Close relationships to major customers, suppliers, research centers, and universities seemed to support high venture performance in the start-up phase.

Siemens (2010) used a qualitative study to investigate challenges for small rural businesses. Market size, labor availability, access to urban centers, and infrastructure gaps were some common themes also discussed by other scholars (e.g., Bhushan, 2018; Tanwar & Bhardwaj, 2022). Social networks have been recognized to support local business development to boost rural economy and grow local talent and workforce. Economic scale could be a barrier for rural entrepreneurs given lower density of population and accessibility to markets. When we look at the entrepreneurs living and serving rural communities, they seem to have a strong sense of family and embeddedness within the communities that they serve. Building a trustworthy relationship with local residents and vendors may help rural entrepreneurs sustain business activities, even under the pressure to grow or expand the business activities to achieve higher profit. Some studies identified entrepreneurial characteristics associated with rural or urban entrepreneurs, and seeking high profit did not seem to rank high on entrepreneurs' priority list (e.g., Liang & Dunn, 2008; Liang & Dunn, 2007a; Liang & Dunn, 2007b). Many nascent entrepreneurs started businesses with family members or friends with whom they have strong ties in a social domain. It would be easier to acquire or gather resources or start-up capital from people who already have a good relationship or convenient communication with. The same situation holds for supplier, vendors, and financial institutions in a rural community. Although the business deal might create negative impacts on existing relationships, it is a common practice for rural entrepreneurs to work with local people or organizations when seeking advice or assistance.

Rural entrepreneurs are often embedded within their communities. Entrepreneurs may be embedded within their communities through social relationships, economic interdependence, cultural integration, and the use of local resources. Embeddedness in rural communities often leads to the development of trust and a good reputation. Rural entrepreneurs often play multiple roles within their communities beyond just being entrepreneurs. They may be involved in local organizations, schools, or government, which enhances their embeddedness within the community. Entrepreneurs who are embedded in rural communities often have a deep understanding of local culture, values, and traditions. This understanding can be a significant asset in marketing their products or services effectively to local customers.

Their strong social networks provide them with access to resources, information, and support that are crucial for business success. Rural entrepreneurs who are well connected and actively involved in their communities are more likely to be trusted by local residents, leading to increased customer loyalty and support. This reciprocity is important as they also rely on local suppliers and service providers. The reliance on local supply chains strengthens their ties to the community and contributes to the local economy by circulating money within the region. Embeddedness within a rural community can also enhance an entrepreneur's ability to adapt to changing circumstances and overcome challenges. Owners who have strong ties within their communities may receive valuable advice and better access to resources during difficult times. Overall, the concept of rural entrepreneurship and embeddedness underscores the interconnectedness between small businesses and the communities in which they operate. It emphasizes the significance of building and maintaining strong relationships, networks, and connections for the mutual benefit of both businesses and rural residents.

There are many aspects to apply social network theory in studying rural entrepreneurship. Researchers could observe the frequency of communications across different actors for various types of businesses. For example, retail, wholesale, manufacturing, and service sectors have protocols to serve and support each other. It would be critical to investigate how actors relate to each other in various levels of business transactions via communication strategies (e.g., frequency, style, and media). Legal contracts, regulatory concerns, organizational governance or structures, and levels of trust directly or indirectly influence how people within or across networks perform under various scenarios (e.g., startup vs maturity stage). All of these factors will trigger different responses to rural entrepreneurs' decisions on market, finance, labor, distribution, and growth.

2.3 Schumpeter and Institutional Theories

Schumpeter's entrepreneurship theory has triggered generations of topics in entrepreneurship research (Schumpeter, 1943). The essential idea of Schumpeter's entrepreneurial perspective is related to "creative destruction" where change and innovation would occur to replace old processes. Schumpeter argued that the economic process would evolve constantly, recessions and conflicts would occur, and creative innovation would be needed to re-establish the balance. Scholars have discussed several contexts regarding the Schumpeter's view of entrepreneurship (Sweezy, 1943). Whether it is from the capitalist's view or economic growth, many scholars recognize that innovation and entrepreneurial activities have been the driving force of our society. Given this thread of discussions, there are many topics that could shed light of modern rural entrepreneurship.

Śledzik (2013) reviewed and analyzed recent entrepreneurship development following Schumpeter's concept of innovation. Schumpeter's notion of innovation seems to match today's entrepreneurial decisions when many entrepreneurs (1) create new products to open new market opportunities; (2) design and implement new production or sale methods; (3) revamp the existing supply chains by creating new business models and new value propositions using new materials; and (4) create new industries that did not exist before (e.g., information, communication, and technology advancement). Schumpeter believed that entrepreneurs seeking profits must innovate and trigger change. While Schumpeter's view of entrepreneurship is still valid, modern entrepreneurship and innovation has become more complex and less reliant on one individual's capacity and perhaps more reliant on a system of collaboration or cooperation to achieve goals. This is particularly important when scholars conduct research in rural entrepreneurship since rural definition has changed significantly based on population migration, technology advancement, living environment mixed within natural contents, and accessibility to knowledge and information completely shifted the control and decision-making process for many rural entrepreneurs.

Andersson et al. (2022), for example, defined four elements in the entrepreneurship framework that could explain various levels of diversity and market integration, which would stimulate entrepreneurship and innovation in different manners. Global versus local market orientations, market integration and cost structures, consumers' profiles and preferences, and market service orientations would significantly influence the types of innovation in rural communities. The COVID-19 pandemic also provided an example of how organizational structures and market orientations shifted dramatically given unexpected disruptions. For example, our food systems and food supply chains were completely disrupted in a very short period of time – fresh produce or milk could not leave the farm gate, transportation and distribution systems were shut down due to lack of workers, consumers could not purchase food from grocery stores due to quarantine orders. The whole food production and supply chain had to evolve quickly to respond to the chaos and new business models surfaced from local themes to accommodate needs. Shorter and effective supply infrastructures such as a growing number of local farmer markets and food hubs have created and re-established food security for rural and urban areas. Rural communities have empowered the direct connections between local farmers and customers. The reactions and responses to the COVID-19 interruptions have proved that rural communities could be vulnerable yet resilient given creative activities. Future research is needed to track key elements in rural entrepreneurship correlating to enterprise resilience, innovative supply and demand connectivity, and impacts of social networks on untimely shocks for rural vs urban markets.

2.4 Finance, Capital, Resources

Several entrepreneurship researchers have taken a different theoretical approach to explain entrepreneurial decisions associated with finance, capital, and resource accessibility. For example, agglomeration theory described benefits for firms to locate near one another in certain types of location clusters (Glaeser, 2010). Some variables used in examining the validities of using agglomeration theory in rural entrepreneurship focus on population density, prices, wages, and transportation costs to move goods and people (Muñoz & Kimmitt, 2019; Goetz et al., 2010). Muñoz and Kimmitt (2019) further provided an empirical study to introduce an integrated framework based on the agglomeration approach, focused on institutional and structural conditions (social, economic, political and cultural) by enabling adequate human capital, financing, innovation, and enterprise supporting systems. Scholars believe that the integrated framework would trigger rural economic development and enhance competitiveness and growth. This integrated approach has also served as the base for more recent studies in food systems from production to supply chain and consumer welfare via entrepreneurial collaborations during the COVID-19 pandemic (e.g., Kansheba, Marobhe & Wald, 2023; Smith et al., 2024).

Resource-based theory and balanced scorecard theory have been mentioned in entrepreneurship studies, although not common in rural entrepreneurship research. Resource-based theory referred to measurement of a firm's performance based on the resources rather than in industry structure (Wernerfelt, 1984). Resources can be tangible or intangible in nature. Tangible resources include capital, access to capital and location (among others). Intangible resources consist of knowledge, skills and reputation, leadership, among others. Few studies have considered small firms from a resource-based view (Lerner and Almor, 2002), yet small firms are likely those which must rely heavily on the owner's skills or other intangible assets. Basco and Suwala (2021) also used resource-based theory to link family businesses to regional and rural development with a regional familiness model. They underscore the importance of understanding the composition of the firms in rural communities and that family firms may have a competitive advantage in rural communities because they are spatially embedded in their local contexts.

The Balanced Scorecard (BSC) was introduced by Kaplan and Norton (1992) to use key elements of a company's strategy mainly financial perspective, customer perspective, internal business perspective, and innovation and learning perspective to identify issues and solve problems related to financial measures and accounting systems. Using the company's historical data, the Balanced Scorecard assists managers to review information about a company's performance at the marketplace, showing if the company is on track or failing due to either internal factors (if production and delivery are on schedule, if customers prefer to buy from other competitors, etc.) The Balanced Scorecard approach is based on existing data or information a company already has, to create a feasible road map for the managers or owners to improve production, distribution, customer relations, and other plans over time. For a start-up entrepreneur, it would be helpful to set up a balanced scorecard as a way to assess/evaluate performance using a baseline scenario such as the start-up costs/investment, initial goals of sales and number of customers to acquire, or internal management structure to involve different personnel at different decision-making level. Some research topics could apply the Balanced Scorecard approach to (1) understand if an entrepreneur has established a proper scale of operation based on production time and resource allocation, (2) guide an entrepreneur to learn about market potential and calculate a reasonable range of expected sales/profits over a certain period of time, and (3) assist an entrepreneur to recover from loss or failure by reviewing the business plan to identify variables or factors triggered the issues (and to fix these problems with alternatives).

2.5 Psychology and Social Behavior

Optimism and positive attitudes toward work seemed to have positive impacts on motivation and performance (Luthans & Youssef-Morgan, 2017). Several studies have introduced entrepreneurial characteristics, and optimism and pessimism were among some variables to explore entrepreneurs' assessment on business progress (Liang & Dunn, 2010; Liang & Dunn, 2008). Utilizing the revised Life Orientation Test (Scheier & Carver, 1985), Liang and Dunn (2010, 2008) examined the entrepreneurial characteristics of optimism and pessimism in the new venture creation process, related to how entrepreneurs perceived their future of profit and individual/family satisfaction. Life Orientation Test consists of 5-point scales to assess individual's perspectives of optimism based on expected outcomes (e.g., expected the best or the worst, counting on good things to happen or not). This tool could be easily adopted or modified to evaluate entrepreneur's perspectives of new venture creation process, business development, or future outlooks.

A discussion in Ma et al. (2022) revealed employees' existing knowledge and organizational abilities to achieve business growth built on resource-based theory. Social capital and strategic resources were driving forces for firms' entrepreneurial performances. Ma et al. (2022) proposed a new approach to study integrated impacts of social and psychological capital related to entrepreneurial performance (e.g., financial outcomes, customer relation, learning and growth) by incorporating variables such as social network, trust, reputation, and sense of self-efficacy. In the social capital domain, common factors being investigated included relationships within and across social networks including family and organizations. Scholars believed that social capital could be established through participation in community and public engagement, which would build trust, harmony, and connectivity to achieve common goals. Ma et al. (2022) also elaborated on psychological capital which related to entrepreneurs' characteristics such as knowledge, sense of satisfaction, emotional intelligence, optimism, and resilience. Future research could examine the role of socioemotional wealth and rural entrepreneurship. Much research is still needed to explore or examine how social and behavioral factors influence rural entrepreneurship and entrepreneurial decisions, how these factors influence business development, and under what conditions these factors would help rural entrepreneurs to become resilient in the long term.

Semkunde et al. (2022) introduced an application of the feminist separatist theory in the context of rural entrepreneurship to investigate how women's groups participated in business activities. Barriers for women entrepreneurs have been well documented in the literature. From local community environment to access to capital and network support, women entrepreneurs in rural regions were more likely facing economic and social stress. Feminist separatist theory described women's challenges in gaining social and economic recognition via independent decision-making and network support compared with their male counterparts. Tillmar et al. (2022) argued that contextual barriers for women had not been fully explored in existing literature. Contextual barriers could be linked to limited information, training, and opportunities for women entrepreneurs in rural areas, who might not proactively seek support. More benefits for women entrepreneurs contributing to rural communities beyond generating incomes related to the stability, service, and care for families. For example, Tilmar et al. (2022) conducted research to investigate women entrepreneurship and contributions to rural viability and gender equality. The research led to several theoretical implications in understanding: (1) how gender relates to business diversification in rural communities, (2) income discrepancies between male and female entrepreneurs, and (3) welfare and gender equality are correlated in the context of family needs and opportunity-driven status while pursuing entrepreneurship.

2.6 Information and Innovation Theories

Technology in recent years has become an integral in business development that aims to improve efficiency, competitiveness, and timely decision-making. Many believe that successful and sustainable businesses probably have access to modern information technology to gain communication advantages with customers, market potential and supply chains. Given the fast-growing technology era, some scholars focused on technology-related entrepreneurship. Many scholars mentioned that information technology needed to be considered beyond the concept of the balanced scorecard discussed in the earlier section to achieve business goals for entrepreneurs. Van Der Zee and De Jong (1999) introduced a framework to integrate information technology into business management strategies as entrepreneurs plan and execute decisions. This framework highlighted the values of integrating information technology at various stages of business management, which would potentially enhance the business performance and efficiency. The researchers cautioned that evaluation for limitations and consequences should be conducted as an element when evaluating business performance. Beckman et al. (2012) argued that technology entrepreneurship was affiliated with the core value of component of a venture development, market development, or network development across industries. These technical advancements or innovations could drive benefits in gaining market potential or lead to disruptive behaviors in commercial exchange. While information technology seems to gain significant attention for entrepreneurs to improve market accessibility, competitiveness, and communications with suppliers/vendors, and customers, challenges and barriers remain for rural entrepreneurs to adopt information technology or integrate information technology into their business management. For example, internet access and infrastructures to support effective information technology development could be an issue to many rural communities. High costs and geographical diversity (e.g., mountain terrain or valleys) sometimes prevent rural entrepreneurs to rely on information technology to keep up day-to-day operations. Other studies (e.g., Olalekan, 2024) revealed that rural entrepreneurs might lack the skills and understanding about how to use digital technologies effectively in business operations. Netrepreneur was defined to represent an entrepreneur or a group of entrepreneurs who apply information and communication technology while establishing businesses in cyberspace (Balachandran & Sakthivelan, 2013; He, 2019). The explosive development and growth of the cyberspace-based businesses have become mainstream in marketing, connectivity, trade, communication, and information exchange between sellers and buyers in all types of products and services. He (2019) proposed a theoretical framework to link factors and characteristics of the rural economy (e.g., poverty, skills, spatial separation, market failure) with the information technology domain regarding entrepreneurial development to improve economic outcomes and prosperity. Some research topics need more attention include linking human behaviors (e.g., mindset and thinking process, willingness to adopt, skills and knowledge for implementation) to technology design, development, and implementations that would improve the overall rural prosperity.

3 Data and Rural Entrepreneurship

The study of rural entrepreneurship relies on data, and researchers have relied on a variety of datasets to study the phenomenon. The Global Entrepreneurship Monitor (GEM) is the most renowned dataset to study entrepreneurs around the world. GEM collects primary data through surveys focused on entrepreneurs and their ecosystems. Yet is has scarcely been used to study rural entrepreneurs. Some rare examples are researchers that have used it to study rural entrepreneurs in Spain (Driga et al., 2009) and Russia (Baldanov et al., 2020). Hechavarría and Ingram (2019) use the GEM data in a general method of moments model to study the effect of entrepreneurial ecosystems on women entrepreneurs in 75 countries.

Scally et al. (2020) discuss how "good" rural data are hard to come by. They note that entrepreneurship data from public data sources may not be reliable. The difficulty may be not only collecting and reporting rural data but also the complication of defining rural communities. Many public sources such as the American Community Survey used to model self-employment income are available at the county and state level and although available at the census tract level they may be suppressed because of lack of population. These difficulties become even more exacerbated if data include regions that include Native American reservations. The lack of "good" data is even worse for those conducting research on rural entrepreneurship. Those who study entrepreneurship have relied on indirect measures of entrepreneurship (Goetz et al., 2010). For example, one of the most often used measures of entrepreneurship is self-employment.

One of the most used data sources in the US is Data.Gov. This is the US government's open data source which includes data, tools, and resources to conduct research in entrepreneurship topics or beyond. This website also provides concepts to develop web-based applications, design various visualizations, and incorporate diverse outputs in reporting/publications. Currently, there are over 290,000 datasets available, and some of the most viewed datasets related to rural entrepreneurship research are in the following categories – local government, climate, older adults, energy, human health, transportation, food resilience, and census of business or population. The data formats include XML, ZIP, HTML, PDF, CSV, Esri REST, EXCEL, TEXT, TIFF, RDF, gml, JSON, QGIS, and others. Some of the datasets introduced in the following sections are available in Data.Gov, and a similar open data source is available for European data (Data.europa.eu).

Aggregate data related to self-employment and small business owners can be accessed through the Small Business Administration's Office of Advocacy (https://advocacy.sba.gov). Research from the Small Business Administration uses economic data that is usually publicly available such as the Bureau of Labor Statistic: Business Employment Dynamics and the Census Bureau's Business Formation Statistics. The Bureau of Labor Statistic: Business Employment Dynamics which provides information on changes in establishments and employment by sector, firm size, and state. The Business Employment Dynamics provides data on new business applications by sector. Some examples of research conducted by the Office of Advocacy include studies focused on the growth of rural firms (Wilmoth, 2019).

The Census Bureau has several datasets that focus on self-employment and small business owners. Self-employment data at the individual level can be accessed through the American Community Survey. The American Community Survey [https://www.census.gov/programs-surveys/acs] is a national survey conducted across a sample of the population. Researchers can study individuals by employment status. The Survey of Business Owners and Self-Employed Persons (SBO), the Annual Survey of Entrepreneurs (ASE), and non-employer statistics are also collected by the Census Bureau (https://www.census.gov/programs-surveys.html). Conroy and Watson (2023) use the American Community Survey and firm birth data from the Bureau of Labor Statistics to study how overeducation affects entrepreneurship and find that overeducation may increase entrepreneurship in rural areas. Deller et al. (2019) use data from Census Bureau's Business Information Tracking System (BITS) with the County Business Pattern database and spatial econometrics to study migration and rural entrepreneurship. Deller et al. (2022) also use these datasets along with information on broadband to determine how rural broadband impacts business startup rates.

A unique dataset collected by the Census Bureau is the Small Business Pulse Survey (https://www.census.gov/data/experimental-data-products/small-business-pulse-survey.html). These unique data were collected to understand the challenges faced by small businesses during the Coronavirus pandemic. The data were collected for a two-year period from April 2020 to April 2022 on a weekly basis. For example, Buffington et al. (2021) used the data to research the effect of the pandemic by business owner characteristics and rural/urban location.

An agency that specifically studies rural communities is the USDA-Economic Research Service (ERS). Researchers that aim to compare metro and non-metro areas often use the Rural-Urban Continuum Codes developed by ERS (these codes can be found here https://www.ers.usda.gov/data-products/rural-urban-continuum-codes/). Researchers may use their county typology codes that describe the socioeconomic conditions of US counties (county codes can be found here https://www.ers.usda.gov/data-products/county-typology-codes/). An ERS data product that is particularly valuable when researchers want to study farm owners is the Agricultural Resource Management Survey (ARMS). This dataset provides information on the management practices and economic well-being of farmers and ranchers. For example, Vogel and Bollman (2017) use the ARMS data to study the impact off-farm businesses run by farmers. The agency also provides various reports on rural America (see for example, Davis et al. 2022). Whitacre et al. (2019) used data from the Economic Research Service-Rural Establishment Innovation Survey from 2014 to develop an innovation index. This restricted dataset consists of businesses with at least five employees and oversampled rural areas. They analyze the effect of their innovation index on business level outcomes.

The Panel Study of Entrepreneurial Dynamics (PSED) is also a national U.S. sample but tracks firm creation across time (http://www.psed.isr.umich.edu/psed/home). Other versions of the PSED are available in Sweden (SE-PSED), Australia, and Canada. Hechavarría et al. (2016) studied the effect of financing on startup speed using event history analysis using samples from PSED I and PSED II. Segantini and Dickes (2021) used the PSED to also study the effect of external funding but on rural entrepreneurs.

Other sources of data that can be used to measure outcomes for rural entrepreneurs focus on establishments, employment, and income. One of these data sources includes the Quarterly Census of Employment and Wages (which has been discontinued), which has data at the county level and was collected by the Bureau of Labor Statistics. Another data source is Bureau of Economic Analysis, which collects data on employment, personal income, and gross domestic product (GDP) (https://www.bea.gov/tools/).

Henderson et al. (2007) use data from the Bureau of Economic Analysis-Regional Economic Information System to calculate the ratio of entrepreneurs in US counties to determine the breadth and depth of entrepreneurship in rural areas. Goetz (2006) also use the BEA-REIS data in spatial econometrics to study the determinants of self-employment rates and the effects of self-employment on economic development.

Interview or focus group data collection is essential for researchers applying qualitative methods. Researchers shouldn't discount the use of qualitative research methods to study rural entrepreneurship (Barkley, 2006). Qualitative research usually involves in-depth interviews, focus groups, observation, or case studies which require smaller sample sizes than quantitative research methods. Qualitative research methods allow researchers to gather rich and detailed data that can help them gain a deeper understanding of the experiences of rural entrepreneurs in their local contexts (Kalantaridis & Bika, 2006). For example, Son and Niehm (2021) use a case study approach to investigate how rural entrepreneurs use social media to navigate changing rural markets. De Guzman et al. (2020) also use a case study approach to explore the perceptions of rural business owners and youth. Their study concurred with previous literature on infrastructure and social challenges of rural communities but also highlighted the social benefits of small communities.

4 Thoughts for Future Research

Rural entrepreneurship in developed world has a lot of potential for scholars to pursue future research opportunities. Most of the literature in entrepreneurship focuses on management strategies, economic growth, decision-making factors, and enterprise characteristics, including owner's demographics. As recognized by some scholars, rural entrepreneurs and their environment are very different from urban or global aspects. Based on the literature reviews of theories and data sources, traditional ways of designing and creating a theory framework from a particular domain would lose some important characteristics and explanation for rural domain about who, what, why, how, and so what. Rural areas may offer a diverse resource base such as land, space, and higher potential to engage with their communities to build a legacy. The downside of starting or establishing businesses in rural area involves lack of proper capital, skilled labor force, distribution channels, markets, or supporting networks. These opportunities and challenges provide the potential for future research in the field such as:

- How do rural entrepreneurs handle the lack of broadband for technology innovation? What are options in supporting rural entrepreneurship with limited access to information technology? What are cost-effective innovative strategies to sustain rural supply chain? (Innovation and technology)
- How do rural communities enhance entrepreneurial ecosystems (i.e., workforce development, resources, technical assistance, customer behaviors, and network)

in supporting rural entrepreneurs? (Agglomeration theory and integration, Network theory)
- What micro/macro factors hinder or enhance rural entrepreneurship from integrated social, economic, political, and cultural aspects? (Integrated approach)
- How do rural entrepreneurs respond to the inter-connectivity between rural and urban divide? (Psychology and behavioral theory)
- What factors trigger rural entrepreneurs' decisions in choosing an ideal location for business? What geographical characteristics are critical to establishing and sustaining successful rural enterprises in various scenarios? (Location theory)

Research has also shown that spatial context matters for rural entrepreneurship (Basco & Suwala, 2021; Deller et al., 2018; Korsgaard et al., 2015). Thus, future research should explore how entrepreneur embeddedness in rural communities affects business outcomes. A large proportion of research focused on entrepreneur embeddedness has used qualitative methods focused on the respondent's social networks. However, some researchers have studied the role of social capital on entrepreneurship outcomes (Li et al., 2013; Deller et al., 2018) using quantitative methods. This stream of research may be more holistically studied through mixed-method research (i.e., combining qualitative and quantitative methods) to study the process of embeddedness across multiple contexts (Wigren-Kristoferson et al., 2022). Rural entrepreneurship is the key to rural economic development, and new theory frameworks would evolve in a historical context building on previous literature and findings to continue broadening the frontier of research.

References

Andersson, D.E., Bögenhold, D., & Hudik, M. (2022). Entrepreneurship in superdiverse societies and the end of one-size-fits-all policy prescriptions. Journal of Entrepreneurship and Public Policy, 11(1), 40–52.

Balachandran, V., & Sakthivelan, M. (2013). Impact of information technology on entrepreneurship. Journal of Business Management & Social Sciences Research, 2(2), 51–56, 89–93.

Baldanov, A., Kiminami, L., & Furuzawa, S. (2020). Situation of human development, human capital, agriculture and rural development in Russia. In Agriculture and rural development in Russia since the 2000s. SpringerBriefs in economics. Singapore: Springer. https://doi.org/10.1007/978-981-15-4665-5_3.

Barkley, D.L. (2006, October). The value of case study research on rural entrepreneurship: Useful method. In Presented Joint ERS-RUPRI conf., exploring rural entrepreneurship: Imperatives opportunities res. Washington, DC.

Basco, R., & Suwala, L. (2021). Spatial familiness and family spatialities—Searching for fertile ground between family business and regional studies. Family business and regional development, 7–32.

Beckman, C., Eisenhardt, K., Kotha, S., Meyer, A., & Rajagopalan, N. (2012). Technology entrepreneurship. Strategic Entrepreneurship Journal, 6, 89–93.

Bhushan, P. (2018). Prospects & challenges of rural entrepreneurship in India. International Journal of Research and Analytical Reviews, 5(4), 1089–1100.
Breiger, R., Carely, K., & Pattison, P. (Eds.). Dynamic social network modeling and analysis (pp. 39–77). Washington, DC: The National Academies Press.
Buffington, C., Chapman, D., Dinlersoz, E., Foster, L., Hunt, J., & Klimek, S. (2021). Small Business Pulse Survey Estimates by Owner Characteristics and Rural/Urban Designation.
Conroy, T., & Watson, P. (2023). Overeducation, natural amenities, and entrepreneurship. Small Business Economics. https://doi.org/10.1007/s11187-023-00734-w.
Davis, J.C., Rupasingha, A., Cromartie, J., & Sanders, A. (2022). Rural America at a glance. Economic Research Service, Economic Information Bulletin Number, 246. https://www.ers.usda.gov/webdocs/publications/105155/eib-246.pdf?v=8108.6.
de Guzman, M.R.T., Kim, S., Taylor, S., & Padasas, I. (2020). Rural communities as a context for entrepreneurship: Exploring perceptions of youth and business owners. Journal of Rural Studies, 80, 45–52.
Deller, S., Whitacre, B., & Conroy, T. (2022). Rural broadband speeds and business startup rates. American Journal of Agricultural Economics, 104(3), 999–1025.
Deller, S.C., Conroy, T., & Markeson, B. (2018). Social capital, religion and small business activity. Journal of Economic Behavior & Organization, 155, 365–381. https://doi.org/10.1016/j.jebo.2018.09.006.
Deller, S., Kures, M., & Conroy, T. (2019). Rural entrepreneurship and migration. Journal of Rural Studies, 66, 30–42.
Driga, O., Lafuente, E., & Vaillant, Y. (2009), Reasons for the Relatively Lower Entrepreneurial Activity Levels of Rural Women in Spain. Sociologia Ruralis, 49, 70–96. https://doi.org/10.1111/j.1467-9523.2008.00475.x
Driga, O., Lafuente, E., & Vaillant, Y. (2009). Reasons for the relatively lower entrepreneurial activity levels of rural women in Spain. Sociologia Ruralis, 49, 70–96. https://doi.org/10.1111/j.1467-9523.2008.00475.x.
Fortunato, M.W.P. (2014). Supporting rural entrepreneurship: A review of conceptual developments from research to practice. Community Development, 45(4), 387–408. https://doi.org/10.1080/15575330.2014.935795.
Frazier, B., Stoel, L., Niehm, L., & Eckerson, N. (2013). Optimism for new business survival in rural communities: An institutional perspective. Journal of Small Business & Entrepreneurship, 26(5), 443–462.
Freeman, L.C. (1996). Some antecedents of social network analysis. Connections, 19, 1–42.
Freeman, L.C. (2003) Finding social groups: a meta analysis of the southern women data.
Freeman, L.C. (2004). The development of social network analysis: A study in the sociology of science. Vancouver: Empirical.
Glaeser, E.L. (2010). Agglomeration economics, editor. The University of Chicago Press. ISBN: 0-226-29789-6.
Goetz, S., Partridge, M., Deller, S., & Fleming, D. (2010). Evaluating U.S. rural entrepreneurship policy. Journal of Regional Analysis & Policy, 40(1), 20–33.
Goetz, S.J. (2006). The place-based structural determinants and effects of self-employment. Final Report to the Kauffman Foundation. Found at https://aese.psu.edu/nercrd/entrepreneurship/research-resources-on-entrepreneurship/publications.
He, X. (2019). Digital entrepreneurship solution to rural poverty: Theory, practice and policy implications. Journal of Developmental Entrepreneurship, 24(1), #1950004, 32.
Hechavarría, D.M., Matthews, C.H., & Reynolds, P.D. (2016). Does startup financing influence startup speed? Evidence from the panel study of entrepreneurial dynamics. Small Business Economics, 46, 137–167. https://doi.org/10.1007/s11187-015-9680-y.

Hechavarría, D.M., & Ingram, A.E. (2019). Entrepreneurial ecosystem conditions and gendered national-level entrepreneurial activity: A 14-year panel study of GEM. Small Business Economics, 53, 431–458. https://doi.org/10.1007/s11187-018-9994-7.
Henderson, J., Low, S.A., & Weiler, S. (2007). The drivers of regional entrepreneurship in rural and metro area. In N. Walzer (Ed.), Entrepreneurship and local economic development. Lexington Books.
Káposzta, J., & Nagy, H. (2022). The major relationships in the economic growth of the rural space. European Countryside, 14(1), 67–86. doi: 10.2478/euco-2022-0004.
Kačar, B., Curić, J., & Ikić, S. (2016). Local economic development in theories of regional economies and rural studies. Economics of Agriculture, UDC, 338(43), 3308.
Kalantaridis, C., & Bika, Z. (2006). Local embeddedness and rural entrepreneurship: Case-study evidence from Cumbria, England. Environment and Planning A, 38(8), 1561–1579.
Kaplan, R., & Norton, D. (1992). The balanced scorecard – Measures that drive performance. Harvard Business Review, January-February, 71–79.
Korsgaard, S., Anderson, A., & Gaddefors, J. (2016). Entrepreneurship as re-sourcing: Towards a new image of entrepreneurship in a time of financial, economic, and socio-spatial crisis. Journal of Enterprising Communities: People and Places in the Global Economy, 10(2), 178–202.
Korsgaard, S., Ferguson, R., & Gaddefors, J. (2015). The best of both worlds: How rural entrepreneurs use placial embeddedness and strategic networks to create opportunities. Entrepreneurship & Regional Development, 27(9–10), 574–598. doi: 10.1080/08985626.2015.1085100.
Korsgaard, S., Müller, S., & Tanvig, H.W. (2015). Rural entrepreneurship or entrepreneurship in the rural – Between place and space. International Journal of Entrepreneurial Behavior & Research, 21(1), 5–26. https://doi.org/10.1108/IJEBR-11-2013-0205.
Li, Y., Wang, X., Huang, L., & Bai, X. (2013). How does entrepreneurs' social capital hinder new business development? A relational embeddedness perspective. Journal of Business Research, 66(12), 2418–2424. https://doi.org/10.1016/j.jbusres.2013.05.029.
Liang, C., & Dunn, P. (2010). Entrepreneurial characteristics, optimism, realism and pessimism: Correlation or collision? Journal of Business and Entrepreneurship, 22(1), 1–22.
Liang, K., & Dunn, J. (2008). Are entrepreneurs optimistic, realistic, both or fuzzy? Academy of Entrepreneurship, 14(1 & 2), 51–76.
Liang, C., & Dunn, P. (2008). Exploring the myths of optimism and realism in entrepreneurship related to expectations and outcomes. Journal of Business and Entrepreneurship, 20(1), March, 1–17.
Liang, C.-L. (Kathleen), & Dunn, P. (2007a). Triggers of new venture creation: A comparison between pre-business and in-business entrepreneurs. Academy of Entrepreneurship Journal, 13(1), 79–88.
Liang, C.-L. (Kathleen), & Dunn, P. (2007b). Multiple aspects of triggering factors in new venture creation: Internal drivers, external forces and indirect motivation. Journal of Business and Entrepreneurship, 19(1), March, 23–39.
Luthans, F., & Youssef-Morgan, C.M. (2017). Psychological capital: An evidence-based positive approach. Annual Review of Organizational Psychology and Organizational Behavior, 4, 339–366.
Ma, H., Zhang, Y.C., Butler, A., Guo, P., & Bozward, D. (2022). Entrepreneurial performance of new-generation rural migrant entrepreneurs in China. International Journal of Entrepreneurial Behavior & Research, 28(2), 412–440. doi: 10.1108/IJEBR-07-2020-0456.
Mohammadifar, Y., Naderi, N., Khosravi, E., & Karamian, F. (2022). Developing a paradigm model for resilience of rural entrepreneurial businesses in dealing with the COVID-19 crisis: Application of grounded theory in western of Iran. Frontier in Public Health, 10, 833909.
Muñoz, P., & Kimmitt, J. (2019). Rural entrepreneurship in place: An integrated framework. Entrepreneurship & Regional Development, 31(9–10), 842–873. https://doi.org/10.1080/08985626.2019.1609593.
Muñoz, P., & Kimmitt, J. (2019). Rural entrepreneurship in place: An integrated framework. Entrepreneurship & Regional Development, 31, 9–10, 842–873. doi: 10.1080/08985626.2019.1609593.

Newbery, R., Siwale, J., & Henley, A. (2017). Rural entrepreneurship theory in the developing and developed world. The International Journal of Entrepreneurship and Innovation, 18(1), 3–4.
North, D. (1955). Location theory and regional economic growth. Journal of Political Economy, 63(3), 243–258.
Olalekan, O.O. (2024). Rural entrepreneurship in the digital age: A systematic review. International Journal of Sustainable Rural Development, 1(1), 1–5.
Peter Kansheba, J.M., Marobhe, M.I., & Wald, A.E. (2023). Cushioning the Covid-19 economic consequences on entrepreneurial ecosystems: The role of Stakeholders` engagement, collaboration, and support. Journal of African Business, 24(2), 214–234. doi: 10.1080/15228916.2022.2078933.
Pinho, J.C., & Smapaio de Sá, E. (2013). Entrepreneurial performance and stakeholders' relationships: A social network analysis perspective. International Journal of Entrepreneurship, 17, 1–19.
Pred, A. (1967). Behaviour and location, foundations for a geographic and dynamic location theory, Part I. Lund: Dep. Geogr. R. Univ. Lund.
Scally, C.P., Burnstein, E., Gerken, M., & Immonen, E. (2020). In Search of "Good" Rural Data. Found at https://www.urban.org/research/publication/search-good-rural-data.
Scheier, M.F., & Carver, C.S. (1985). Optimism, coping, and health: Assessment and implications of generalized outcome expectancies. Health Psychology, 4(3), 219–247.
Segantini, M., & Dickes, L.A. (2021). An examination of rural and female-led firms: A resource approach. Journal of Small Business Strategy, 31(4), 20–39. https://doi.org/10.53703/001c.29472.
Semkunde, M.A., Elly, T., Charles, G., Gaddefors, J., & Chiwona-Karltun, L. (2022). Rural entrepreneurship and the context: Navigating contextual barriers through women's groups. International Journal of Gender and Entrepreneurship, 14(2), 213–234. doi: 10.1108/IJGE-01-2021-0013.
Shields, J. (April, 2005). Does rural location matter? The significance of a rural setting for small businesses. Journal of Developmental Entrepreneurship, 10(1), 49–63. DOI: 10.1142/S1084946705000057
Shields, J. (2005). Does rural location matter? The significance of a rural setting for small businesses. Journal of Developmental Entrepreneurship, 10(1), 49–93.
Siemens, L. (2010). Challenges, responses and available resources: Success in rural small businesses. Journal of Small Business and Entrepreneurship, 23(1), 65–80.
Śledzik, K. (2013). Schumpeter's view on innovation and entrepreneurship, management trends in theory and practice. In S. Hittmar (Ed.), Faculty of management science and informatics (Vol. 2013). University of Zilina & Institute of Management by University of Zilina, ISBN 978-80-554-0736-4.
Smith, A.M., Steiner, A., Steinerowska-Streb, I., & Tiwasing, P. (2024). Challenges and opportunities for rural entrepreneurship in times of crisis. The International Journal of Entrepreneurship and Innovation, 25(2), 73–75. https://doi.org/10.1177/14657503241252434.
Son, J., & Niehm, L.S. (2021). Using social media to navigate changing rural markets: The case of small community retail and service businesses. Journal of Small Business and Entrepreneurship, 33(6), 619–637.
Sweezy, P. (1943). Professor Schumpeter's theory of innovation. The Review of Economics and Statistics, 25(1), 93–96.
Tanwar, D.S., & Bhardwaj, M.S. (2022). Challenges and opportunities for rural entrepreneurship. The Journal of Contemporary Issues in Business and Government, 28(3), 612–620, Retrieved from. https://cibgp.com/au/index.php/1323-6903/article/view/2398.
Terluin, I.J. (2003). Differences in economic development in rural regions of advanced countries: An overview and critical analysis of theories. Journal of Rural Studies, 19(3), 327–344. ISSN 0743-0167. https://doi.org/10.1016/S0743-0167(02)00071-2.
Tillmar, M., Sköld, B., Ahl, H., Berglund, K., & Pettersson, K. (2022). Women's rural businesses: For economic viability or gender quality? – A database study from the Swedish context. International Journal of Gender and Entrepreneurship, 14(3), 323–351.

Van Der Zee, J.T.M., & De Jong, B. (1999). Alignment is not enough: Integrating business and information technology management with the balanced business scorecard. Journal of Management Information Systems, 16(2), 137–158. https://doi.org/10.1080/07421222.1999.11518249.

Vogel, S., & Bollman, R.D. (2017). The multifunctional farm household enterprise: Using farm microdata to assess the rural economy impacts generated by farmer-operated off-farm businesses. In Proceedings of the seventh international conference on agricultural statistics, Rome 26–28, 2016. Available at SSRN: https://ssrn.com/abstract=3091326.

Wigren-Kristoferson, C., Brundin, E., Hellerstedt, K., Stevenson, A., & Aggestam, M. (2022). Rethinking embeddedness: A review and research agenda. Entrepreneurship & Regional Development, 34(1–2), 32–56. https://doi.org/10.1080/08985626.2021.2021298.

Wilmoth, D. (2019). Growth in number of rural establishments. https://cdn.advocacy.sba.gov/wp-content/uploads/2020/02/04111621/Rural-Business-Growth-Fact-Sheet1.pdf.

Don Macke

Rural Entrepreneurship: Half a Century of Learning

e2 Entrepreneurial Ecosystems

Abstract: Fieldwork with rural communities and their builders has been the foundational source of insight into rural entrepreneurship for a diverse group of North American economic development practitioners. Since the 1970s, the team at e2 Entrepreneurial Ecosystems (e2) has collaborated with this practitioner group to understand the dynamics of rural entrepreneurship. This chapter is an account of that multi-decade learning journey.

Following is a chronological review of e2 leadership's keystone experiences, including collaboration and research with the community of Ord, Nebraska, and the resulting lessons and policy considerations for building, growing, and sustaining a robust rural entrepreneurial ecosystem. To fully understand the characteristics of rural entrepreneurship, it is helpful to first establish a common understanding of the terminology.

Keywords: entrepreneur, entrepreneurship, entrepreneurial, entrepreneur ecosystems, rural, learning, economic competitiveness, diversification, resilience, prosperity, development capacity, network, models, HomeTown Competitiveness

1 Defining "Rural" and "Entrepreneur"

Rural and entrepreneur each have many meanings. A shared definition of these concepts is important for a fruitful discussion of the attributes of rural entrepreneurs and their distinct opportunities and challenges.

When defining "entrepreneur," the Entrepreneurial Ecosystems (e2) team ascribes to the view that most residents in rural communities are potential entrepreneurs, and most never become entrepreneurs. It also employs Jay Kayne's definition of an entrepreneur as a ". . . person or team that creates and grows a venture" (Kayne, n.d.). Building on Kayne's definition, e2 considers entrepreneurship to be the process of creating and growing a venture across the full spectrum of entrepreneurial talent, from aspiring entrepreneurs to those with high growth potential. Furthermore, the term ventures is understood to comprise for-profit businesses, nonprofit organizations, and government enterprises (Macke & Chaffin, 2020a).

Defining "rural" also requires the consideration of several factors and can be challenging because of the many perceptions regarding what is considered "rural" in

Don Macke, e2 Entrepreneurial Ecosystems, www.energizingentrepreneurs.org, email: don@e2mail.org

https://doi.org/10.1515/9783110791396-011

North America. It is depreciative to define rural as simply "non-urban" or "non-metropolitan." Likewise, current U.S. urban and rural delineations basically encompass the classifications of metropolitan, micropolitan, and rural by default – or what is not metro or micro (Iaquinta, 2022). David Iaquinta, however, proposes that these classifications include the concept of nanopolitan, which offers a more useful, nuanced label when defining rural areas. Nanopolitan areas are smaller in population size when compared to micropolitan statistical areas yet include both rural and urban community components. Thousands of rural communities across North America are nanopolitan, including Ord, Nebraska, and its surrounding region, discussed in more detail in this chapter (Iaquinta, 2022).

Entrepreneurial Ecosystems (e2) also considers rural areas to fall within the U.S. Census Bureau's "urban to rural continuum" (U.S. Department of Agriculture, 2020). This continuum includes small and mid-sized metros that anchor rural regions, such as Missoula, Montana; urban-adjacent rural communities; dense rural regions found in the Northeast and South; micropolitan areas; lower-density rural regions common in the Mountain West and the Great Plains regions; nanopolitan areas (Iaquinta, 2022); and frontier communities still common in Alaska, the Great Plains, and Maine. e2 has worked with communities in nearly every rural region in North America that spans the urban to rural continuum.

The town of Ord, Nebraska, is a helpful backdrop for considering these definitions of entrepreneurship and rural. e2 began its work with Ord in the late 1990s. Many of the core components of rural entrepreneurial ecosystem building put forth by e2 can be observed through the team's engagement and research with Ord.

2 Ord, Nebraska

The small rural town of Ord, Nebraska, has provided some of the greatest revelations into rural entrepreneurial ecosystem building for e2. This community of about 2,000 residents in north-central Nebraska anchors a rural region of about 10,000 residents.

The e2 team began its work with Ord in the late 1990s (Macke et al., 2020a). At this time, Ord was in crisis. Like many other rural communities, it had been in a state of slow decline that was exacerbated by the agricultural crisis of the 1980s (see Table 1 for Ord's complete development chronology). With the community's decline accelerating, deep conflict brewed, and there was a lack of vision for how to move forward. However, unlike so many rural communities across North America that faced similar challenges, Ord was able to realize transformative change. e2 observed and recorded the critical role of entrepreneurship in Ord's revitalization through an in-depth case study of the town and the Valley County region in which it resides (Macke et al., 2020d).

Today, Ord has reshaped its once narrow economy, rooted in two sectors (i.e., commodity agriculture and regional hub city), into a higher value, more diversified, and resilient rural economy and society supported by eight economic sectors (i.e., commodity agriculture, value-added agriculture, regional hub city, destination tourism, growth entrepreneurial ventures, retiree services and amenities, and health care) (Macke et al., 2020c).

Table 1: Ord's Development Chronology.

1970s **Slow decline**	Like many rural communities in the 1970s, Ord was experiencing a slow decline and depopulation. For much of rural America at this time, undiversified economies were rooted in single industries like agriculture, forestry, mining, and manufacturing. As these industries changed and automated, the very rationale for many rural communities' existence eroded.
1980s **Agricultural crisis**	The agriculture crisis drove Ord, which was already experiencing a slow decline, into deep stress with accelerating agricultural consolidation, venture losses, and net outmigration and depopulation. This time of crisis seeded community conflict that divided and inhibited necessary community investment and change. Other rural communities have experienced similar crisis events when a furniture manufacturing plant closes or access to forests becomes constricted, for example. [10]
1990s **Search for colutions**	Out of the crisis emerged a group of local leaders who were committed to the community's future. This small, courageous, dedicated group evolved into a committee of 100 that has strengthened resident agency and envisioned and driven complex development. Learning from other communities and engaging outside partners, including e2, fueled Ord's search for solutions. Too many rural communities fail to reach out to other communities and external resources for help.
2000 **The pivot year**	In so many ways, 2000 was a watershed year for Ord. The community gained enough consensus to get organized, generate funding for development, and commit to a sophisticated development game plan that included entrepreneur-focused economic development.
2000s **Commitment &** **investment**	In the 2000s, Ord invested in its community economic development, staffing, and leadership. It also embraced community philanthropy and began working one-on-one with area entrepreneurs, which contributed to e2's early learning around what it now calls the "ground game." Ord backed up its commitments with real investment, including increased tax support.
2010s to present **Transformative** **change**	In the 2010s, Ord and its region began to realize a transformative impact measured in a robust ground game, new investments, and commitments to quality of life placemaking, all of which resulted in a larger, higher value, and more diverse economy. Depopulation is the greatest threat for Ord, and the community and its region have achieved dramatic net gains in the 30- to 40 year-old age range to support population stabilization and growth.

Source: Macke et al. (2020b). Reproduced with permission.

Ord's story prompts consideration of the increasing importance of resilience in rural community economic development work. Rural communities regularly experience "once-in-time shocks" and "structural shocks." Once-in-time shocks include both environmental (e.g., tornadoes, hurricanes, floods, wildfires) and economic (e.g., loss of a major employer, a new highway bypass) events. Structural shocks include long-term trends like climate change, industrial automation and associated job loss, depopulation, and loss of water supplies undermining irrigated agriculture.

Shocks deeply stress communities and their regions, often reducing the vitality of a community during and after the event. Many rural communities never fully recover following a major shock, reflecting a lack of resiliency. Resident, venture, and community resiliency enable communities to not only survive a shock but also rebound to become stronger following it. There are examples of this resiliency throughout Ord's history, including the community's response to the coronavirus pandemic. David Iaquinta examines Ord and Valley County's response to the pandemic in *Weathering the Pandemic in Ord*, illustrating how Ord has become a resilient community that empowers residents, ventures, and institutions to thrive through stressful times (Iaquinta, 2021).

Entrepreneurial Ecosystems' partnership with Ord has resulted in a case study and story capture project that spans 50 years and two-generations. In many ways, the core concepts of entrepreneurial ecosystem building that e2 has recorded and supported in this community mirror the team's broader learning journey and ongoing research and fieldwork across North America (Iaquinta et al., 2009).

3 Rural Entrepreneurial Ecosystem Development – e2's Learning Journey

Like the Ord story, the e2 team chronicles their learning journey through formative experiences beginning in the late 1970s and continuing through to the current day. This period encompasses six learning cycles, informed by field tests of the **e2 Development Framework and Process** [11] (Macke, 2020) in rural regions and communities throughout North America. The e2 team has refined the e2 Development Framework and Process after each learning cycle based on the results of field tests.

1970s

Living Rural. Many members of the e2 team grew up in rural areas, including Senior Vice President Don Macke. Macke was raised in the Central High Plains of Colorado and Nebraska and experienced firsthand the powerful forces undermining rural community vitality, like agricultural automation and consolidation. Macke's experiences as a resident in both struggling and prospering rural communities seeded his commitment to supporting more effective rural development.[1]

Nebraska Unicameral. Members of the e2 team and its network have engaged in policy work throughout the years. Macke worked in and consulted with the Nebraska Unicameral (a single-house, nonpartisan system unique to the state) and staffed the Unicameral's Special Committee on Energy and Economic Development during the turbulent late 1970s. At this time, he began to realize the futility of focusing on business attraction as Nebraska's primary rural economic development game plan. It became increasingly apparent to Macke that the opportunity for, the cost of, and the competition with interstate and inter-local business attraction did not make economic or social sense. Related policy work began to document that business attraction for most rural communities was not viable.[2]

1980s

North American Work. During the 1980s, Macke worked with a private for-profit consulting firm called Economic Research Associates that engaged in energy and economic development work from the Caribbean to British Columbia and locations throughout the United States. This work afforded him new lessons in the art and science of rural community economic development. During this same period, Deborah Markley was establishing her credentials in the field of rural capital and finance. Markley's experiences contributed to e2's scientific approach to learning and fieldwork, and the all-important role of capital access in rural entrepreneurship.[3] Markley and Macke later co-founded the Center for Rural Entrepreneurship.

1990s

HomeTown Competitiveness. In the mid-1990s, Maxine Moul and Jeff Yost with the Nebraska Community Foundation, Milan Wall with the Heartland Center for Leadership Development, Rick Foster with the W.K. Kellogg Foundation, Don Macke with the Center for Rural Entrepreneurship, and others came together to envision and deploy the HomeTown Competitiveness (HTC) initiative. HTC focused on the four strategic rural development "pillars" of community philanthropy, leadership development, youth engagement, and entrepreneur-led development. Ord, Nebraska, was the first community to partner with HTC, which was expanding its work across Nebraska into

1 Don Macke's personal journals and research files informed these recollections.
2 Ibid.
3 Ibid.

Kansas with HomeTown Prosperity, and then across the country from Indiana to border communities in Texas.[4]

The Nelson administration and Nebraska Rural Development Commission. Ben Nelson took office as Nebraska's governor in 1991 with Maxine Moul as lieutenant governor, serving two 4-year terms. Governor Nelson and Lieutenant Governor Moul both grew up in rural Nebraska and, early in their administration, made rural development a priority. The first executive order of the Nelson administration created the Nebraska Rural Development Commission (RDC). Macke co-developed the RDC with Moul and became its first executive director.

The RDC was a robust, well-funded, well-staffed, and supported organization. It worked closely with the Nebraska Department of Economic Development, the University of Nebraska, and other rural-facing development entities. The RDC began discovery work around community-centered entrepreneurial development. Its collaboration with the Center for Rural Affairs in Nebraska and the center's Rural Enterprise Assistance Program (REAP), established in 1990, allowed for deep learning about community-centered microlending and technical assistance strategies that were ascendant across the United States at the time. This early work with REAP and microlending demonstrated that significant rural economic development was possible and desirable. Additionally, this early work began to stimulate "systems" thinking that evolved into Entrepreneurial Development Systems and later **Entrepreneurial Ecosystems.**[5]

Partnership for Rural America. During the 1990s, there was a national refocusing on rural development. President George H.W. Bush, through the U.S. Department of Agriculture and its Rural Development agency, created the Partnership for Rural America. The Clinton administration continued the Partnership for Rural America. The RDC became a founding member of the decade-long partnership. This national network advanced e2's learning around community-centered business development that was foundational to later exploration of entrepreneur-led development.[6]

2000s

Discovery States and Legacy Rural E-Initiatives. Before the creation of the **Center for Rural Entrepreneurship** in 2001, the Rural Policy Research Institute (RUPRI) and the Ewing Marion Kauffman Foundation teamed with Macke and Markley to sponsor

4 Ibid.
5 Ibid.
6 Ibid.

two important pieces of work. The first was the **Rural Entrepreneurship Discovery States Initiative**. Working with Maine, Minnesota, Missouri, West Virginia, and later Colorado and Texas, the initiative explored the "state of rural entrepreneurship" in these partner states and approaches to foster state and community ecosystem-building strategies and policies. As the Center for Rural Entrepreneurship was forming, Macke and Markley undertook the second effort to explore legacy rural entrepreneurship building programs, including those facilitated by Kentucky Highlands, Coastal Enterprises in Maine, and Northern Initiatives in Michigan, among other well-established and demonstrated rural entrepreneurship initiatives. Markley captured this work in a collection of entrepreneur stories and case studies. These experiences informed initial answers to the "why," "what," and "how" questions of community-centered ecosystem building and operations.[7]

Institutes. In the early years up to the Great Recession that began in 2007, the Center for Rural Entrepreneurship hosted dozens of 24-hour to week-long institutes with HomeTown Competitiveness throughout the United States and Canada. These institutes were powerful vehicles for generating income, advancing learning, and marketing the e2 team's development models.[8,9]

First Book Published. The Center for Rural Entrepreneurship published *Energizing Entrepreneurs: Charting a Course for Rural Communities* that focused on answering, "why entrepreneurship?" and provided development framework insights from early field learning (Markley et al., 2005).

Kansas Influence. Wally Kearns with the Kansas Small Business Development Center and Patty Clark with the Kansas Department of Commerce became interested in the HomeTown Competitiveness initiative. In partnership with the Kansas Farm Bureau and others, the Center for Rural Entrepreneurship launched the Kansas HomeTown Prosperity initiative. In time, the organization partnered with Kearns, Clark, and others to advise on the formation of NetWork Kansas. Since 2004, and particularly 2007, members of the e2 have actively partnered with NetWork Kansas and its E-Communities Program. This relationship has informed work in Kansas and the e2 Development Framework and Process. Along with Ord, NetWork Kansas is e2's longest-running partnership (Markley & Binerer, 2014).

7 Ibid.

8 Ibid.

9 With the Great Recession and travel bans, and later the coronavirus pandemic, institutes transitioned from in-person gatherings to webinar events and then Zoom sessions. Today, however, there is a renewed interest in restarting institutes where people can immerse themselves in more networking opportunities that support learning and action planning.

Other Relevant Fieldwork. During the 2000s, the e2 team also engaged in deep learning in North Carolina,[10] Georgia,[11] the Mid-South,[12] Arizona,[13] Wisconsin,[14] South Dakota,[15] Iowa,[16] and Montana.[17] These engagements informed the team's entrepreneurship ground game protocols and education on demand-driven entrepreneurial ecosystem building.

2010s

Second Book Published. The second Center for Rural Entrepreneurship book, *Transfer of Wealth in Rural America: Understanding the Potential, Realizing the Opportunity, and Creating Wealth for the Future* made strong connections between rooted entrepreneurs creating community wealth and serving as major donors and supporters of entrepreneur-centered development (Macke, Markley & Binerer, 2011).

Nebraska and Indiana Prosperity Development Framework. The idea of greater and more broadly held community prosperity first surfaced in Kansas with the HomeTown Prosperity initiative. From 2017 to 2020, the e2 Development Framework and Process evolved in response to collaborations with Nebraska Extension (Macke,

10 There were two cycles of work in partnership with the North Carolina Rural Center supporting entrepreneurial communities demonstration projects.

11 The Georgia Entrepreneurial Communities Initiative was undertaken with Georgia Tech University, The Georgia Chamber of Commerce and the Georgia Department of Commerce. Georgia created a unique entrepreneurial communities certification program and trained many state and local economic developers using the 2005 book and framework.

12 This work was undertaken in partnership with Communities Unlimited, based in Fayetteville, Arkansas.

13 Partnering with Christina Hamelton Pennell and the University of Arizona in Tucson, this entrepreneurial communities project was based in Sahuarita, Arizona between Tucson and the Mexico border.

14 For a number of years, the Center for Rural Entrepreneurship partnered with Envision Fond du Lac in east central Wisconsin. Envision is this region's economic development group and had been employing Economic Gardening and in engaging the e2 development framework and had created a community-centered strategic plan.

15 Deuel County is located in East Central South Dakota near the Minnesota border. It is rural and for nearly a decade Don Macke worked with this community on their entrepreneur-led economic development game plan.

16 The Western Iowa Development group (WIDA) is the rural economic development agency in Pottawattamie County, Iowa. This is a geographically large county and is home to Council Bluffs, which is part of the Omaha Metropolitan Area. WIDA partnered with us to first employ HomeTown Competitiveness in the approximately one dozen rural villages in the county and then the e2 development framework. With this work, the organization dramatically refined its coaching knowledge.

17 This e2 work was in partnership with the Greater Missoula Montana region. During this work, the organization refined resource mapping tactics and evolved the hub and spoke organization model.

2020a) and the **Rural Communities Prosperity initiative** that engaged eight rural Nebraska communities, and later rural Indiana communities through support from the Lilly Endowment Inc. The result was a framework consisting of the following four essential activities to help communities achieve the endgame of community prosperity:

- Resident attraction, development, and retention
- Quality of life placemaking (both physical and cultural)
- Entrepreneur led economic development
- Community capacity building for development

The framework builds on four pillars established earlier through the HomeTown Competitiveness initiative and has been incorporated into the Energizing Entrepreneurial Ecosystems (E3) initiative in Nebraska (Macke, 2020a).

Third Book Published. Macke, Markley, and John Fulwider authored *Energizing Entrepreneurial Communities: A Pathway to Prosperity*. This was the first comprehensive guide to e2's Development Framework and Process, rooted in previous cycles of field learning (Macke, Markley & Fulwider, 2014).

Transition and Rebuilding. Virginia Community Capital (VCC) acquired the Center for Rural Entrepreneurship in 2017. By the end of 2018, VCC made the strategic decision to end its entrepreneurship work and began discussions with NetWork Kansas to find a new home for these efforts. In January 2019, VCC transferred the center's entrepreneurship resources and work to NetWork Kansas, rebranding it as e2 Entrepreneurial Ecosystems (e2). This period resulted in disruption and rebuilding as well as the development of an e2 vision and strategy. This process of renewal and refinement is ongoing.[18]

2020s and Beyond

National e2 Practitioners Network. In 2020, e2 updated and enhanced the **e2 Development Framework and Process** and **e2 University Resources**. The resources are a public good accessible to those who join e2's free **National e2 Practitioners Network**. In turn, the e2 team learns from engagement with and feedback from practitioners network members. Although membership growth has been slow due to disruptions from the coronavirus pandemic and uncertainties around inflation, the practitioners network remains an opportunity area for both e2's public mission and its compensated work.[19]

18 Ibid.
19 For background on the National e2 Practitioners Network and e2 University Resource Library go to https://www.energizingentrepreneurs.org/library/e2university/.

Pathways to Rural Prosperity Podcast. Rural people have a strong oral culture, in part due to routine, longer travel times via motor vehicles. To better serve and reach its rural audience, e2 launched its semimonthly **Pathways to Rural Prosperity Podcast** in 2021. The podcast's audience is growing slowly, and the response provides encouragement that this communications channel will generate greater awareness of and interest in the e2 Development Framework and Process.[20]

Ord, Nebraska Case Study. With funding support from e2, the Kettering Foundation, and particularly the Ewing Marion Kauffman Foundation, e2 led a comprehensive case study of Ord and its region from 2020 through 2022 and converted it into online learning courses.[21]

LEDOs. In 2021 and 2022, e2 developed its Likely Entrepreneurial Development Opportunities (LEDO) framework, informed by analytics from the organization's **Development Opportunity Profiles**. The LEDO framework includes the following 11 free strategy guides and their companion podcasts:[22]
1. Area Spending Capture
2. Commuters
3. Hub City Development
4. New Resident Attraction
5. Retiree-Led Development
6. Growth-Oriented Es
7. Larger Employer Retention and Expansion
8. Natural Resources
9. Tourism and Hospitality
10. Transportation Corridors
11. Regional Development

Seventh Cycle of Field Learning. e2, in partnership with NetWork Kansas, is engaged in renewed fieldwork with the Southern Minnesota Initiative Foundation through the Rural Entrepreneurial Venture (REV) initiative;[23] ongoing collaboration with NetWork Kansas' extensive network of E-Communities;[24] Growing Rural Oregon

20 For additional information on e2 Pathways to Rural Prosperity Podcasts go to http://www.energizingentrepreneurs.org/podcast.
21 For additional information on e2's Ord, Nebraska case study and resources go to https://www.energizingentrepreneurs.org/library/theme-papers/subjects/ord-nebraska.html.
22 For additional information on e2's Likely Entrepreneurial Development Opportunity Strategy Guides and resources go to https://www.energizingentrepreneurs.org/library/theme-papers/subjects/likely-edev-opps.html.
23 For additional information on REV or the Rural Entrepreneurial Venture initiative go to https://smifoundation.org/programs/economic-development-2/.
24 To learn more about NetWork Kansas and its E-Communities initiative go to https://www.networkkansas.com/.

(GRO) with The Ford Family Foundation;[25] and Energizing Entrepreneurial Ecosystems (E3)[26] with the Nebraska Community Foundation. In many ways, this seventh cycle of fieldwork and learning is among the most robust and allows for deployment of the latest e2 Development Framework and Process.

Reflecting on the knowledge gained over the past five decades of extensive research, fieldwork, and collaboration, the e2 team has made several discoveries with critical bearing for communities seeking to increase their prosperity through entrepreneur-focused economic development and ecosystem building.

4 Lessons Learned

At the end of the day, rural communities and the people who call them home engage in community economic development because they want their community to prosper. Furthermore, for a community to be successful in rural entrepreneur-focused economic development, first and foremost, residents must seriously take on the responsibility. Additionally, rural communities that are successful in rising to this responsibility, like Ord, can help other communities find their "right way" forward to their own prosperity.

Legacy Ord leader Robert Stowell was asked what advice he would give to other rural communities based on his experience with Ord's success. His three-fold response[27] was swift and passionate...

1. **Commit to and invest in community leadership development.** Ord has created and supports the world-class **Synovation Valley Leadership Academy** with deep engagement throughout the community.[28]
2. **Be willing to invest.** Over the past 25 years, Ord has invested a documented $250 million in public and private investment. Additionally, for a community historically opposed to increasing taxes, Ord has consistently passed tax increases and bond issues to support its development (Macke et al., 2020d).
3. **Make community-centered entrepreneurship the primary economic development game plan.** Ord has demonstrated success with business attraction and existing venture development and expansion; however, it has also invigorated its economy and society through entrepreneur-led entrepreneurial development,

25 To learn more about The Ford Family Foundation go to https://www.tfff.orb/ and learn more about GRO or Growing Rural Oregon go to https://www.tfff.org/.

26 To learn more about Nebraska E3 or the Energizing Entrepreneurial Ecosystems initiative go to https://www.energizingentrepreneurs.org/podcast/exploring-e3-in-nebraska.html.

27 To listen to Robert Stowell's podcast go to https://www.energizingentrepreneurs.org/podcast/episode-29.html.

28 For additional information on e2's Ord, Nebraska case study and resources go to https://www.energizingentrepreneurs.org/library/theme-papers/subjects/ord-nebraska.html.

documented in 100 entrepreneurial development deals ranging from main street ventures to growth enterprises (Macke et al., 2020d).

In addition to Stowell's guidance, the e2 team offers the following curated list of 25 learnings most relevant to the *Handbook of Rural Entrepreneurship*:

1. **A Community Has a Job to Do!** Etched into the stone of Nebraska's capitol are Aristotle's words, "A community, like an individual, has a work to do."[29] In the United States, the primary responsibility for a community's development rests with the community. This is not the case in other mature economies in Europe, Canada, and Japan, where regional, provincial, and federal agencies play larger roles. This important learning is forcing work inward with respect to what communities can do with and without external help.
2. **Rural is Diverse, Complex, and Requires Customized Strategies.** Throughout North America, there are many rural regions with unique development assets, histories, and cultures. Some of these regions enjoy robust external support, as is the case with Minnesota Initiative Foundations.[30] The e2 Development Framework and Process provides structure and research-based strategies and tactics, but rural communities must customize it to their unique assets, capacities, and preferences.
3. **Entrepreneur-Led Development Is Foundational.** During his time with the Corporation for Enterprise Development, Brian Dabson posited that human talent development is foundational to community development, which empowers optimal economic development.[31] Dabson advocates that entrepreneurship is not just one more economic development approach, but rather it is the foundation for all economic development, enabling better large employer retention and expansion and ultimately venture attraction. e2's fieldwork and research embrace Dabson's counsel, including that entrepreneur-led development is foundational for all rural community development.
4. **Community Leadership Is Key.** There is great truth in Margaret Mead's famous quote, "Never doubt that a small group of thoughtful, committed citizens can change the world; for, indeed, that's all who ever have."[32] When the e2 team reflects on its accumulated experience, the primary differential between failure

29 To learn more about quotations carved into the stone of Nebraska's State Capitol building check out: https://capitol.nebraska.gov/building/artwork/panels-and-sculptures/.

30 To learn more about Minnesota's Initiative Foundations go to https://www.greaterminnesota.net.

31 Brian Dabson in e2's view is among a group of contemporary entrepreneurship thought leaders. Hailing from England, Brian led the Corporation for Enterprise Development and the Rural Policy Institute and now lives in North Carolina where he continues his research, lecturing, writing and consulting.

32 For more background on Margaret Mead and her quotations see the Library of Congress Biography and Works, https://www.loc.gov/exhibits/mead.

and success is the empowerment of community leaders who, in turn, create resident agency to spawn and grow community economic development.

5. **The e2 Development Framework and Process.** The 7th generation e2 Development Framework and Process, embracing lessons shared in this chapter, among others, has demonstrated value in empowering transformative rural change. Creating a more competitive, diverse, higher value, and resilient economy that democratizes opportunity is core to this entrepreneur-focused development framework (Mack, 2020b; Macke, Markley & Binerer, 2011).
6. **Understanding Entrepreneurial Talent.** Entrepreneurial talent (E-talent) is the foundational asset for entrepreneur-led development. Although every community has E-talent, there are not universal levels of it. Increasing E-talent is central to growing an entrepreneurial economy and community quantitatively and qualitatively over time. This work starts with the talent a community has at the beginning of its journey (Macke & Chaffin, 2020a).
7. **E-talent and Entrepreneurial Ecosystems.** Energizing talent through various established and emergent strategies (e.g., capital access, incubation, acceleration, clusters, etc.) and tactics embedded in the e2 ground game is paramount to generating desired community economic development outcomes, beginning with increased deal flow and continuing with the creation of more and better ventures, new investments, jobs, and the like (Macke & Chaffin, 2020a).
8. **The Basic Transaction and the Community Ground Game.** The North Star of the e2 Development Framework and Process is simple – engage with entrepreneurs. e2 refers to this as the "basic transaction" and the establishment of a ground game, which is a community's commitment to and capacity for regularly reaching out to entrepreneurs and networking them to assistance. e2's current call for paid "resource networkers" and entrepreneur coaches seeks to empower a more scaled-up and sustainable ground game (Macke & Chaffin, 2020a).
9. **Area Venture Services.** Most rural communities, and particularly smaller rural communities, can fulfill the vast majority of entrepreneurs' needs and wants from within the immediate area. Investing in and supporting area venture services (e.g., commercial lending, gap financing, mentors, attorneys, bookkeepers, CPAs, etc.) helps create an optimal entrepreneurial ecosystem. With the area ecosystem engaged, the community can then focus on networking entrepreneurs to more specialized resources that are often external to the community (Macke, 2022).
10. **Supporting All Three Venture Types.** With entrepreneurship, there is a dominant focus on for-profit businesses; however, all three venture types – for-profit businesses, nonprofit organizations, and governmental enterprises – present entrepreneurial opportunities and are important to community-centered development.
11. **Demand-Driven Ecosystem Building.** Every community has elements of an entrepreneurial ecosystem. Entrepreneurial ecosystems in most rural communities are fractured and lack access and transparency. An **E-Demand-Driven** approach can help address these challenges through the curation of local, regional, and ex-

ternal E-Resource Networks that provide access to "Go To" Resources, "Pathway Resources," "Business Services," and the like (Macke & Chaffin, 2020a; Macke, 2020c).

12. **Development Pacing.** Pacing within the e2 Development Framework and Process is important. Likewise, e2 has become more aggressive and directed in its advice to communities about pacing and shares the following pacing goals (Macke & Chaffin, 2020a; Macke, Markley & Binerer, 2011):

Take up to a year to determine readiness.

Within the first six months:
- Early organizing and stakeholder engagement
- Stakeholder assessment
- Community engagement
- Development opportunity profile
- E-Talent mapping and targeting
- E-Resource mapping and engagement
- Early outreach to entrepreneurs

Within the next six months:
- Working with entrepreneurs
- Funding, staffing, and capacity building
- Technical assistance cost-sharing program
- Capital access
- Early impacts and testimonials

13. **The Power of Community Learning and Sharing.** Relatable stories are powerful and can inspire and inform other communities. For example, Ord's stories are moving other rural communities to explore what they can and need to do to be more successful. e2 advocates for more community stories and accessible case studies (Macke & Chaffin, 2020b).
14. **Catalysts.** There are several catalysts that can empower a more entrepreneurial economy and community, including those listed in the following progression: creativity, innovation, invention, commercialization, scale-up and growth, value-chains, and economic clusters. Entrepreneurs are particularly important for capturing innovation and invention, driving commercialization, or the useful and monetized deployment of new ideas. Collective agency, however, is necessary to grow value-chains and economic clusters.[33]

33 Ibid.

15. **Accelerators.** Resource navigators, capital access, financial packagers, youth entrepreneurial strategies, and technical assistance cost-sharing programs are all accelerators of entrepreneur-centered development.[34]
16. **Role of Research and Analytics.** e2 curates and refines a collection of analytics on an ongoing basis to provide resources for data-driven decision-making. These analytics are generically and specifically employed in the e2 Development Framework and Process (Macke, n.d.). Primary analytics resources include profiles on:
    - Development opportunity
    - Market opportunity
    - Venture dynamics
    - Growth-entrepreneurs
    - Demographics
    - Philanthropy
    - Specialized topics
17. **The Technologies.** Effectively working with communities should consider both art and science. Based on e2's fieldwork, "the technologies" that are central to community engagements include (Macke, 2020c):
    - Development road maps
    - Progress scorecards
    - Entrepreneur portfolios
    - Use of video conferencing to increase engagement and reduce isolation from resources
    - Action planning
18. **Metrics.** Metrics as defined by e2 include statistics and stories/testimonials. As the old Forbes saying goes, "You are what you measure." The e2 Development Framework and Process uses a collection of metrics to help demonstrate "cause and effect," and also employs Milan Wall's **Hierarchy of Community Impacts** concept, which provides insights into community-based evaluation for community and economic development (Macke & Chaffin, 2020b; Wall & Macke, 2014).
19. **The Prosperity Community Framework Is Empowering.** The **Prosperity Community Framework** provides an empowering way for most rural communities to organize for transformative change. This framework includes a commitment to greater and widely shared prosperity measured in income and household wealth. The four essentials of the framework – embedded in e2's Change Model – include (Macke, 2020a):
    - New resident attraction, development, and retention
    - Quality of life placemaking (both physical and cultural)
    - Entrepreneur-focused economic development
    - Community capacity building for development

34 These sections were informed by Don Macke's personal journals and research files.

20. **Hierarchy of Community Impacts Framework.** Milan Wall, with the Heartland Center for Leadership Development, curated the **Hierarchy of Community Impacts Framework**, working with the HomeTown Competitiveness initiative. Over the years, e2 has employed and evolved the hierarchy in its fieldwork and case and natural studies. There are five levels in the hierarchy (Wall & Macke, 2014):
    - Level 1 – Smart Activities
    - Level 2 – Resulting Outputs
    - Level 3 – Commitments and Investment
    - Level 4 – Outcomes Like Deal Flow
    - Level 5 – Indicators of Transformative Change
21. **Ripple Effect Mapping, Celebration, and Momentum. Ripple Effect Mapping** (REM) is a powerful tool and experience for communities that provides a foundation for community evaluation and celebration and contributes to community momentum. REM captures intended and unintended outputs, outcomes, and impacts. This activity is fun and energizes community participants as they discover their progress and success (Chazdon et al., 2017).
22. **Development Capacity.** One of the greatest inhibitors to rural community economic development is the lack of efficient, effective, and sustained development capacity. For rural communities to realize transformative change, there must be robust and sustained development capacity. e2 focuses serious attention on mapping and building a community's development capacity (Macke, 2021).
23. **Hub and Spoke Organizational Model.** The Energizing Entrepreneurial Ecosystems (E3) initiative encourages and supports communities to evolve a **Hub and Spoke Organizational Model** once they have engaged in priority development actions (Macke & Spillers, 2021). This model has been successfully tested in expansive work with the Appalachian Regional Commission (Entreworks Consulting, 2018).
24. **Sustained Effort.** Communities, their residents, and ventures operate in a dynamic, ever-changing world economy and society. For communities to realize sustained and broadly shared prosperity, they must maintain their development at a smart and elevated level. **Community Economic Development** (CED) requires a 24-7-365 commitment. It is never-ending, and in rapidly changing economic, social, and environmental climates, continuous CED ensures community relevancy and success (Macke & Chaffin, 2020b).
25. **Rural Communities Need More Useful Help.** Important, but not foundational, to Ord's transformative change has been its employment of external help (Hansen, 2021). Other progressive communities inspired and informed Ord, while outside partners like Nebraska Public Power District and Nebraska Extension provided expertise, facilitation, and networking to resources. There are extensive examples of external play benefiting communities on their journeys to prosperity.

The time- and field-tested key learnings e2 has identified can aid rural communities in building and sustaining a successful entrepreneurial ecosystem that undergirds their economic development objectives. However, any discussion regarding strengthening rural entrepreneur-focused economic development is incomplete without consideration of the policy landscape and the opportunities that lie within it.

5 Policy Considerations

As discussed, external support has an important role to play in enabling rural entrepreneur-focused economic development. As such, the following are e2's top 10 recommendations for national and state/provincial leaders and development agencies, including foundations and corporations, to contribute in meaningful ways to rural community economic development (RCED).[35]

1. **Understanding the Seed Grant System Flaw.** Based on decades of work in rural North America (e.g., United States, Canada, and the Caribbean), e2 has come to conclude that current federal and state RCED support through **seed grants** is flawed. The e2 team has worked with nearly all federal and many state grant programs, including those administered by USDA Rural Development, the U.S. Economic Development Administration, and the U.S. Department of Housing and Urban Development (e.g., Community Development Block Grants). While the team's experience is not comprehensive, it is expansive as members have made a living advising rural communities and regions on using these funds. Unfortunately, these investments typically were not sustained and never realized transformative desired change. Following are three prevalent flaws the e2 team has identified with this funding mechanism:
   - **Lack of a system to provide ongoing support is necessary for realizing transformative change**. Most federal and state RCED grants range from one to a maximum of 3 years. To realize transformative change, interventions require a minimum of 5 to 10 years of commitment.
   - **Insufficient grant funds**. The dollars were not robust enough to make a real difference.
   - **Absence of capacity-building consideration**. These grants rarely build the sustained development capacity necessary for advancing RCED work.
2. **From Seed Grants to Systemic Regionalism.** There is an untapped opportunity to invest in rural community capacity building that will enable rural communities to take on and own their development, embracing a regional approach to RCED.

35 While these recommendations are specifically relevant to the United States, they also may hold value for international efforts.

e2 recommends federal and state RCED funding evolve from an under-resourced collection of disorganized, cumbersome grant programs to:
- Dedicate at least 50% of all federal and state RCED funding streams to systemic funding for regional development organizations, providing them with discretionary resources and greater capacity to work with rural communities and their regions.
- Devolve at least 50% of all federal and state RCED funding to more flexible grant funding to support, first, community and area development capacity building, and second, community and area-defined systemic development projects.

These two adjustments would empower greater RCED impact to help realize transformative positive change and ensure the sustainability of RCED work.

3. **Federal Agency Targets.** As part of e2's proposed "pivot" demonstration policy project, the organization recommends targeting the following federal agency spending streams:
   - U.S. Economic Development Administration – Commerce
   - U.S. Small Business Administration – Commerce
   - Community Development Block Grants – Housing and Urban Development
   - Rural Development – U.S. Department of Agriculture

e2 recognizes that this early policy change demonstration could include other agencies.

4. **Foster Regional Collaboration.** Over the years, the federal government, often in collaboration with state governments, has created and supported a wide range of governmental and nonprofit regional organizations. Historically, these organizations were intended to be a federal, state, and local community collaboration. Examples include:
   - U.S. Economic Development Administration's Development Districts
   - U.S. Small Business Administration's Small Business Development Centers
   - Community Action Agencies
   - Regional Public Health Agencies
   - Regional Disability Agencies
   - U.S. Department of Agriculture's Resource Conservation and Development Areas

However, with federal and state policy trends to defund and deauthorize governmental and some nonprofit regional development organizations, other entities have begun to operate in this space. Based on fieldwork, e2 has observed that often higher-impact regional development groups are largely outside of federal and state oversight and funding. This includes:
- Regional community foundations
- Regional private and/or family foundations
- State-authorized regional development organizations with dedicated funding

Bottom line, federal and state RCED policy should foster regional collaboration that drives meaningful cooperation, if not articulation, with every rural region's regional development groups.

5. **Intentional Partnership with Regional and Community Philanthropy.** If the government is engaged with RCED, it should strive to create the optimal beneficial impact, which requires empowering citizens. Only rural communities and their regions can effectively and efficiently determine and execute their own development. In America, absent more direct federal and state policy engagement (as is the case in Canada), federal and state government RCED funding should focus on growing both regional and community development capacity.

e2 recommends the development of intentional partnerships with regional and community philanthropy, employing the well-established community foundation policy framework. Community foundations can become impactful, rooted, and community-directed RCED partners. There are numerous successful examples to inform how federal and state policy could support community foundation development and ensure that these institutions remain community-driven and centered, thereby embracing the tried and true 4 H value, "Never do to. Work hard to not do for. Always do with."[36]

Support for community foundations must inspire, inform, and ensure that this ethical approach to development is a guiding principle of this work. It would be a profound innovation in federal and state RCED policy to embrace and empower community foundations across rural America, just as the Kansas Health Foundation has done in rural Kansas, for example.

6. **New Funding Streams.** The following three demonstrated new funding sources have the potential to bring massive and sustained capitalization to RCED:
   - Dedicating gaming dollars
   - Industry severance taxes
   - Philanthropic endowments

Dedicating Gaming Dollars. Iowa dedicates gaming revenues to fostering community and regional philanthropy with the intent that these investments will grow permanent endowments to provide lasting community and regional development support. As more states adopt gaming, they should give serious consideration to allocating all or some of these new dollars to regionally empowered RCED.

Industry Severance Taxes. In 1941, the governor and state of Minnesota created an innovative rural development policy through the Iron Range Resources and Rehabilitation Board (IRRRB) and fund. The state levied a tax on the mining of iron ore in northern Minnesota's Iron Range and created a trust fund that thrives to this day. Funds from the IRRRB trust fund have supported three goals:

36 See https://4-H.org.

- Innovations in the iron ore mining industry
- Rehabilitation of environments impacted by mining activity.
- Economic diversification and quality of life placemaking.

Rural America continues to be a major producer of natural resources, from energy to minerals, timber, agricultural commodities, and recreational tourism. A modest value-added tax on these resources could capitalize on trust funds and/or endowments that are regionally oriented and used to support smart, transformative development, including socio-economic diversification, in environments dependent on natural resources.

Consider the following example from the Bakken oil patch in western North Dakota:

The Bakken Region: From Depopulation to Economic Boom

When the e2 team first started working with communities in western North Dakota through Dickinson State University, the region faced long-term, chronic, and severe depopulation and economic contraction. In time, however, its challenges shifted to dealing with an economic boom as massive investment flowed in to produce oil and natural gas from the Bakken formations.

The U.S. Geological Survey estimates that the Bakken has between 4.4 and 11.4 billion barrels of oil that can be recovered. Consider the following scenario:

Assume the Bakken Region can produce 8 billion barrels of oil at a value of at least $100 per barrel over time, resulting in an estimated gross value of $1 trillion. Likewise, assume a 1 percent gross severance tax on the $1 trillion value, resulting in $10 billion that could be dedicated to an RCED trust fund. This provides the potential for an annual perpetual payout at 4 percent of $400 million annually in perpetuity.

It may take 50 to 100 years to exploit all oil and natural gas resources associated with the Bakken Region. Sometime in the future, that resource will be depleted, and the economic activity will transition to other oil patches or maybe renewables. Regardless, there are present and future development needs and opportunities that the region could capitalize on with just a small slice of this resource's value dedicated to regionally empowered and community-centered RCED work.

Philanthropic Endowments. The Ford family created wealth through the harvesting and processing of timber resources in rural Oregon and Northern California. In 1957, Kenneth and Hallie Ford established The Ford Family Foundation. Now with an estimated $1 billion in assets, The Ford Family Foundation has been investing in rural Oregon communities and people for decades.[37] The foundation is community-oriented and empowers transformative change at the personal and community level. Across America, there are hundreds, if not thousands, of private, corporate, and community foundations that focus on rural regions and communities. Federal and state policies should incentivize and advantage rural donors and foundations that are investing in the best in RCED work. Doing so will increase sustainable RCED funding sources.

37 See https://www.tfff.org/.

7. **Regional Models.** Although by no means comprehensive of all the remarkable regional development organizations, the following is a list of ten development organizations that e2 believes merit study to inform possible federal and state RCED policy:
   - Communities Unlimited – seven southern U.S. states, including many rural communities
   - The Ford Family Foundation – rural Oregon
   - HoChunk Inc. – Winnebago Tribe of Nebraska
   - Iowa Area Development Group – statewide
   - Iron Range Resources and Rehabilitation Board – rural Minnesota
   - Kentucky Highlands Investment Corporation – southeastern Kentucky
   - Minnesota Initiative Foundations – rural Minnesota
   - Nebraska Community Foundation – rural Nebraska
   - NetWork Kansas – statewide
   - Northern Initiatives – Michigan
8. **Universal Broadband.** Trails, rivers, railroads, highways, and telephone lines have all served as critical infrastructure that enabled or constrained the development of communities. Likewise, today, access to high-speed, affordable broadband is essential to competitive communities. There remain huge differences in broadband capacity, access, and cost across the United States. The primary differential is the area broadband provider. Current state and federal broadband policies are undermined by their support of the broadband providers that are unwilling to provide high-quality, affordable service. Focusing funding on community-selected, willing broadband providers is a key, necessary policy shift for universal broadband.
9. **Leadership and Organization Building.** Colleagues with the Heartland Center for Leadership Development demonstrate that entities on the leading edge of successful RCED are empowering community leaders and are integrated, adequately funded, and professionally staffed development organizations. It should be a state, national, and international priority to deploy world-class leadership and organizational development support to every rural community.
10. **Professionalization of Rural Community Economic Developers.** Across the board in rural communities, dedicated, capable, and passionate leaders and staffers work hard to support their community's development. At the same time, with the erosion of business attraction opportunities beginning in the early 1980s, rural communities have disinvested in their community economic development infrastructure. During the peak of the business attraction era, local economic developers were among the highest-salaried persons in a community. They stayed in their jobs for years and acquired the experience and skills to excel in the business attraction game. Today, community economic developers often are not well paid and lack competitive benefits. The field faces destructively high turnover. The time has come to reinvest in our community economic development leaders and staff. Central to this is providing them with a development game plan that

> can generate desired impacts. Entrepreneurship-focused development is that game plan for achieving success. National, state, and regional development groups should focus on revitalizing RCED through the restored professionalization of its leaders and staff.

Although rural communities have primary responsibility for their own development and success, smarter regional, state, and national policies and programs can empower greater and quicker success. The clock is ticking for many rural communities that are approaching the tipping point when they will lack the opportunity and capacity for renewal.

Recommended Resources

e2 Entrepreneurial Ecosystems, and the Center for Rural Entrepreneurship before it, is a nonprofit corporation with U.S. Internal Revenue Service 501(c)(3) charitable status. As such, a critical part of e2's mission is public service and the advancement of impactful rural community economic development strategies. Visit the e2 Entrepreneurial Ecosystems website[38] to explore its free resources, including the following:

- Ord Sidney Nebraska Case Study, Nebraska, stories and case study, including an accompanying online curriculum.
- Entrepreneurial Ecosystem Building in Rural America – Four Decades of Learning
- Pathways to Rural Prosperity Podcasts are no longer being produced, but all episodes are available through the e2 website which is active at www.enertizingentrepreneurs.org.
- e2 National Practitioners Network and Resource Library

References

Chazdon, S., Emery, M., Hansen, D., Higgins, L., & Sero, R. (2017). A field guide to ripple effects mapping. University of Minnesota Libraries Publishing.

Entreworks Consulting, Center for Rural Entrepreneurship, Center for Regional Economic Competitiveness. (2018). Building an entrepreneurial future: Ideas for Appalachia's ecosystem builders and champions. Retrieved on July 28, 2022 from https://www.arc.gov/wp-content/uploads/2018/09/EntrepreneurialEcosystemsEntrepFuture2018.09.pdf.

Hansen, M. (2021). The long drive home: How Bob Stowell and allies made Ord's future. e2 Entrepreneurial Ecosystems.

Iaquinta, D. (2022). Weathering the pandemic in Ord, Nebraska. How a well-functioning entrepreneurial ecosystem came back better. e2 Entrepreneurial Ecosystems. Retrieved from https://www.energizingentrepreneurs.org/file_download/6af87233-5117-4331-b33d-17c28087189a

Iaquinta, D.L. (2022). What Kind of Place is Ord: Rural, Urban, Periurban?e2 Entrepreneurial Ecosystems. November 1.

38 https://www.energizingentrepreneurs.org/

Iaquinta, D.L. (2021). Weathering the Pandemic, Pivoting to Abundance Amidst Crisis. e2 Entrepreneurial Ecosystems. November 5.
Iaquinta, D., Wehrbein, W., Donahue, T., Koehn, J., Partington, J., Decker, C., & Fransecky, R. (2009). Strategic Discussions for Nebraska, UNL Digital Commons. Accessed from: https://digitalcommons.unl.edu/sdn/4/.
Kayne, J. (n.d.). Jay Kayne served as the Vice President for the Center for Entrepreneurial Leadership at the Ewing Marion Kauffman Foundation and shared this definition, widely used by the Center for Rural Entrepreneurship with e2.
Macke, D. (n.d.). Rural Community Prosperity Development. e2 Entrepreneurial Ecosystems. Retrieved July 28, 2022, from https://www.energizingentrepreneurs.org/library/theme-papers/subjects/community-prosperity-development-framework.html.
Macke, D. (2022). Entrepreneurial communities and business services. Entrepreneurial Ecosystems. e2 Entrepreneurial Ecosystems. Retrieved from: https://files.constantcontact.com/c84c5a8b001/76b1cd73-6d12-49d9-a513-40b8d580e915.pdf?rdr=true.
Macke, D. (2021) Community capacity building. Shaping the future of hometowns. e2 Entrepreneurial Ecosystems. Retrieved from: https://www.energizingentrepreneurs.org/file_download/f049a803-fbe3-4eff-b4b0-73011e0cd54b.
Macke, D. (2020a). e2's rural community prosperity development framework. e2 Entrepreneurial Ecosystems. Retrieved from https://www.energizingentrepreneurs.org/library/theme-papers/subjects/community-prosperity-development-framework.html.
Macke, D. (2020b). Entrepreneurial ecosystem building in rural America: Four decades of learning. e2 Entrepreneurial Ecosystems.
Macke, D. (2020c). Key e2 technologies. e2 Entrepreneurial Ecosystems. Retrieved from https://www.energizingentrepreneurs.org/file_download/63921613-9d15-4387-911d-17b2c0d44eb6.
Macke, D., & Chaffin, A. (2020a). Working with Entrepreneurs Guide. e2 Entrepreneurial Ecosystems. Retrieved from https://www.energizingentrepreneurs.org/file_download/36e3ba5f-ee31-4caf-8f09-702b036d531c.
Macke, D., & Chaffin, A. (2020b). Metrics, stories, and sustainability guide. e2 Entrepreneurial Ecosystems. Retrieved from: https://www.energizingentrepreneurs.org/file_download/3f51091b-091f-43bd-9ddd-209a6fd89b59.
Macke, D., Iaquinta, D., Kottwitz, C., Stowell, R., & Chaffin, A. (2020a). Defining Ord and its economy. e2 Entrepreneurial Ecosystems. Retrieved from https://www.energizingentrepreneurs.org/library/theme-papers/subjects/ord-nebraska.html.
Macke, D., Iaquinta, D., Kottwitz, C., Stowell, R., & Chaffin, A. (2020b). Development chronology – Ord: Ord's journey to becoming an entrepreneurial community in Nebraska. e2 Entrepreneurial Ecosystems. Retrieved from https://www.energizingentrepreneurs.org/library/theme-papers/subjects/ord-nebraska.html.
Macke, D., Iaquinta, D., Kottwitz, C., Stowell, R., & Chaffin, A. (2020c). Ord comparative performance analysis: An entrepreneurial community. e2 Entrepreneurial Ecosystems. Retrieved from https://www.energizingentrepreneurs.org/library/theme-papers/subjects/ord-nebraska.html
Macke, D., Iaquinta, D., Kottwitz, C., Stowell, R., & Chaffin, A. (2020d). Ord, Nebraska, an entrepreneurial community. e2 Entrepreneurial Ecosystems. Retrieved from https://www.energizingentrepreneurs.org/library/theme-papers/subjects/ord-nebraska.html.
Macke, D.W., Markley, D.M., & Binerer, A. (2011). Transfer of wealth in rural America: Understanding the potential, realizing the opportunity, creating wealth for the future. Lincoln, Nebraska: Center for Rural Entrepreneurship.
Macke, D., & Spillers, K. (2021). Hub city development: A likely entrepreneurial development opportunity strategy guide. e2 Entrepreneurial Ecosystems. Retrieved from https://www.energizingentrepreneurs.org/file_download/a5f11cac-0f4d-4496-be86-4e15f52ff065.

Macke, D., Markley, D., & Fulwider, J. (2014). Energizing entrepreneurial communities. A pathway to prosperity. Lincoln, NE: Center for Rural Entrepreneurship.

Markley, D., & Binerer, A. (2014). Creating entrepreneurial communities in kansas, listening, learning and adapting. e2 Entrepreneurial Ecosystems. Retrieved from https://www.energizingentrepreneurs.org/library/eimpact/success.html

Markley, D., Macke, D., Luther, V., & Wall, M. (2005). Energizing entrepreneurs. Charting a course for rural communities. Heartland Center for Leadership Development.

U.S. Department of Agriculture (2020). Rural-urban continuum codes. Retrieved from https://www.ers.usda.gov/data-

Wall, M., & Macke, D. (2014). Hierarchy of community impacts: A concept paper on community-based evaluation for community and economic development. Center for Rural Entrepreneurship. Retrieved from: https://energizingentrepreneursorg.presencehost.net/file_download/f8e64271-0ea9-4f3f-8935-f7077c5d6445.

Arjan van Dorsselaer, Niels Bosma and Mara van Twuijver

Rural Roots and Urban Aspirations: Spatial Influences on Entrepreneurial Motivations in Europe

Abstract: This chapter explores the spatial influences on entrepreneurial motivations across urban, peripheral, and rural regions in Europe. Using data from the Global Entrepreneurship Monitor (2019–2021), it examines distinct motivations for engaging in entrepreneurship, emphasizing how contextual factors shape entrepreneurial activity. Rural areas, often characterized by limited access to financial and human capital, weaker markets, and institutional constraints, tend to foster necessity-driven entrepreneurship. In contrast, urban regions, with their more resource-rich ecosystems, encourage opportunity-driven ventures aimed at wealth creation, autonomy, and social impact. Applying Maslow's hierarchy of needs, the study identifies four key motivational drivers: earning a living due to scarce job opportunities, continuing a family tradition, achieving financial independence, and creating social value. The findings reveal that necessity-driven entrepreneurship is less prevalent in urban regions, where entrepreneurs are more likely to pursue great wealth and societal impact. Gender, education, and age further shape these motivations. Whereas women and lower-educated people most often engage in entrepreneurship out of necessity, young rural entrepreneurs are motivated by family traditions, and younger and highly educated individuals in urban regions are more inclined toward opportunity-based entrepreneurship. These insights contribute to a deeper understanding of regional entrepreneurial dynamics, highlighting policy implications for fostering entrepreneurship in different spatial contexts.

Keywords: regional entrepreneurship dynamics, rural entrepreneurship, entrepreneurial motivations, Global Entrepreneurship Monitor

1 Introduction

Entrepreneurial activity takes shape through interaction with factors in its environment (Welter, 2011; Gaddefors & Anderson, 2019). This acknowledgment has led to a growing interest in research into the relation between context and entrepreneurial activity (Autio et al., 2014; Zahra et al., 2014, Korsgaard et al., 2015). In this light, the

Arjan van Dorsselaer, Utrecht University, email: a.vandorsselaer@uu.nl
Niels Bosma, Utrecht University, email: N.S.Bosma@uu.nl
Mara van Twuijver, University College Cork, email: MVanTwuijver@ucc.ie

https://doi.org/10.1515/9783110791396-012

field of rural entrepreneurship has emerged as a response to contextualizing the spatial dimension within entrepreneurship (Müller & Korsgaard, 2018; Gaddefors & Anderson, 2019). For rural areas, this spatial dimension is often characterized by remoteness, uniformity, limited access to financial and human capital, weak local markets and institutional frameworks, and unbalanced power dynamics that negatively affect local citizens (Baumgartner et al., 2013; Fortunato, 2014). At the same time, local identity, territorially rooted skills and knowledge, and social capital from, for example, family ties, can be seen as characteristics that can be conducive to entrepreneurship (Muñoz & Kimmitt, 2019).

Entrepreneurship is linked in different ways to regional development (Müller, 2016). With regards to the contribution that rural entrepreneurs can have on rural development, it is important to consider their socio-economic factors as they influence the extent to which entrepreneurs' foster economic growth through local employment and innovation (Acs, 2006). Here, a distinction can be made between necessity-driven and opportunity-driven entrepreneurship. Whereas necessity-driven entrepreneurship covers the "venture creation activities by individuals who seek to fulfill their basic physiological and safety needs" (Dencker et al., 2021b, p. 63) and thus highlights the income-generating aspect of entrepreneurship, opportunity-driven entrepreneurship is about the ventures that are created to reach higher levels of fulfillment, in which non-monetary needs are prioritized, such as more autonomy, broader skill development, and even reaching self-actualization (Liang & Dunn, 2014).

Various studies have looked into how the spatial dimension has influenced the motivational drivers of entrepreneurs, since promoting opportunity-driven entrepreneurship is argued to further advance regional development further than necessity-driven entrepreneurship (Wennekers et al., 2005). For example, for the United States, it was found that rural entrepreneurs mainly start a business out of necessity, having no or only unsatisfactory job alternatives (Tsvetkova, Partridge & Betz, 2017). For the Canadian rural context, however, Bousmah (2021) showed that nascent entrepreneurs are seemingly more driven by opportunities than necessities. Yet, he further found that higher age and lower education levels of entrepreneurs decrease this effect. Sohns and Revilla Diez (2018) stated that, for Vietnam, especially opportunity-driven entrepreneurship cannot evolve in every regional setting. When areas are remote or very poor due to far distances to markets, entrepreneurs are thus forced to practice necessity-driven entrepreneurship.

When considering the European context, Bosma and Sternberg (2014) noted that opportunity-driven entrepreneurship is highest in urban areas. This was reiterated by Kedmenec et al. (2015), who concluded that human capital is an important driver for opportunity recognition. Therefore, in Slovenia, business opportunities are more often foreseen by the urban population than by its rural counterpart (25.6% compared to 18.6%). It thus seems that within Europe, necessity-driven entrepreneurship is relatively more prevalent in rural areas. Yet, up till now, no study has focused on motivational drivers while adopting a spatial lens in the setting of European regions. This chapter will therefore investigate how spatial dimensions influence characteristics of entrepreneurial activities and their underlying motivations by considering urban, peripheral, and rural regions in Europe. In drawing on survey data from the Global Entrepreneurship Monitor Adult Population Survey (2019–2021), this study sheds light on the relation between spatial factors and the development of specific types of entrepreneurship.

In doing so, this chapter offers a broader picture and a deeper understanding of the spatial context of (rural) entrepreneurship (Müller & Korsgaard, 2018; Gaddefors & Anderson, 2019) and the role of different types of entrepreneurship in regional development (Müller, 2016).

2 Entrepreneurial Motivations

Entrepreneurial motivations can be understood as lying along a continuum where, on one end, necessity-based entrepreneurs create their ventures driven out of basic needs (Dencker et al., 2021), and, on the other, opportunity entrepreneurs can primarily be driven by an aim to fulfill higher-level needs (Dencker, Bacq & Gruber, 2021). Rather than simply studying this dichotomy, we believe that the necessity/opportunity dynamics take shape in different forms, and certain subprofiles can be found within these two extremes (Giacomin et al., 2011). Therefore, in this section, we will nuance this understanding of necessity and opportunity-based entrepreneurship and distinguish between different motivational factors for entrepreneurs.

Motivational factors for the creation of firms can be distinguished between push (necessity-based) and pull (opportunity-based) factors (Reynolds et al., 2001). Dencker et al. (2021) apply Maslow's hierarchy of needs (1943) to explain the decisional push factors. Here, we extend their approach by also understanding the pull factors through Maslow's 'pyramid'. We thus distinguish the five tiers: (1) physiological needs; (2) safety and security; (3) love and belonging; (4) esteem; (5) self-actualization. Accordingly, the first two layers are considered push factors for starting an enterprise, whereas the last three are pulling individuals, as depicted in Figure 1.

Hence, when looking at the motivations of necessity entrepreneurs in developed countries, individuals establish businesses mainly because they are "pushed" to fulfill their security and safety needs due to layoffs and struggles with finding employment. Their basic physiological needs are often already met through governmental welfare programs (Dencker et al., 2021). Therefore, we formulate our first motivational factor:

Motivation 1: Pushed into entrepreneurship to earn a living because jobs are scarce.

The third layer of love and belonging can be seen as both a push and pull factor (O'Donnell et al., 2021), especially when relating it to the family element of this tier. People can become entrepreneurs as they grow up in an entrepreneurial family, which can pull individuals into entrepreneurship as they are better at spotting oppor-

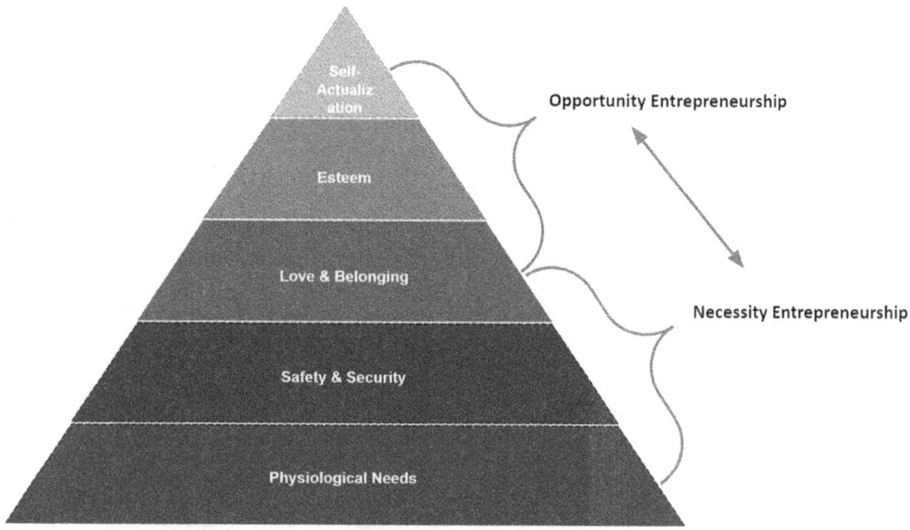

Figure 1: Maslow's pyramid of needs as entrepreneurial motivations.
Source: (based on Maslow, 1943)

tunities (Bhola et al., 2006; Dencker et al., 2021; Molina, 2020; Wagner, 2005). However, perpetuating the family tradition and living up to family expectations are also pushing factors that obligate individuals to take over the family business (Bhola et al., 2006; Giacomin et al., 2011; Molina, 2020). Yet, studies suggest that the pulling aspect of family is generally higher, as they provide the entrepreneur with encouragement, financial capital, and a social network (Bhola et al., 2006; Molina, 2020). In this study, we recognize both sides of the coin. Therefore, building on the role that family plays in deciding to become an entrepreneur, we formulate our second motivational factor as follows:

Motivation 2: Engaged in entrepreneurship for continuing a family tradition.

The fourth layer of Maslow's hierarchy, esteem, is about the need for achievement that drives individuals to become entrepreneurs. Having "a strong desire to assume personal responsibility, to set and meet moderately difficult goals, and to receive performance feedback" (p. 64), as well as gaining more autonomy, are important indicators of esteem (Dencker et al., 2021b). Liñan et al. (2013) note that in developed countries, both intellectual (e.g., being curious, open-minded, and creative) and affective (e.g., experiencing pleasure as well as a varied and exciting life) autonomy are important for opportunity entrepreneurs. The pursuit of higher levels of esteem through entrepreneurship is thus often translated to being independent by becoming self-employed, creating a job that allows one to be creative and flexible, and gaining high levels of financial capital to eventually pursue dreams (Giacomin et al., 2011; Pato & Teixeira, 2016; Tuzun & Takay, 2017). This leads us to the third motivational factor we formulate for founding a business, namely:

Motivation 3: Pulled into entrepreneurship for building a great wealth or a very high income to gain autonomy.

The final hierarchical need layer is self-actualization, which encompasses the motivations that are about reaching fulfillment directly from being an entrepreneur itself, also known as self-fulfillment (Dencker et al., 2021b). Here, the opportunity entrepreneur is searching for personal growth and peak experiences and wants to realize their own potential. Moreover, the individual can be motivated by values that transcend the personal self. Examples of entrepreneurs who are striving for self-actualization through entrepreneurship are the "lifestyle entrepreneurs." This subtype of opportunity entrepreneur builds on esteem and self-actualization as decisive factors for beginning a business. They pursue entrepreneurship so that they can afford a certain lifestyle or live in a certain community by operating businesses that are closely aligned with their personal values, interests, or passions (Fortunato, 2014; Pato & Teixeira, 2016). Linked to this idea of focusing on more than personal profits is the sub-typology of the social entrepreneur who combines resources in an innovative way to exploit opportunities for addressing societal needs (Fortunato, 2014). Put differently, this group of entrepreneurs is thus more interested in creating value than in capturing it (Santos, 2012). The last decisive factor we will therefore study is:

Motivation 4: Pulled into entrepreneurship to create value for others and to make a difference in the world.

3 Entrepreneurial Motivations from a Spatial Perspective

As argued in the previous section, the existing evidence suggests that the European rural entrepreneur is more often pushed than pulled into entrepreneurship compared to its urban counterpart (Bosma & Sternberg, 2014; Kedmenec et al., 2015). In general, rural spaces are considered to be "sparse" entrepreneurial ecosystems, defined by their limited resources, covering infrastructure, human capital, information spillovers, less access to investment, government support, or migrant entrepreneurship, fewer differences in economic activity, and more costly access to markets and demand, whereas urban areas are considered to be "munificent" (Miles & Morrison, 2020). Muñoz and Kimmitt (2019) note that indeed rural areas are deprived of entrepreneurial resources in some ways; however, they partially make up for this in other ways. Here, local identity, traditions, history, and territorially rooted skills and knowledge are mentioned as the most important drivers for entrepreneurship (Muñoz & Kimmitt, 2019, p. 863). Another factor contributing to this local embeddedness is the notion of family businesses. Business families are relatively unlikely to move their ventures, making them disproportionately important for rural areas. In many cases, the role of farms as the original business is key, as family-farms with ownership spanning over multiple generations comprise a substantial part of the agricultural sector (Seaman, 2015). In these enterprises, hard work is linked to personal and family amelioration (Muñoz & Kimmitt, 2019).

A study conducted in Finland by Huovinen and Koiranen (2011) also found that being motivated by identity and traditions translates to a logic of working hard and trying one's best, which dominated in the rural areas. They furthermore noted that urban entrepreneurs seem to adopt a logic that emphasizes strong faith in one's own leadership skills, which pursues esteem by gaining a superior position and running multiple companies alongside each other (Huovinen & Koiranen, 2011). This self-oriented focus of the urban entrepreneur goes against the conceptualization of the urban entrepreneur by Osorio and Özkazanç-Pan (2014). They noted that urban areas, characterized by their high population density, are increasingly experiencing disparities (e.g., access to food security, unequal wealth distribution). In this socioeconomic space, the urban entrepreneur is viewed as a social engineer whose role it is to ensure the sustainability or resilience of the area. This, thus, positions urban entrepreneurs as empathic individuals that found their business aiming to create value, not only for themselves but also for the rest of their community.

Building on the various motivations outlined above, and at the same time adopting a spatial lens, this study formulates four general hypotheses concerning urban-rural distinctions and entrepreneurial motivations:

H1A: In rural areas, early-stage entrepreneurs are motivated more often by push factors (motivation 1) than in urban areas.

H1B: In rural areas, early-stage entrepreneurs are motivated more often by continuing a family tradition (motivation 2) than in urban areas.

H1C: In urban areas, early-stage entrepreneurs are motivated more often by the desire to build wealth or a very high income (motivation 3) than in rural areas.

H1D: In urban areas, early-stage entrepreneurs are motivated more often by the desire to make a difference in the world (motivation 4) than in rural areas.

4 Socio-economic Motivational Drivers

When keeping Maslow's hierarchy of needs in mind and considering the different motivations that push and pull individuals into entrepreneurship, it becomes clear that there are various socio-economic factors influencing this decision (Block & Wagner, 2010; Giacomin et al., 2011; Liñan et al., 2013; Poschke, 2013; van der Zwan et al., 2016). In the following, three key demographic characteristics of the individual entrepreneur will be discussed, as these have been found to either strengthen or weaken the push and pull factors. Our focus herein lies on the spatial dimension. We examine these factors in conjunction with regional differences, and in particular, the expected differential effects for urban, peripheral, and rural regions.

4.1 Gender

As the field of women's entrepreneurship is growing rapidly in both importance and size, it has become clear that initial motivations to undertake entrepreneurial activities are affected by the sex of the entrepreneur, as venture creation itself is gendered (de Bruin, Brush & Welter, 2007). Gender discrimination, lack of education, and access to capital are pushing women in rural areas into entrepreneurship, whereas inferior status, limited decision-making power, early marriages, culture and traditions, and lack of family support are keeping women from enterprising (Li et al., 2019). Generally, women do not have the same access to their entrepreneurial ecosystem as their male counterparts, which limits their opportunity recognition (Cukier & Hassannezhad Chavoushi, 2020; Memon, 2020), yet a distinction should be made here between developed and undeveloped countries (Kobeissi, 2010).

In developing (non-OECD) countries, it is shown that women living in both urban and rural areas are more likely to be necessity-based entrepreneurs who start businesses to increase their household income (Hernandez et al., 2012; Rijkers & Costa, 2012). In developed (OECD) countries, research is less congruent on women entrepreneurs' motivations. Covering the entirety of Europe, the findings of Bosma & Sternberg (2014) hint towards urban females especially being unlikely to engage in opportunity-motivated entrepreneurship. Moreover, Martinez-Rodriguez et al. (2022) found that the COVID-19 pandemic has especially affected women and demonstrated that between 2018 and 2021, more women entered into entrepreneurship because of necessity.

In a Norwegian island setting, Rytkönen et al. (2023) describe how rural female entrepreneurs are discouraged from becoming opportunity entrepreneurs. On the one hand, their permanent employment is demanded by lenders to reduce the financial risks associated with their husbands' companies (often farms). On the other hand, when being the only entrepreneur (or breadwinner), employment alongside their enterprise is necessary for attracting investment, limiting opportunity entrepreneurship (for women) in rural areas. Yet, Poschke (2013) researched necessity-based entrepreneurs in OECD countries and found that women are slightly more likely to be opportunity-driven. Figueroa-Armijos and Johnson (2013) noted that in the American context, both men and women in rural counties are more likely to engage in opportunity-based entrepreneurship than in urban regions. In Turkey, rural female entrepreneurs are more necessity entrepreneurs, as they aim to increase their family income, whereas urban women strive more often for self-actualization. Further, no matter the region, women, more than men, have a desire to gain independence (Tuzun & Takay, 2017).

The latter is in line with Laure Humber and Drew (2010), who studied the Irish context. Yet, they found that women, just like men, are more often opportunity entrepreneurs. They do, however, note the importance of gender on motivation but emphasize the importance of marital status, having children (or not), and age as the more decisive factors. Baycan Levent, Masurel, and Nijkamp (2003), who studied Turkish women entrepreneurs in Amsterdam, noted family tradition as an important driving force for venturing, where entrepreneurial spirit showed more influence than experience. Conroy and Low (2022) examined the interplay between gender and income and noted that women entrepreneurs mainly arise in high and low-income situations, where the high income allows for lucrative business opportunities, whereas in low-income households the woman often becomes an entrepreneur to satisfy the need for income. For rural female entrepreneurs in Turkey, contributing to the household income is even mentioned as their most important driver for founding their enterprise, whereas in urban areas this plays a less important role (Tuzun & Takay, 2017). Therefore, we hypothesize:

H2A: In rural areas, women entrepreneurs are more often motivated by push factors (motivation 1) in comparison to women entrepreneurs in urban areas.

H2B: In urban areas, women entrepreneurs are more often motivated by continuing a family tradition (motivation 2) than women in rural areas.

4.2 Educational Level

Another very important factor driving the difference between being an opportunity versus a necessity entrepreneur, according to the literature, is the level of human capital an individual possesses. When assessing the opportunity recognition abilities of individuals, it is important to consider that person's stock of prior knowledge and experience. Moreover, at the exploitation stage, human capital endowments are argued to firstly influence the amount of resources one can acquire, secondly determine how these are bundled into capabilities, and lastly how these are then leveraged into value that is created and/or captured (Dencker et al., 2021b).

Regarding necessity-based entrepreneurship, the literature somewhat agrees that higher levels of education lessen the chances of becoming an entrepreneur in this category, and thus also, lower levels heighten the chances of ending up in this typology (Bergmann & Sternberg, 2007; Bourlès & Cozarenco, 2018; Bousmah, 2021; Chang et al., 2023; Poschke, 2013). Bousmah (2021) found, for example, that individuals in Canada with a graduate education are 31.5% more likely to end up being an opportunity entrepreneur than entrepreneurs who did not enjoy secondary education. However, other studies showed similar levels of education between the two entrepreneur typologies (Block & Wagner, 2010; van der Zwan et al., 2016). Block and Wagner (2010) therefore differentiate the explanatory power of human capital for the two entrepreneurship typologies, elaborating that high levels of general human capital (like formal education) are particularly linked to opportunity entrepreneurs, whereas lacking specific human capital (e.g., being educated in the particular vocation pursued by the individual) explains necessity entrepreneurship.

Considering various motivations for becoming an entrepreneur, Zhang, Duysters, and Cloodt (2014) found that entrepreneurial education has a direct effect on entrepreneurial intention. Saeed et al. (2013) elaborate on the increased intention by explaining the influence education has on self-efficacy. Al-Mamary and Alshallaqi (2022) found a strong relationship between entrepreneurial intention and more autonomy, innovativeness, risk-taking, and proactiveness, which is in line with Maslow's need for esteem as described in motivation 3.

When approaching human capital from a spatial perspective, it is assumed that urban regions generally have a younger and more highly educated population than rural areas, meaning that "the rural" seems to push individuals more into (necessity) entrepreneurship than urban contexts. Lavesson (2018) researched the Swedish environment on a regional level and noted a positive effect between education and start-up rates, both for necessity and for opportunity entrepreneurship. In the Slovenian setting, Kedmenec et al. (2015) found similar results, stating that most entrepreneurs enjoyed post-secondary formal education and lived in both urban and rural areas. Yet, they did find lower levels of education in rural areas and higher levels of entrepreneurial experience, knowledge, and skills amongst urban populations. On average, having completed a secondary education or less translated into being only 0.8 times as likely to identify a promising entrepreneurial opportunity as those who had had a post-secondary education (Kedmenec et al., 2015). Additionally, Eliasson and Westlund (2013) found that for both rural and urban regions, the level of education is positively related to the entry into self-employment, and thus becoming an entrepreneur. Especially in urban areas, a significant effect was found even for postgraduates over university education. Building on the predominant literature (Baumgartner et al., 2013; Fortunato, 2014; Kedmenec et al., 2015) we therefore hypothesize the following:

H3A: In rural areas, highly-educated entrepreneurs are more often motivated by push factors (motivation 1) than highly-educated entrepreneurs in urban areas.

H3B: In urban areas, highly-educated entrepreneurs in are more often motivated by the pursuit of autonomy and great wealth (motivation 3) than highly-educated entrepreneurs in rural areas.

4.3 Age

Age is related to entrepreneurial activity and its underlying motivations in several ways. Coming with age are several intangible benefits like increased experience, knowledge, and stronger social networks (Chang et al., 2023). At the same time, among others, decreased physical abilities and family commitments might decrease entrepreneurial activity or alter motivations (Chang et al., 2023). Overall, evidence on the relation between age and entrepreneurial activity remains inconclusive (Chang et al., 2023; Zhang & Acs, 2018).

In a German setting, Bergmann and Sternberg (2007) find that age does not affect the probability of becoming a necessity entrepreneur, while there is an inverted

U-shaped relation between age and opportunity entrepreneurship. Using GEM-data in the UK, Stephan et al. (2015) find a U-shaped relation between age and opportunity-based entrepreneurship, and an inverted U-shaped relation between age and necessity-based entrepreneurship. In the US, Zhang and Acs (2018) do not find a significant effect of age on either necessity versus opportunity-driven entrepreneurship. In the Canadian context, Bousmah (2021) finds that those under 65 years of age living in rural communities have a higher probability of becoming an opportunity-driven entrepreneur than those of the same age living in urban communities. However, when age progresses, this effect becomes less pronounced, and around 65 years of age, this effect disappears. Drawing on GEM data for 60 countries, Chang et al. (2023) find an inverted U-shaped relationship between age and both necessity and opportunity entrepreneurship. Their study indicates that the probability of becoming an opportunity-driven entrepreneur peaks at age 30, while the probability of becoming a necessity-driven entrepreneur peaks at age 35. It can be noted that youth and young adults are more optimistic about their ability to contribute to improving the world and creating social value compared to older generations. In general, they are more comfortable taking big risks and experience an increased capacity to empathize with the rest of society (Bublitz et al., 2021). Keeping in mind that rural areas are recognized by an aging population, we hypothesize the following:

H4A: In rural areas, younger entrepreneurs are more often motivated by push factors (motivation 1) than younger entrepreneurs in urban areas.

H4B: In urban areas, younger entrepreneurs are more often motivated by the opportunity to make a difference (motivation 4) than younger entrepreneurs in rural areas.

5 Data & Methods

5.1 Data

For exploring patterns of entrepreneurship and underlying motivations, we use novel data from the Global Entrepreneurship Monitor (GEM). The GEM database, normally used for comparing and contrasting entrepreneurship indicators across countries (and over time), has recently been analyzed at the regional level (GEM, 2023). For this purpose, all GEM individual-level data from the GEM Adult Population Surveys (APS) from 2015 to 2021 have been merged into a large, pooled sample involving more than 500,000 individual data points. Based on these data, we provide regional-level entrepreneurship indicators for 231 regions encompassing 28 European countries, as well as the underlying motivations as discussed above.

We first present our data, obtained from rigorous, harmonized data collection methods based on representative samples of the adult population (18–64 years old). The GEM methodology (Reynolds et al., 2005; Bosma, 2013) was designed to measure entrepreneurship across countries, rather than within countries. The sample sizes required to make comparisons between economies

At least 2,000 adults per economy are typically insufficient to make comparisons between regions within an economy (France, for example, has 14 regions). The countries and regions included in our analysis are listed in Appendix I. Aligning with European standards for regional data collection, we have adopted the NUTS categories of EUROSTAT, and a standard classification adopted in most European data collection efforts, for our regional classification.[1] The default spatial level is the NUTS2 level. For some smaller economies, we opted for NUTS3, particularly when the NUTS2 level presented rather limited geographic detail (e.g., less than three NUTS2 regions). In larger economies such as France, Germany, and the United Kingdom, we resort to NUTS1, as for these economies adopting NUTS2 would result in limited sample sizes per region.

Figure 2 shows patterns of early-stage entrepreneurial activity across European regions. To be more precise, these data reflect the percentage of the population between 18 and 64 that is currently (at the moment of the survey) actively in the process of starting a business, or currently owning and managing a business that exists for up to 42 months. For more information on patterns of entrepreneurial activity and entrepreneurial perceptions, see GEM (2023).

5.2 Dependent Variables

Whereas the indicators in Figure 2 are based on 2015–2021 data, our focus is on the underlying motivations of early-stage entrepreneurship. For our analysis, we therefore focus on early-stage entrepreneurs and take as dependent variables their (self-reported) motivations; these measures have been available since 2019, and hence our analysis is based on 2019–2021. The phrasing of the set of questions on entrepreneurial motivation is as follows: "Please tell me the extent to which the following statements reflect the reasons you are involved in this business. You can strongly agree, somewhat agree, neither agree nor disagree, somewhat disagree, or strongly disagree."

1. To make a difference in the world.
2. To build great wealth or a very high income.
3. To continue a family tradition.
4. To earn a living because jobs are scarce.

All GEM questions are translated into the local language under the supervision of the GEM National Team. This procedure involves back-translations (into English) by a third party in order to check if both versions align.

1 See https://ec.europa.eu/eurostat/web/nuts/background

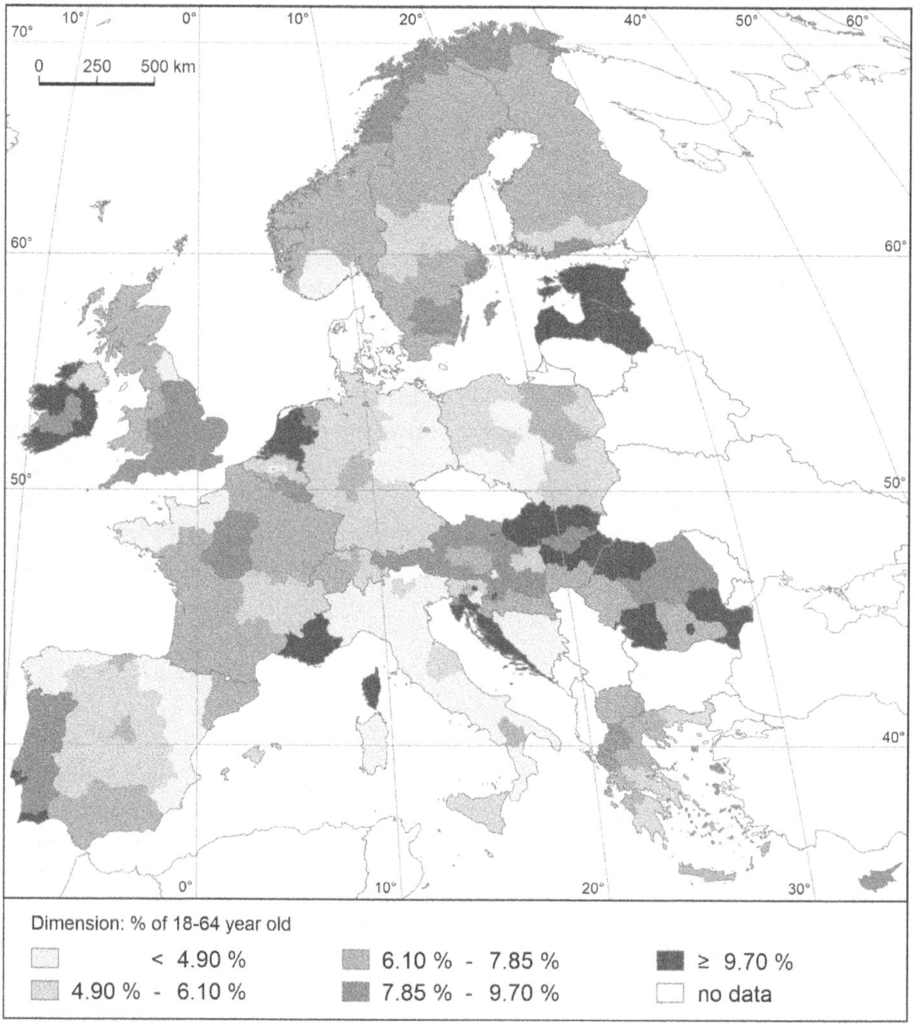

Figure 2: Total early-stage Entrepreneurial Activity (TEA) across European regions, based on GEM 2015–2021 data.
Source: GEM 2022.

5.3 Independent Variables

In order to discern rural, peripheral, and urban regions, we adopt a classification by Eurostat. Hence, all regions entrepreneurs in our sample reside in are classified as either rural, peripheral, or urban. Other key independent variables include the demographic indicators: gender, age, and education. Age is measured in five different age categories. We use the youngest available age category, 18–24 years, as our focus for

H4. Adopting age categories yields higher response rates (not all respondents are willing to indicate their exact age) and also allows for the possibility of non-linear effects. As discussed in Section 4, the relationship between age and entrepreneurial activity is rarely a linear one, and the same may hold for entrepreneurial motivations. Highest educational attainment was locally coded to fit with local education classifications. These have been translated by the GEM Data Team, in collaboration with the GEM National Teams, into the classification adopted by the United Nations. In order to ensure consistency and simplicity, we only discern three levels of education.

5.4 Control Variables

We include household income (in three categories that represent tertiles within the national context) and main occupation, as these tend to be relevant indicators for explaining entrepreneurial activity. In this chapter, explaining the impact of national (institutional) contexts is beyond our focus. In order to control for these contexts, we include fixed effects (dummy variables) at the country level. Finally, we control for an indicator that measures the respondent's self-perceived fear of failure when it comes to entrepreneurship, based on the answers to the statement: "fear of failure would prevent you from starting a business." In most of our regressions, this indicator turns out to be positive, but its inclusion does not affect the main results.

Table 1 shows the correlation of the main indicators. As can be seen, the motivation that most clearly separates individuals in urban and rural regions is motivation 2 (engaged in entrepreneurship to continue a family tradition), which is linked in particular to rural settings.

5.5 Methodology

In this chapter, we use the GEM data, as described above, to (i) analyze to what extent different motivations play a role, and (ii) how this plays out for rural versus urban and intermediate regions. We do this by adopting ordinal logit regressions on the individual (self-reported) responses by early-stage entrepreneurs concerning these four types of motivations. This way, we account for the ordinal nature of the data and can test if the thresholds between these categories are statistically significant (Hedeker, 2008).

Consistent with the theoretical argumentation in Sections 3 and 4, we run four distinct sets of regression models, each set using one of the four identified motivation types as dependent variables. We start each set with a regression that includes all main effects (independent variables and controls). We then augment this by adding

Table 1: Correlation table.

	1	2	3	4	5	6	7	8
1 TEA_mot1 (pushed)	1							
2 TEA_mot2 (family)	0.0946*	1						
3 TEA_mot3 (indiv wealth)	0.0586*	0.0523*	1					
4 TEA_mot4 (better world)	−0.0438*	0.0970*	0.2053*	1				
5 Urban	−0.0033	−0.0788*	0.0013	0.0242*	1			
6 Rural	0.0196	0.0659*	0.0417*	−0.0032	−0.5091*	1		
7 Female	0.0542*	−0.0375*	−0.0967*	0.0332*	−0.0004	0.002	1	
8 Young	−0.0119	0.0270*	0.0756*	0.0594*	−0.0053*	0.0090*	−0.0097*	1
9 High education	−0.0786*	−0.0563*	0.0327*	0.0526*	−0.0162*	0.0412*	0.0184*	−0.0812

relevant interaction effects of urban and rural (with intermediate regions taken as the reference group) and specific groups of interest across the indicators of gender, age, and education. This allows us to test all hypotheses developed above.

6 Results

6.1 Entrepreneurship Motivated by Push Factors

In Table 2, we observe in model 1A that, compared to peripheral regions, urban regions tend to exhibit significantly fewer entrepreneurs who mention being active as entrepreneurs (partly) because of the need to earn a living and lack of job alternatives. This is in line with H1a, stating that we expect to find more early-stage entrepreneurs in rural rather than urban areas being pushed into entrepreneurship. We also observe that females tend to be pushed into entrepreneurship more often than males. However, when we look into urban-rural differences, we do not observe a particular, distinctive gender effect. The same can be said for younger entrepreneurs versus their older counterparts (model 1C); living in either a rural or urban region does not seem to imply a higher or lower chance of being pushed into entrepreneurship, other than the main effects already discussed with model 1A. We do observe that higher-educated rural entrepreneurs are less likely to be motivated by push factors in comparison to highly educated entrepreneurs in peripheral regions (model 1D). By and large, the estimates of the threshold parameters are statistically significant and suggest the relevance of appreciating the ordinal nature of the dependent variable in the analysis.

Table 2: Entrepreneurship motivated by push factors (motivation 1).

Motivation among early-stage entrepreneurs: to earn a living because jobs are scarce	**(1A)**	**(1B)**	**(1C)**	**(1D)**
Region: rural	−0.0207 (0.0487)	−0.0477 (0.0585)	−0.0215 (0.0510)	0.0362 (0.0582)
Region: urban (H1A)	−0.0791** (0.0394)	−0.0484 (0.0515)	−0.0740* (0.0416)	−0.0661 (0.0500)
Gender: female	0.104*** (0.0316)	0.109* (0.0578)	0.104*** (0.0316)	0.106*** (0.0316)
Rural × female (H2A)		0.0708 (0.0797)		
Urban × female		−0.0696 (0.0756)		
Age: 25–34	−0.0437 (0.0552)	−0.0434 (0.0552)	−0.0572 (0.0922)	−0.0447 (0.0552)
Age: 35–44	0.0546 (0.0560)	0.0545 (0.0560)	0.0411 (0.0927)	0.0539 (0.0560)
Age: 45–54	0.145** (0.0580)	0.145** (0.0581)	0.132 (0.0937)	0.145** (0.0580)
Age: 55–64	0.0942 (0.0650)	0.0943 (0.0650)	0.0809 (0.0981)	0.0939 (0.0650)
Rural × young			0.00869 (0.119)	
Urban × young (H4A)			−0.0452 (0.118)	
Education: level 1	0.368*** (0.106)	0.370*** (0.106)	0.367*** (0.106)	0.381*** (0.107)
Education: level 2	0.197** (0.1000)	0.198** (0.1000)	0.197** (0.1000)	0.209** (0.100)
Education: level 3	0.0618 (0.0989)	0.0623 (0.0989)	0.0616 (0.0989)	0.134 (0.112)

Table 2 (continued)

Motivation among early-stage entrepreneurs: to earn a living because jobs are scarce	(1A)	(1B)	(1C)	(1D)
Rural × educ level 3 (H3A)				−0.143* (0.0808)
Urban × educ level 3				−0.0366 (0.0767)
Year of survey: 2019	−0.467*** (0.0391)	−0.468*** (0.0391)	−0.467*** (0.0391)	−0.468*** (0.0391)
Year of survey: 2020	0.0153 (0.0411)	0.0160 (0.0411)	0.0156 (0.0411)	0.0141 (0.0411)
Threshold fully/somewhat disagree	−1.960*** (0.177)	−1.953*** (0.178)	−1.970*** (0.188)	−1.921*** (0.178)
Threshold somewhat disagree/neutral	−1.152*** (0.176)	−1.144*** (0.177)	−1.162*** (0.187)	−1.112*** (0.178)
Threshold neutral/somewhat agree	−0.576*** (0.176)	−0.569*** (0.177)	−0.586*** (0.187)	−0.536*** (0.178)
Threshold somewhat/fully agree	0.507*** (0.176)	0.515*** (0.177)	0.497*** (0.187)	0.547*** (0.178)
Observations	14,274	14,274	14,274	14,274

Standard errors in parentheses.
***p < 0.01, **p < 0.05, *p < 0.1.
Reference categories: Region (intermediate), Age (18–24), Education (not reported), Year of survey (2021). Additional control variables included in the regression but not reported in this table are self-perceived fear of failure, main occupation, household income, and country; the full table is available on request.

6.2 Entrepreneurship Motivated by the Desire to Continue a Family Tradition

Model 2A in Table 3 confirms that entrepreneurs in urban areas are less inclined to be motivated by continuing a family tradition. The results in this column furthermore show that females and highly educated individuals tend to be linked less to this motivation. Model 2C indicates that young rural entrepreneurs are particularly motivated by the desire to continue a family tradition. This does not necessarily mean that they take over a family business. In fact, since they indicate they are starting or owning and managing a young firm, it is more likely that they start a different firm, having been influenced by entrepreneurial ancestors. Model 2D, finally, suggests that there is no differential rural-urban effect among highly educated entrepreneurs, who have already been seen to report family tradition as an underlying motivation to a limited extent.

Table 3: Entrepreneurship motivated by the desire to continue a family tradition.

Motivation among early-stage entrepreneurs: to continue a family tradition	**(2A)**	**(2B)**	**(2C)**	**(2D)**
Region: rural	0.000775 (0.0515)	0.0166 (0.0614)	−0.0390 (0.0540)	0.0226 (0.0608)
Region: urban (H1B)	−0.185*** (0.0426)	−0.173*** (0.0551)	−0.194*** (0.0450)	−0.216*** (0.0534)
Gender: female	−0.117*** (0.0339)	−0.0922 (0.0621)	−0.116*** (0.0339)	−0.116*** (0.0339)
Rural × female		−0.0397 (0.0844)		
Urban × female (H2B)		−0.0295 (0.0818)		
Age: 25–34	−0.0222 (0.0582)	−0.0220 (0.0582)	0.114 (0.0984)	−0.0224 (0.0582)
Age: 35–44	−0.0377 (0.0593)	−0.0375 (0.0593)	0.0986 (0.0991)	−0.0372 (0.0593)
Age: 45–54	−0.152** (0.0618)	−0.152** (0.0618)	−0.0157 (0.100)	−0.151** (0.0618)
Age: 55–64	0.0507 (0.0692)	0.0511 (0.0692)	0.186* (0.105)	0.0511 (0.0692)
Rural × young			0.308** (0.125)	
Urban × young			0.0688 (0.127)	
Education: level 1	0.174 (0.110)	0.174 (0.110)	0.174 (0.110)	0.183* (0.110)
Education: level 2	−0.0710 (0.104)	−0.0708 (0.104)	−0.0689 (0.104)	−0.0622 (0.104)
Education: level 3	−0.295*** (0.102)	−0.294*** (0.103)	−0.294*** (0.102)	−0.296** (0.116)
Rural × educ level 3				−0.0546 (0.0859)
Urban × educ level 3				0.0753 (0.0834)
Year of survey: 2019	0.150*** (0.0414)	0.150*** (0.0414)	0.149*** (0.0414)	0.149*** (0.0414)

Table 3 (continued)

Motivation among early-stage entrepreneurs: to continue a family tradition	(2A)	(2B)	(2C)	(2D)
Year of survey: 2020	−0.112** (0.0446)	−0.112** (0.0446)	−0.112** (0.0446)	−0.115** (0.0447)
Threshold fully/somewhat disagree	−0.427** (0.178)	−0.417** (0.179)	−0.303 (0.191)	−0.419** (0.180)
Threshold somewhat disagree/neutral	0.173 (0.178)	0.182 (0.179)	0.297 (0.191)	0.181 (0.180)
Threshold neutral/somewhat agree	0.524*** (0.178)	0.533*** (0.180)	0.649*** (0.191)	0.532*** (0.180)
Threshold somewhat/fully agree	1.374*** (0.179)	1.383*** (0.180)	1.498*** (0.192)	1.382*** (0.181)
Observations	14,244	14,244	14,244	14,244

Standard errors in parentheses.
***$p < 0.01$, **$p < 0.05$, *$p < 0.1$.
Reference categories: Region (intermediate), Age (18–24), Education (not reported), Year of survey (2021). Additional control variables included in the regression but not reported in this table are self-perceived fear of failure, main occupation, household income, and country.

6.3 Entrepreneurship Motivated by Building Wealth and Generating Income

Moving toward higher levels in Maslow's pyramid, Table 4 confirms that this motivation is more frequently mentioned in urban areas compared to rural and peripheral regions. The effect for urban regions in models 3A–3D is rather significant and robust for different model specifications. Interestingly, females in rural areas seem to be relatively often motivated by building wealth and generating high income (in particular compared to entrepreneurs in peripheral regions, see model 2B), but this effect is only weakly significant. We do not observe any particular differential effect related to rural/urban differences for young and/or highly educated entrepreneurs.

Other factors that are seen to be important and support earlier reported evidence are gender (males are clearly more motivated) and age (motivation is less prevalent as age progresses). Even though not presented in Table 4, substantial variation exists among countries. Countries that (controlling for the effect of all other factors) show the highest rate of entrepreneurs who self-report being motivated by building great wealth or generating high incomes include Cyprus, Italy, and Romania. Norway, Finland, Latvia, and Slovakia were the countries with the lowest country "fixed" effects for this motivation.

Table 4: Entrepreneurship motivated by the desire to generate wealth and develop high income.

Motivation among early-stage entrepreneurs: to build great wealth or a very high income	**(3A)**	**(3B)**	**(3C)**	**(3D)**
Region: rural	0.0234 (0.0478)	−0.0359 (0.0575)	0.00371 (0.0501)	0.0399 (0.0569)
Region: urban (H1C)	0.155*** (0.0387)	0.112** (0.0506)	0.154*** (0.0409)	0.176*** (0.0491)
Gender: female	−0.319*** (0.0312)	−0.404*** (0.0568)	−0.319*** (0.0312)	−0.319*** (0.0312)
Rural × female		0.144* (0.0782)		
Urban × female		0.0990 (0.0743)		
Age: 25–34	−0.180*** (0.0543)	−0.181*** (0.0543)	−0.125 (0.0906)	−0.181*** (0.0543)
Age: 35–44	−0.419*** (0.0554)	−0.419*** (0.0554)	−0.363*** (0.0912)	−0.419*** (0.0554)
Age: 45–54	−0.679*** (0.0572)	−0.679*** (0.0572)	−0.624*** (0.0922)	−0.679*** (0.0572)
Age: 55–64	−0.909*** (0.0646)	−0.910*** (0.0646)	−0.854*** (0.0967)	−0.909*** (0.0646)
Rural × young			0.156 (0.117)	
Urban × young			0.00179 (0.116)	
Education: level 1	−0.0451 (0.106)	−0.0430 (0.106)	−0.0436 (0.106)	−0.0447 (0.106)
Education: level 2	−0.0309 (0.100)	−0.0296 (0.100)	−0.0287 (0.100)	−0.0301 (0.100)
Education: level 3	−0.00300 (0.0992)	−0.00304 (0.0991)	−0.00176 (0.0992)	0.0321 (0.111)
Rural × educ level 3				−0.0430 (0.0795)
Urban × educ level 3 (H3B)				−0.0532 (0.0754)
Year of survey: 2019	−0.162*** (0.0382)	−0.162*** (0.0382)	−0.161*** (0.0382)	−0.162*** (0.0382)
Year of survey: 2020	−0.168*** (0.0404)	−0.168*** (0.0404)	−0.168*** (0.0404)	−0.168*** (0.0404)

Table 4 (continued)

Motivation among early-stage entrepreneurs: to build great wealth or a very high income	**(3A)**	**(3B)**	**(3C)**	**(3D)**
Threshold fully/somewhat disagree	−2.095*** (0.173)	−2.128*** (0.174)	−2.043*** (0.184)	−2.081*** (0.174)
Threshold somewhat disagree/neutral	−1.136*** (0.172)	−1.168*** (0.173)	−1.084*** (0.183)	−1.122*** (0.174)
Threshold neutral/somewhat agree	−0.474*** (0.172)	−0.506*** (0.173)	−0.421** (0.183)	−0.460*** (0.174)
Threshold somewhat/fully agree	0.941*** (0.172)	0.909*** (0.173)	0.994*** (0.183)	0.955*** (0.174)
Observations	14,273	14,273	14,273	14,273

Standard errors in parentheses.
***$p < 0.01$, **$p < 0.05$, *$p < 0.1$.
Reference categories: Region (intermediate), Age (18–24), Education (not reported), Year of survey (2021). Additional control variables included in the regression but not reported in this table are main occupation, household income, and country.

6.4 Entrepreneurship Motivated by Making a Difference in the World

We finally turn to motivations that go beyond the individual entrepreneur: becoming active as an entrepreneur in the pursuit of making a difference in the world (whether this is a modest contribution or a very ambitious one). Table 5 confirms that, as with the previously discussed motivation, early-stage entrepreneurs in urban areas tend to report this motivation more than those in rural or peripheral regions (model 4A). The size of the effect is also comparable. It should be stressed that, with all four motivations discussed, aligning with one motivation does not rule out the others. Indeed, in the data, we see a variety of combinations of motivations. A striking difference with the results in Table 4 is the opposite effect of gender. Concerning the motivation of making a difference in the world, female entrepreneurs are more likely to express this in comparison to males. This gender effect does not seem to deviate between rural, peripheral, or urban regions. The same goes for age; while also here (as with table R3) this motivation seems to be less prominent as age increases, there is no distinct pattern when it comes to urban or rural characteristics. Model 4D suggests that education might be a more relevant factor, as rural higher-educated entrepreneurs report lower motivations linked to making a difference in the world than higher-educated entrepreneurs in peripheral or urban regions.

Table 5: Entrepreneurship motivated by the desire to make a difference in the world.

Motivation among early-stage entrepreneurs: to make a difference in the world	**(4A)**	**(4B)**	**(4C)**	**(4D)**
Region: rural	−0.0388 (0.0483)	−0.0687 (0.0579)	−0.0634 (0.0506)	0.0671 (0.0576)
Region: urban (H1D)	0.113*** (0.0390)	0.108** (0.0509)	0.0972** (0.0412)	0.160*** (0.0494)
Gender: female	0.107*** (0.0312)	0.0782 (0.0577)	0.107*** (0.0312)	0.110*** (0.0312)
Rural × female		0.0746 (0.0788)		
Urban × female		0.0120 (0.0749)		
Age: 25–34	−0.207*** (0.0542)	−0.207*** (0.0542)	−0.0930 (0.0908)	−0.209*** (0.0542)
Age: 35–44	−0.402*** (0.0552)	−0.402*** (0.0552)	−0.288*** (0.0913)	−0.403*** (0.0552)
Age: 45–54	−0.525*** (0.0573)	−0.525*** (0.0574)	−0.412*** (0.0925)	−0.527*** (0.0573)
Age: 55–64	−0.698*** (0.0647)	−0.699*** (0.0647)	−0.585*** (0.0970)	−0.698*** (0.0647)
Rural × young			0.189 (0.117)	
Urban × young (H4B)			0.132 (0.116)	
Education: level 1	−0.568*** (0.105)	−0.567*** (0.105)	−0.567*** (0.105)	−0.547*** (0.105)
Education: level 2	−0.426*** (0.0992)	−0.426*** (0.0992)	−0.425*** (0.0992)	−0.406*** (0.0995)
Education: level 3	−0.261*** (0.0980)	−0.262*** (0.0980)	−0.261*** (0.0980)	−0.105 (0.111)
Rural × educ level 3				−0.270*** (0.0800)
Urban × educ level 3				−0.125 (0.0761)
Year of survey: 2019	0.0488 (0.0382)	0.0484 (0.0382)	0.0476 (0.0382)	0.0471 (0.0382)

Table 5 (continued)

Motivation among early-stage entrepreneurs: to make a difference in the world	**(4A)**	**(4B)**	**(4C)**	**(4D)**
Year of survey: 2020	−0.300*** (0.0407)	−0.300*** (0.0407)	−0.301*** (0.0407)	−0.302*** (0.0407)
Fear of failure (self-reported)	−0.118*** (0.0324)	−0.117*** (0.0324)	−0.118*** (0.0324)	−0.117*** (0.0324)
Threshold fully/somewhat disagree	−0.918*** (0.172)	−0.928*** (0.173)	−0.820*** (0.183)	−0.841*** (0.173)
Threshold somewhat disagree/neutral	−0.202 (0.172)	−0.212 (0.173)	−0.104 (0.183)	−0.124 (0.173)
Threshold neutral / somewhat agree	0.414** (0.172)	0.405** (0.173)	0.513*** (0.183)	0.493*** (0.173)
Threshold somewhat/fully agree	1.631*** (0.172)	1.621*** (0.173)	1.729*** (0.183)	1.710*** (0.174)
Observations	14,200	14,200	14,200	14,200

Standard errors in parentheses.
***p < 0.01, **p < 0.05, *p < 0.1.
Reference categories: Region (intermediate), Age (18–24), Education (not reported), Year of survey (2021). Additional control variables included in the regression but not reported in this table are main occupation, household income, and country.

7 Discussion

The present study has contributed to the ongoing debate about entrepreneurial drivers, by adopting a spatial lens to examine necessity and opportunity-based entrepreneurship. Here, our contributions are threefold. Firstly, recognizing that the dichotomy between necessity and opportunity entrepreneurship is an oversimplified representation of the entrepreneur's main motivations to initially found their business venture (Dencker et al., 2021ab; Dencker et al., 2021b; Giacomin et al., 2011), we presented a framework which distinguishes five motivational sub-typologies. Building on Maslow's hierarchy of needs (1943), we identified four main motivations for being pushed and pulled into entrepreneurship (Reynolds et al., 2002) that prevail in developed countries: being pushed to earn a living because jobs are scarce; being pulled to continue a family tradition; being pulled to gain great wealth and autonomy; and being pulled to create value and make a difference in the world.

Secondly, we acknowledge the influence that socio-material features have in opportunity provision, which in turn impacts the sort of engagement entrepreneurs have with their environment (Gaddefors & Anderson, 2019; Müller, 2016; Müller &

Korsgaard, 2018). Building on this idea that socio-economic spaces influence entrepreneurial driving forces, we found that European rural areas, considered "sparse" entrepreneurial ecosystems (Miles & Morrison, 2020), produce more necessity entrepreneurs than their urban "munificent" counterparts (Bosma & Sternberg, 2014; Conroy & Low, 2022; Kedmenec et al., 2015; Sohns & Revilla Diez, 2018; Tsvetkova, Partridge & Betz, 2017). This follows from our first hypothesis (H1A), where we found fewer entrepreneurs to be pushed into entrepreneurship in urban than in rural areas. We further found a difference in the types of opportunity entrepreneurship that is leading in the rural versus the city. In line with H1B, it seems that the motivation to continue a family tradition is more predominant for rural opportunity entrepreneurs (Muñoz & Kimmitt, 2019). For urban opportunity entrepreneurs the motivations to generate great wealth and autonomy (H1C) (Huovinen & Koiranen, 2011) as well as to create value to make a difference in the world (H1D) (Osorio & Özkazaç-Pan, 2014) seem to be more popular, as they are more prevalent there than in rural areas.

Finally, we contribute to the existing literature by studying how socio-economic factors are further spurring entrepreneurial motivations (Block & Wagner, 2010; Giacomin et al., 2011; Liñan et al., 2013; Poschke, 2016; van der Zwan et al., 2016). We examined the influence of various key factors by formulating three more sets of hypotheses, namely gender; education; and age. Regarding the role of gender, we found in contrast to most research (Cukier & Hassannezhad Chavoushi, 2020; Hernandez et al., 2012; Li et al., 2019; Memon, 2020; Rijkers & Costa, 2012), that, in pre-COVID times, European men were more likely to be pushed into entrepreneurship than women. This thus confirms the findings of Poschke (2010), who studied all OECD-countries. Interestingly, the pandemic seems to have hit women harder than men, as in accordance with Martinez-Rodriguez et al. (2022), the year 2019 seems to have marked a turning point, where relatively more women became necessity entrepreneurs. While zooming in on women entrepreneurs specifically, we find evidence that indeed urban women entrepreneurs in Europe are less often pushed into entrepreneurship than their rural counterparts (in line with H2A). As noted before, Conroy and Low (2022) linked gender with household income, stating that in lower income households women aim to contribute to a better income, and in higher income households women rather pursue entrepreneurship for lucrative purposes. This disparity seemed to hold for the Turkish context, where richer urban areas produce fewer women necessity entrepreneurs than rural areas (Tuzun & Takay, 2017). We theorize that this might be the case for the entirety of Europe. Interestingly, we found no support for our second hypothesis (H2B), that rural women entrepreneurs were more likely to be motivated by continuing a family tradition. We found that in general, women are less often motivated by this driver than men. Potentially because family firm succession is often still considered to be a role for the son rather than the daughter. Even though the amount of female CEO's in family firms is on the rise, they still only make up 24% of the family firm leaders worldwide (Kubíček & Machek, 2019). Additionally, women are also less motivated by generating great wealth or high incomes, yet more so by making a difference in the world. Using these results, the well-documented literature on gender gaps in entrepreneurship (de Bruin et al., 2007) may be enriched, as the (so far) untapped potential among women may contribute to an entrepreneurial society that is more focused on contributing to others and to the planet. From a policy angle this suggests that appealing more to female entrepreneurship might be a good strategy for stimulating social and sustainable entrepreneurship.

Concerning the part that education plays, we found some interesting general insights. First, with regards to necessity entrepreneurship we found a positive correlation with education, where a lower level of education increases the chances to be pushed into entrepreneurship, which was in line with the literature (Bergmann & Sternberg, 2007; Bourlès & Cozrenco, 2018; Bousmah, 2021; Chang, 2023; Poschke, 2010). No significant difference, however, was found on a regional level, and thus showing no support for H3A nor H3B. This shows that there are also enough reasons for urban entrepreneurs to become necessity entrepreneurs. Next, with regards to family traditions, it can be noted from the data, that higher educated are less likely to be motivated to continue a family legacy, perhaps because entrepreneurship education favors autonomy more in their programs than family values (van Gelderen, 2010). Another explanation could be that higher educated people tend to be more focused on creating value for society at large and aim to change the world, for example through social entrepreneurship (Audretsch et al., 2022; Estrin et al., 2016). This is in line with our last findings on education that indeed find that higher educated are more inclined to become entrepreneurs for reaching self-actualization (Fortunato, 2014).

With regards to age as a socio-economic factor, two interesting findings can be noted. When coming of age, entrepreneurs become less and less motivated by generating great wealth and neither by changing the world. This thus links closely to the findings of Bergmann and Sternberg (2007) who also noted that age does not affect the probability of becoming a necessity entrepreneur. However, they found an inverted U-shaped relation between age and opportunity entrepreneurship, whereas we find a negative correlation. As Bublitz et al. (2021) argued, older generations are less comfortable taking big risks and have issues empathizing with the rest of society. This could explain why they will not pursue the risky business ideas associated with great wealth generation, nor start a social enterprise. Furthermore, we did not find any support for our last hypothesis set (H4A & B), which means that for younger entrepreneurs no differences were found on a regional level for being pushed into entrepreneurship or becoming entrepreneurial for changing the world. However, linking to the earlier discussions on family tradition, we did find that this is more often a driver for young rural entrepreneurs than for their urban counterparts.

Limitations and Future Research

Given that the study of necessity and opportunity entrepreneurship is highly debated, but at the same time, still in an emerging state, clear theoretical frameworks that extend this dichotomy were limited. In terms of theory building, this study aimed to develop an integrated model, based on the foundation that was laid by Dencker et al. (2021b), who theorized on necessity-based entrepreneurship. However, it should be mentioned that the hierarchy of needs model, on which our four formulations were based, allows for other unexamined motivations per tier. For example, the opportunity-based tier of "esteem" also includes these entrepreneurs that found their venture to express their creativity, something that was not included in our study. Future research could thus extend our model by including more motivations, which will provide even better insights into the motivations of entrepreneurs.

Besides our theorizing, this study relied heavily on the newly assembled regional Global Entrepreneurship Monitor data available in Europe. At the moment, these regions are categorized using the Eurostat NUTS labels. Here, it was noted that some countries are analyzed on a NUTS-1 level, whereas others allowed for a NUTS-3 level analysis. This means that some countries would benefit from a richer data set, so that clearer distinctions can be made between rural and urban areas. This would on the one hand benefit the analysis, as differences in motivations could be more apparent than presented in our study, but on the other hand it would also benefit the countries themselves, as they have a better understanding of how to influence regional entrepreneurship through governmental support and policy making.

In addition to the limitations mentioned before, it can be noted that there are a lot of socio-economic factors that drive the motivations for initially engaging in entrepreneurial activities. Even though our study controlled for a couple of those (including fear of failure, main occupation, household income, and country), we only directly hypothesized on three of them, namely gender, education and age. Future research could examine the direct effects of these other factors as well, and can even enlarge the scope by including other drivers that we failed to include.

Appendix 1 Regions included in the analysis

Eastern Europe	
Hungary	HU10: Közép-Magyarország HU21: Közép-Dunántúl HU22: Nyugat-Dunántúl HU23: Dél-Dunántúl HU31: Észak-Magyarország HU32: Észak-Alföld HU33: Dél-Alföld
Romania	RO11: Nord-Vest RO12: Centru RO21: Nord-Est RO22: Sud-Est RO31: Sud - Muntenia RO32: Bucure?ti - Ilfov RO41: Sud-Vest Oltenia RO42: Vest
Poland	PL11: Łódzki PL12: Mazowieckie PL21: Małopolskie PL22: Śląskie PL31: Lubelskie PL32: Podkarpackie PL33: Świętokrzyskie PL34: Podlaskie PL41: Wielkopolskie PL42: Zachodniopomorskie PL43: Lubuskie PL51: Dolnośląskie PL52: Opolskie PL61: Kujawsko-Pomorskie PL62: Warmińsko-Mazurskie PL63: Pomorskie
Croatia	HR02: Panonska Hrvatska HR03: Jadranska Hrvatska HR05: Grad Zagreb HR06: Sjeverna Hrvatska
Slovakia	SK01: Bratislavský kraj SK02: Západné Slovensko SK03: Stredné Slovensko SK04: Východné Slovensko

Southern Europe	
Greece	EL30: Attiki EL41: Voreio Aigaio EL42: Notio Aigaio EL43: Kriti EL51: Anatoliki Makedonia, Thraki EL52: Kentriki Makedonia EL53: Dytiki Makedonia EL54: Ipeiros EL61: Thessalia EL62: Ionia Nisia EL63: Dytiki Ellada EL64: Sterea Ellada EL65: Peloponnisos
Spain	ES11: Galicia ES12: Principado de Asturias ES13: Cantabria ES21: País Vasco ES22: Comunidad Foral de Navarra ES23: La Rioja ES24: Aragón ES30: Comunidad de Madrid ES41: Castilla y León ES42: Castilla-La Mancha ES43: Extremadura ES51: Cataluña ES52: Comunidad Valenciana ES53: Illes Balears ES61: Andalucía ES62: Región de Murcia ES63: Ciudad Autónoma de Ceuta ES64: Ciudad Autónoma de Melilla ES70: Canarias
Italy	ITC1: Piemonte ITC2: Valle d'Aosta/Vallée d'Aoste ITC3: Liguria ITC4: Lombardia ITF1: Abruzzo ITF2: Molise ITF3: Campania ITF4: Puglia ITF5: Basilicata ITF6: Calabria ITG1: Sicilia

(continued)

Western Europe	
Netherlands	NL11: Groningen NL12: Friesland NL13: Drenthe NL21: Overijssel NL22: Gelderland NL23: Flevoland NL31: Utrecht NL32: Noord-Holland NL33: Zuid-Holland NL34: Zeeland NL41: Noord-Brabant NL42: Limburg
Belgium	BE10: Bruxelles-Capitale BE21: Prov. Antwerpen BE22: Prov. Limburg (BE) BE23: Prov. Oost-Vlaanderen BE24: Prov. Vlaams-Brabant BE25: Prov. West-Vlaanderen BE31: Prov. Brabant Wallon BE32: Prov. Hainaut BE33: Prov. Liège BE34: Prov. Luxembourg (BE) BE35: Prov. Namur
France	FR1: Ile-de-France FRB: Centre – Val de Loire FRC: Bourgogne-Franche-Comte FRD: Normandie FRE: Hauts-de-France FRF: Grand Est FRG: Pays de la Loire FRH: Bretagne FRI: Nouvelle-Acquitaine FRJ: Occitanie FRK: Auvergne-Rhône-Alpes FRL: Provence-Alpes-Côte dAzur FRM: Corse FRY: Régions Ultrapériphériques Françaises
Switzerland	CH01: Région lémanique CH02: Espace Mittelland CH03: Nordwestschweiz CH04: Zürich CH05: Ostschweiz CH06: Zentralschweiz

Southern Europe	
	ITG2: Sardegna ITH2: Provincia Autonoma di Trento ITH3: Veneto ITH4: Friuli-Venezia Giulia ITH5: Emilia-Romagna ITI1: Toscana ITI2: Umbria ITI3: Marche ITI4: Lazio
Portugal	PT11: Norte PT15: Algarve PT16: Centro (PT) PT17: Lisboa PT18: Alentejo
Slovenia	SI031: Pomurska SI032: Podravska SI033: Koroška SI034: Savinjska SI035: Zasavska SI036: Posavska SI037: Jugovzhodna Slovenija SI038: Primorsko-notranjska SI041: Osrednjeslovenska SI042: Gorenjska SI043: Goriška SI044: Obalno-kraška
Bosnia and Herzegovina	BA01: Bosnia & Herz
Macedonia	MK00: Macedonia
Cyprus	CY00: Cyprus

Northern Europe	
United Kingdom	UKC: North East UKD: North West UKE: Yorkshire and the Humber UKF: East Midlands UKG: West Midlands UKH: East of England UKI: London

(continued)

Western Europe	
	CH07: Ticino
Austria	AT11: Burgenland AT12: Niederösterreich AT13: Wien AT21: Kärnten AT22: Steiermark AT31: Oberösterreich AT32: Salzburg AT33: Tirol AT34: Vorarlberg
Germany	DE1: Baden-Württemberg DE2: Bayern DE3: Berlin DE4: Brandenburg DE5: Bremen DE6: Hamburg DE7: Hessen DE8: Mecklenburg-Vorpommern DE9: Niedersachsen DEA: Nordrhein-Westfalen DEB: Rheinland-Pfalz DEC: Saarland DED: Sachsen DEE: Sachsen-Anhalt DEF: Schleswig-Holstein DEG: Thüringen
Luxembourg	LU00: Luxembourg

(continued)

Northern Europe	
	UKJ: South East UKK: South West UKL: Wales UKM: Scotland UKN: Northen Ireland
Sweden	SE11: Stockholm SE12: Östra Mellansverige SE21: Småland med öarna SE22: Sydsverige SE23: Västsverige SE31: Norra Mellansverige SE32: Mellersta Norrland SE33: Övre Norrland
Norway	NO01: Oslo og Akershus NO02: Innlandet NO03: Sor-ostlandet NO04: Agder og Rogaland NO05: Vestlandet NO06: Trøndelag NO07: Nord-Norge
Ireland	IE041: Border IE042: West IE051: Mid-West IE052: South-East IE053: South-West IE061: Dublin IE062: Mid-East IE063: Midland
Finland	FI19: Länsi-Suomi FI1B: Helsinki-Uusimaa FI1C: Etelä-Suomi FI1D: Pohjois- ja Itä-Suomi
Latvia	LV003: Kurzeme LV005: Latgale LV006: Rīga LV007: Pierīga LV008: Vidzeme LV009: Zemgale

(continued)

Northern Europe	
Estonia	EE001: Põhja-Eesti EE004: Lääne-Eesti EE006: Kesk-Eesti EE007: Kirde-Eesti EE008: Lõuna-Eesti

References

Acs, Z. (2006). How is entrepreneurship good for economic growth?. Innovations, 1(1), 97–107.

Al-Mamary, Y.H., & Alshallaqi, M. (2022). Impact of autonomy, innovativeness, risk-taking, proactiveness, and competitive aggressiveness on students' intention to start a new venture. Journal of Innovation & Knowledge, 7(4), 100239.

Audretsch, D.B., Eichler, G.M., & Schwarz, E.J. (2022). Emerging needs of social innovators and social innovation ecosystems. International Entrepreneurship and Management Journal, 1–38.

Autio, E., Kenney, M., Mustar, P., Siegel, D., & Wright, M. (2014). Entrepreneurial innovation: The importance of context. Research Policy, 43(7), 1097–1108.

Baumgartner, D., Schulz, T., & Seidl, I. (2013). Quantifying entrepreneurship and its impact on local economic performance: A spatial assessment in rural Switzerland. Entrepreneurship & Regional Development, 25(3–4), 222–250.

Baycan Levent, T., Masurel, E., & Nijkamp, P. (2003). Diversity in entrepreneurship: Ethnic and female roles in urban economic life. International Journal of Social Economics, 30(11), 1131–1161.

Bergmann, H., & Sternberg, R. (2007). The changing face of entrepreneurship in Germany. Small Business Economics, 28, 205–221.

Bhola, R., Verheul, I., Thurik, R., & Grilo, I. (2006). Explaining engagement levels of opportunity and necessity entrepreneurs.

Block, J.H., & Wagner, M. (2010). Necessity and opportunity entrepreneurs in Germany: Characteristics and earning s differentials. Schmalenbach Business Review, 62, 154–174.

Bosma, N. (2013). The Global Entrepreneurship Monitor (GEM) and its impact on entrepreneurship research. Foundations and Trends® in Entrepreneurship, 9(2), 143–248.

Bosma, N., & Sternberg, R. (2014). Entrepreneurship as an urban event? Empirical evidence from European cities. Regional Studies, 48(6), 1016–1033.

Bourlès, R., & Cozarenco, A. (2018). Entrepreneurial motivation and business performance: Evidence from a French microfinance institution. Small Business Economics, 51(4), 943–963.

Bousmah, I. (2021). L'entrepreneuriat au Canada rural : Motivé par la nécessité ou l'opportunité ? Innovation. Science and Economic Development Canada.

de Bruin, A., Brush, C.G., & Welter, F. (2007). Advancing a framework for coherent research on women's entrepreneurship. Entrepreneurship Theory and Practice, 31(3), 323–339.

Bublitz, M.G., Chaplin, L.N., Peracchio, L.A., Cermin, A.D., Dida, M., Escalas, J.E., . . . Miller, E.G. (2021). Rise up: Understanding youth social entrepreneurs and their ecosystems. Journal of Public Policy & Marketing, 40(2), 206–225.

Chang, Y.Y., Sanchez-Loor, D.A., Hsieh, H.C., & Chang, W.S. (2023). How aging affects opportunity-necessity entrepreneurship: Demographic and perceptual view. Australian Journal of Management, 48(1), 67–89.

Conroy, T., & Low, S.A. (2022). Entrepreneurship, broadband, and gender: Evidence from establishment births in rural America. International Regional Science Review, 45(1), 3–35.
Cukier, W., & Hassannezhad Chavoushi, Z. (2020). Facilitating women entrepreneurship in Canada: The case of WEKH. Gender in Management: An International Journal, 35(3), 303–318.
Dencker, J.C., Bacq, S., & Gruber, M. (2021a). Basic needs as the boundary condition for a reconceptualization of necessity entrepreneurship across contexts. Academy of Management Review, 46(4), 830–835.
Dencker, J.C., Bacq, S., Gruber, M., & Haas, M. (2021b). Reconceptualizing necessity entrepreneurship: A contextualized framework of entrepreneurial processes under the condition of basic needs. Academy of Management Review, 46(1), 60–79.
Eliasson, K., & Westlund, H. (2013). Attributes influencing self-employment propensity in urban and rural Sweden. The Annals of Regional Science, 50, 479–514.
Estrin, S., Mickiewicz, T., & Stephan, U. (2016). Human capital in social and commercial entrepreneurship. Journal of Business Venturing, 31(4), 449–467.
Figueroa-Armijos, M., & Johnson, T.G. (2013). Entrepreneurship in rural America across typologies, gender and motivation. Journal of Developmental Entrepreneurship, 18(02), 1350014.
Fortunato, M.W.P. (2014). Supporting rural entrepreneurship: A review of conceptual developments from research to practice. Community Development, 45(4), 387–408.
Gaddefors, J., & Anderson, A.R. (2019). Romancing the rural: Reconceptualizing rural entrepreneurship as engagement with context (s). The International Journal of Entrepreneurship and Innovation, 20(3), 159–169.
van Gelderen, M. (2010). Autonomy as the guiding aim of entrepreneurship education. Education+ Training, 52(8/9), 710–721.
Giacomin, O., Janssen, F., Guyot, J.L., & Lohest, O. (2011). Opportunity and/or necessity entrepreneurship? The impact of the socio-economic characteristics of entrepreneurs.
Hernandez, L., Nunn, N., & Warnecke, T. (2012). Female entrepreneurship in China: Opportunity-or necessity-based?. International Journal of Entrepreneurship and Small Business, 15(4), 411–434.
Huovinen, J., & Koiranen, M. (2011). Achievement motivation among habitual entrepreneurs in urban and rural areas. Liiketaloudellinen Aikakauskirja, (3).
GEM (Global Entrepreneurship Monitor) (2023). Global Entrepreneurship Monitor 2021/22 European Regional Report. London: GEM.
Hedeker, D. (2008). Multilevel models for ordinal and nominal variables. In Handbook of multilevel analysis (pp. 237–274). New York, NY: Springer New York.
Kedmenec, I., Šebjan, U., & Tominc, P. (2015). Effect of rurality and human capital resources in the entrepreneurial opportunity identification process. Naše gospodarstvo/Our Economy, 61(2), 35–44.
Korsgaard, S., Müller, S., & Tanvig, H.W. (2015). Rural entrepreneurship or entrepreneurship in the rural–between place and space. International Journal of Entrepreneurial Behavior & Research, 21(1), 5–26.
Kobeissi, N. (2010). Gender factors and female entrepreneurship: International evidence and policy implications. Journal of International Entrepreneurship, 8, 1–35.
Kubíček, A., & Machek, O. (2019). Gender-related factors in family business succession: A systematic literature review. Review of Managerial Science, 13, 963–1002.
Lavesson, N. (2018). How does distance to urban centres influence necessity and opportunity-based firm start-ups?. Papers in Regional Science, 97(4), 1279–1303.
Laure Humbert, A., & Drew, E. (2010). Gender, entrepreneurship and motivational factors in an Irish context. International Journal of Gender and Entrepreneurship, 2(2), 173–196.
Li, C., Ahmed, N., & Qalati, S.A. (2019). Impact of gender-specific causes on women entrepreneurship: An opportunity structure for entrepreneurial women in rural areas. Journal of Entrepreneurship & Organization Management, 8(1), 1–9.

Liñán, F., Romero Luna, I., & Fernández Serrano, J. (2013). Necessity and opportunity entrepreneurship: The mediating effect of culture. Revista de Economía Mundial, 33, 21–47.
Liang, C.L., & Dunn, P. (2014). Entrepreneurial profile, characteristics, expectations, and outcomes-An Empirical study to compare rural entrepreneurs with Urban Entrepreneurs. American Journal of Entrepreneurship, 7(2).
Martínez-Rodríguez, I., Quintana-Rojo, C., Gento, P., & Callejas-Albinana, F.E. (2022). Public policy recommendations for promoting female entrepreneurship in Europe. International Entrepreneurship and Management Journal, 18(3), 1235–1262.
Maslow, A. H. (1943). A theory of human motivation. Psychological Review, 50(4), 370–396.
Memon, A. (2020). Analyzing the entrepreneurial ecosystem for women entrepreneurs: A study of rural Jamshoro, Pakistan. Indian Journal of Commerce and Management Studies, 11(3), 45–59.
Miles, M.P., & Morrison, M. (2020). An effectual leadership perspective for developing rural entrepreneurial ecosystems. Small Business Economics, 54, 933–949.
Molina, J.A. (2020). Family and entrepreneurship: New empirical and theoretical results. Journal of Family and Economic Issues, 41, 1–3.
Müller, S. (2016). A progress review of entrepreneurship and regional development: What are the remaining gaps?. European Planning Studies, 24(6), 1133–1158.
Müller, S., & Korsgaard, S. (2018). Resources and bridging: The role of spatial context in rural entrepreneurship. Entrepreneurship & Regional Development, 30(1–2), 224–255.
Muñoz, P., & Kimmitt, J. (2019). Rural entrepreneurship in place: An integrated framework. Entrepreneurship & Regional Development, 31(9–10), 842–873.
O'Donnell, P., O'Gorman, C., & Clinton, E. (2021). Rethinking the "necessity" in necessity entrepreneurship. Academy of Management Review, 46(4), 827–830.
Osorio, A.E., & Özkazanç-Pan, B. (2014). Defining the 'urban'in urban entrepreneurship: Implications for economic development policy. In Academy of Management Proceedings (Vol. 2014, No. 1, p. 12486). Briarcliff Manor, NY 10510: Academy of Management.
Pato, M.L., &Teixeira, A.A. (2016). Twenty years of rural entrepreneurship: A bibliometric survey. Sociologia Ruralis, 56(1), 3–28.
Poschke, M. (2013). 'Entrepreneurs out of necessity': A snapshot. Applied Economics Letters, 20(7), 658–663.
Reynolds, P., Bosma, N., Autio, E., Hunt, S., De Bono, N., Servais, I., . . . Chin, N. (2005). Global entrepreneurship monitor: Data collection design and implementation 1998–2003. Small Business Economics, 24, 205–231.
Reynolds, P.D., Bygrave, W.D., Autio, E., Cox, L.W., and M. Hay (2001). Global Entrepreneurship Monitor, 2001 Executive Report.
Rytkönen, P.I., Oghazi, P., & Mostaghel, R. (2023). Food entrepreneurship and self-employment in an island context. British Food Journal, 125(13), 237–252.
Rijkers, B., & Costa, R. (2012). Gender and rural non-farm entrepreneurship. World Development, 40(12), 2411–2426.
Saeed, R., Nayyab, H.H., Lodhi, R.N., Baqir, R., Rehman, M.A., & Mussawar, S. (2013). Impact of retention factors on organizational commitment in general education division of Pakistan. Middle-East Journal of Scientific Research, 17(4), 539–545.
Santos, F.M. (2012). A positive theory of social entrepreneurship. Journal of Business Ethics, 111(3), 335–351.
Seaman, C. (2015). Creating space for the business family: Networks, social capital & family businesses in rural development. Journal of Family Business Management, 5(2), 182–191.
Sohns, F., & Revilla Diez, J. (2018). Explaining micro entrepreneurship in rural Vietnam – A multilevel analysis. Small Business Economics, 50, 219–237.
Stephan, U., Hart, M., & Drews, C.C. (2015). Understanding motivations for entrepreneurship: A review of recent research evidence.

Tsvetkova, A., Partridge, M., & Betz, M. (2017). Entrepreneurial and employment responses to economic conditions across the rural-urban continuum. The ANNALS of the American Academy of Political and Social Science, 672(1), 83–102.

Tuzun, I.K., & Takay, B.A. (2017). Patterns of female entrepreneurial activities in Turkey. Gender in Management: An International Journal, 32(3), 166–182.

Wagner, J. (2005). Nascent and infant entrepreneurs in Germany: Evidence from the Regional Entrepreneurship Monitor (REM). Available at SSRN 684007.

Welter, F. (2011). Contextualizing entrepreneurship – Conceptual challenges and ways forward. Entrepreneurship Theory and Practice, 35(1), 165–184.

Wennekers, S., Van Wennekers, A., Thurik, R., & Reynolds, P. (2005). Nascent entrepreneurship and the level of economic development. Small Business Economics, 24, 293–309.

Zahra, S.A., Wright, M., & Abdelgawad, S.G. (2014). Contextualization and the advancement of entrepreneurship research. International Small Business Journal, 32(5), 479–500.

Zhang, T., & Acs, Z. (2018). Age and entrepreneurship: Nuances from entrepreneur types and generation effects. Small Business Economics, 51, 773–809.

Zhang, Y., Duysters, G., & Cloodt, M. (2014). The role of entrepreneurship education as a predictor of university students' entrepreneurial intention. International Entrepreneurship and Management Journal, 10, 623–641.

van der Zwan, P., Thurik, R., Verheul, I., & Hessels, J. (2016). Factors influencing the entrepreneurial engagement of opportunity and necessity entrepreneurs. Eurasian Business Review, 6, 273–295.

Hassan Shahraki

Rural Entrepreneurship at the Cross Point of Cultural Turn and Planetary: A Geosocial Critique of Rural Entrepreneurship

Abstract: In this study, while looking at entrepreneurship through the lens of critical social thought, I will attempt to analyze rural entrepreneurship from the standpoint of geographical and spatial implications and put it at the cross point of cultural and geographical turn. This study challenges traditional economic-centric viewpoints and highlights the need for a more comprehensive understanding by taking into account how rural entrepreneurial activities are interwoven in local cultural practices, environmental conditions, and spatial relationships. The novel concept of planetary social thought introduced by Nigel Clark and Bronislaw Szerszynski has been used as the key concept in the provided analysis, and it is regarded as a conceptual tool that can open a completely modern window on rural entrepreneurship studies. This study is an effort to open the gates and new paths for critical entrepreneurship studies, particularly rural entrepreneurship. Although considerable evidence used to document the claims and to explain the concepts are specific to Iran, the inter-local, national, and global connection through nature, environment, and geography causes them to benefit from the global dimension. The example of digging deep wells has been employed as an appropriate case study to provide the reader with the presented theoretical and abstract subjects and matters in a more concrete and understandable manner. It also emphasizes going beyond rural entrepreneurship to realize the ruralization of entrepreneurship.

Keywords: rural entrepreneurship, ruralization of entrepreneurship, planetary social thought, anthropocene, deep well

1 Introduction

Currently, as I am writing these lines, both the whistle of bullets in all cities of Iran and the howling wind sound and sand storm with a speed of 70 km/h in the Sistan region have echoed in my ears, and this is a lived experience at the frontline of both women's liberation (freedom of women) and saving the earth from the climate crisis. These two cases have transformed the political and the earth system, respectively, and their more detailed analysis and explanation require something called planetary social thought (Clarke & Szerszynski, 2021). My life and residence as an entrepreneurial researcher in a suburb and rural area on the border of Iran and Afghanistan, which after nearly 20 years of intolerable drought, as well as a decade of starting entrepreneurial plans and projects, now is caught up in a catastrophic environmental

https://doi.org/10.1515/9783110791396-013

crisis, have been the prelude to my motive to provide an antagonistic and geosocial critique of rural entrepreneurship. The use of the adjective "rural" for entrepreneurship somehow represents the creation of an obligation or condition for entrepreneurship; an obligation or condition that, according to the new and discourse definitions of rural and rurality (Cloke, 2006; Dabson, 2005; Rosenqvist, 2020), is imposed on entrepreneurship by the rural identity and culture, social relations, and the rural body and space (geography). The use of an adjective also implies a form of criticism. Just as post-development implies the kind of anthropological and cultural critique of development, rural entrepreneurship – at least in this chapter – will mention a geosocial critique of entrepreneurship. It should be noted that entrepreneurship, in turn, is not a constant phenomenon and requires an evolutionary trajectory; from the food trade 50 years before Christ to attributing entrepreneurship to engineers and architects between 1,000 to 1,500 AD, participating in dangerous military missions in the sixteenth century AD, and adding the concept of innovation and risk to entrepreneurship practice and definition in the twentieth century. Currently, in the twenty-first century, regarding environmental crises, the geography and space component and its association with the social matter – and policymaking – it is required to become involved in entrepreneurial discussions as accurately, comprehensively, and quickly as possible, particularly rural entrepreneurship-related studies. When the evolutionary trajectory of entrepreneurship is suggested in a paper, it means that the meaning and concept of entrepreneurship, and accordingly, the entrepreneurial practice, have changed over time. Therefore, the role that entrepreneurship has played and continues to play in various economic systems should be considered from a critical perspective. Dey (2020) differentiates two critical perspectives on entrepreneurship from each other: Antagonistic critique and Agonistic critique. The first one seeks to antagonize and make enemies, and the second one, while accepting the existence of a competitor, does not regard it with hostility and seeks respect and admiration of others. (Can criticism be respected, at least in a situation where an environmental crisis swallows both me and the other at the same time?) The antagonistic infrastructure of the geosocial critique of rural entrepreneurship means that there is something wrong in understanding and implementing, at least in Iran and in the projects cited in this study, and it consists of neglecting the mutual and dynamic relationship between the environment (the planet) and the people who live on it, as well as imposing and implementing a merely economic version inattentive to the environment based on the climate crisis. Such a process converts entrepreneurship into an enemy of the ecosystem; into the other who is either inattentive to the environmental disasters in the village or, as explained in the disaster capitalism theory (Klein, 2008; Loewenestein, 2015), only wants to profit from the disaster/opportunity. Accordingly, the planetary turn – which is indeed based on an antagonistic critique – and has been introduced as an expander and processor of the postmodern cultural turn in this study; intends to provide a biocentric perspective of rural entrepreneurship instead of a profit-based critique. For this reason, some theorists (Shepherd, 2019; Jones & Spicer, 2009) emphasize the negative aspects of entrepreneurship, in a sense, "dark entrepreneurship." In other words, when an antagonistic approach is adopted for entrepreneurship, it is not possible to talk only about a positive economic activity. On the contrary, much institutionalization and knowledge acquisition regarding entrepreneurship is fundamentally questioned; therefore, entrepreneurship can lead to failure, waste of resources, environmental crisis, deviation from the development process (Shahraki & Keikha, 2022), and unethical or irrational behavior. Hence, this study asserts that entrepreneurship is an ideological smokescreen – as has been the same in many cases in Iran – wherein planetary deadlocks can lurk. The fundamental critiques of entrepreneurship, especially critical studies addressing entrepreneurship from the perspective of environmental crises, are scarce, in the number of drops; these drops must be turned into a stream (Shepherd, 2019). This chapter does not intend to be only satisfied with rhetorical quotations and to take a Pontius Pilate approach, as stated in the post-development literature (Ziai, 2015); rather, both throughout the text, particularly, where it evaluates the digging deep wells project in Sistan, Iran[1] and in the conclusion and suggestions section, it will offer a series of specific solutions to break the deadlock that the mainstream of entrepreneurship has yielded and draw paths for future research.

2 Entrepreneurship and Rural Entrepreneurship: Elapsed Time

If we accept that in many studies (Audretsch 2002; McElwee, 2005) entrepreneurship is considered a development strategy; thus, the origin or root of the positivistic or mechanistic view of entrepreneurship lies in the analysis of development within the framework of such a view – a reductionist, linear, positivistic, mechanistic, teleological, measurable, and eventually evolutionary view. In presenting an effective and historical classification of development, Ronaldo Munk (2021), while denying the univocal and unilinear viewpoint, advocates retaining Marx's dialectic method in the discussion of development and addresses this issue by indicating the concept of aleatory materialism introduced by the French philosopher Louis Althusser. This concept explains that many phenomena do not possess a predetermined destination. Accordingly, it can be argued that attributing a fixed historical essence to entrepreneurship primarily represents an affirmation of the change in its nature and essence; therefore, it can lead to failure and waste of resources instead of economic development or welfare.

1 Three wells are currently running. Two wells are in areas called Hamoon and Ramshar, and the third one is in a city called Adimi. Well No. (1) is exploratory and has a depth of 3,120 meters. Well No. (2) was dug at a distance of 250 m from the first well and has a depth of 1,600 m. Well No. (3) was dug in Adimi or Nimruz County and has a depth of 2,100 m. The RO water softener has been installed on this third well and is in operation.

Historically, as briefly mentioned in the introduction section, the conceptual history of the entrepreneurship subject can be divided into three junctures: prehistoric (from ancient times to the sixteenth century), historical-economic (from the sixteenth to the twentieth century), and the multidisciplinary juncture (from the beginning of the twentieth century up to now). Therefore, entrepreneurship has shifted from the business domain to economics, and then to a specific type of neoliberal capitalism over many centuries. From Birch's viewpoint (2017: 131), entrepreneurship and entrepreneurialism highly correlate with neoliberalism. Given that we become more entrepreneurial under the influence of neoliberalism, the rentiership[2] rate in the economy increases equally; hence, the spread of rent and corruption can be traced under the banner of entrepreneurship. Except for the cultural, social, and geographical context in which it wants to step, entrepreneurship, like today, has not always been held by a single maximum-oriented person or is monopolized by a company. According to Neil Smelser and Richard Swedberg (2005: 3), many of the beliefs held by Joseph Schumpeter, who is considered among contemporary economic sociologists like Karl Polanyi and Talcott Parsons, especially in the book *Capitalism, Socialism, and Democracy* (1942), have a sociological character. This book, indeed, is a sociological work regarding the institutional structure of society and the beginning of the analysis or cultural and social turn of entrepreneurship. Schumpeter's analysis of perfect competition, large business, and monopoly, and how people relate to their property represents a completely sociological character. The keywords of Schumpeter, including "creative destruction" and "business cycles," are interdependent and somehow refer to "processes" and "operations" within an economic system; such processes indicate the historical and process dimensions of the economy, which, in turn, have paved the way for contextual studies in the field of entrepreneurship, Especially since the early 1990s and introducing the creation theory, against the discovery theory. However, in general, Schumpeterian entrepreneurship is also realized based on a capitalist system. Schumpeter explicitly envisions the transformation of old mills to modern power plants and from pony express to the current airmail as a mutation in industrial structure, which consistently transforms and destroys itself fundamentally and creates a new structure again. This is a brief definition of creative destruction proposed by Schumpeter, who considers it a necessary and definite truth about capitalism. Some philosophers (Knudsen & Swedberg, 2009) also regard entrepreneurship as a new combination (innovation) in the entire economic process to make a profit. The cultural turn in entrepreneurship studies coherently started almost from the 1990s under the influence of opinions provided in the field of economic sociology and social

2 A person who derives unearned income from ownership of existing assets or resources is known in political economy as a rentier. Rentiership is characterized by the social dominance of ownership in the economy, at least over production. Actually, rentirship involves the appropriation of value through government fiat (e.g. laws, regulations, standards), monopoly rights (e.g. location), and organizational reconfiguration (e.g. mortgage securitization). (Birch, 2017:143–146)

interpretations suggested by Schumpeter's works. In this regard, Thornton's studies can be mentioned (Thornton, 1999; Thornton et al., 2011). Thornton indicates two important perspectives in dealing with entrepreneurship and its associated research: the supply perspective, which refers to filling entrepreneurial roles, and the demand perspective, which emphasizes the number and quantity of entrepreneurial roles to be performed or played by individuals. The comprehensive framework provided by Thornton for the sociological analysis of entrepreneurship is a combination of the embeddedness theory (Granovetter,1985), ecological and institutional theories, and the levels suggested include individual, organizational, market, and environmental levels. The cultural turn focuses on concepts and variables such as social interactions, agency of people, context, diversity, difference, process, discourse, and institution and examines the extent of their contribution in explaining entrepreneurship or leaning toward entrepreneurship among different nations and cultures. The cultural turn led to critical and valuable studies on entrepreneurship. Some philosophers (Ogbor, 2000; da Costa & Silva Saraiva, 2012; Goss, 2005) have criticized and deconstructed the discourse of entrepreneurship and have attempted to ignore or retest the categories that are often postulated in the entrepreneurship literature, including an extraordinary entrepreneur, the origin of entrepreneurship in the white western culture, masculine, heteronormative, originating from Europe and North America, and looking at the entrepreneur from a gender perspective. A number of researches (Nicholson & Anderson, 2005), with a postmodern perspective on culture, have also remarked on its hegemonic character in entrepreneurship texts and demonstrated that the meanings are not completely fluid and floating; however, regarding entrepreneurship, they provoke a culture that promotes individualism, thereby strengthening capitalist structures. While adopting a completely interpretive perspective, Frederic Bill et al. (2010: 1–11) state that the term "creative destruction" coined by Schumpeter means that entrepreneurship is not necessarily a positive phenomenon and should be questioned. Some studies (Shahraki et al., 2016) have also criticized the sociological and anthropological aspects of rural entrepreneurship and have endeavored to provide a type of discourse analysis of the phenomenon. However, the overemphasis of the cultural turn on the element of culture and discourse made it possible to note about addressing the space and geography and the involvement of environmental preventive crises in analyzing the entrepreneurial process as a missing link and a structural defect in such studies. It may be stated that environmental economy and its effort for ecologizing the economy is considered the only case in the history of entrepreneurship bringing environment (nature) and agriculture (village) to entrepreneurship studies. While recovering the roots of environmental economy in France in the eighteenth century and the start of the Age of Enlightenment in the German historical school and American institutionalism, Paula Kyrö (2014) emphasizes that the idea of entrepreneurship and nature almost faded out in the scope of economics and under the influence of the classical economists and Adam Smith with the beginning of the modern era and industrialization during the eighteenth and nineteenth centuries. Although we observe that the concept of nature is highlighted in the works of the Romanian economist/ecologist Nicholas Georgescu-Roegen, it should be noted the liberation of entrepreneurship from organizational and corporate monopolies and its return to nature, Unlike in the past, particularly in the sixteenth century, when small-scale farmers engaged with nature to produce raw materials for craftsmen and artisans, the current neoliberal economy—arguably the ideological superstructure of extractivism—has driven the expansion of industrialized and intensified agriculture on a massive scale. Therefore, it could be mentioned that even in the environmental economy, due to the susceptibility of the productivism approach and extraction/nature-based development, it is the only source of extraction and hence, this special and only remained type of economy also considers the sustainability plan and entropy pessimism – which was welcomed by Schumpeter, just as a warning. It is worth mentioning that the Roegen school had various psychological labels and waned in the following years.

3 Rural: From a Physical Viewpoint to Figurative Critique

In the entrepreneurship literature, the alertness concept, which was introduced for the first time in the Austrian school, means identifying an opportunity that is hidden before initiating entrepreneurial activity and is revealed and even created by market conditions. In the present study, rural entrepreneurship does not mean conducting entrepreneurial activities in the village or developing such activities from city to village, or even formulating and implementing a green and sustainable entrepreneurship; however, it comprises a kind of consciousness before initiating the entrepreneurship process; consciousness regarding the components and complex dimensions of the rurality concept and its geographical implications. The cultural turn entailed a kind of democratic and egalitarian view of the rural concept; in other words, the old and physical view of the village was transformed into the concept of the rural society and then rural domain (Dabson, 2005; Clock, 2006). In the physical view, considering the village from the geographical and spatial dimension (and not planetary or geological) was the criterion. Village (*Deh* in Persian) was a remote place, consisting of the minimum population engaged in agriculture, horticulture, or animal husbandry. What was achieved before the work of humans on nature (agriculture) and also the specific spatial features such as remoteness were important, not the earth as a planet or the internal dynamics of the earth and its relations with humans. From the distant past to the present day, the definition of village provided in Iran is within the framework of this physical view (Vosooghi & Eemani, 2010). However, the concepts of rural society and rural domain include components such as values, culture, rural identity, integration of village and city, hyperreal communities, lived experience of the rural and generally constructionism, meanings, and signs and symbols related to the rural. Dobson (2005), in a definition of American rural communities, adopted a stand similar to the one described above, which considers a rural society to consist of three components: economy, values and environment, and finally atmosphere or climate. He maintains that agriculture is the most important pillar of the rural economy in explaining the economy component. Values are explained by cases such as religion, tradition, self-reliance, and self-sufficiency. Accordingly, the environment includes beautiful and enjoyable spaces that are filled with livestock and animals and are covered with trees and farms. Eventually, the climate refers to a more comfortable and safer lifestyle and an appropriate place to nurture children. Hence, the cultural turn involved egalitarian elements that, according to Clock (2006), under the influence of postmodern and post-structuralist thought, the village was no longer considered as a form of urban-rural dichotomy, or a place to produce grains that should be transported to the city for consumption (functional view of the village); however, it was regarded as a place of consumption. Now, due to spatial mixing, phenomena such as ruralization of urban (urban agriculture) and urbanization and industrialization of rural can be provided. In cultural turn-based studies, it was no longer acceptable that all the events occurred in the rural environment were dependent on the dynamics of the national and international political economy, and therefore, they were affected by factors beyond the rural environment; an issue that is one of the main assumptions of rural entrepreneurship. Hence, the cultural turn entailed a new definition of the rural environment, which to some extent, was able to provide the field of critical studies on the rural environment, including research into rural entrepreneurship. As mentioned in a study (Shahraki, et al., 2016), by emphasizing rural resistance and polyphony of discourse and development practice, a critical view of rural entrepreneurship can allow raising the issue of rural colonization and confronting it (anticolonialization), avoiding the homogenization of rural environments by focusing on the rural identity and traditions and lived experience (heterogenization), and contributing to the diversity in agriculture by highlighting the production for niche markets and multifunctional agriculture (diversification). It can be briefly stated that despite the emphasis on rural identity, diversity in agriculture, as well as agency and resistance against external forces, the cultural turn fails to propose and analyze the concept of relations between humans and the environment, and from a more general viewpoint, between humans and the planet, and the geological agency cannot explain the concept of geologizing the social appropriately, accurately, and comprehensively except for considering the rural place as a space for the passivity test (the concept of geographic remoteness). For this reason, the explanation of rural entrepreneurship should go further while it can represent geologizing the entrepreneurship or development, which in turn depends on the radical conceptualization of the rural and rurality concept. One of the most illustrious studies regarding the design of a complex and modern understanding of rurality and its association with space and geography is the study by Rosenqvist (2020). This author revised the concept of rural in the form of a holistic understanding using a philosophy known as hermeneutical realism. According to Rosenqvist's perspective and from an ontology viewpoint, the space in the world is manifested in two ways: literal and figurative. Literal manifestation represents the geographic and physical space; and the meaning of the figurative manifestation of space is an abstraction existing separately from physical space. Rosenqvist's hermeneutical and holistic analysis of space aims to correlate both human and things limitations owing to their placement in mental and cultural structures (such as time, language, and awareness) with the abilities retrieved from this placement by using the concept of situatedness of an object. Rosenqvist insists on both the importance of time and objectivity or reality of space by providing a three-component definition of life world with the components such as being, living, and understanding. Now, we are affected by the memories of the past and the expectations that we have for the future. This retrospective and prospective consideration, as we will observe in the next section, is considered one of the basic components of planetary social thought. Additionally, from Rosenqvist's viewpoint, objectivity means that things outside the life world draw our attention and demand something or action from us and accordingly, mere being turns into living. As phenomenologists have stated, awareness is always intentional: awareness is always aware of something. We interpret things and phenomena and hence, act toward them. Therefore, it can be suggested that if the planet turns into our horizon or our awareness belonging and like the forest that disappears when we look at the trees, since it is everywhere and obviously, it does not stay out of our eyes; then we enter the understanding space of planetary social thought. Rosenqvist's perception of the third element of the life world means that the element of understanding is the nature within us; indeed, what occurs inside us. Understanding means that we desire to specify our life world boundaries while interacting with what is outside our lifeworld. Understanding has been placed between the reader and the text, the speaker and the listener, and the interpreter and the interpreted. This perception of understanding is associated with the threshold concept in the planetary social thought; in other words, it is the transition from the border or threshold that creates a disaster. The conceptualization of rurality suggested by Rosenqvist represents other geographical implications, like criticizing the concept of living on the edge of the world or being wild; concepts that are considered a bridge between researches conducted in the area of cultural turn and planetary studies.

4 Rural Entrepreneurship: From Cultural Criticism to Geosocial Criticism in the Anthropocene Era

By introducing a new concept of planetary social thought, Nigel Clark and Bronislaw Szerszynski, in their fantastic book with the abbreviated title of *Planetary Social Thought* (2021) – which I have used a lot to write this part of the study – seek to answer the question: What kind of a planet do we live on? What was the past of this planet, and what will be its future? What kind of beings are we, and What should be the relations between us and the planet? This particular type of thought represents the thought regarding the social matter through the earth; through the interhuman and non-human contact zone and going deep into the times and spaces of the earth itself. Planetary social thought attempts to analyze the exchange between the self-transformation and self-differentiation of the earth (which the authors called geologic or planetary multiplicity) and how human groups experience, encounter, recognize, and understand the earth (which is called social matter or earthly multitude). Although the authors do not claim that this particular kind of thought will lead to resolving the current climate deadlocks in the Anthropocene era, since such exchange is, indeed, to socialize the Anthropocene and to geologize the social matter simultaneously, it will definitely lead to the creation of a new view of the climate crisis and, based on the opinion of the author of this study, will result in rural entrepreneurship. Therefore, instead of rural entrepreneurship, it is necessary to discuss the ruralization of entrepreneurship, namely the combination of entrepreneurship (economic and social) with planetary processes. Hence, it should be seen whether there is mainly anything remaining from the current mainstream of rural entrepreneurship, and we have adopted a hostile attitude toward it in the present study. Ruralization of entrepreneurship means identifying and analyzing the planetary and geologic dimensions of the entrepreneurship process. The re-recognition of rural involves something that was once abandoned with the beginning of the development and urbanization era. This is a revolutionary transition in time and in the life-planet system that attempts to return entrepreneurship not to the market-origin, but to the earth-origin and then raise the question of what is the impact of entrepreneurial activities on the past and present of the earth and how the surface and depth of the earth can change by the influence of these activities. In the case study of the deep well in the Sistan region, it will also be noted how the dominant debate of rural entrepreneurship has caused fundamental changes in the surface and depth of the earth and caused the future of the region's ecosystem to encounter unpredictable consequences by neglecting the issue of the permanent change in the Hirmand river flow by the ruling Taliban delegation in Afghanistan, national and local policy-makers. Here, the rural entrepreneurship rhetoric only acts as a justifier device for destructive measures and human-created artifacts, which is one of the prominent manifestations of the development in the Anthropocene period and can significantly affect the strata-forming processes in the Sistan plain. Therefore, rural entrepreneurship should be regarded on a geosocial basis and considering geological developments of at least several decades to understand well how it affects the relations between humans and the planet; this is the planetary turn in the entrepreneurship literature that leads to the ruralization of entrepreneurship. Ruralization of entrepreneurship through the planetary turns also means focusing on and analyzing the situatedness of social groups in their cultural and historical context; something that affects the special displays and manifestations of the Anthropocene. This last case is strongly specified in the case study of a deep well in Sistan, Iran; digging a deep well is like a project that completely occults the emotional aspects and body of science and development in addition to the planetary aspects, and thus separates the story of entrepreneurship from the story of humans and the earth. Hence, today, the geosocial critique of rural entrepreneurship and development has a double necessity, in both Iran and the whole world. Although there is not sufficient time to address all aspects of the ruralization of entrepreneurship in one chapter, at least it can be proposed and suggested as a completely new area in rural entrepreneurship studies.

4.1 Revolutionizing the View of Entrepreneurship

From the perspective of planetary social thought, the analysis of rural entrepreneurship involves a revolutionary view of entrepreneurship through the earth. Revolutionizing the view of entrepreneurship in the present study is to provide a two-step critique of it: (1) cultural-anthropological critique affected by the postmodern period and (2) planetary social critique. Previously, it was discussed about the first critique, including critical-discourse analyses and studies of entrepreneurship. In addition to the studies mentioned earlier, other studies (Shahraki & Movahedi, 2017) can also be suggested, which were conducted by the author of this chapter, and they have attempted to provide a discourse and anthropological critique of entrepreneurship in the form of the cultural turn. In this series of studies, which are all conducted in Iran, after specifying and examining the evolvement of Joseph Schumpeter's opinion, some cases regarding reformatory critiques and radical critiques of entrepreneurship have been mentioned. Some of the reformatory critiques are as follows: revising and reassessing Schumpeter's thoughts, for example, using the Schumpeterian concept of resistance to entrepreneurship in the sociological analysis of rural entrepreneurship, analyzing dualities such as individual/social and balance/innovation in the discussion of the political economy of entrepreneurship (rural), improving the business environment simultaneously with further and more detailed monitoring of lending mechanisms, emphasizing the group and not individual entrepreneurship, class analysis of the rural entrepreneurs, and finally training modern marketing techniques for entrepreneurs. Some of the radical measures include looking at rural entrepreneurship as a discourse and deconstructing it, analyzing the basic concept of opportunity and focusing on it instead of the concept and strategy of job creation, critical analysis of rural entrepreneurship as a developmental project of government or discarding it and returning to discourse and classical rural development practice with the aims of eradicating poverty, unemployment, and inequality, continuous, broad, and comprehensive fight against administrative corruption with the aim of replacing the contradictory and government project of rural entrepreneurship development with the discourse and government project of multifunctional agriculture, and finally, institutional measures regarding the creation and reproduction of rural identity based on the spontaneous and autonomous rural movements. Campbell Jones and André Spicer (2009) are the pioneers of this type of view and critique (the first critique) of entrepreneurship who have attempted to put entrepreneurship in the center of political and social conflicts and somehow reconstruct it by providing functionalist, interpretive, and critical approaches to entrepreneurship while analyzing the actions. Since the cultural turn in entrepreneurship synchronizes with the emergence of the postmodern school, many similarities can be traced between the cultural turn and postmodernism, including belief in a dynamic and indefinite concept of culture, historicity of social realities, as well as replacing ideology with nature. Previously, the author of this chapter employed the critical theory of Jones and Spicer in other articles (Shahraki & Keikha, 2022) to replace the concept of rural entrepreneurship with another concept called Rural Prosperity, which can be considered an introduction to the second critique, which is geologizing the entrepreneurship and enjoying the planetary critical thought in explaining rural entrepreneurship. The three-way paradigm of rural prosperity is based on three pillars, including rural embodiment, history and economy, and sustainability; while among them, sustainability is more closely associated with the planetary-critical critique of rural entrepreneurship. For example, concepts such as multifunctional agriculture, protecting the rights of animals and plants, preserving the space (ecosystem) in its figurative sense (in completing the physical concept of space), and finally territorial community are mentioned. Meanwhile, multifunctional agriculture and territorial community can have some contradictory aspects around the concept of threshold. In the skeptical post-development approach (Ziai, 2019), the rural environment is regarded as a territorial community. Territorial community includes both concepts of urban-rural integration and ecological awareness of this integration, thereby maintaining its borders with the outside environment. However, on the contrary, in multifunctional agriculture, only a kind of transition (from threshold to border) is observed; transition from agriculture and traditional cultivation pattern to service or industrial production, from productivism to post-productivism, and from ideological essentialism to culture and constructed rurality. Such transitions can be appropriate and aligned with environmental considerations and reinforce the forces of the earth; for example, shifting from production-based extractivism to post-productivism, as well as emphasizing the prevention of agricultural waste and promotion of accurate and urban agriculture. They can also be harmful and damage the environment through strengthening industrial production and services in rural areas, imposing a different operational state on the earth and affecting its dynamics. Indeed, it can be stated that the ratio of multifunctional agriculture to traditional one is similar to the ratio of rural entrepreneurship to the capitalism system. In other words, multifunctional agriculture means that agriculture is still important for human beings, and its development should be continued, even if it crosses the threshold. Therefore, geosocial critique rewrites rural entrepreneurship through the earth. As mentioned in the above lines, one of the rewriting axes can be the protection of animals and plants' rights, which has been referred to as an Inhuman Modernity expansion (Clarke & Szerszynski, 2021). The protection of animal rights is generally absent in the rural entrepreneurship literature. Kamran Neiri (2018), in designing a plan for establishing a kind of ecocentric socialism, states that the process of domestication, which is one of the pillars of today's capitalism civilization, has resulted in the forced invasion of at least half of the planet's land surface and sea from wildlife. Neiri notices that the systematic and multilateral domestication has dealt a deathblow to plants and wild animals. Due to this process, breeding, fattening, incubation, and in-vitro fertilization of only a dozen crops (banana, barley, corn, cassava, potato, rice, sorghum, soybean, sugar beet, sugarcane, sweet potato, and wheat) and just five large livestock (cow, sheep, goat, pig, and horse) have led to the destruction of 70% of wild species. This process has laid the groundwork for the Anthropocene sixth extinction, at a rate of 1,000 times higher than the natural rate. Thus, in rural prosperity or any other concept resulting from the radical critique of rural entrepreneurship from the perspective of planetary social thought, the component of "opportunity" must be rewritten in a way that is transferred from the market to nature, and savagery should be considered not as the domesticated and close other and something dwelt there in far distance, but as a reality that is an integral part of the earth like a dynamic planet. What I understand by the concept of planetary multiplicity is an emphasis on the unpredictability, immeasurability, irrepressibility, and in a word, savagery of the forces and dynamics of the earth, especially when such forces cross the threshold through human actions. The ruralization of entrepreneurship will be realized when it can bear a planetary explanation of savagery and remoteness concept. Therefore, it is more revealed that the cultural turn studies are somehow agonistic, and planetary critique is somehow antagonistic (Dey, 2020). Such antagonism not only seeks to reflect the cultural dynamics, dissimilarity, and difference in the earth's dynamic and self-transformed or vice versa, but also always considers that transition from gradualism attitude in geology and discarding it as well as adopting a catastrophic approach in the earth system science will require a revolutionary view of both the earth and entrepreneurship and transition from past to present (and future), from human to non-human, from dictatorship to democracy, and from the surface (morphology) to the depth (geology). These transitions will be impossible except through an antagonistic encounter with market-based, monolithic, uniformed, profit-oriented, unilateral, positivistic routines and discourses available in the rural entrepreneurship climate. Such an encounter necessitates accepting and acting on planetary ethics along with its own epistemology and ontology. Such an ethic is not only limited to cases like property rights, rights of accumulation and transfer of wealth, company establishment and registration rights, and fair trade, but also looks for reviewing the meaning of good and bad, virtue and ethical vice in the context of the relations between humans (society), the relations between humans and animals (zoopolis), and humans with the planet (human as geo-power). The author previously represented ethics in one study (2016) as one of the key components of rural entrepreneurship. While conducting this research in the west of the country, it was perceived that rural entrepreneurs, who had come to woodcarving and making tables and chairs – and had become so-called multifunctional or multi-occupational – cut the trees of the pastures around the village indiscriminately without being controlled by local authorities. Considering the discussion about ethics, to avoid over-abstraction, we will indicate an obvious example that will further demonstrate the aim of using planetary social thought in the rural entrepreneurship critique.

4.2 Sistan and a Brief History of Rural Entrepreneurship

The province of Sistan and Baluchistan – the location of three deep wells – is situated in the southeast of Iran. Out of 2,775,014 people who lived in this province, approximately 1,427,332 people (approximately 51%) live in rural areas. There are 9,285 villages in this province, of which 2,732 (approximately 30%) have been desolated during the last 15 years of drought. The economic activity rate and unemployment rate in this province are 32.9% and 13.8%, respectively (the values of these indices for the whole country are 40.4% and 12.7%, respectively); thus, according to these two criteria, this province is ranked in the lowest rating of the economic activity rate, and it is ranked 25 out of 31 provinces in terms of unemployment (Statistical Center of Iran, Population and Housing Census, 2016). Approximately 64,003 landless farming households exist in this province, being relatively 9% of all farmer households in the country. The Sistan region is located in the north of Sistan and Baluchistan Province, an ancient region dating back thousands of years. The economic system of Sistan is based on subsistence farming and suffered irreparable damage during a severe and long drought. Furthermore, 223,146 people (approximately 57%) out of 349,029 people living in the whole region of Sistan reside in rural areas (the rural population rate in the whole country is 26%). The 15 year drought has not only caused serious damage to infrastructure facilities, including roads, agricultural fields, and schools in Sistan, but also led to severe air pollution and the occurrence and spread of eye and respiratory diseases in this region (Dahmardeh, 2016, Miri et al., 2010). According to the summary report of studies on the planning program of Sistan and Baluchistan Province (PBO, 2019), 60,951 people have left the province and 27,267 have entered during the years 2006–2011. Thus, Sistan and Baluchistan is an immigrant-first province and ranks 10th among the 31 provinces of the country in terms of being immigrant-first. Meanwhile, Zabol County – the center of the Sistan region – has the second-highest rank of being immigrant-first in the province with a population of 5,235 people, after Zahedan, the capital of the province. Furthermore, during the same period when the economy and environment of Sistan suffered stagnation and destruction, the entrepreneurial turn in the country was ongoing with a special focus on rural areas. This demonstrates that entrepreneurial plans and projects, if not failed, have not been able to achieve desirable results, at least in rural areas in Sistan. Approximately 40 million dollars from the total of 1.5 billion dollars have been allocated to Sistan and Baluchistan Province from the National Development Fund of Iran for rural development and job creation in rural areas in August 2018; this is a high amount. However, according to the statistics gathered from entrepreneurial consulting companies that have registered people on the KARA website, only 17% of qualified native people living in Sistan are registered, and almost 3% of the registered individuals have been able to receive a 4% rural loan to start a business (Shahraki & Sarani, 2019). However, the main problem has been focusing on lending and neglecting the reinforcement of entrepreneurial institutions, reforming business regulations, lack of attention to the pursuit of water rights from the Hirmand River, and focusing too much on digging deep wells. The blocking of water from the Hirmand River by the government of Ashraf Ghani – the fugitive president of Afghanistan – and then by the Taliban as the new ruling body in Afghanistan, has completely stopped the flow of life in rural Sistan.

4.3 Deep Well and Three Disastrous Transitions

The author, as a university professor and citizen of Sistan, who has lived and worked in this area for many years, maintains that digging a deep well is a new kind of encroachment on the ground, which is unprecedented in the history of Sistan. A deep well is a clear example that illustrates how the rhetorical emphasis on entrepreneurship and rural resilience, regardless of the planetary aspect, culture, local customs, and the earth, can lead to the destruction of a region and its people. Nevertheless, the issue of deep wells can be considered an opportunity to examine a new relationship between humans and nature, which is based on the destruction caused by crossing thresholds: (a) political threshold (Who are the main administrators of development in the region?), which resulted in individual decisions in the context of regional development; (b) cultural threshold (Where is the mythical position of the Hirmand River in local and national culture, and who we/Sistanis are?), which resulted in neglecting the fears, motives, expectations, and experiences, and in general, the lived experience of people residing in Sistan; and (c) geologic threshold (What is the morphology and geology of the Sistan Basin and what kind of place is the planet we live on?), which led to movement from the surface and morphology of the earth (changes in the historical and successive course of the Hirmand River) to the depth (digging deep wells), thereby changing the historical water regime in Sistan. Meanwhile, what has been the main stimulus of the disastrous crossing of these three thresholds includes the dominant discourse monopoly of rural entrepreneurship on loan payments, and consequently, the catastrophic neglect of guaranteeing sustainable water rights from the Hirmand River as the main component of planetary multiplicity and an expression of the earth's dynamics and self-organization.

4.3.1 Deep Well in Contrast to Participatory Democracy

Today, Buen Vivir – means living well, collective wellbeing, cohabitation with others and nature – has been introduced as a new paradigm for development (Walsh, 2010, Gudynass, 2011; Chassagne, 2021). One of the components of this new development pattern, which is especially compatible with rural environments, includes deepening democracy and citizenship in every member of society, equality, and participation. Hence, Buen Vivir correlates with a regime of development that is more subject-based than object-based. In the analysis of numerous environmental experts, it can be found that there is no possibility to resolve dilemmas like global warming except by establishing a general well that goes beyond the level of psychological and individual apocalyptic concerns about the future of the planet and the earth and involved governments. Hence, the democratization of governments, which is one of the pillars of people-based patterns of development like Buen Vivir, enables the manifestation of the general will in the domain of the planet/earth. While with the beginning of neoliberal policies in Iran since 1989 until now, the importance of the social issue in policymaking has gradually diminished, and two provincial governance institutions, namely governor-generalship and the management and planning organization, are regarded as the pulse of policymaking and budget regulation and allocation for every province. The decision to dig deep wells as a development project has not even gone through any of the decision-making levels in these two governance institutions and is the result of an individual decision. Clark and Szerszynski (2021: 38) clearly demonstrated that establishing a planetary social thought requires disbanding the authoritarian social regulation. Albeit, according to the author's findings, scientific data on deep wells are neither available nor confidential, thereby ascertaining the governance processes as non-participatory in this regard. According to Clark and Szerszynski (Ibid), if the issue is to confront human, the wrath of nature or the energy hidden in it, the thinking and decision-making system equally inclines toward a closed-system thinking. According to the findings, the generality of data and information related to deep wells is classified as confidential and security. Note at the end of the chapter presents the few findings provided by some local experts.

4.3.2 Deep Well in Contrast to the Lived Experience of Sistani's Residents (Transition from Cultural Threshold)

Digging deep wells as a resilience strategy for residents of Sistan and as a means of reviving agriculture after a prolonged 15-year drought directly undermines the region's cultural dependence on and historical connection to the Hirmand River. This practice not only challenges traditional water management systems but also disrupts the natural and cultural heritage of the river. In a priceless book titled *Natural-Historical Geography of Sistan*, written by Ahmadi (2015), the sanctity of the river and the mention of its name in Avesta and Zoroastrian texts are discussed. The name of the river in Avesta is rich in dams (هئه‌تومنت), a river that was celebrated in a special manner and was considered the soul of Sistan or Sakastan. Ahmadi (Ibid: 133) quoted from Ibn Faghih writes, "the river of Sistan is handmaid and the people of Sistan say, a thousand streams flow into it and it does not increase, and a thousand streams rise from it and it does not decrease." This is the reflection of the Hirmand's mythical nature as a dynamic geological force; this is a kind of dynamism frozen and stabilized in the mythological view: water that neither decreases nor increases. A drought in such a river means the transformation of the calmness and quietness arising from the myth into the restlessness caused by the disaster. Terminologically, it is also stated that Hir 'هیر' or Eer 'ایر' means benevolent and blessing, and Hirmand means owner of blessing. In the story of Rostam and Esfandiar in Shahnameh, the mythical element of water can be observed in the form of the Hirmand River and even the name of Rostam in Pahlavi is rodestahm, which is in the form of ruatah us-taxman in ancient Iran, meaning a river that outflows (Mohseni-nia & Amiri-far, 2014). A river that is like a threshold, while crossing it can mean both death and life (Jafari & Ashrafzadeh, 2016).

4.3.3 Deep Well in Contrast to the Historical Water Regime of the Sistan Plain (Transition from the Geological Threshold)

More specifically, this threshold has linked the story of the land to the rural entrepreneurship narrative and has established a kind of geologizing rural entrepreneurship. The notion of water regime in this study is one of the manifestations of earthly multitude, that is, how people in Sistan have encountered the river, used its water, faced its droughts and floods, and understood and imagined it. Moreover, what have been the collective responses of the people to the opportunities and threats resulting from successive changes in the Hirmand River throughout history? This water regime has been a reaction to the many changes in the course of the Hirmand River over many years; changes in the course of the river reflect a unique planetary multiplicity, which has been both destructive and constructive. Sometimes the residents in the Sistan region have borne and have adapted to these changes, and sometimes not. One of the sudden and surprising earthly dynamisms is the change in the course of Hirmand to the northern delta in a place called Qala-e-Bost in Helmand Province, Afghanistan, the last of which occurred in 1692 AD (Ahmadi, 2015: 399) as a self-transformed change, and led to the destruction of the old Sistan and creation of the present-day Sistan around the Hamoon Lake. Every time the course of Hirmand changed, the previous course was filled with quicksand, so that the river never returned to that course. The residents in Sistan, like geological subjects, have changed their activities according to this change in the course of the river as much as they can and have adapted to it. The last change in the course of the river in Qala-e-Bost and Kamal Khan Dam was made completely by hand by the Taliban during the days when this chapter was written and led to the intensification of drought in Sistan and the transfer of water to the Godzareh depression; a saltwater lake with a length of 100 km and a width of 15 km. Therefore, it can be concluded that Hirmand's water regime, as a social and human structure, has always been a reaction to morphological changes and geological forces on the surface of the earth. Digging deep wells for the first time transfers this water regime from the surface of the earth to its depth and, since it has no record in the natural and cultural history of the river, can cause devastating anthropogenic effects in the Sistan basin, and probably in the entire eastern plateau of Iran. Moving from surface to depth is a reflection of moving from morphology to geology. The geology of Sistan is also not very compatible with the main stream hard rock geology. First, changing the conditions and the degraded environment of the Sistan from marine to riverine, and then from riverine to lacustrine, from the end of the third geological period (Miocene to Pliocene) until now, second, two opposing assumptions regarding the presence of coarse and fine sediments in the depth of the earth, and third, the occurrence of a volcanic event below the Hamoon Lake and the formation of a mass of granite called the Khajeh Mountain, all three indicate special geological events that, according to Ahmadi (2015: 6–87), caused the assumption of existing a rich aquifer or huge underground water reservoir in the Sistan plain to be discarded; an assumption that has been the fundamental principle of digging deep wells in Sistan and around the city of Zabol.

5 Conclusions and Suggestions

In this chapter, an effort was made to address a geosocial critique of rural entrepreneurship using some concepts raised by planetary social thought and to explain the concept of ruralization of entrepreneurship instead of the concept of rural entrepreneurship. The conceptual trajectory of the chapter included the transition from the cultural and discourse critique of rural entrepreneurship to geosocial critique and linking the story of the earth and the narrative of entrepreneurship to each other. As mentioned, the cultural critique in the post-development period provided an introduction to the deconstruction of the discourse and practices of both entrepreneurship and rurality. The unilateral, economic, people-oriented, and discriminatory discourse of rural entrepreneurship, which describes the rural environment as a place to offer services to the city, the opportunities restricted to the market, and the entrepreneur as a profit- and maximum-based person, has been criticized in the critical studies and theories of rural entrepreneurship. However, according to the researches by the author in Iran, these studies have not been able to significantly affect rural resilience and revenue enhancement due to the structural defect of neglecting environmental dilemmas and having a rhetorical aspect. Intensifying neoliberal economic policies has led to more and more destruction of the environment, and the discourse and entrepreneurial practices, particularly in the rural environments, have been limited to the lending process. This process has increased the large number of bank debtors along with the corruption in the banking system. In the Sistan region of Iran, due to neglecting the consideration of geological dimensions of rural entrepreneurship and development, with the changes in the water regime of the Hirmand River and the crossing of three thresholds, the future of Sistan will involve unknown geosocial forces and transformations. The native inhabitants of Sistan have lived in this region for thousands of years, and they have organized their economic and social lives based on the special situation of the Hirmand River, and accordingly have established their water regime. The deep well has never been part of the management practices and the use of water resources in Sistan. The end of the chapter discusses some of the suggestions and draws future directions of research in the field of rural entrepreneurship and development. It is an inevitable necessity in the future that the attitude regarding rural entrepreneurship and thinking about it should be in a different way and fundamentally different from the perspective of the earth. Meanwhile, considering the lived experience of the inhabitants who are at the forefront of the climate crisis is regarded as an important point to implement this key issue – geosocial analysis of rural entrepreneurship. The case study of digging deep wells in the Sistan region of Iran indicates that fundamental institutional-political reforms, as well as geological considerations, are simultaneously required to describe the future paradigms and approaches of rural development and can yield completely new concepts and findings. For example, wastewater from water softeners located by the deep well and the creation of new physical and chemical pollution can take the discourse of development in the Sistan region of Iran from deficiency to excess; this requires speculating about completely new emerging issues[3]. The addition of salt to the ecosystem of the region and human invasion into the depth of the earth is unprecedented in the planetary history of this region and is therefore completely problematic for rural environments. The deep well demonstrates that the power of water, like the power of fire and explosion, can relate everyday lived experiences to forces and dynamisms beyond routine life. Finally, it must be acknowledged that analysis of rural entrepreneurship and development from the viewpoint of planetary social thought indicates that both entrepreneurial awareness and opportunity should be generalized from the economic arena to culture – culture as something constructed and not a rigid and fixed phenomenon – and then to the uncertainties and unpredictability of the earth, geopower, and cosmos. According to Marx, everything that is hard and stable will disappear, even supposed results of rural entrepreneurship.

References

Ahmadi, H. (2015). The natural and historical geography of Sistan: Based on historical writings and field studies. Maziar Publishing.

Audretsch, D. (2002). Entrepreneurship: A survey of the literature. Institute for Development Strategies, Indiana University & Centre for Economic Policy Research (CEPR).

3 The results of analyzing the physical and chemical parameters of the water samples from the deep well in Adimi County (Nimruz) and wastewater of the RO water softener indicate that the amounts of salts in the deep well, including CI and EC, sulfate, calcium carbonate, calcium, magnesium, and iron, are higher than the environmental standards quantity allowed for drinking and agriculture. Additionally, due to the high amount of physical and chemical parameters, the wastewater of the RO water softener does not meet the required standard for discharge to surface water, absorbing wells, and agricultural utilization. Thus far, the project contractor has sent no explanatory plans and proposed mechanisms for wastewater disposal of the water softener to the Water and Sewage Company and the General Department of the Environment of the province.

Bill, F., Bjerke, B., & Johansson, A. W. (Eds.). (2010). (De)Mobilizing the entrepreneurship discourse. Edward Elgar.
Birch, K. A. (2017). Research agenda for neoliberalism. Edward Elgar.
Chassagne, N. (2021). Buen Vivir as an alternative to sustainable development: Lessons from Ecuador. Routledge.
Clark, N., & Szerszynski, B. (2021). Planetary social thought: The anthropocene challenge to the social sciences. Polity Press.
Cloke, P. (2006). Conceptualizing rurality. In P. Cloke, T. Marsden, & P.H. Mooney (Eds.), Handbook of rural studies (pp. 18–29). Sage.
Dabson, B. (2005). Entrepreneurship as a real community and economic development strategy. Columbia, MO: Rural Policy Research Institute, University of Iowa College of Public Health/Truman School of Public Affairs, University of Missouri.
da Costa, A.D.S.M., & Silva Saraiva, L. (2012). Hegemonic discourses on entrepreneurship as an ideological mechanism for the reproduction of capital. Organization, 19, 587–614.
Dahmarde, M. (2016). Assessment of drought damage of Hamoun wetland on health condition of inhabitants of Sistan region. World Review of Science, Technology and Sustainable Development, 12, 335–352.
Dey, P. (2020). What does it mean to be against entrepreneurship? From antagonistic to agonistic critique. In A. Örtenblad (Ed.), Against entrepreneurship: A critical examination (pp. 267–278). Palgrave Macmillan.
Goss, D. (2005). "Schumpeter's legacy? Interaction and emotions in the sociology of entrepreneurship." Entrep. Theory Pract., 29, 205–218.
Granovetter, M. (1985). Economic action and social structure: The problem of embeddedness. American Journal of Sociology, 91, 481–510.
Jones, C., & Spicer, A. (2009). Unmasking the Entrepreneur. Edward Elgar.
Gudynas, E. (2011). Buen Vivir: Today's tomorrow. Development, 54, 441–447. https://doi.org/10.1057/dev.2011.86.
Jafari, M., & Ashrafzadeh, R. (2016). Rivers in Shahnameh. Persian Literature Journal, 12(6), 7–26.
Klein, N. (2008). The shock doctrine: The rise of disaster capitalism. Penguin Books.
Knudsen, T., & Swedberg, R. (2009). Capitalist entrepreneurship: Making profit through the unmaking of economic Orders. Capitalism and Society, 4(2), Article 3.
Kyrö, P. (2014). To Grow or Not to Grow? Entrepreneurship and sustainable development. In P. Kyrö (Ed.), Handbook of entrepreneurship and sustainable development research (pp. 3–29). Edward Elgar.
Loewenstein, A. (2015). Disaster capitalism: Making a killing out of catastrophe. Verso.
McElwee, G. (2005). Developing entrepreneurial skills of farmers. ESOF series (SSPE-CT-2005-006500). University of Lincoln.
Miri, A., Moghaddamnia, A., Pahlavanravi, A., & Panjehkeh, N. (2010). Dust storm frequency after the 1999 drought in the Sistan region, Iran. Clim Res, 41, 83–90.
Mohseni Nia, N., & Amiri Far, A. (2014). Mythical decoding of water in Virgil's Aeneid and Shahnameh. Journal of Prose Studies in Persian Literature, 17, 317–343. doi: 10.22103/jll.2014.788.
Munck, R. (2021). Rethinking development: Marxist perspectives. Palgrave MacMillan.
Nayyeri, K. (2018). "How stop the sixth extinction." Retrieved from https://pecritique.com on 1st February 2022.
Nicholson, L., & Anderson, A. R. (2005). News and nuances of the entrepreneurial myth and metaphor: Linguistic games in entrepreneurial sense-making and sense-giving. Entrepreneurship Theory and Practice, 29(2), 153–172.
Ogbor, J.O. (2000). Mythicizing and reification in entrepreneurial discourse: Ideology-critique of entrepreneurial studies. Journal of Management Studies, 37(5), 605–635.

Planning and Budgeting Organization of Iran (PBO). (2019). Spatial development report. Retrieved from https://sb.mporg.ir on March 20, 2021.

Rosenqvist, O. (2020). Deconstruction and hermeneutical space as keys to understanding the rural. Journal of Rural Studies, 75, 132–142.

Schumpeter, J.A. (2003 [1941]). Capitalism, socialism and democracy. Routledge.

Shahraki, H., Movahedi, R., & Yaghoubi Farani, A. (2016). From Arturo Escobar's development theory to Antony Giddens's structuration theory: A social constructionist analysis of rural entrepreneurship and multifunctional agriculture. International Journal of Agricultural Resources, Governance and Ecology, 12, 406–426.

Shahraki, H., & Movahedi, R. (2017). Reconceptualizing rural entrepreneurship discourse from a social constructionist perspective: A case study from Iran. Middle East Critique, 26(1), 79–100.

Shahraki, H., & Sarani, V. (2019). Development and its devil twin: The situational analysis of rural entrepreneurship in Sistan Region. Journal of Community Development, 11(1), 173–196.

Shahraki, H., & Keikha, A. (2022). How the entrepreneurship can set aside the rural development process: A historical and discursive reflection on rural entrepreneurship and development policies in Iran. J Glob Entrepr Res, doi: 10.1007/s40497-022-00323-3.

Shepherd, D.A. (2019). Researching the dark side, downside, and destructive side of entrepreneurship: It is the compassionate thing to do! Academy of Management Discoveries, 5(3), 217–220.

Smelser, N.J., & Swedberg, R. (2005). Introducing economic sociology. In N.J. Smelser & R. Swedberg (Eds.), Handbook of economic sociology (pp. 3–26). Princeton University Press.

Statistical Center of Iran. (2016). National population census.

Thornton, P.H. (1999). The Sociology of entrepreneurship. Annual Review of Sociology, 25, 19–46.

Thornton, P.H., Ribeiro-Soriano, D., & Urbano, D. (2011). Socio-cultural factors and entrepreneurial activity: An overview. International Small Business Journal, 29(2), 105–118.

Vosooghi, M., & Eemani, A. (2010). Future of rural development and sustainability challenges. Rural Development Journal, 1(2), 23–45.

Walsh, C. (2010). Development as Buen Vivir: Institutional arrangements and (de)colonial entanglements. Development, 53, 15–21. https://doi.org/10.1057/dev.2009.93.

Ziai, A. (2015). Post-Development: Premature burials and haunting ghosts. Development and Change, 46(4), 833–854.

Ziai, A. (2019). Gharbzadegi in Iran: A reactionary alternative to 'development'? doi: 10.1057/s41301-019-00221-4.

Concluding Thoughts

This handbook is the culmination of many ideas, concepts, experiences, and reflections that provide a broad perspective on rural entrepreneurship in developed economies. During the process of gathering information, the world has experienced tragedies and shocks across countries and regions. Significant climate variations and price instability, for example, have triggered inflation and natural disasters that force individuals and organizations in rural communities to plan, prepare, and respond to the "unknown." Entrepreneurs and entrepreneurial thinkers are the leaders of any efforts to deal with uncertainty and the unknowable because they take action and reflect upon and learn from that action so that they can make the necessary adjustments. Their work is invaluable to building rural economies and ensuring quality of life.

We are grateful to the authors who contributed their knowledge and experiences working within the rural entrepreneurship domain. Each chapter could be treated as an independent topic for researchers, teachers, and practitioners who are seeking ideas to pursue future entrepreneurship-focused studies or programming. The linkages between each chapter naturally form an integrated platform for scholars to identify connections and interactions across different topics that could simultaneously impact the development of rural entrepreneurship from various domains.

Deller and Conroy (Chapter 1) open the discussion of rural entrepreneurship by providing a review of historical concepts related to economic development. Their treatment of economic growth in rural versus urban environments focuses on different approaches and factors such as people's thinking, policies, and strategies. Their support of the concept that entrepreneurship development is an economic development strategy is highly relevant, as rural entrepreneurs directly allocate the existing resources in a rural setting and bring about economic change. They note the various definitions of "rural" and how different definitions could lead to mixed interpretations of who rural entrepreneurs are, what they do in communities that fit into various entrepreneurial activities, and how to capture contributions and impacts from those activities.

Alter and Fortunato (Chapter 2) re-visit the traditional view of entrepreneurial ecosystems and argue that this perspective is predominantly based on an urban viewpoint. Entrepreneurial ecosystems have been studied by various scholars across a wide range of situations. Many studies and frameworks discuss features and functions of the entrepreneurship ecosystem from both micro and macroeconomic perspectives. Alter and Fortunato introduce the proto-ecosystem, or nascent ecosystem development, in rural communities. They caution scholars and practitioners in the rural entrepreneurship field to develop scenario-proper frameworks or best practices when exploring this topic. This echoes the introduction of the rural concept in the previous chapter.

https://doi.org/10.1515/9783110791396-014

Lyons (Chapter 3) dives deeper into the microfoundations of ecosystem development by examining the skills and relevant training for successful rural entrepreneurship. He recognizes the flexible nature of the skills needed for rural entrepreneurs to succeed, depending on time and place. Lyons builds on previous studies that explored important properties of skills such as being learnable, actionable, reproducible, and repeatable, which were important to establishing successful ventures. For rural entrepreneurs, it seems to be essential to develop skills via formal or informal education and training in workplaces. Some skills in the rural entrepreneurship space have not been fully examined, including mentorship, coaching, and learning from experiences and engagement in action. Lyons addresses these deficiencies. The author concludes with a system to bring skill definition, meaningful measurement, and development, using a practical tool as an example.

Zoller and Makino (Chapter 4) discuss an interesting process of new value creation that could demonstrate the development of "entrepreneurs in rural areas" and "entrepreneurs of rural areas." Using primary and secondary data collected in Italy, the authors explore how family members, values, and mindset can nurture and strengthen the development of rural entrepreneurs. Participation and experiences, similar to what has been highlighted in previous chapters, are embedded in socio-economic aspects, including culture and creative promotional strategies. Both economic and non-economic motivational factors are crucial and closely linked to rural communities.

Chapter 5 by Cowan turns our attention to technology and provides an example to show how technologies have influenced rural entrepreneurship development. The author introduces the new concept of Technology Roadmapping, building on existing research using Smart Grid concepts, to demonstrate how scholars can design and analyze similar roadmapping strategies across industries in rural environments. Recent calls for innovative energy design and development have generated much interest and action grounded in community-based initiatives. Smart technology has become a reality, not a dream, in many entrepreneurship domains (e.g., engineering, construction, appliances, and automobiles). It would be interesting to project how the smart technology concepts and applications might impact the formation of policies that could assist rural entrepreneurs in reducing barriers to business transactions.

While several of the previous chapters touch upon the entrepreneurial ecosystem, Chapter 6, by Theodoraki, Messeghem, and Carayannis, addresses some gaps in studying this topic and proposes the alternative view of an ecosystem constituted of sub-systems. The authors build on the Quadruple Helix model to re-visit the entrepreneurial ecosystem from a regional perspective. Some factors have been introduced by scholars to characterize an entrepreneurial ecosystem, including components, domains, elements, and attributes associated with people, places, and actions. The authors propose two approaches based on Quadruple Helix principles to interpret conditions, coordination, and cross-connectivity of the sub-ecosystems, which often provide in-between services and support to entrepreneurship development.

Once we understand these different perspectives regarding entrepreneurship and rural connections, it raises the question: "What role does education play in fostering successful entrepreneurship?" Jacobson (Chapter 7) discusses how institutions of higher education could play a key role in supporting entrepreneurial ecosystems within a rural context. Workforce development, in general, has been a challenge for rural communities. Barriers exist for individuals and families in rural areas to access information (e.g., lack of communication media and connectivity), acquire assistance (e.g., limited staff and specialists), and gain knowledge of new opportunities offered by federal or state agencies. Public entities such as Land-Grant institutions and Small Business Development Centers in the U.S. are good examples of approaches to cultivating rural entrepreneurship. This author concludes that more research is needed to understand the dynamics and shared responsibilities among these educational entities.

Being mission-driven is one of the characteristics mentioned by scholars when discussing the unique nature of social entrepreneurs. Collins and Taylor (Chapter 8) introduce an example of the mission-driven approach to rural entrepreneurship, based on farming activities in Southeastern Ontario. Social entrepreneurs are driven by purpose, service, and impact beyond the traditional economic value of currency. This chapter offers an insightful description of an analytical framework that could be applied to study social entrepreneurship in a rural setting. Examples in the discussion also demonstrate how rural entrepreneurs deploy innovative business strategies toward ecological sustainability and community resilience.

To assist scholars in broadening the theoretical foundation, Liang and Marshall (Chapter 9) share examples of different theories that could support the foundation of rural entrepreneurship studies. These theories cover both the micro- and macroeconomic domains; for example, location theory, institutional theory, finance/resource theory, psychology theory, and information or technology theory have served as the underpinning frameworks for many entrepreneurship literatures. Many datasets also exist to facilitate empirical analysis in the rural entrepreneurship field. By combining robust theoretical frameworks and reliable data sources, scholars could generate new knowledge and understanding of rural entrepreneurs, their decisions, and their impacts on rural development.

As we continue to share examples of empirical contexts, Macke (Chapter 10) provides an example of a specific entrepreneurship program to energize the entrepreneurial ecosystem in rural areas. This chapter affords details of a program with a history of supporting rural entrepreneurs in the US. The historical reviews, steps, and lessons learned show the challenges, opportunities, and impacts of rural prosperity. Chapter 11 (van Dorsselaer, Bosma, and van Twuijver) provides a set of European examples of entrepreneurial aspirations. Using the 2023 Global Entrepreneurship Monitor database, Chapter 11 presents interesting evidence related to entrepreneurial drivers, entrepreneurial engagement, and socioeconomic factors linking to entrepreneurial motivations.

Finally, Chapter 12 (Shahraki) looks at rural entrepreneurship through social lenses and examines the geographical and spatial implications. Rural entrepreneurship represents diverse individual characteristics, enterprise development strategies, societal profiles, and cultural aspirations. Although economic development seems to be the most commonly explored topic among entrepreneurship scholars, the overall impacts and linkages between rural entrepreneurs, their decisions, their actions, and their contributions to rural areas are complex and deserve further attention.

Through this Handbook of Rural Entrepreneurship, we hope to stimulate and encourage new topics for furthering our understanding of rural entrepreneurs and their environment. There are new strategies, innovative methods, and creative data available for us to jointly expand the frontier of knowledge and application. Our ultimate goal should be to provide timely and effective services to achieve rural prosperity and long-term resiliency for rural communities.

Additional Thoughts to Stimulate Applications – Examples, Cases, and Stories

From Chapter 2: The Sociological Imagination and Theories of the Middle Range in Rural and Non-traditional Entrepreneurial Ecosystems

An Engineer and a Gardener at Work in an Entrepreneurial Ecosystem

We sincerely hope our readers do not think that we are (a) simply opposed to any kind of sophisticated statistical models, (b) believe that experts (and proponents of urban-style ecosystems) are somehow overblown and misguided – or worse, (c) think the field of ecosystem research has decayed into a hopeless abyss of useless studies or ill-fitting grand theories. Not true. The true elegance of middle-range theory is that such theories seek *pragmatic meaning* within our science, applying the best of our findings differentially and appropriately to a variety of social systems that operate under different histories, paradigms, and social milieux. There may indeed be a great deal of similarity among certain classes of ecosystems, such as rural ecosystems over a wide area (compared to more dense urban ecosystems), or proto-ecosystems in Western nations compared with the rest of the world. Perhaps the best way to find out what kind of ecosystem we are dealing with is through direct engagement. This is best demonstrated through an example, using a music-based entrepreneurial ecosystem.

Situation: Community X has an unusual number of talented musicians in its small, rural community. This situation is historical, as the community has long been a stopping place between larger cities and a regular stop for entertaining travelers and traders. It is a proto-ecosystem: several businesses and a few nonprofits exist, but they are relatively disconnected from one another. The community agrees, however, that music is their strongest attractor to the community, a placemaking centerpiece, and there is room to grow a connected cluster of music-oriented businesses that serves as an economic cluster.

Problem: How do we connect diverse actors into some semblance of a self-reinforcing ecosystem capable of sectoral growth?

Engineer Approach: Well-established blueprints for growing into a music city already exist. Looking at the stories of Nashville, for example, the community became a hub for country music due to the presence of radio shows like the Grand Ole Opry, prominent studios like RCA Studio B, and music publishing companies that could sign new acts. Charismatic producers followed, cultivating legendary acts. Austin, by contrast, focused on venues for country musicians that shied away from the Nashville sound, taking a venue-and-festival approach incrementally over time. Both started small and slowly filled

https://doi.org/10.1515/9783110791396-015

in what we now know to be a complete, thriving music ecosystem with entrepreneurial efforts prominent throughout its history.

Engineer Research: A structural equation model (SEM) was conducted using categories drawn from the literature, including "music leaders," "music feeders," and "non-music feeders." Results clustered well, and many gaps were found in the local music entrepreneurship ecosystem, especially around funding, and all will require some development. The research is used to inductively support broader theories on ecosystems, particularly those focusing on ecosystem structure.

Engineer Practice: Since Nashville and Austin are ideal music cities and very prosperous, the data suggest that creating a balanced mix of venues, small publishing firms, and modern production facilities for online distribution (the new radio) will lead to increased momentum. Research shows that creating a diverse industry that communicates fluidly (through meetups, conferences, etc.) helps to catalyze ongoing growth. Local arts organizations should focus on pairing investment with local entrepreneurs, driving toward right-sized projects of these types to create the genesis of a music entrepreneurship ecosystem over time. Governments should shift toward musician-friendly policies like Nashville, Austin, and Seattle, whatever that means in a small community.

Gardener Approach: Upon visiting Community X, it is clear that local musicians and venues are visibly sickened by the idea of becoming a "Little Nashville or Austin," and besides, it is unlikely to be reproducible, and their efforts will never be taken too seriously next to industry giants. Culturally, this community wishes to remain small but sees promise in selling its rural music culture as a packaged experience complete with artisan retail, great restaurants, and cozy inns to meet its fullest potential. Sustainability and slow growth are preferable over rapid development. They recognize that, while also unpalatable, a reasonable amount of tourism will be required to achieve this dream. Several venues are already very successful, along with several local bands – but retail, restaurants, and inns are largely disconnected from this world, and most are not tourist-focused.

Gardener Research: A grounded approach is taken to understand citizen viewpoints and to take stock of what is already working well. Social network analysis is chosen as a means of finding gaps in communication and relationship-building across diverse actors. A mix of qualitative and quantitative data are compared with other case studies in non-traditional, smaller cities with music as a leading developmental factor, including Leiper's Fork, TN; Taos, NM; Muscle Shoals, AL; and Denton, TX. Relational dynamics from the research are used to build middle-range theory about non-traditional, grassroots music ecosystems in smaller environments, with a general store approach to understanding the contributions of relationships built across and beyond the music scene.[1] Connections are also made to the mainstream literature, identifying which areas

1 See Balfour et al. (2016) for an example of middle-range theory building in an arts context.

of the entrepreneurial ecosystem literature are most appropriate in this type of non-traditional ecosystem, and which diverge from the middle-range theory.

Gardener Practice: This is not a standard "music city," but it can still be very successful when it comes to entrepreneurship with music at the center. The goal is not music output (i.e., getting attention as a place that spawns national acts or a new entrant in the mainstream music industry), but rather moving from output to creating whole experiences. Music becomes a leading factor in a more holistic tourist environment, including retail, inns, and restaurants. Focus should shift toward building bridges to other tourist-focused entities and understanding how to enhance participation behind a common vision. Investment should be grassroots and appropriate to place, and may take the form of new restaurant, retail, and lodging offerings – especially if these can be generated locally among latent entrepreneurs that understand the culture. Fusion with music can take the form of a new downtown organization committed to small business development with music as a theme, incorporating members of the already-strong music scene as leaders along with others in the community. This organization can take leadership in attracting local investment, supporting small business development and education, music education, tourist promotion, and attracting grant funds as appropriate.

From Chapter 3: What Skills Do Rural Entrepreneurs Need for Success, and How Can They Develop Them?

Chapter 3 describes a clinical tool for assessing entrepreneurship called the Readiness Inventory for Successful Entrepreneurship (RISE). A forerunner of this assessment tool, the Entrepreneurial League System Assessment (ELSA), was used in an entrepreneur coaching pilot program in a rural region spanning counties in western West Virginia, eastern Kentucky, and southern Ohio. This part of central Appalachia is known as the Advantage Valley.

In this pilot, all participating entrepreneurs had their skill levels assessed. They were then placed into groups of eight to ten, all at the same skill level. A coach worked with them individually to create an action plan for addressing their skill weaknesses. They also came together in their peer groups to meet regularly to share information and resources and to provide mutual support. The coach acted as the facilitator of these meetings. Once or twice per year, they came together across skill levels to celebrate successes, share stories, and enable role-modeling and mentoring opportunities among themselves. A survey of entrepreneurs and coaches in the pilot identified important successes in entrepreneur and business development (Kutzhanova, Lyons & Lichtenstein, 2009).

This model is replicable in any rural community or region, using the RISE. It offers a tool and a coaching system for facilitating rural entrepreneurship as an economic development strategy. It also provides a tool for objectively measuring entrepreneurship skill development, which can be used in research. Finally, institutions of higher education, such as Santa Barbara City College and the University of Tennessee at Chattanooga, have successfully used this approach to develop student entrepreneurs through the strategic application of curriculum, co-curricular activities, and community resources (Lyons, Lyons & Samson, 2021).

References

Kutzhanova, N., Lyons, T.S., & Lichtenstein, G.A. (2009). Skill-based development of entrepreneurs and the role of personal and peer group coaching in enterprise development. Economic Development Quarterly, 23(3), 193–210.

Lyons, T.S., Lyons, J.S., & Samson, J.A. (2021). Entrepreneurship skill building: Focusing entrepreneurship education on skills assessment and development. Springer/Palgrave-Macmillan.

From Chapter 4: From Entrepreneurship "in" Rural Areas to Entrepreneurship "of" Rural Areas: The Interplay between Entrepreneurship and Place for Rural Community Revitalization

Applying Rural Entrepreneurship Concepts: Insights from Place-Embedded Ventures

Rural entrepreneurship plays a crucial role in revitalizing local economies by fostering innovation, leveraging unique regional characteristics, and strengthening community resilience. Chapter 4 discusses the significance of place-embedded entrepreneurship and highlights how rural businesses can thrive by engaging with their local cultural, historical, and economic ecosystems. Here are some tips on how the concepts and content of the chapter can be applied practically, both in entrepreneurial ventures and academic research.

1. **Key concept: place-embedded rural entrepreneurship**
   The chapter emphasizes that rural entrepreneurship is not merely about running a business in a rural area, but rather about leveraging the unique resources, culture, and community of the place to create value. This is illustrated through the case of Centro Studi Italiani (CSI) in Urbania, which integrates local culture, history, and networks into its business model. From a teaching perspective, insights from this chapter can be valuable for students across multiple disciplines. Business students can learn about sustainable entrepreneurship models, while rural sociology and human geography students can explore the social and spatial dynamics of rural enterprises. Additionally, students in environmental studies and tourism management can analyze how place-based entrepreneurship may support ecological sustainability and local development.
2. **Practical application: starting a rural cultural tourism business** This study could be useful for an entrepreneur wanting to apply the concept of place-

embedded rural entrepreneurship by establishing or enriching a cultural tourism business in a rural town. Using insights from the chapter, they could:
- identify unique cultural, historical, and natural resources in the area
- collaborate with local artisans, farmers, and historical sites to create hands-on experiences (e.g., local cooking classes, heritage walks, or artisan workshops)
- develop partnerships with educational institutions to bring students for field studies or cultural immersion programs
- foster community involvement by engaging local residents as guides, hosts, or mentors, ensuring a deeper integration of the business into the local (entrepreneurial) ecosystem

3. **Research application: investigating the impact of embedded entrepreneurship**
   For researchers looking to build on this work, potential research questions include:
   - how does rural entrepreneurship influence local community resilience and identity?
   - what factors determine the level of place-embeddedness in rural ventures?
   - how do rural entrepreneurs balance local embeddedness with external market connections and the need to 'survive' economically?
   - what role does social capital play in the success of rural businesses?

4. **Case study application: comparing rural business models**
   A useful research direction could involve comparing multiple rural businesses with similar 'place-based features,' such as:
   - farm-to-table restaurants sourcing from local farms
   - heritage-based homestay networks that integrate cultural experiences/storytelling
   - rural co-working or co-living spaces for digital nomads that attempt to connect them with the local community

By comparing case studies, researchers can assess how different levels of embeddedness and bridging strategies influence success and sustainability.

From Chapter 7: Rural Everyday Entrepreneurial Ecosystems and Higher Education

In the chapter, Rural Everyday Entrepreneurial Ecosystems and Higher Education, the focus is on the role higher education institutions can and should be playing in terms of infrastructure, human capital, policies, and more in rural everyday entrepreneurial ecosystems. The chapter highlights the rural, everyday entrepreneur context, discusses potential rural entrepreneurial ecosystem contributors, and then makes the case for three organizations as key entrepreneurial ecosystem builders – land-grant universities, Small Business Development Centers (SBDCs), and Women's Business Centers (WBCs). The chapter includes two examples of what can happen when key players in a rural entrepreneurial ecosystem come together to support everyday rural entrepreneurs by highlighting what is happening in Utah with the Utah Rural Leadership Academy and Banking on Women.

The Utah Rural Leadership Academy is a partnership between the Utah Association of Counties (UAC), Utah's Governor's Office, and Southern Utah University (SUU) with funding from the Utah legislature. The aim of the program is to provide professional development and leadership training for Utah's rural county elected and appointed officials (27 of Utah's 29 counties are designated as rural) The program includes learning modules (virtual and in-person) on intergovernmental relations and partnerships, public budgeting and finance, and concludes with a rural government entrepreneurship incubator.

A partnership between Synchrony Bank, the Utah Microloan Fund, and Westminster University, Banking on Women has since 2010 provided Utah women entrepreneurs and business owners with financial literary classes, business plan development training, mentoring, and an opportunity to apply for a microenterprise loan. During that time, the program has had 18 in-person cohorts that included over 240 participants. Perhaps most importantly given the mission of the program, at least 70% of participants have household incomes that fall below the low to moderate income (LMI) parameters and approximately 15% of participants are women of color including: Native American, Asian, Black, and Hispanic. During the core years of the COVID pandemic (2020 and 2021), virtual courses were run for the cohorts. Given the success of the virtual programming and the needs of women entrepreneurs in rural Utah, Westminster University, in partnership with the WBC Utah office in rural Cedar City, Utah, proposed a second cohort for 2023 – a virtual cohort for rural Utah. Given the vast geographical distances in rural Utah, this virtual programming will include weekly virtual classes but keep the mentoring component and add a competency-based model (which Westminster already does well) for financial literacy and business plan development. The ultimate goal, with Westminster leading, will be to deepen the level of financial and entrepreneurship literacy for women entrepreneurs in all of Utah and developing pathways for additional training and education at Westminster and beyond.

From Chapter 8: How Alternative Farmers in Southeastern Ontario Mobilize Mission-driven Approaches for Rural Revitalization and Resilience

To improve the applicability of our research to a wider audience, we wish to share some insights that steered our methodology for carrying out semi-structured interviews with farmers. While our research was regionally specific to Southeastern Ontario, we feel that these insights will apply to researchers who are working with farmers in diverse settings.

1. Farmers' busiest periods are during their growing seasons. Therefore, we concluded that it would be most appropriate to schedule interviews in the winter. While there is still plenty of work to be done on the farm in the winter, farmers were more likely to take time out of their day to speak with us during this period.
2. We tried to be very mindful of time, stating that interviews would last around 30 min. On some occasions, interviews lasted much longer if the farmer was open to continuing our discussion, occasionally stretching the meeting to two hours. We also performed shorter follow-up interviews a few weeks or months later. After we interviewed every farmer and started identifying trends, we felt it would be useful to go back to each farmer for a shorter interview to ask any lingering questions and cover anything we missed the first time.
3. To reduce the burden on the farmer, all our meetings took place on location at their farm. While some farmers invited us to speak in their houses, others suggested roaming their grounds. This had the dual benefit of letting the farmer showcase some of their operations.
4. To find new farmers who were willing to participate, we utilized a snowball sampling technique. After each interview, we asked the farmers if they knew anyone within their networks who fit the type of farm specialization we were seeking. On multiple occasions, farmers were happy to suggest potential participants and provided their contact information. Some even sent an email introduction to these farmers, which helped us establish credibility and open communication channels with potential farmers to join our research.
5. Our interview framework borrowed from the 1989 book Farmer First by Robert Chambers (1989), which advocates participatory farmer research as an excellent source of information for learning about agricultural issues and solutions. We valued learning about farmers' own lived experiences and capacities for innovation as an insightful method for researching social entrepreneurship in our study area. We also believe taking a 'Farmer First' approach to be a critically useful tool for studying other research domains in the rural space as well.

From Chapter 9: Examples of Theories and Data Sources in Conducting Research of Rural Entrepreneurship

Trust in Institutions: Using the NCR-Stat Database

The North Central Regional Center for Rural Development (NCRCRD) collects data to understand the challenges facing rural and urban communities within the North Central Region (NCR) of the U.S. Data are collected across households and small businesses and focus on demographics, economics, health, housing, community development, and social behavior. NCR-Stat: Baseline Survey (Bednarikova et al., 2022) includes data collected on 4,668 households for the 12 states (IA, IN, IL, KS, MI, MO, MN, ND, NE, OH, SD, and WI) in the NCR. The NCR-Stat: Small Business Survey includes over 1,287 small businesses (Wiatt et al., 2024). The NCRCRD surveys households in rural and urban areas but oversamples rural households and businesses.

An important aspect of rural entrepreneurship is rural embeddedness and social capital. Both require a certain amount of trust in institutions and networks. This made me reflect that trust is built by individuals who represent institutions. And I asked myself the question, do individuals in the NCR trust institutions?

During the pandemic, there were many reports on distrust of government, education, healthcare, and police. And those reports were not unfounded based on a series of questions about trust in the NCR-Stat: Baseline (2022) survey. Only 38% stated they trust their local government. This is similar to the 36% that trust the local news media and better than the 24% that trust the federal government. In fact, 45% stated they did not trust the federal government and 27% did not trust their local government. The national news media did worse with 40% distrusting and only 27% trusting national media.

But let's go back to basics, do people trust their neighbors and others in their community? Yes, they do. At least 56% of individuals trust their neighbors (only 11% said they distrust their neighbors) and 65% trust their co-workers. Of those that attend religious services, 73% trust the people that attend with them. Not only that, but 63% trust those who educate their children, 74% trust their healthcare provider, and 61% trust their local police. The data reveals a "trust gradient" where confidence is highest in immediate social circles and local institutions, and then decreases as institutions become more distant or abstract.

Small business owners follow a similar pattern, showing higher trust in their immediate community (67% trust in neighbors) compared to institutions (41% trust in local government, 26% in federal government). This suggests that the trust dynamics observed in the general population are consistent across different segments of society in the NCR.

The data challenges the narrative of complete social division, suggesting instead that while there may be a crisis of confidence in larger institutions, the fundamental social fabric at the community level remains relatively strong. This has important implications for rural entrepreneurship and community development, as it indicates that the foundation for social capital formation exists at the local level, even if trust in broader institutions is limited.

References

Bednarikova, Z., Marshall, M.I., Wiatt, R.D., & Wilcox, M.D. Jr. (2022). North central region household data (NCR-Stat): Baseline survey. Purdue University Research Repository. doi: 10.4231/2DEM-Z333.

Wiatt, R.D., Marshall, M.I., Jr, M.D., Bednarikova, Z., Adams, N., Katare, B. (2024). NCR-Stat: Small Business Survey. Purdue University Research Repository. doi: 10.4231/6VG5-5386.

Rural Entrepreneurship and the Interface of Technology for Supporting a Resilient Food Supply Chain – An Example of the National MarketMaker Program

Many studies recognized the challenges and barriers for rural entrepreneurs to conduct day-to-day business. Technology and information seem to be at the center of such discussion. How would technology change the paradigm of rural entrepreneurship? An informal conversation with the leaders of the National MarketMaker Program could provide insight to re-energize the food supply chain for small farm enterprises in rural communities. Darlene Knipe, Richard Knipe, and Richard Warner are co-founders and leaders of MarketMaker. Darlene and Richard Knipe co-manage and operate the collaborative network, and Richard Warner is a professor emeritus at the University of Illinois and also a partner in Global Food and Ag Network, GFAN LLC the umbrella company that holds and manages the MarketMaker license.

MarketMaker was started 21 years ago, and it was a University of Illinois Extension project. It was grown through cooperation and collaboration from 23 different Land Grant Institutions in the US.[1] The relationships among partners form a foundation of this network, and MarketMaker maintains a trusted and neutral status that is essential to grow this community and engage farmers and entrepreneurs. What makes MarketMaker even more unique is that it builds on networking capacities within the networks as well. This program creates an information hub relying on secured technology platforms to meet the needs of our modern online community. MarketMaker is based on a model that is 80% relationships and 20% technology. The emphasis on grass roots engagement through a broad range of partnerships enables MarketMaker to adapt and evolve to the needs of a diverse group of stakeholders. A similar example is LinkedIn, which supports and creates professional networking capacity for individuals and companies.

So what is the MarketMaker program? It is an online platform providing various types of opportunities for farmers and vendors working in the agricultural and food sectors to conduct day-to-day business (e.g., find products and services across the food and agricultural systems, connect directly with growers, buyers, and service vendors across the supply chain). For example, farmers and businesses can sign up for free to create a strong business profile, list location/products/services for buy/sell forum, seek new market opportunities and advice, and reach out to buyers/growers/vendors at local/regional/national level. In the US, each state partner can customize their state profile, highlight state product/events, promote what is in season, recruit labor and other needed services, and showcase the success of farmers and agribusiness activities. The platform of MarketMaker has an interactive nature with direct communication between individuals and businesses with 100% secured data management. The website also has a new component to offer food discount and donation feature which could potentially offer savings and services to communities with special needs.

The leaders of MarketMaker believe some components of MarketMaker aligned themselves very well with rural economic development. Many of their clients, people who are part of the network, have prospered in rural areas because of MarketMaker, and some reasons are: (1) it opens up possibilities for them to live in rural areas, it exposes their value-added products, not only in rural areas, but urban areas. (2) MarketMaker offers a robust direct communications infrastructure for people to connect using tailored filters to pinpoint what they are looking for, to gain information in the most effective manner. This significantly reduces stress and time for farmers and businesses searching for information and connectivity. For example, MarketMaker's Buy Sell Forum allows one to make products available, but also learn of products that are available somewhere else. (3) MarketMaker offers consistent and secured data structure such as infrastructure and capacity of organizing and harmonizing data in a way that people can really expose their products and their businesses at their pace. This really allows people to gain networks, networks within their communities of interest in practice.

The unique characteristic of MarketMaker helps to overcome what has always been a challenge with rural entrepreneurship, when proximity becomes a barrier. If businesses are not in the proximity of markets, it can become a barrier. In essence, MarketMaker has mastered the logistics of information sharing. Its hub and spoke network allows interaction at the community level but can connect rural entrepreneurs to regional and national markets as they grow their operations.

Although information and location barriers are not unique to rural areas, rural entrepreneurs such as farmers face more challenges to access markets and opportunities without timely information. With modern technology and platform infrastructure, MarketMaker can help farmers and businesses in rural communities to capitalize on the information and create an exciting rural culture interacting with a digital environment related to food and agriculture beyond the traditional domain. For example, the users of MarketMaker platform benefit from the fact that they can better refine their business opportunities and the support infrastructure that they need. As one example of that MarketMaker is an integral part of the USDA-supported Ag Marketing Resource Center (AgMRC) based at Iowa State University. Its mission is to provide reliable and research-based marketing information to farmers who engage in the production of value-added and differentiated products that often represent emerging market opportunities for rural entrepreneurs.

The estimated number of users of MarketMaker in 2024 included 2.9 million page views. In any typical week, there were 15,000 profile views of the people who have profiles in MarketMaker. And any typical week in the Ag Marketing Research Center, the food searcher tool receives more than 5000 commodity searches every week. This statistic implies approximately 15,000 visits to entrepreneurs and food and farm businesses through the MarketMaker system which could help exposures weekly in connections to potential customers, buyers, and other service providers including researchers. As more connectivity and actions adding to the MarketMaker platform as the market demand grows, the network of supply chain will expand to respond to building a more resilient agricultural and food supply chain to support rural entrepreneurs.

From Chapter 10: Rural Entrepreneurship: Half a Century of Learning

eReady?

Since the late 1990s, the Center has partnered with and learned from Ord and its Valley County Region. In 2000, Ord pivoted to comprehensive entrepreneur-focused community economic development. Over the next 20 years Ord and its region transformed from crisis and deep conflict to socio-economic renewal. The Center working with Ord captured this 30-year-long story incorporating it into an Articulate 360 interactive learning platform. The Ord Case Study is a powerful example of a smaller, rural, and distressed community achieving revitalization by employing an entrepreneurship-centered development game plan.

Working with the International Economic Development Council, the Southern Minnesota Initiative Foundation (Minnesota REV), Compeer Financial, and Wisconsin Extension, the Ord Case Study was employed to support an entrepreneurial readiness (eReady?) process with candidate Wisconsin rural communities curating the first cohort of entrepreneurial communities within Wisconsin REV. Wisconsin REV is now planning for a second cohort of rural entrepreneurial communities including the use of the eReady? Resource to onboard both a new group of community coaches and teams.

Entrepreneurial community case studies like Ord, Nebraska can be used to help other rural communities and regions explore entrepreneur-focused development including improving readiness and enhancing strategy development.

e2 Development Framework

Beginning in the 1990s with HomeTown Competitiveness, the process of curating the ***e2 Development Framework and Process*** rooted in learning from rural communities and innovative rural entrepreneurship initiatives like Nebraska's Rural Enterprise Assistance Program, Maine's Coastal Enterprises, Michigan's Northern Initiatives, and the Kentucky Highlands Investment Corporation. As a framework for envisioning, developing and scaling rural community and regional-centered entrepreneurial ecosystems these insights and building blocks for rural entrepreneurial ecosystems can be customized to a community's preferences and unique assets and circumstances.

The e2 Framework has now been employed throughout North America from Alberta to Georgia, and Maine to Arizona. The evolved e2 Framework is currently being effectively demonstrated with the two REV (Rural Entrepreneurial Venture) initiatives in both Southern Minnesota and statewide in Wisconsin. As a no-cost public resource today, the e2 Framework has been customized and adapted by numerous development groups and foundations throughout North America over the years.

The recent (2020 through 2024) Nebraska E3 (Energizing Entrepreneurial Ecosystems) initiative hosted by the Nebraska Community Foundation with funding from the Ewing Marion Kauffman Foundation employed the e2 Framework. Three of the six cohort communities including Ord and Valley County, Ogallala and Keith County, and particularly Sidney, excelled with the e2 Framework. Sidney has evolved a community revitalization following the 2017 loss of Cabela's Outfitters (loss of 2,000 jobs in a community of 6,000) via acquisition by Bass Pro Shops. e2 is curating a comprehensive case study of the Sidney experience and how the e2 Framework was instrumental.

From Chapter 11: Rural Roots and Urban Aspirations: Spatial Influences on Entrepreneurial Motivations in Europe

De KetchupFabriek and Pieter Pot: A Case of Rural Roots and Urban Aspirations in the Netherlands

The stories of **De KetchupFabriek** and **Pieter Pot** highlight the interplay between entrepreneurial motivations and the spatial contexts in which enterprises emerge. These two Dutch companies, rooted in vastly different ecosystems – one rural, the other urban – illustrate how necessity and opportunity drive entrepreneurship in unique ways while addressing pressing societal challenges.

De KetchupFabriek: Necessity and Sustainability in Rural Zeeland

Founded by Patrick Keizer in the small village of Graauw, Zeeland, **De KetchupFabriek** is a prime example of rural entrepreneurship born out of necessity while set to make a difference in the world. Keizer's transition from graphic designer to ketchup maker began in 2012 during the financial crisis. With fewer design clients and limited alternatives in his rural community, Keizer began experimenting with ketchup production as both a creative outlet and a way to make ends meet. At 51 years old, he had to reinvent himself, using his hobby of cooking to launch a business that now produces over 8,000 bottles annually.

De KetchupFabriek leverages the resources of its rural environment. Keizer works closely with local farmers to source second-choice tomatoes and peppers – produce rejected by supermarkets due to aesthetic imperfections but perfectly suitable for consumption. This not only reduces food waste but also aligns with the broader push for sustainable food practices. The ketchup is handmade without artificial additives, appealing to modern consumers' preference for authenticity and natural ingredients.

De KetchupFabriek's success is also tied to its close-knit rural community and the reputation Keizer has built as a small-scale entrepreneur. Awarded with the regional social entrepreneurship prize in 2018, the business has become a symbol of innovation and resilience in Zeeland. Keizer's story reflects the role of necessity in rural entrepreneurship, demonstrating how local resources and constraints can inspire sustainable solutions that create both economic value and social impact.

Pieter Pot: Urban Opportunity-Driven Sustainability in Rotterdam

In contrast, **Pieter Pot**, based in Rotterdam, showcases urban opportunity-driven entrepreneurship. Founded by Jouri Schoemaker and Martijn Bijmolt during their master's studies, Pieter Pot is the Netherlands' first zero-waste grocery delivery service. The business offers products in reusable jars, eliminating single-use packaging and appealing to environmentally conscious urban consumers.

Pieter Pot's urban ecosystem provided fertile ground for growth. Rotterdam's dense population of sustainability-minded residents offered a ready market for their service, while the city's robust infrastructure facilitated efficient delivery logistics. Moreover, the founders capitalized on urban networks to attract funding and partnerships, allowing them to scale quickly and expand their impact.

Unlike De KetchupFabriek, which grew out of financial necessity, Pieter Pot was born from an opportunity to innovate and address a societal challenge: reducing waste in the food system. Schoemaker and Bijmolt's motivation to "make a difference in the world" reflects the urban context's emphasis on scaling solutions to global problems. Pieter Pot's success also underscores the role of urban consumers in driving demand for sustainable innovations.

Insights and Implications

The stories of De KetchupFabriek and Pieter Pot illustrate how the dichotomy between necessity and opportunity entrepreneurship is oversimplified, and how entrepreneurial motivations often blend both push and pull factors, shaped by spatial, socio-economic, and personal contexts. The stories reveal how entrepreneurial motivations and strategies are shaped by rural and urban contexts in the following ways:

1. **Rural Necessity and Resource Utilization**: De KetchupFabriek illustrates how rural entrepreneurs leverage local resources to address economic and environ-

mental challenges. Keizer's use of second-choice produce and his focus on small-scale production reflect the constraints and opportunities of a rural ecosystem.
2. **Urban Opportunity and Market Innovation**: Pieter Pot highlights the role of urban ecosystems in fostering opportunity-driven entrepreneurship. Rotterdam's consumer base, infrastructure, and networks enabled Schoemaker and Bijmolt to scale their zero-waste concept, demonstrating the potential for urban businesses to address global challenges.
3. **Contrasting Entrepreneurial Backgrounds**: Keizer's journey as an older, self-taught entrepreneur contrasts with Schoemaker and Bijmolt's experiences as young, highly educated founders. This highlights how different personal and professional backgrounds influence entrepreneurial paths, particularly in relation to their spatial and socio-economic contexts.
4. **Shared Commitment to Sustainability**: Despite their differences, both ventures share a commitment to sustainability, showcasing how entrepreneurs in diverse contexts can contribute to societal goals in unique ways.

Conclusion and Policy Implications

The contrasting stories of De KetchupFabriek and Pieter Pot illustrate the diverse paths entrepreneurs take in response to their spatial environments, personal circumstances, and societal challenges. Rural entrepreneurs like Patrick Keizer often rely on local resources and the necessity to innovate, while urban entrepreneurs like Jouri Schoemaker and Martijn Bijmolt leverage opportunities for scaling and market impact. Despite their differences, both ventures share a commitment to sustainability, contributing to broader societal goals in unique ways.

These examples offer several **policy implications** for fostering entrepreneurship across different contexts:

1. **Spatially Aware Entrepreneurial Supports:** In creating support structures that take into account socio-material circumstances, policy makers can enable entrepreneurship in different socio-material environments. Rural areas with limited resources, infrastructure, and markets require different types of entrepreneurial supports than well-connected urban areas. For rural areas, for instance, initiatives like grants for sustainable practices, technical support for small-scale producers, and incentives to repurpose surplus agricultural products could help ventures like De KetchupFabriek thrive while addressing rural unemployment and food waste.
2. **Encouraging Diverse Entrepreneurship**: Tailored programs recognizing the distinct needs of entrepreneurs from different educational and demographic backgrounds can bridge gaps in entrepreneurial ecosystems. For example, mentorship opportunities for older or less formally educated entrepreneurs can help them

navigate complex business landscapes, while young, highly educated entrepreneurs may benefit from startup incubators and access to venture capital.
3. **Promoting Cross-Spatial Collaboration**: Encouraging partnerships between rural and urban entrepreneurs could amplify impact. For instance, urban companies like Pieter Pot might collaborate with rural ventures like De KetchupFabriek to create integrated supply chains that reduce waste and support local producers.

By recognizing the unique contributions of rural and urban entrepreneurs, and addressing the structural barriers they face, policymakers can build more inclusive and resilient entrepreneurial ecosystems.

From Chapter 12: Rural Entrepreneurship at the Cross Point of Cultural Turn and Planetary: A Geosocial Critique of Rural Entrepreneurship

Despite the fact that entrepreneurship is typically an economic phenomenon, the idea of nature is particularly entwined with the conceptualization and policymaking around rural entrepreneurship. Consequently, in order for the readers to comprehend and utilize the ideas covered in this article, it is advised that they:
1) Put aside the division between the social and natural worlds and embrace a relational viewpoint,
2) It is important to have a figurative understanding of space rather than only understanding geography,
3) Adopt an interdisciplinary viewpoint and focus on the points where geography and sociology converge,
4) What is considered and regarded as an entrepreneurial opportunity is directly and significantly influenced by the historical geography of the research as well as the dominant subcultures. The deep well drilling in Sistan, southeast Iran, for example, has no historical precedent in the area and will therefore undoubtedly be rejected by the Helmand River as an actor as well as by human actors and the space-geography itself,
5) I implore the reader to break free from the damaging belief that entrepreneurship is a panacea that works in all eras and locations. In the Anthropocene, entrepreneurship, particularly in rural areas, has negative features and has the potential to destroy the environment. In the instance of Sistan, the Islamic Consultative Assembly representative for this region, who was also in charge of the deep well drilling project, supported local rural business initiatives. The area became water bankrupt as a result of the government drilling at least three deep wells and numerous semi-deep wells drilled by rural residents. The high salinity and water temperature caused the deep wells to be permanently abandoned, and the con-

flict between Helmand and the deep wells hampered diplomatic attempts to secure Helmand's water rights from Afghanistan,

The adage "Sistan is the paradise of unfinished projects" is well-known in Iran. The list of unsuccessful and incomplete initiatives now includes the deep well drilling project. The link below will take readers to one of my articles on the https://anthropologyandculture.com, where they may read more about the water situation between Iran and Afghanistan. Readers can select from three different languages on this website: French, Persian, or English,

https://anthropologyandculture.com/%d8%b3%db%8c%d8%b3%d8%aa%d8%a7%d9%86%d8%8c-%d8%b3%d8%a7%d9%84-%d8%b5%d9%81%d8%b1/ You can also search for the Persian phrase “ سیستان، سال ” صفر on the website, go to the article, and then switch the language from Persian to English or French if the link didn't work.

The Company Lab's Rural Outreach Program Lunch & Learns

In 2023, The Company Lab's (CO.LAB) rural outreach program was scattered, time-consuming, and inefficient. Only one person was leading the initiative who attempted to identify partners, build relationships, recruit participants, and execute programming across 10 counties surrounding Chattanooga, TN. At the time, we measured success primarily by the number of program participants, but with an average of only two people attending each event – and only five total events in 2023 – it was clear our approach wasn't working.

From these challenges, we learned valuable lessons: building relationships with rural communities requires time, consistency, collaboration, and delivering on promises. After consistently low numbers and canceled programs, we realized we needed a more structured, high-quality, low-barrier-to-entry resource to build trust in communities where we weren't actively present.

We reassessed our approach by evaluating existing partnerships, local entrepreneurial ecosystems, and capacity constraints. Instead of spreading resources too thin, we focused on four rural counties – Marion, Rhea, Bradley, and McMinn – which showed the most readiness for CO.LAB's entrepreneurial resources. These locations were also geographically central to other areas we serve, making them accessible to surrounding counties. Since many rural residents regularly commute for work and services, we hypothesized they might also travel for valuable business resources.

The Lunch & Learn Strategy

To better serve these communities, we launched a series of Lunch and Learns – free, in-person, hour-and-a-half workshops designed to equip participants with actionable skills for starting or scaling their businesses. These workshops cover a range of entrepreneurial topics, including Canva, Grant Writing, AI for Small Businesses, Finding Your Customer, and more. We actively source topic suggestions from participants and partners to make sure our events are addressing the community's ongoing needs and wants.

Currently, we host one Lunch and Learn per community every other month, bringing in local experts to lead sessions. After each event, we send a feedback form to attendees, providing space for future topic suggestions. Most importantly, we follow through on common suggestions to reinforce trust and responsiveness.

Building Partnerships for Sustainable Growth

We partnered with key local organizations to maximize impact and build credibility in each community:

- Marion County: Chattanooga State Community College & Marion Chamber of Commerce
- Rhea County: Clyde W. Roddy Library & MainStreet Dayton
- Bradley County: Tennessee Small Business Development Center (TSBDC) & Cleveland Bradley County Library
- McMinn County: Tennessee Wesleyan University & The LITE House

By collaborating with these organizations, we increase awareness and event attendance through their established networks. Co-branding our events with these trusted partners has strengthened our reputation and provided a familiar point of connection for attendees.

Results & Takeaways

Since implementing this strategy, our average event attendance has grown from two people to 19 per event, with about 30 events per year. This approach has reinforced that building trust, staying consistent, and working alongside community partners are the keys to fostering meaningful entrepreneurial growth in rural areas.

www.ingramcontent.com/pod-product-compliance
Lightning Source LLC
Chambersburg PA
CBHW081442091025
33802CB00006B/259
* 9 7 8 3 1 1 0 7 9 1 2 8 0 *